Competence
in the Law

Competence in the Law

From Legal Theory to Clinical Application

Michael L. Perlin
Pamela R. Champine
Henry A. Dlugacz
Mary A. Connell

John Wiley & Sons, Inc.

Library of Congress Cataloging-in-Publication Data

Competence in the law : from legal theory to clinical application / by Michael L. Perlin . . . [et al.].
   p. ; cm.
 Includes bibliographical references.
 ISBN 978-0-470-14420-6 (cloth : alk. paper)
 1. Competency to stand trial—United States. 2. Insanity (Law)—United States. I. Perlin, Michael L., 1946–
 [DNLM: 1. Mental Competency—legislation & jurisprudence—United States.
 2. Mentally Ill Persons—legislation & jurisprudence—United States. 3. Commitment of Mentally Ill—legislation & jurisprudence—United States. 4. Expert Testimony—legislation & jurisprudence—United States. WM 33 AA1 C695 2008]
   KF9242.C66 2008
   345.73'04—dc22
                              2007034469

Printed in the United States of America.
10 9 8 7 6 5 4 3 2 1

For Linda, Julie, and Alex . . . like it was written in my soul . . .

MICHAEL PERLIN

For Isabella

PAMELA R. CHAMPINE

For Luisa, Isaac, and Noah

HENRY DLUGACZ

For all the people whose lives have been affected by Professor Perlin's contributions.

MARY CONNELL

Contents

Introduction: The Expanding Role of the Expert Witness in Questions of Competence

Some 30 years ago, Loren Roth and colleagues famously said that the search for a unitary competency standard was a "search for a holy grail."[1] If anything, the intervening 3 decades have underscored the prescience and continued vitality of this observation. Developments in every relevant area of the law—criminal law, mental disability law, private law—have yielded multiple definitions and meanings of "competency," many of which have arisen in areas legally unknown (and perhaps not conceived of) when Roth and his colleagues wrote.

By way of a vivid example, the week before the manuscript of this book was submitted to the publisher, the United States Supreme Court ruled, in a death penalty case, that a prisoner with a severe, documented mental illness had a right to a hearing at which he could allege that he was too mentally ill to be executed because delusions interfered with his understanding of the reason for his execution.[2] Less dramatically, hundreds of reported appellate cases each year explore the meaning of the term "competency" in cases involving, variously, a criminal defendant's right to waive counsel,[3] a psychiatric patient's right to sexual inter-

---

1. Loren H. Roth et al., *Tests of Competency to Consent to Treatment,* 134 Am. J. Psychiatry 279, 283 (1977).

2. *See* Panetti v. Quarterman, 127 S. Ct. 2842 (2007), *reversing* Panetti v. Dretke, 448 F. 3d 815 (5th Cir. 2006); *see generally,* Michael L. Perlin & Henry A. Dlugacz, Mental Health Issues in Jails and Prisons: Cases and Materials, chapter 10B (in press) (2008). *See generally infra* Chapter 2H.

3. *See, e.g.,* Godinez v. Moran, 509 U.S. 389 (1993).

action,[4] a testator's right to bequeath money as she sees fit,[5] a hospital patient's right to consent to experimental treatment,[6] the right of institutionalized civil psychiatric patients to make autonomous treatment decisions,[7] the right of a currently incompetent-to-stand-trial jail detainee to refuse medication that would make him competent to be tried,[8] or the right to decide to marry.[9] And this short list barely scratches the surface.[10]

There is one constant in all of these cases: in virtually every instance (both in the hundreds of reported cases and the thousands of nonreported ones), there is expert testimony offered as to whether the "central player" (perhaps a plaintiff, perhaps a defendant, perhaps another) is competent to exercise a right (or to refuse state intervention). And, in each of these cases, the expert witness must offer her expertise—through a submitted report, a deposition or live testimony—on this question.[11] In a significant number of these cases, there are experts on both sides of the issue.[12]

Forensic mental health expertise holds a particularly important place in these areas of law because the case law tends to emphasize the importance of evidentiary facts in individual cases that bear on the applicable legal standard, as opposed to the theoretical definition of mental competence. Thus, the role of expert witnesses—especially witnesses who draw upon psychological or other behavioral science expertise in their testimony—continues to expand, as the significance of the resolution of the cases takes on greater social import, and as the entire role of

---

4. *See, e.g.,* Foy v. Greenblott, 190 Cal. Rptr. 84, 90–91 n.2 (Cal. Ct. App. 1983); *see generally,* Michael L. Perlin, *Hospitalized Patients and the Right to Sexual Interaction: Beyond the Last Frontier?* 20 NYU Rev. L. & Soc'l Change 302 (1993-94).

5. *See, e.g.,* Estate of Doris Duke, N.Y.L.J., at 24, col. 6 (Aug. 6, 1997) (challenge to trust established under will of tobacco heiress Doris Duke for the benefit of her dogs).

6. *See, e.g.,* Femrite v. Abbott Northwestern Hosp., 568 N.W.2d 535, 543 (Minn. Ct. App. 1997).

7. *See, e.g.,* Rennie v. Klein, 462 F. Supp. 1131, 1147 (D.N.J. 1978), suppl., 476 F. Supp. 1294 (D.N.J. 1979), modified, 653 F.2d 836 (3d Cir. 1981), vacated, 458 U.S. 1119 (1982); Rivers v. Katz, 495 N.E.2d 337(N.Y. 1986).

8. *See, e.g.,* Sell v. United States, 539 U.S. 166 (2003).

9. *See, e.g.,* Ivery v. Ivery, 129 S.E. 2d 457 (N.C. 1963).

10. *See, e.g.,* Michael L. Perlin & Heather Ellis Cucolo, Mental Disability Law: Civil and Criminal (2007 Cum. Supp.) (discussing cases).

11. On the question of whether experts should ever (or even) offer an opinion on the "ultimate question," See, e.g., Ric Simmons, *Conquering the Province of the Jury: Expert Testimony and the Professionalization of Fact-Finding,* 74 U. Cin. L. Rev. 1013(2006). In federal insanity defense cases, by way of example, experts are forbidden to answer the ultimate question (see Fed. R. Ed 704), although anecdotal evidence (and case reports) suggests that this is still a common occurrence. See, e.g., United States v. Samples, 456 F.3d 875 (8th Cir. 2006) (prosecutorial question to government expert that verged on asking ultimate question regarding defendant's sanity did not deprive defendant of fair trial).

12. In some cases—e.g., a suit over a will that is contested by multiple parties—there may be more (often many more) than two sides. *See, e.g.,* Toon v. Gerth, 735 N.E. 2d 314 (Ind. App. 2000).

expert testimony comes under greater court (and public) scrutiny in all areas of the law.[13] Not surprisingly, this state of affairs can cause confusion—not only to students grappling with these issues for the first time in an academic context—but also to seasoned forensic psychologists and psychiatrists, to lawyers representing parties in such cases, and to jurors and judges.[14] The question of legal competency—an individual's capacity to engage in or enter into certain sorts of important decision making, both in court proceedings and in daily life decisions—is, intuitively, an important one to lawyers, forensic mental health professionals, and the justice system (not to mention the persons about whose competency a question has been raised). Yet, extreme confusion remains.

It is clear that demands on forensic mental health professionals to understand the underlying legal concepts, to be able to contextualize them with other legal-psychological structures, and to be able to assist lawyers and judges in cases in which these issues are central will intensify. The need for students in graduate programs in psychology to master this subject matter will also accelerate. Yet, remarkably, there has been, until now, no single volume devoted to this issue. By writing this book, we hope to assist in this important venture.

The book will proceed in this manner. Chapter 1 introduces the subject matter by providing a brief history of the relationship between competency and the law, by briefly looking at those landmark cases that have set the boundaries in this area of the law, by predicting areas of future development in this area, and by focusing on why this question is so important to mental health professionals. It does this, in part, by introducing the reader to the concepts of *sanism* and *pretextuality*. Sanism is an irrational prejudice of the same quality and character of other irrational prejudices that cause, and are reflected in, prevailing social attitudes of racism, sexism, homophobia, and ethnic bigotry. Sanism infects jurisprudence and lawyering practices in a largely invisible and largely socially acceptable way. It is based predominantly upon stereotype, myth, superstition, and deindividualization. It is sustained and perpetuated by our use of the false concept of "ordinary common sense" and heuristic reasoning in an unconscious response to events both in everyday life and in the legal process.[15] Pretextuality refers to the way in which courts accept—either implicitly or explicitly—testimonial dishonesty and engage in similarly dishonest and frequently meretricious decision-making, specifically where witnesses, especially expert witnesses, show a high propensity to purposely distort their testimony in order to achieve desired

---

13. *See, e.g.,* Harold J. Bursztajn, Milo Fox Pulde, Darlyn Pirakitikulr, & Michael Perlin, *Kumho for Clinicians in the Courtroom: Inconsistency in the Trial Courts,* 24 MED. MALPRACTICE L. & STRATEGY 1 (Nov. 2006).

14. By way of example, on the Supreme Court's confusion over the meaning of "mental disorder," see 1 MICHAEL L. PERLIN, MENTAL DISABILITY LAW: CIVIL AND CRIMINAL, § 2A-3.3, at 75–92 (2d ed. 1998).

15. *See, e.g.,* MICHAEL L. PERLIN, THE HIDDEN PREJUDICE: MENTAL DISABILITY ON TRIAL 21–58 (2000).

ends.[16] These concepts best explain why the law of competency has developed as it has.[17]

Chapter 2 deals with the criminal competencies: the competency-to-stand-trial decision, the disposition of cases of persons found permanently incompetent to stand trial, competency to plead guilty, competency to waive counsel, and other criminal competencies. Chapter 3 considers the relationship between competency and the institutionalization of persons with mental disabilities, and considers the relationship between competency and involuntary civil commitment, competency and the right to refuse treatment, competency and other institutional rights, and competency and correctional decision-making. Chapter 4 then turns to questions of competency in civil law matters (torts; wills, trusts, and estates; contracts; domestic relations, and guardianship cases). Finally, Chapter 5 concludes by identifying commonalities between court decisions in these discrete areas of the law, and offers some modest suggestions—keeping in mind the discussion of sanism and pretextuality in Chapter 1—for forensic psychologists to adopt in their approaches to such cases.

16. *Id.* at 59–75.
17. *See, e.g.,* Pamela R. Champine, *A Sanist Will?,* 46 N.Y.L. Sch. L. Rev. 547 (2002–2003); Heather S. Ellis, *"Strengthen the Things That Remain": The Sanist Will,* 46 N.Y.L. Sch. L. Rev. 565 (2002–2003); Michael L. Perlin, *"Things Have Changed": Looking at Non-Institutional Mental Disability Law Through the Sanism Filter,* 46 N.Y.L. Sch. L. Rev. 535 (2002–2003).

1

Overview: The History, Present Scope, and Future Implications for Legal Competency

A. THE HISTORY OF THE RELATIONSHIP BETWEEN COMPETENCY AND THE LAW

As is discussed in greater detail in Chapter 2, the legal system worldwide has dealt with questions of competency in criminal law for centuries, dating to at least mid-seventeenth century England,[1] perhaps for even 400 years before that.[2] Other questions of competency date to the time of the Code of Hammurabi.[3] Social historians tell us that the relationship between competency and issues related to psychiatric hospitalization was first considered some 2,500 years ago in the Twelve Tables of Rome.[4] The question of the relationship between civil law and competency is similarly venerable: Guardianship has ancient origins in Roman and English common law, for example, as does the law of wills.[5] These, in

---

1. *See* Bruce Winick & Terry DeMeo, *Competency to Stand Trial in Florida,* 35 U. MIAMI L. REV. 31, 32 n.2 (1980).

2. *See* RONALD ROESCH & STEPHEN GOLDING, COMPETENCY TO STAND TRIAL 10 (1980).

3. *See* Thomas R. White, *Oaths in Judicial Proceedings and Their Effect Upon the Competency of Witnesses,* 51 U. PA. L. REV. 373, 375, 395 (1903).

4. *See* 1 MICHAEL L. PERLIN, MENTAL DISABILITY LAW: CIVIL AND CRIMINAL, § 2A-2.1a, at 46 (2d ed. 1999), citing THE MENTALLY DISABLED AND THE LAW 6 (F. Lindman & D. McIntyre eds. 1961).

5. *See, e.g.,* Patricia McManus, *A Therapeutic Jurisprudential Approach to Guardianship of Persons with Mild Cognitive Impairment,* 36 SETON HALL L. REV. 591 (2006) (guardianship); 3 SIR WILLIAM HOLDSWORTH, A HISTORY OF ENGLISH LAW 541–44 (3d ed. 1923) (wills).

short, are inquiries that have concerned lawyers, mental health professionals, and policymakers for centuries.

Yet, in at least two of the three major substantive areas with which this volume is concerned, the most important developments in competency and the law have come within the past 35 years—in the landmark cases of *Jackson v. Indiana*[6] and *Rivers v. Katz*.[7] In *Jackson*—a case nominally involving the competency to stand trial of a criminal defendant who was profoundly mentally retarded, deaf, and mute—the U.S. Supreme Court, for the first time, applied the due process clause to all matters involving the nature and duration of commitment to psychiatric institutions.[8] In *Rivers*—a case nominally about a civil patient's right to refuse the involuntary administration of antipsychotic medications—the N.Y. Court of Appeals seriously considered the relationship between an individual's competency and his right to exercise autonomy in institutionally based decision-making.[9] The impact of both of these cases transcended the circumstances of the narrow legal issues presented, and, in effect, opened the courthouse doors[10] to multiple new inquiries about competency in all relevant aspects of public law.

Simultaneously, researchers and behavioral scholars launched a series of complex, multijurisdictional studies designed to illuminate the multiple layers of competency, to better understand the relationship between competency and mental illness, between competency and decision-making, and between competency and the legal process. These studies—many of which were undertaken under the aegis of the MacArthur Foundation—shone new light on the clinical concepts involved in legal competency decisions and clarified the relationships between competence and mental illness, concluding that mental patients are not always incompetent to make rational decisions and that mental patients are not inherently more incompetent than nonmentally ill patients.[11] In fact, on "any given measure of decisional abilities, the majority of patients with schizophrenia did not perform more poorly than other patients and nonpatients."[12] By way of example, the judicial presumption that there is both a de facto and de jure presumption of

6. 406 U.S. 715 (1972).

7. 495 N.E. 2d 337 (N.Y. 1986).

8. *Jackson*, 406 U.S. at 738.

9. *Rivers*, 495 N.E. 2d at 341–42.

10. *Cf.* David Bazelon, *Veils, Values and Social Responsibility,* 37 AM. PSYCHOLOGIST 115, 115 (1982) (courts should "open the courthouse doors" to mental health professionals but "never hand over the keys").

11. Michael L. Perlin, *Therapeutic Jurisprudence and Outpatient Commitment: Kendra's Law as Case Study,* 9 PSYCHOL. PUB. POL'Y & L. 183, 193–94 (2003), relying on, inter alia, Paul S. Appelbaum & Thomas Grisso, *The MacArthur Treatment Competence Study. I: Mental Illness and Competence To Consent to Treatment,* 19 LAW & HUM. BEHAV. 105 (1995); Thomas Grisso et al., *The MacArthur Treatment Competence Study. II: Measures of Abilities Related to Competence To Consent to Treatment,* 19 LAW & HUM. BEHAV. 127 (1995); Thomas Grisso & Paul S. Appelbaum, *The MacArthur Treatment Competence Study. III: Abilities of Patients To Consent to Psychiatric and Medical Treatments,* 19 LAW & HUM. BEHAV. 149 (1995).

12. Grisso & Appelbaum, *supra* note 11, at 169.

incompetency to be applied to medication decision-making appears to be based on an empirical fallacy[13]; psychiatric patients are not necessarily more incompetent than nonmentally ill persons to engage in such independent medication decision-making.[14]

Also, state legislatures began to consider questions of competency in their efforts to create new solutions to vexing legal-social-clinical problems (e.g., the proliferation of so-called "assisted outpatient treatment" laws, most famously exemplified by New York's Kendra's Law;[15] the creation of so-called "Problem-Solving Courts" such as drug treatment courts or mental health courts, which are conceived as ways of diverting certain individuals from the criminal justice system into more treatment-focused tribunals;[16] and the proliferation of sexually violent predator laws, mandating civil commitment following completion of terms of criminal sentences.[17]

In addition, scholars have increasingly begun to turn their attention to "therapeutic jurisprudence." Therapeutic jurisprudence (TJ) presents a model by which we can assess the ultimate impact of case law and legislation that affects individuals with mental disabilities. Therapeutic jurisprudence studies the role of the law as a therapeutic agent, recognizing that substantive rules, legal procedures, and lawyers' roles may have either therapeutic or antitherapeutic consequences, and questions whether such rules, procedures, and roles can or should be reshaped so as to enhance their therapeutic potential while not subordinating due process principles.[18] Several researchers have focused the therapeutic jurisprudence lens directly on questions of competence in matters related to criminal and institu-

---

13. *See, e.g.,* Michael L. Perlin, *"You Have Discussed Lepers and Crooks": Sanism in Clinical Teaching,* 9 Clinical L. Rev. 683, 696 (2003) (Perlin, *Lepers*)(discussing literature); Michael L. Perlin, *"Make Promises by the Hour": Sex, Drugs, the ADA, and Psychiatric Hospitalization,* 46 DePaul L. Rev. 947, 973–74 (1997) (same).

14. Perlin, *supra* note 11, at 194; *see generally,* Bruce J. Winick, *The MacArthur Treatment Competence Study: Legal and Therapeutic Implications,* 2 Psychol., Pub. Pol'y & L. 137 (1996).

15. *See, e.g.,* N.Y. Mental Hyg. Law §9.60(5)–(6) (constitutionality upheld in In re K. L., 806 N.E.2d 480 (N.Y. 2004)).

16. *See, e.g.,* Pamela M. Casey & David B. Rottman, *Problem-solving Courts: Models and Trends,* 26 Just. Sys. J. 35 (2005).

17. *See, e.g.,* 1 Perlin, *supra* note 4, § 2A-3.3, at 75–92.

18. Michael L. Perlin, *"For the Misdemeanor Outlaw": The Impact of the ADA on the Institutionalization of Criminal Defendants with Mental Disabilities,* 52 Ala. L. Rev. 193, 228 (2000). *See generally,* Therapeutic Jurisprudence: The Law as a Therapeutic Agent (David B. Wexler ed. 1990); Essays in Therapeutic Jurisprudence (David B. Wexler & Bruce J. Winick eds. 1991); Law in a Therapeutic Key: Recent Developments in Therapeutic Jurisprudence (David B. Wexler & Bruce J. Winick eds. 1996); Therapeutic Jurisprudence Applied: Essays on Mental Health Law (Bruce J. Winick ed. 1997). The scope of therapeutic jurisprudence now goes far beyond questions of mental disability law. *See, e.g.,* 1 Perlin, *supra* note 4, § 2D-3, at 540 nn. 133–43 (discussing applications of TJ to, inter alia, domestic violence law, family law, labor arbitration, workers' compensation law, probate law, and policies about disclosure of sexual orientation).

tional law,[19] and courts are also beginning to consider principles of therapeutic jurisprudence in deciding cases and rewriting court rules.[20]

It is certainly reasonable to anticipate that this confluence of case law, behavioral investigation, legislative action, and scholarly ferment will continue and will expand in the future.[21]

B. FUTURE GROWTH

We can confidently predict that these areas of law and psychology will continue to evolve in future years. As we discuss in the subsequent parts of this book, it is entirely foreseeable that competency-related case law will continue to grow in the areas of criminal procedure (especially in matters involving [a] the pretrial process,[22] [b] post-guilty verdict stages,[23] and [c] the death penalty),[24] sexually violent predator laws,[25] the laws related to psychiatric institutionalization (the relationship between competency and, variously, civil commitment,[26] the right to refuse treatment,[27] and deinstitutionalization, especially as that relates to the Americans with Disabilities Act),[28] correctional law as it relates to questions of inmate discipline and segregation,[29] and those areas of civil law that focus on trusts and estates,[30] contractual obligations,[31] domestic relations,[32] and guardianships.[33] In short, we expect that this will be a growth area for the foreseeable future.

---

19. *See, e.g.,* Bruce Arrigo, & Jeffrey Tasca, *Right to Refuse Treatment, Competency to be Executed, and Therapeutic Jurisprudence: Toward A Systematic Analysis,* 24 L. & PSYCHOL. REV. 1, 1–47 (1999); Patricia McManus, *A Therapeutic Jurisprudential Approach to Guardianship of Persons with Mild Cognitive Impairment,* 36 SETON HALL L. REV. 591 (2006); Richard Barnum & Thomas Grisso, *Competence to Stand Trial in Juvenile Court in Massachusetts: Issues of Therapeutic Jurisprudence,* 20 NEW ENG. J. ON CRIM. & CIV. CONFINEMENT 321 (1994); Bruce J. Winick, *Competency to Consent to Treatment: The Distinction Between Assent and Objection,* 28 Hous. L. Rev. 15, (1991).

20. *See, e.g.,* Amendment to the Rules of Juvenile Procedure, Fla. R. Juv. P. 8.350, 804 So.2d 1206 (Fla. 2001); In re Mental Health of K.G.F., 29 P.3d 485 (Mont. 2001).

21. *See infra* Chapter 1 B.

22. *See infra* Chapter 2 D 1.

23. *See infra* Chapter 2 D 3.

24. *See infra* Chapter 2 H.

25. *See infra* Chapter 2 G.

26. *See infra* Chapter 3.

27. *See infra* Chapter 3.

28. *See infra* Chapter 3.

29. *See infra* Chapter 3.

30. *See infra* Chapter 4 C.

31. *See infra* Chapter 4 B.

32. *See infra* Chapter 4 D.

33. *See infra* Chapter 4 E.

C. WHY THE QUESTION OF COMPETENCE IS SO IMPORTANT TO MENTAL HEALTH PROFESSIONALS

1. Introduction

Because mental health professionals are often called upon to assist the court in its determination of competency, the way that competency is defined by the law is of great interest. In order to accomplish a forensic assessment of any kind, the first task of the examiner is to understand the legal question. The definitions provided by the law (What is the meaning of "insanity"? What is the standard for involuntary civil commitment? Does a person need to be "competent" to enter into a contractual relationship with another?) may incorporate terms that are ambiguous or concepts that have disparate meanings when used in clinical settings.[34]

To clarify the focus of the examination, the mental health examiner must operationalize the concept or term so that its functional components can be identified for evaluation.[35] For example, the term "reasonable appreciation of available pleas" is ambiguous and must be conceptualized by examining the functional capacities at play. Is it enough to be able to name the pleas, "guilty" and "not guilty?" Or should the accused be expected to know each plea and the nature and quality of the evidence that would justify that plea, along with likely consequences of entering the plea? What constitutes a reasonable appreciation? Is it sufficient to memorize the answers, through participation in a program designed to restore competency, or must the person be able to demonstrate an actual understanding of what each plea means?[36]

2. Legal Implications

When the mental health examiner has operationalized *which* competency is to be assessed and has accomplished the assessment, the resulting opinion may have significant implications that may involve incarceration, court-ordered treatment, or, potentially, the death penalty.[37] The legal concept of competency may embrace values or principles held by society; clearly, the legal implications of a finding of "competent-or-not-competent" are reflections of society's determination about who should and who should not be held responsible for their own behavior.[38]

---

34. Or terms, such as "insanity," that are no longer used in clinical settings. See, e.g., Richard Lowell Nygaard, *On Responsibility: Or, the Insanity of Mental Defenses and Punishment,* 41 VILL. L. REV. 951, 955 n.11 (1996) ("the word insanity anachronistically survives in our legal vocabulary, notwithstanding the fact that this construct has no medical counterpart").

35. *See* THOMAS GRISSO, EVALUATING COMPETENCIES 22, 52–54 (2d ed. 2003).

36. *See generally infra* Chapter 2.

37. *See infra* Chapter 2 H.

38. See, for example, GRISSO, *supra* note 35, at 477: "An expert opinion that answers the ultimate legal question is not an 'expert' opinion, but a personal value judgment. No amount or type of empirical and scientific information alone can answer the question of legal competence, because the degree of ability required for legal competence is not definitive, absolute, or

These value determinations are beyond the expertise of mental health professionals and are best left to the law. The mental health professional can offer an opinion about whether the individual possesses the capacities identified as operational definitions of the legal construction of competency, and can explain the basis of the opinion, but the mental health professional must then stop short of making the final step—whether the individual is, as a matter of fact, competent. That is a determination to made by the law. Put simply, an opinion regarding competency is not a finding of competency—the ultimate issue is the determination of the court.

3. Clinical Implications

Clinical implications of an individual's competency to stand trial are irrelevant when they are unmoored from the legal context. That is, incompetence to stand trial is not a clinical condition that requires treatment or for which there is an established intervention regimen.[39] An infinite number of clinical conditions may contribute to incompetence to stand trial, including cognitive impairment such as mental retardation or brain disorders that may have an impact on a person's reasoning ability or memory, as well as those conditions of psychosis that may distort the individual's reasoning ability or capacity for interpersonal communication or impair contact with reality to such an extent that the person cannot properly assist counsel's efforts to mount a defense.[40]

Those conditions, in and of themselves, each have clinical implications apart from the competency question. There may be a need for ongoing medication management, inpatient or outpatient treatment, or special support and assistance for independent living. A clinical condition—the nature of which contributes to a judicial finding of incompetence—is not, standing alone, the basis for the finding.[41] Competence assessment hinges on specific functional deficits, which *may* be

---

consistent across cases; *see also,* GARY MELTON ET AL., PSYCHOLOGICAL EVALUATIONS FOR THE COURTS , §1.04 (2d ed. 1997), and *id.* at 17 :

> [A]lthough the range of opinions with which mental health professionals provide the courts should be narrowed to exclude opinions of a purely moral or legal nature, the door should be left open to professional opinions, including formulations of legally relevant behavior, that might assist (as opposed to overwhelm) the trier of fact. At the same time, mental health professionals should be careful to indicate the level of scientific validity or certainty attached to their opinions.

The use of the word *responsible* in this context is used in a far broader sense than simply whether a defendant is to be held *criminally* responsible for an act because of his or her mental state.

39. On the confusion that persists in this specific area of the law and policy, *see* Perlin, *supra* note 18.

40. On the question of the ability of the defendant to assist counsel, *see* 4 PERLIN, *supra* note 4, § 8A-2.3, at 23–24 (2d ed. 2002).

41. *See* Perlin, *supra* note 18, at 202–08 (on how findings of incompetence to stand trial— regardless of severity of crime or defendant's clinical condition—leads to lengthy institutionalization in maximum security facilities, often ones inappropriate and countertherapeutic for the defendant).

present along with each of a number of clinical conditions, but which also *may* be absent in the cases of other individuals suffering from the same clinical conditions. For example, one person who suffers from paranoid schizophrenia may be so affected by delusions that she believes her attorney has entered into a conspiracy with the prosecutor to bring about her imprisonment. This suspiciousness may cause her to withhold critical information from her attorney, information that would clearly assist in her defense. By contrast, another person suffering from paranoid schizophrenia may have periods of lucidity that allow for active participation in the defense effort, or delusions focusing on a specific group of feared persecutors, excluding defense counsel who are—instead—trusted. The diagnosis of a psychiatric condition is, itself, insufficient to establish incompetence.[42]

4. Constraints Potentially Limiting Adequacy of Assessment

A forensic mental health assessment is a snapshot of the examinee's functioning at a specific time and with regard to whatever functional capacities are at issue. The clarity of the image depends on the tools available—the snapshot may be a fuzzy image when the functional capacities are ill defined or difficult to measure. The sources of data may also limit the examiner—a defendant may be unwilling to cooperate by answering questions, may try to control the outcome by faking incapacity, or may be so disturbed or cognitively impaired that it is not possible to reasonably assess understanding. Medication may affect performance in the examination.[43]

Conditions of the assessment may be less than optimal in other ways—examinations conducted in noisy visiting areas of jails, or in attorney consultation areas with glass separating examiner and defendant, may constrain assessment.[44] Language barriers, cultural differences, or mistrust bred of mental illness may interfere with communication.[45] There are sometimes pressures to complete an assessment in a short time, or access to the examinee may be limited so that the

42. *See* 4 PERLIN, *supra* note 4, § 8A-2.3, at 20–22 (discussing levels of mental disability that, in and of themselves, have, in certain cases, not been seen as a sufficient basis for an incompetency finding).

43. On the question of whether a currently incompetent defendant may be involuntarily medicated so as to make him or her competent to stand trial, *see infra* Chapter 2 A 1 d.

44. The *Standards for Educational and Psychological Testing* (1999), authored by the American Educational Research Association, American Psychological Association, and National Council on Measurement in Education notes that psychologists are obligated to create a testing environment relatively free of distractions. Standard 5.4 states, "The testing environment should furnish reasonable comfort and minimal distractions." *Id.* at. 83. Many test manuals also include a statement to this effect in the instructions for administration. For example, the *WAIS-III Manual* states, "As a rule, no one other than you and the examinee should be in the room during the testing." *See* DAVID WECHSLER, WESCHSLER ADULT INTELLIGENCE SCALE-III 29 (1997).

45. Mark D. Cunningham, *The Role of the Forensic Psychologist in Death Penalty Litigation,* presented January 19, 2007, at the American Academy of Forensic Psychology Continuing Education Workshop Series, in San Diego, CA (PowerPoint slides of paper on file with authors).

assessment must be accomplished in one or two visits when several would have been ideal. Third-party information, a staple of forensic assessment, may be limited. Records of previous functioning, earlier evaluations, school and medical records, and other objective sources of data are generally consulted, and this time-consuming process, in the absence of adequate consent to access information, requires a court order, further protracting the process.

Finally, the rate of reimbursement for competency assessment may be insufficient to encourage some skilled practitioners to participate in them, and may drive those who do the assessments to give them less than their due. When a 10-hour assessment might be barely adequate, for example, the established rate of reimbursement may be more nearly the hourly rate for 2 hours of the clinician's time. While it is assumed that a clinician who agrees to do a competency evaluation will provide the time and attention required to do an adequate job, it is naïve to assume that the rate of reimbursement will not have an impact, directly or indirectly, on the quality of examinations available to the court. Court clinics employ forensically trained evaluators who provide these assessments in many urban communities, potentially resolving this tension. The advantage of having trained and experienced examiners available to do the assessments may be somewhat compromised, however if caseloads are unreasonable. Additionally, there is the risk that clinic staff may become enmeshed with the process of prosecution and lose their neutrality.[46]

5. Informed Consent on the Part of the Examinee[47]

The process of gaining informed consent—a knowing and voluntary decision to participate in a proposed treatment—raises several considerations when competence is being assessed. First, the examinee whose competency is at question cannot be assumed to have the capacity to knowingly evaluate the proposed treatment. In some cases, the examinee may have limitations that could exert an impact on the capacity of the examiner to understand some aspects of the informed consent discussion. Even cognitively unimpaired litigants may not be able to anticipate the consequences of refusing to participate in the assessment, of discussing uncharged offenses, or of admitting to or denying a juvenile adjudication record that is understood to have been sealed. It is with counsel that this informed consent discussion must first occur, so that counsel can carefully evaluate the potential impact of each prong on the defendant's position and make the informed decision about whether to go forward with the assessment as it is being described. Second, voluntariness, in the true sense of the concept, is not

---

46. On the futility of demanding authentic "neutrality" in many such settings, *see* Michael L. Perlin, *"They're An Illusion To Me Now": Forensic Ethics, Sanism and Pretextuality*, in PSYCHOLOGY, CRIME AND LAW: NEW HORIZONS AND INTERNATIONAL PERSPECTIVES (David Canter & Rita Zukauskien eds. 2007) (in press).

47. *See infra* Chapter 4 A 1.

totally possible when the assessment is court ordered; generally, it the rare examinee who voluntarily decides to undergo an assessment of competency. Whether the examiner is legally obligated to obtain informed consent or the examinee is legally capable of giving it, the examiner may be ethically obligated to ensure that the examinee or the legal representative of the examinee has had the opportunity to contemplate the nature and potential consequences of the examination and has had time to raise any objections.[48] Prof. Kirk Heilbrun has wisely used the term "Notification of Purpose" to describe the process by which an involuntary examinee is notified of the elements that would normally be included in informed consent.[49]

6. The Difference between Expert as Forensic Witness and Expert as Therapist

Forensic examination and *clinical* examination and treatment are two distinctly different kinds of mental health services. Historically, the courts have often relied on testimony from medical and mental health treatment providers to assist in making determinations of matters important to the administration of justice. As it became increasingly common to invoke expert testimony in a wide variety of court cases, the profession of forensic examination began to take shape. Mental health professionals—whose data include the patient's self-report—became increasingly aware that an assessment for a court matter differed significantly from an assessment for clinical purposes.[50] In the clinically driven examination, the examinee or the examinee's guardian (if one has been appointed) often initiates the examination and treatment to relieve suffering. The examinee is often, but not always, cooperative, and may stand to benefit from the treatment, specifically by gaining relief from some debilitating condition.[51] The examination and treatment generally occur in the context of a trusting relationship and some assurance of confidentiality. The cost may be borne by the examinee or a third party with whom the examinee has an established relationship, such as a guardian, employer, or insurance provider. Participation in the service generally remains voluntary and the examinee or service recipient can expect to benefit or to leave the treatment relationship if no benefit accrues, if trust falters, or for any reason.

---

48. APA Ethics Code, 3.10 Informed Consent (c), "When psychological services are court ordered or otherwise mandated, psychologists inform the individual of the nature of the anticipated services, including whether the services are court ordered or mandated and any limits of confidentiality, before proceeding."

49. Kirk Heilbrun, Principles of Forensic Mental Health Assessment 141–153 (2001).

50. *See generally,* Stuart Greenberg & Daniel Shuman, *Irreconcilable Conflict Between Therapeutic and Forensic Roles,* 28 Prof'l Psychol: Res. & Prac. 30 (1997); Michael L. Perlin, *Power Imbalances in Therapeutic and Forensic Relationships,* 9 Behav. Sci. & L. 111 (1991).

51. Or, paradoxically, he may wish to exercise his right to personal autonomy by *refusing* certain treatment that his treating mental health professional may recommend. *See infra* Chapter 3.

By contrast, the forensic mental health assessment is generally initiated by someone other than the examinee. The court, the attorney, or an agency may cause the assessment to occur. The examinee's wishes about the assessment may be of little concern. The assessment is intended to provide information that will assist a court or administrative body in answering a legal question or establishing some competency or fitness. The results may specifically thwart the aims of the examinee. Data collected as part of the assessment will necessarily be shared with others, and the examinee generally has no control over how they are distributed or utilized. The cost of the assessment may be borne by the examinee, as in parenting assessments or lifetime assessment of testamentary competency, or may be paid by a party with an opposing interest.

With these differences driving the forensic assessment, special considerations are warranted to ensure that the examinee's rights are not violated and that the resulting opinions are sufficiently reliable and relevant to the court or administrative body to warrant their consideration. The forensic assessment is ideally conducted in an objective, dispassionate way by a neutral examiner who actively seeks data to confirm or disconfirm each reasonable hypothesis.[52] The examiner will not be preserving a traditional treatment relationship in providing courtroom testimony, her courtroom presentation, and traditional concepts of treater confidentiality are not typically betrayed by the examiner's presentation,[53] a subtle but powerful

---

52. *See, e.g.,* HEILBRUN, *supra* note 49; and see Greenberg & Shuman, *supra* note 51, at 56:

> Therapists do not ordinarily have the requisite database to testify appropriately about psycholegal issues of causation (i.e., the relationship of a specific act to claimant's current condition) or capacity (i.e., the relationship of diagnosis or mental status to legally defined standards of functional capacity).
>
> These matters raise problems of judgment, foundation, and historical truth that are problematic for treating experts.

See also, Committee on Ethical Guidelines for Forensic Psychologists, *Specialty Guidelines for Forensic Psychologists,* 16 LAW & HUM. BEHAV. 655, 658 (1991) (Guideline IV §A, "Relationships") (*Specialty Guidelines*):

> During initial consultation with the legal representative of the party seeking services, forensic psychologists have an obligation to inform the party of factors that might reasonably affect the decision to contract with the forensic psychologist. These factors include, but are not limited to . . . (2) prior and current personal or professional activities, obligations, and relationships that might produce a conflict of interests.

We use the word "ideally" as a recognition that this goal is not always met. *See, e.g.,* Michael L. Perlin, *Therapeutic Jurisprudence: Understanding the Sanist and Pretextual Bases of Mental Disability Law,* 20 N. ENG. J. CRIM. & CIV. CONFINEMENT 369, 380–81 (1994) (discussing matter of Dr. James Grigson, "who testified [in multiple death penalty cases] in defiance of all existing professional ethical guidelines").

53. *See* Kirk Heilbrun et al., *Pragmatic Psychology, Forensic Mental Health Assessment, and the Case of Thomas Johnson,* 10 PSYCHOL. PUB. POL'Y & L. 31, 37 (2004):

> For example, when performing a court-ordered evaluation, the forensic clinician must provide the individual being evaluated with basic information regarding (a) the nature and purpose of the evaluation, (b) who authorized the evaluation, and (c) the associated

consideration in the treating professional's provision of courtroom testimony.[54] Matters disclosed in a treatment relationship with no anticipation of litigation were, undoubtedly, shared without the forewarning that they might be disclosed in court in a way that could be harmful. Where the treatment professional may rightly be concerned that the "patient" will feel betrayed when private matters disclosed in treatment are now revealed during cross-examination, the forensic examiner has, from the outset, clearly conveyed an absence of confidentiality in the process of assessment and the potential that anything disclosed could be used in court in a way that would compromise the aims of the examinee.[55]

The fact finder may believe that treatment providers can offer useful clinical information about someone who is well known to them and that this information, derived for treatment purposes rather than litigation, is more reliable. The forensic expert may be viewed as a hired gun, and the treating clinician viewed as a helping professional whose motives are altruistic. However, the treating clinician has generally not conducted an assessment of the capacities or competencies at question in the legal matter. The careful assessment of relevant capacities, derived from multiple data sources selected for their objectivity and reliability, is quite different from clinical assessment. Clinical assessment, conducted in anticipation of providing remedial intervention, relies principally on the presentation of the patient, which is assumed to be driven by a wish to get help with symptoms. The clinician,

---

limits on confidentiality, including how the individual's information might be used. In this context, however, the individual's participation in the evaluation is not voluntary, and it would therefore be inappropriate for the forensic clinician to seek informed consent. By contrast, when an attorney retains a forensic clinician to conduct an evaluation of that attorney's client, the evaluation is voluntary, and informed consent should therefore be obtained from the individual before proceeding.

54. When a forensic witness takes the stand, there can be no blanket assurances of confidentiality, and, in anticipation of this testimony, the witness cannot promise to an examinee that she or he will not disclose certain information. This, of course, is a separate matter from attorney-client confidentiality, a topic beyond the scope of this volume.

55. There is a significant difference between the empathetic skills used in therapeutic relationships and the interviews used in forensic encounters, where the employment of such empathy may be highly inappropriate. *See, e.g.,* Donald Judges, *The Role of Mental Health Professionals in Capital Punishment: An Exercise in Moral Disengagement,* 41 Hous. L. Rev. 515, 589 n.411 (2004), quoting Stuart A. Greenberg & Daniel W. Shuman, *Irreconcilable Conflict Between Therapeutic and Forensic Roles,* 28 Prof. Psychol.: Res. & Prac. 50, 53 (1997) (explaining that while "[t]he therapist is a care provider and usually supportive, accepting, and empathic; the forensic evaluator is an assessor and usually neutral, objective, and detached as to the forensic issues"), and Alan M. Goldstein, *Overview of Forensic Psychology,* in 11 Handbook of Psychology: Forensic Psychology 3, 5 (Alan M. Goldstein ed., 2003) (observing that "in forensic assessments, the motivation [of the client] to consciously distort, deceive, or respond defensively is readily apparent" compared to nonforensic clinical evaluations).

While clinicians should be professionally skilled at drawing people out and invoking dependency and trust, in the forensic examination, it may be disingenuous for forensic examiners to use that posture. *See generally,* Daniel W. Shuman, *The Use of Empathy in Forensic Examinations,* 3 Ethics & Behav. 289 (1993).

wanting to be helpful to the patient and to the court and unschooled in evidentiary standards, may stretch to try to answer the question before the court.

Treating clinicians may have information that illuminates some aspect of the question before the court. Taken for what it is, appropriately limited by the clinician and given the weight it merits by the fact finder, this information may be salient. The difficulty is that clinicians routinely fail to articulate those limits, either because they are not asked the relevant questions or because they do not appreciate the difference between a forensically driven and a clinically driven assessment. Just as routinely, the legal setting calls for the clinician to offer opinions on matters beyond those that the clinical examination addressed. For these reasons, mental health testimony is sometimes viewed as "junk science."[56] The thoughtfully conducted forensic mental health examination and resultant carefully limited testimony, by contrast, can form reliable and relevant evidence of direct assistance to the court.

7. Absence of Confidentiality

There is little confidentiality afforded the forensic examinee. The data collected in the forensic examination forms the basis for expert opinion that is to be offered, and the parties involved have the expectation that they can probe it for completeness and accuracy. Thus, with limited exceptions, the examinee should be led to understand that there will be no confidentiality afforded in the assessment process.[57] This runs counter to the expectations generally held about mental health practitioners—not only examinees, but even counsel, may assume that psychologists, psychiatrists, or counselors *always* keep the confidences of people to whom they provide services. When services are provided in the anticipation of litigation, this is almost never the case.

8. Potential for Outcome to Be Unhelpful or Harmful to the Examinee's Interests

Clinicians generally are trained to do no harm. The forensic assessment may, however, result in failure to have one's property distributed as one wished, incarceration, involuntary commitment, or, ultimately, even death—consequences that might logically be seen by the examinee as quite harmful. How does the forensic mental health examiner reconcile this potential harm with principles of nonmalfeasance and beneficence?

---

56. *See, e.g.,* Paul C. Giannelli, *The Abuse of Scientific Evidence in Criminal Cases: The Need for Independent Crime Laboratories,* 4 Va. J. Soc. Pol'y & L. 439 (1997); Mike Redmayne, *Expert Evidence and Scientific Disagreement,* 30 U.C. Davis L. Rev. 1027 (1997).

57. Melton et al., *supra* note 38, § 3.04, at 46: "In the purely evaluative relationship, however [contrasted to the typical *therapetuic* relationship], confidentiality is close to nonexistent. The clinician-patient privilege does not apply when the clinician-'patient' relationship is the creature of the court, as is the case with court-ordered evolutions."

The task of the mental health professional who undertakes examinations that will be relied upon by a court is to conduct the examination in a way that respects the examinee's autonomy, the system of justice, and the principle of fairness.[58] The examiner has an obligation to carefully assess the relevant capacities, explore all rival hypotheses, actively seek data that would test each hypothesis, and arrive at an objective assessment of the matter.[59] The examiner can then forcefully present that finding, disclosing all data underlying the opinion and data that argued for a different opinion. What happens beyond that is out of the control of the examiner, but is in the hands of the fact finder. The outcome, presumably, is a reflection of how society has construed the issue, rather than how the mental health professions construe it or how the particular evaluator sees it.

In order to perform forensic mental health assessments, the clinician must accept this dichotomy and achieve some comfort with it. The examiner cannot attempt to thwart justice as the law styles it by offering opinion testimony in order to achieve a certain outcome for the examinee.[60] The evaluation must be done with neutrality and objectivity rather than from an advocacy stance.

9. The Special Circumstances of Mandated Reporting

In most jurisdictions, mandated-reporter status requires the examiner to make a report to authorities when there is a reason to believe abuse or neglect of an elder or a child has occurred.[61] There are generally no exceptions for mental health professionals. The attorney may assume that the retained examiner is working under the work-product shield and instruct the examiner not to disclose anything about the assessment to anyone without the attorney's express permission, but this instruction may run counter to the mental health professional's legal

58. American Psychological Association, *Ethical Principles of Psychologists and Code of Conduct,* 57 AM. PSYCHOLOGIST 1060 (2002) ("Principle E: Respect for People's Rights and Dignity").

59. *Specialty Guidelines, supra* note 52, Guideline VII, Public and Professional Communications, (D) "When testifying, forensic psychologists have an obligation to all parties to a legal proceeding to present their findings, conclusions, evidence, or other professional products in a fair manner. This principle does not preclude forceful representation of the data and reasoning upon which a conclusion or professional product is based. It does, however, preclude an attempt, whether active or passive, to engage in partisan distortion or misrepresentation. Forensic psychologists do not, by either commission or omission, participate in a misrepresentation of their evidence, nor do they participate in partisan attempts to avoid, deny, or subvert the presentation of evidence contrary to their own position."

60. *Id.*

61. Mary Connell, et al., *Expert Opinion—Does Mandatory Reporting Trump Attorney-Client Opinion?* 24 AMERICAN PSYCHOLOGY–LAW SOCIETY NEWS, 10, 15 (2005), accessible at http://www.ap-ls.org/publications/newsletters/fall2004.pdf and at http://home.comcast.net/~slgolding/publications/Mandated_reporting.htm (both last accessed June 20, 2007). See generally, Maryann Zavez, *The Ethical and Moral Considerations Presented by Lawyer/Social Worker Interdisciplinary Collaborations,* 5 WHITTIER J. CHILD & FAM. ADVOC. 191, 203 (2005) (on the question of whether mandatory reporting obligations "might still trump" what otherwise would be protected attorney-client communications).

and ethical obligation to report. The case of *Tarasoff v. Regents of the University of California*[62] raises a further potential mandated-reporting requirement in many jurisdictions. The mental health professional may have a duty to take preventative measures when it would appear, to a reasonable and competent clinician, that an examinee is likely to harm another person in the near future. There is generally no duty unless the potential victim is specifically identifiable.[63] It may be acceptable to provide the warning by notifying authorities or committing the examinee, or, in examining an already incarcerated individual, by providing the warning in the report to be submitted to the court.[64]

What, then, must counsel do in securing expertise when there is risk that the examiner may discover an uncharged offense? And in fact, even details of the charged offense must, according to the mandated-reporter statute, generally be reported when they come to the attention of the mandated reporter. In most states, the statutes do not excuse the mandated reporter from the obligation to report on the basis that the case is already being investigated by a protective service or public service agency. The statutes are ordinarily construed very simply, requiring anyone who becomes aware of or has reason to believe a child or adult is in danger of being abused or neglected, or has been abused or neglected, to report to the appropriate agency within a specified period of time.[65]

---

62. Tarasoff v. Board of Regents of University of California, 551 P.2d 334 (Cal. 1976).

63. Thompson v. County of Alemeda, 614 P.2d 728 (Cal. 1980).

64. *See generally,* Michael L. Perlin, Tarasoff, *and the Dilemma of the Dangerous Patient: New Directions for the 1990's,* 16 LAW & PSYCHOL. REV. 29 (1992); Michael L. Perlin, *"You Got No Secrets to Conceal": Considering the Application of the Tarasoff Doctrine Abroad,* 75 U. CIN. L. REV. 611 (2006).

65. In Texas, by way of example, state family law provides that "[a] person having cause to believe that a child's physical or mental health or welfare has been adversely affected by abuse or neglect by any person shall immediately make a report as provided by this subchapter." Tex. Fam. Code Ann. § 261.101(a) (Vernon 2002); see White v. State, 50 S.W.3d 31, 47 (Tex. App.-Waco 2001, pet. ref'd) ("cause" means "sufficient reason"). The same law "imposes a mandatory requirement upon any person, not merely law enforcement officers, to report child abuse, whether it is physical abuse, sexual abuse, or other conduct included in the definition of 'abuse.'" Tex. Fam. Code Ann. § 261.101(a); see State v. Harrod, 81 S.W.3d 904, 908 (Tex. App.-Dallas 2002, pet. ref'd) (prosecution for failure to immediately report child sexual abuse), Rodriguez v. State, 47 S.W.3d 86 (Tex. App.-Houston [14th Dist.] 2001, pet. ref'd) (conviction for failure to immediately report child abuse); Tex. Att'y Gen. Op. No. DM-458 (1997) at 3 (section 261.101(a) does not allow sex offender treatment providers to decide whether or not to report "incomplete or dated" information received from client).

Section 261.101(b) of the family law act establishes a specific reporting requirement for "a professional," defined as "an individual who is licensed or certified by the state or who is an employee of a facility licensed, certified, or operated by the state and who, in the normal course of official duties or duties for which a license or certification is required, has direct contact with children," including "teachers, nurses, doctors, day-care employees, employees of a clinic or health care facility that provides reproductive services, juvenile probation officers, and juvenile detention or correctional officers." (3) Tex. Fam. Code Ann. § 261.101(b) (Vernon 2002). If a professional has cause to believe that a child has been abused or neglected or may be abused or neglected, or that a child is a victim of an offense under Section 21.11, Penal Code, and the

From the examiner's perspective, there is arguably an obligation to introduce this issue during the informed consent process with counsel, before the examination begins, so that the attorney can take whatever steps are required in contemplation that the statute may be triggered. Finally, the examiner, in discussing the contours of the examination with the examinee, is duty bound to notify the examinee of what will be done with any information obtained in the examination, including that covered under mandated-reporter status.[66]

10. "Door-Opening Considerations" and the Instant Case

In criminal cases in some jurisdictions, the defendant's examination by a defense-retained mental health expert may "open the door" to a prosecution-retained expert examination. Within this issue, however, is a secondary one. Acting anticipatorily, counsel may instruct the defendant not to discuss the instant offense with the defense expert because to do so would open the door to the examination of it by the prosecution expert. This matter raises both legal and ethical considerations for the forensic examiner. It is imperative that counsel make the decision about whether to allow the defendant to discuss the alleged offense—this is a legal matter and may invoke the defendant's constitutional rights against self-incrimination.[67]

---

professional has cause to believe that the child has been abused as defined by Section 261.001, the professional shall make a report not later than the 48th hour after the hour the professional first suspects that the child has been or may be abused or neglected or is a victim of an offense under Section 21.11, Penal Code.

See http://www.oag.state.tx.us/opinions/op50abbott/ga-0106.htm (last accessed June 20, 2007).

66. APA Ethics Code, 3.10, Informed Consent:

(a) When psychologists conduct research or provide assessment, therapy, counseling, or consulting services in person or via electronic transmission or other forms of communication, they obtain the informed consent of the individual or individuals using language that is reasonably understandable to that person or persons except when conducting such activities without consent is mandated by law or governmental regulation or as otherwise provided in this Ethics Code. (See also Standards 8.02, Informed Consent to Research; 9.03, Informed Consent in Assessments; and 10.01, Informed Consent to Therapy.)

(b) For persons who are legally incapable of giving informed consent, psychologists nevertheless (1) provide an appropriate explanation, (2) seek the individual's assent, (3) consider such persons' preferences and best interests, and (4) obtain appropriate permission from a legally authorized person, if such substitute consent is permitted or required by law. When consent by a legally authorized person is not permitted or required by law, psychologists take reasonable steps to protect the individual's rights and welfare.

(c) When psychological services are court ordered or otherwise mandated, psychologists inform the individual of the nature of the anticipated services, including whether the services are court ordered or mandated and any limits of confidentiality, before proceeding.

67. *See* 4 Perlin, *supra*, §§ 10-2 to 2.4a.

There may be costs to the perceived credibility of the defense retained expert, however, in not discussing the alleged offense—the fact finder may perceive the expert as partisan for having failed to do so because of the door-opening potential.[68] This should be counsel's carefully considered determination.[69] When counsel makes the decision, the expert must then determine whether the examination can be done at all, under the terms decided by retaining counsel. If the examiner believes there is some prohibition to doing an assessment under constrained conditions, this should be revealed as early as possible in the process to allow counsel time to seek another expert.[70]

11. Dilemma of the Uncooperative Examinee

The mental health examiner faced with an unwilling or uncooperative examinee must take a number of steps to protect the rights of the examinee and to ensure that the examination produces useful results. First, no examination should proceed before counsel is available to the examinee,[71] and if the court orders an examination to go forth before counsel has had an opportunity to consult with the examiner and examinee, the examiner should make known to the court the ethical obligation to delay the assessment until this has been accomplished.[72] Assuming that appropriate consideration has been given to the individual's right to consult with counsel and counsel has supported the examination effort and instructed the examinee to submit to the examination, but the examinee nevertheless fails to cooperate, the examiner carefully considers the next course of action. The examinee

68. See, for example, Specialty Guidelines, supra note 52, Guideline VI, Methods and Procedures, (C), "In providing forensic psychological services, forensic psychologists take special care to avoid undue influence upon their methods, procedures and products. . . . As an expert conducting an evaluation, treatment, consultation or scholarly/empirical investigation, the forensic psychologist maintains professional integrity by examining the issue at hand from all reasonable perspectives, actively seeking information which will differentially test plausible rival hypotheses."

69. Mark D. Cunningham, *Informed Consent in Capital Sentencing Evaluations: Targets and Content*, 37 PROF'L PSYCHOL.: RES. & PRAC., 452, 457–458 (2006).

70. Mark D. Cunningham and Thomas J. Reidy, *A Matter of Life or Death: Special Considerations and Heightened Practice Standards in Capital Sentencing Evaluations.* 19 BEHAV. SCI. & L. 473, 485, 486 (2001).

71. Specialty Guidelines for Forensic Psychology, *supra* note 52, Methods and Procedures, § D, at 661:

Forensic psychologists do not provide professional forensic services to a defendant or to any party in, or in contemplation of, a legal proceeding prior to that individual's representation by counsel, except for persons judicially determined, where appropriate, to be handling their representation pro se. When the forensic services are pursuant to court order and the client is not represented by counsel, the forensic psychologist makes reasonable efforts to inform the court prior to providing the services.

(See http://www.ap-ls.org/links/currentforensicguidelines.pdf)

72. APA ETHICS CODE, *Principle E: Respect for People's Rights and Dignity* (2002).

may need further consultation with counsel to be apprised of the potential consequences of not cooperating with the examination.[73] Mental health professionals are not in a position to alert examinees to the potential legal consequences of not cooperating with an examination and should not attempt to do so.

If the examinee remains uncooperative, the examiner has next to decide what to do with the information that has been obtained, including the examinee's resistant behavior and communications. A lack of cooperation often so constricts available data that no opinion can be offered about the examinee. Sometimes, however, this is not the case. If, for example, an examinee refuses to cooperate in a court-ordered examination of competency, but in so doing lays forth a coherent and logical set of reasons and demonstrates capacities that bear relevance to an assessment of competency, the examiner may be in a position to offer opinion about those specific capacities. There remains the question whether the examinee is *sufficiently* competent to assist counsel in planning his or her own defense, however, if counsel has advised the examinee to cooperate and the examinee has not done so. Thus, the opinion may be attenuated by further explanation of the limits in apparent functional capacities making up competency to stand trial, and the fact finder can then determine whether sufficient information is available to make a finding.

Thus far, we have explored explicit uncooperativeness. The examinee may, however, give overt signs of cooperating with the examination but covertly withhold relevant information or present a skewed picture of functioning. This covert uncooperativeness is anticipated in most forensic assessments. That is, the examinee has a significant stake in the outcome of the assessment and might naturally be expected to attempt to control that outcome by feeding the examiner the necessary impression. *Impression management* is anticipated, and forensic assessment always includes evaluation of how forthcoming or cooperative the examinee has been in providing an accurate representation of functioning.[74] The assessment of response style may occur through testing that specifically addresses response style, through examination of the individual's internal consistency across interviews and other indicia of statements, and through comparison of data obtained from third-party sources.

Impression management may include attempting to feign mental illness or mental retardation, or other impairment of cognition or behavior. *Malingering*

73. *Specialty Guidelines for Forensic Psychologists, supra* note 52, IV Relationships, (E)(1), 1.

Unless court ordered, forensic psychologists obtain the informed consent of the client or party, or their legal representative, before proceeding with such evaluations and procedures. If the client appears unwilling to proceed after receiving a thorough notification of the purposes, methods, and intended uses of the forensic evaluation, the evaluation should be postponed and the psychologist should take steps to place the client in contact with his/her attorney for the purpose of legal advice on the issue of participation.

74. HEILBRUN, *supra* note 49, at 165.

refers to conscious fabrication or gross exaggeration of symptoms for secondary gain, such as to obtain medication, to avoid responsibility for one's actions, or to invoke sympathy and nurturing.[75] Conversely, impression management may be aimed at appearing to have competencies or positive attributes one does not actually possess. An individual undergoing assessment for parenting competency in a child protection proceeding, or in a battle over parenting time and responsibility at marital dissolution, for example, may "fake good," claiming virtues or qualities that might favorably affect the outcome of the assessment.

Impression management may be conscious or unconscious. The individual may be acutely aware of the potential importance of the outcome of the assessment and deliberately present a distorted impression, or may habitually attempt to portray an exaggeratedly positive image. Consider the person who has difficulty acknowledging any weakness and swaggers self-confidently, with pseudo-bravado, or the person who simply covers over anxieties and fears. Conversely, picture the perpetual victim, who routinely focuses on assumed injuries others have perpetrated, or aches and pains, seeking the attention that comes from the sympathetic listener. Neither person is consciously attempting to fool the listener, and yet each presents a distorted picture, exaggerating certain traits while camouflaging others.

The examiner makes a routine assessment of this impression management, or what may at times be covert uncooperativeness, and incorporates this data into the overall assessment. Generally, mental health examiners refrain from concluding that someone is deliberately lying, or is deceitful, but rather attempt to explicate any apparent distortions and offer hypotheses about possible bases for the distortion.[76]

12. Conclusion

In summary, the courts rely upon mental health expertise in competence determination, and this contribution is enhanced by adherence to general ethical principles of beneficence or nonmalfeasance, respect for the rights and dignity of the examinee, and regard for the system of justice within which the examination occurs. Forensic examinations represent a unique kind of mental health service, posing challenges to the examiner and raising concerns not always an-

75. Richard Rogers, *Introduction*, in CLINICAL ASSESSMENT OF MALINGERING AND DECEPTION, 1, 11 (Richard Rogers ed., 2d ed. 1997). On the "ease" with which skilled clinicians can detect malingerers, *see* Perlin, *supra* note 18, at 236–37; Michael L. Perlin, *"There's No Success Like Failure/and Failure's No Success at All": Exposing the Pretextuality of* Kansas v. Hendricks, 92 Nw. U. L. REV. 1247, 1259 (1998).

76. Rogers, *supra* note 75, at 11 (hypotheses could include a range of possible response styles including malingering, defensiveness, irrelevant responding, random responding, honest responding, and hybrid responding).

ticipated by the court or counsel. The defendant, whose capacity to make informed and voluntary decisions may be limited, requires the protection of early notification to counsel of elements of the examination process that invoke special consideration. The examination that follows is ideally an objective, neutral, and thorough consideration of relevant and, where possible, reliable data that is synthesized or integrated to address functional capacities at issue in the court's consideration of competence. The examiner distinguishes between the beliefs or opinions that flow from that data to form expert opinion and the personally held beliefs or values that are irrelevant to the court. For that reason, the examiner may describe the elements of an individual's competence without formulating an opinion on whether the person is, by the law's reckoning, competent.

D. AN INTRODUCTION TO SANISM AND PRETEXTUALITY

Sanism is an irrational prejudice of the same quality and character as other irrational prejudices that cause and are reflected in prevailing social attitudes of racism, sexism, homophobia and ethnic bigotry. It permeates all aspects of mental disability law and affects all participants in the mental disability law system: litigants, fact finders, counsel, and expert and lay witnesses. Its corrosive effects have warped mental disability law jurisprudence in involuntary civil commitment law, institutional law, tort law, and all aspects of the criminal process (pretrial, trial, and sentencing). It reflects what civil rights lawyer Florynce Kennedy has characterized as the "pathology of oppression."[77]

Pretextuality means that courts accept (either implicitly or explicitly) testimonial dishonesty and engage similarly in dishonest (frequently meretricious) decision-making, specifically when witnesses, especially expert witnesses, show a "high propensity to purposely distort their testimony in order to achieve desired ends."[78] This pretextuality is poisonous; it infects all participants in the judicial system, breeds cynicism and disrespect for the law, demeans participants, and reinforces shoddy lawyering, blasé judging, and, at times, perjurious and/or corrupt testifying.[79]

One of the authors of this volume (MLP) has explored the relationships be-

---

77. *See, e.g.,* Michael L. Perlin, *"Half-Wracked Prejudice Leaped Forth": Sanism, Pretextuality, and Why and How Mental Disability Law Developed As It Did,* 10 J. CONTEMP. LEGAL ISSUES 3 (1999); MICHAEL L. PERLIN, THE HIDDEN PREJUDICE: MENTAL DISABILITY ON TRIAL (2000);Perlin, *Lepers, supra* note 14; Michael L. Perlin, *On "Sanism,"* 46 S.M.U L. REV. 373 (1992).

78. Michael L. Perlin, *Morality and Pretextuality, Psychiatry and Law: Of "Ordinary Common Sense," Heuristic Reasoning, and Cognitive Dissonance,* 19 BULL. AM. ACAD. PSYCHIATRY & L. 131, 135 (1991).

79. *See generally,* PERLIN, *supra* note 77.

tween sanism and pretextuality in matters involving, inter alia, competency to stand trial,[80] sexual autonomy,[81] the right to refuse treatment,[82] autonomous decision-making,[83] and competency to plead guilty or waive counsel.[84] In this volume, we will demonstrate how these factors are relevant to—and, in some instances, control—virtually all jurisprudential developments.

---

80. *E.g.*, Michael L. Perlin,*"Everything's a Little Upside Down, As a Matter of Fact the Wheels Have Stopped": The Fraudulence of the Incompetency Evaluation Process*, 4 Houston J. Health L. & Pol'y 239 (2004); Michael L. Perlin, *Pretexts and Mental Disability Law: The Case of Competency*, 47 U. Miami L. Rev. 625 (1993).

81. *E.g.*, Michael L. Perlin, *Hospitalized Patients and the Right to Sexual Interaction: Beyond the Last Frontier?* 20 N.Y.U. Rev. L. & Soc'l Change 302 (1993–94).

82. *E.g.*, Michael L. Perlin, *"And My Best Friend, My Doctor/ Won't Even Say What It Is I've Got: The Role and Significance of Counsel in Right to Refuse Treatment Cases,"* 42 San Diego L. Rev. 735 (2005); Michael L. Perlin & Deborah A. Dorfman, *"Is It More Than Dodging Lions and Wastin' Time?" Adequacy of Counsel, Questions of Competence, and the Judicial Process in Individual Right to Refuse Treatment Cases*, 2 Psychology, Pub. Pol'y & L.114 (1996).

83. *E.g.*, Perlin, *Lepers, supra* note 13.

84. *E.g.*, Michael L. Perlin, *"Dignity Was the First to Leave":* Godinez v. Moran, *Colin Ferguson, and the Trial of Mentally Disabled Criminal Defendants*, 14 Behav. Sci. & L. 61 (1996).

2

Criminal Competencies

INTRODUCTION

The relationship between competency and the criminal trial process is, and has traditionally been, robust. Numerically, the most significant inquiry has been the most well known: whether a criminal defendant is competent to stand trial.[1] But, in the nearly 15 years since the Supreme Court's still-controversial decision in *Godinez v. Moran*[2]—establishing a unitary test for competency to plead guilty and competency to waive counsel that, under federal standards, is identical to that of competency to stand trial[3]—consideration of the full range of competency issues (pretrial, at trial, and post trial) has expanded.[4] Finally, the relationship between competency and the death penalty has come under close judicial scrutiny;[5] examination of this question will likely grow more intense in the coming years as a result of the Supreme Court's decision in *Panetti v. Quarterman*,[6] that a prisoner with a severe, documented mental illness has a right to a hearing at which he could allege that he was too mentally ill to be executed because delusions interfered with his understanding of the reason for his execution.[7]

In this subchapter we examine questions related to competency to stand trial: We believe that an understanding of this issue is a condition precedent to the understanding of all other competency matters.

---

1. *See infra* Chapter 2 A.
2. 2509 U.S. 389 (1993).
3. *See generally infra* Chapter 2 B.
4. *See generally infra* Chapter 2 C 1–7.
5. *See generally infra* Chapter 2 C 8.
6. Panetti v. Quarterman, 127 S. Ct. 2842 (2007), *reversing* Panetti v. Dretke, 448 F. 3d 815 (5th Cir. 2006).
7. *Id.* at 28 57–63.

A. COMPETENCY TO STAND TRIAL

1. The Determination of Competency

a. Substantive standards[8]

(1) Historical background Few principles are as firmly embedded in Anglo-American criminal jurisprudence as the doctrine that an "incompetent" defendant may not be put to trial.[9] The doctrine is traditionally traced to mid-seventeenth-century England,[10] with commentators generally focusing on: (1) the incompetent defendant's inability to aid in his defense;[11] (2) the parallels to the historic ban on trials in absentia;[12] and (3) the parallels to the problems raised by defendants who refused to plead to the charges entered against them.[13]

The primary purpose of the rule was, under all theories, to "safeguard the accuracy of adjudication,"[14] and as early as 1899 a federal court of appeals held that it was "not 'due process of law' to subject an insane person (sic) to trial upon an

---

8. This section is largely adapted from 4 MICHAEL L. PERLIN, MENTAL DISABILITY LAW: CIVIL AND CRIMINAL, §§ 8A-2.1 to 2.3 (2d ed. 2002); *see also,* Michael L. Perlin, *Incompetency to Stand Trial,* in CRIME AND THE MIND (Robert Sadoff & Frank Dattillio, eds., 2008) (in press).

9. The incompetency-to-stand-trial determination has always been a numerically significant one. *See, e.g.,* HENRY STEADMAN, BEATING A RAP? DEFENDANTS FOUND INCOMPETENT TO STAND TRIAL 4 (1979) (approximately 9,000 defendants adjudicated incompetent yearly; 36,000 potentially incompetent defendants evaluated). For other empirical surveys, *see* sources cited in Bruce Winick, *Restructuring Competency to Stand Trial,* 32 UCLA L. Rev. 921, 922–23 (1985); *see generally* GARY MELTON ET AL., PSYCHOLOGICAL EVALUATIONS FOR THE COURTS: A HANDBOOK FOR MENTAL HEALTH PROFESSIONALS AND LAWYERS (2d ed. 1997).

Professor Winick characterizes the costs of competency evaluations as "staggering." Winick, *supra,* at 928. The numerical significance of incompetency determinations contrasts sharply with the remarkably few insanity defense cases adjudicated yearly. *See, e.g.,* Joseph Rodriguez et al., *The Insanity Defense under Siege: Legislative Assaults and Legal Rejoinders,* 14 RUTGERS L.J. 397, 401 (1983) (of 32,500 criminal cases studied in 1982, insanity defense raised in only 50, and was successful in only 15). *See also* MYTHS AND REALITIES: A REPORT OF THE NATIONAL COMMISSION ON THE INSANITY DEFENSE 16 (1983) (paraphrasing testimony by Dr. Alan Stone that insanity defense is "a pock mark on the nose of justice, while the patient is dying of congestive heart failure").

10. *See* Bruce Winick and Terry DeMeo, *Competency to Stand Trial in Florida,* 35 U. MIAMI L. REV. 31, 32 n.2 (1980). Professor Slovenko has suggested that, historically, the incompetency plea emerged as a means by which to "undercut the [death] penalty." Ralph Slovenko, *The Developing Law on Competency to Stand Trial,* 5 J. Psychiatry & L. 165, 178 (1977).

11. *See, e.g.,* 4 BLACKSTONE, COMMENTARIES 24 (9th ed. 1783); HALE, THE HISTORY OF THE PLEAS OF THE CROWN 34 (1847).

12. *See, e.g.,* People v. Berling, 251 P.2d 1017 (Cal. App. 1953).

13. Until the late eighteenth century, if the court concluded that a defendant was remaining "mute of malice," it could order him subjected to the practice of *peine forte et dure,* the placing of increasingly heavy weights on the defendant's chest to "press" him for an answer. *See, e.g.,* Slovenko, *supra* note 10, at 168–69. *See also* Winick, *supra* note 9, at 952. This practice was abolished in 1772.

14. Note, *The Identification of Incompetent Defendants: Separating Those Unfit for Adversary Combat from Those Who Are Fit,* 66 KY. L.J. 666, 668 (1978).

indictment involving liberty or life."[15] Contemporaneously, a state supreme court has suggested, "It would be inhumane, and to a certain extent a denial of a trial on the merits, to require one who has been disabled by the act of God from intelligently making his defense to plead or to be tried for his life or liberty."[16]

Thus, it became black-letter law that the "trial and conviction of a person mentally and physically incapable of making a defense violates certain immutable principles of justice which inhere in the very idea of a free government."[17] *First,* an incompetent defendant might alone have exculpatory information that he is incapable of transmitting to counsel.[18] *Second,* to try an incompetent defendant has been likened to permitting an adversary contest "in which the defendant, like a small boy being beaten by a bully, is unable to dodge or return the blows."[19] *Third,* it has been suggested that the trial of an incompetent transforms the adversary process "from a reasoned interaction between an individual and his community" into "an invective against an insensible object."[20] *Fourth,* "it seems essential to the philosophy of punishment that the defendant knows why he is being punished, and such comprehension is to a great extent dependent on involvement with the trial itself."[21] Such actions were decried over three centuries ago by Lord Coke as "a miserable spectacle, both against law, and of extreme inhumanity and cruelty, and can be no example to others."[22]

American courts quickly adopted the common law test for assessing competency to stand trial: "Does the mental impairment of the prisoner's mind, if there such be, whatever it is, disable him . . . from fairly presenting his defense, whatever it may be, and make it unjust to go on with the trial at this time, or is he feigning to be in that condition. . . ."[23] To answer this question, courts considered whether the defendant was "capable of properly appreciating his peril and of rationally assisting in his defense."[24]

(2) The Supreme Court standard   This standard—accepted by virtually every jurisdiction, either on statutory or case law bases[25]—was slightly modified by the U.S. Supreme Court in *Dusky v. United States,*[26] when the Court asked whether the defendant "has sufficient present ability to consult with his lawyer with a

---

15. Youtsey v. United States, 97 F. 937, 941 (6th Cir. 1989).
16. Jordan v. State, 135 S.W. 327, 328 (Tenn. 1911).
17. Sanders v. Allen, 100 F. 2d 717, 720 (D.C. Cir. 1938).
18. *See, e.g.,* United States v. Chisolm, 149 F. 284, 287 (S.D. Ala. 1906).
19. *See, e.g.,* Frith's Case, 22 How. State Trials 307, 318 (1790).
20. Note, *Incompetency to Stand Trial,* 81 Harv. L. Rev. 454, 458 (1967–68).
21. *Id.*
22. 3 Coke, Institutes 6 (1644). *See* Nobles v. Georgia, 168 U.S. 398 (1897).
23. *Chisolm,* 149 F. at 298.
24. United States v. Boylen, 41 F. Supp. 724, 725 (D. Or. 1941).
25. *See* Note, *supra* note 14, at 671–72 & *id.* at nn.27–29.
26. 362 U.S. 402 (1960). Although *Dusky* established the test only for federal cases, several circuits and state supreme courts adopted it as also setting out minimal *constitutional* standards. *See* Note, *supra* note 14, at 674 n.35.

reasonable degree of rational understanding—and whether he has a rational as well as a factual understanding of the proceedings against him."[27] This emphasis on rationality extended earlier doctrine as to the requisite level of a defendant's "understanding"; under *Dusky,* he must also be able to "appraise and assess the proceedings."[28] Some states and professional associations have endorsed more elaborate and specific tests,[29] yet *Dusky* is still perceived to be the national standard.[30]

Dusky—which was commonly seen as confusing and "less than helpful"[31]—was supplemented by *Drope v. Missouri*[32] to require that the defendant be able to "assist in his defense."[33] The *Drope* court ruled:

> [E]vidence of a defendant's irrational behavior, his demeanor at trial, and any prior medical opinion on competence to stand trial are all relevant in determining whether further inquiry is required, but . . . even one of these factors standing alone may, in some circumstances, be sufficient. There are, of course, no fixed or immutable signs which invariably indicate the need for further inquiry to determine fitness to proceed; the question is often a difficult one in which a wide range of manifestations and subtle nuances are implicated. That they are difficult to evaluate is suggested by the varying opinions trained psychiatrists can entertain on the same facts.[34]

(3) Later litigation   Subsequently, a New York court listed six factors to be considered in determinations of incompetency:

> [W]hether the defendant: (1) is oriented as to time and place; (2) is able to perceive, recall, and relate; (3) has an understanding of the process of the trial and the roles of judge, jury, prosecutor and defense attorney; (4) can establish a working relationship with his attorney; (5) has sufficient intelligence and judgment to listen to the advice of counsel and, based on that advice, appreciate (without necessarily adopting) the fact that one course of conduct may be more beneficial to him than another; and (6) is sufficiently stable to enable him to withstand the stresses of the trial without suffering a serious prolonged or permanent breakdown.[35]

27. *Dusky,* 362 U.S. at 402.

28. Note, *supra* note 14, at 672. *See, e.g.,* People v. Swallow, 803 (N.Y. Sup. Ct. 1969) (word "understanding" requires "some *depth* of understanding, not merely surface knowledge of the proceedings") (emphasis added).

29. *See* Gerald Bennett, *A Guided Tour through Selected ABA Standards Relating to Incompetence to Stand Trial,* 53 Geo. Wash. L. Rev. 375, 377–78 (1985) (discussing N.J. Stat. Ann. §2C:4-4 (West 1981); Wieter v. Settle, 193 F. Supp. 318, 321–22 (W.D. Mo. 1961); State v. Guatney, 299 N.W.2d 538, 545 (Neb. 1980) (Krivosha, C. J., concurring)).

30. Debra Whitcomb & Ronald Brandt, Competency to Stand Trial 1 (1985). *But compare,* Grant Morris et al., *Competency on Trial on Trial,* 4 Hous. J. Health L. & Pol'y 193(2004) (on the significant differences in tests in some states).

31. Bennett, *supra* note 29, at 376.

32. 420 U.S. 162 (1975).

33. *Id.* at 171.

34. *Id.* at 180.

35. People v. Picozzi, 482 N.Y.S. 2d 335, 337 (A.D. 1984), *appeal den.,* 64 N.Y.2d 1137 (1985).

To be able to assist counsel, a defendant should have the ability to communicate,[36] the capacity to reason "from a simple premise to a simple conclusion,"[37] the ability to "recall and relate facts concerning his actions,"[38] and the ability "to comprehend instructions and advice, and make decisions based on well-explained alternatives."[39] Several courts have also considered whether a defendant is particularly susceptible to deterioration during the course of a trial.[40] Factors to be considered include "the defendant's tendency towards violence, the presence and extent of acute psychosis, suicidal depression, regressive withdrawal, and organic deterioration."[41]

Formulaic standards, however, do not end inquiries. As noted in this text's introduction, Roth and colleagues have suggested, for instance, that the search for a single test of competency "is a search for a Holy Grail";[42] on the other hand, Burt has speculated that "the conflicting motives provoked by the spectre of mental illness— . . . solicitude and fear—appear to have induced state paralysis [in dealing with mental incompetency to stand trial]."[43] These two observations focus attention on the dual problems to be considered in assessing any question of competency to stand trial:

> [T]he difficulties inherent in the phraseology outlining the elements of the test and, as with most other areas in which law interacts with psychiatry, the realization that hidden areas of motivation and unconscious impulses are usually far more significant than what appears on the surface. . . .[44]

b. Procedural standards[45]

It is axiomatic that the conviction of an accused person who is mentally incompetent violates due process, as was stated in *Pate v. Robinson.*[46] In addition, if there is a "bona fide doubt" as to the defendant's competence,[47] the trial judge

36. Peter Silten & Richard Tullis, *Mental Competency in Criminal Proceedings*, 28 HASTINGS. L.J. 1053,1062 (1977).

37. *Id.* at 1064.

38. Allen Wilkinson & Arthur Roberts, *Defendant's Competency to Stand Trial*, 40 P.O.F.2d 171, 187 (1974).

39. *Id.* at 187.

40. *See, e.g.,* Hamm v. Jabe, 706 F.2d 765 (6th Cir. 1983). *See also* People v. Vallen, 488 N.Y.S.2d 994, 995 (Cty. Ct. 1985).

41. Wilkinson & Roberts, *supra* note 38, at 187.

42. Loren Roth et al., *Tests of Competency to Consent to Treatment*, 134 AM. J. PSYCHIATRY 279, 289 (1977).

43. Robert Burt, *Of Mad Dogs and Scientists: The Perils of the Criminal-Insane*, 123 U. PA. L. REV. 258, 276 (1974).

44. Michael L. Perlin, *Psychiatric Testimony in a Criminal Law Setting*, 3 BULL. AM. ACAD. PSYCHIATRY & L. 143, 147–48 (1975).

45. This section is adapted from 4 PERLIN, *supra* note 8, § 8A-2.3.

46. 383 U.S. 375, 385 (1966).

47. *See, e.g.,* United States v. Hollis, 569 F.2d 199, 205 n.8 (D.C. Cir. 1977); State v. Spivey, 319 A.2d 461, 469 (N.J. 1974). *See also, e.g.,* United States v. Davis, 365 F.2d 251, 254–55 (6th Cir. 1966) (obligation to order hearing rests on trial judge if court "is on notice that something

must raise the issue *sua sponte*[48] and weigh it at a "suitable hearing"[49] safe-guarded with procedures adequate to "permit a trier of fact reasonably to assess an accused's competency against prevailing medical and legal standards."[50] Once such a hearing is ordered, the proceedings must be stayed.[51] The mere submission of *ex parte* letters by examining physicians cannot take the place of such a hearing.[52]

Other courts have couched this test in terms of whether the doubt as to a defendant's competency is "substantial,"[53] "sufficient,"[54] or "clear and unequivocal,"[55] or "real and substantial,"[56] or "to positively, unequivocally, and clearly generate a real, substantial and legitimate doubt,"[57] so as to determine whether there is a "reasonable doubt" as to whether the defendant is not fit to stand trial.[58]

There need not be "a full-blown competency hearing every time there is the slimmest evidence of incompetency."[59] Under the federal statutory system, for example, a motion to determine competency can be denied "only if the trial judge correctly determines that the motion is frivolous, is not in good faith, or does not set forth the grounds for believing that the accused may be incompetent."[60] As one federal court has phrased the issue, "*Pate* does not require that a trial judge be an omniscient psychiatrist, but that he act reasonably on the objective facts before him."[61]

The fact that a defendant is psychotic does not mean that he is necessarily incompetent to stand trial. Thus, courts have variously found that defendants with these conditions are not necessarily incompetent to stand trial:

---

is amiss"). This is rephrased as "reasonable grounds to doubt" in, inter alia, State v. Saddler, 549 So. 2d 1236, *reh'g denied*, 552 So. 2d 376 (La. 1989).

48. *Pate*, 383 U.S. at 378.

49. *E.g.*, United States v. Masthers, 539 F. 2d 721, 725 (D.C. Cir. 1976).

50. *See* Holmes v. King, 709 F.2d 965, 967 (5th Cir. 1983) (quoting Fulford v. Maggio, 692 F.2d 354, 361 (5th Cir. 1982), *rev'd on other grounds*, 462 U.S. 111 (1983)).

51. *See* State v. Calais, 615 So. 2d 4 (La. App. 1993), *writ denied*, 617 So. 2d 1180 (La. 1993).

52. *E.g.*, Gibson v. State, 474 So. 2d 1183 (Fla. 1985).

53. *See generally* Acosta v. Turner, 666 F.2d 949, 954 (5th Cir. 1982); Spencer v. Zant, 715 F.2d 1562, 1567 (11th Cir. 1983), *rev'd on other grounds*, 781 F.2d 1458 (11th Cir. 1986) (en banc).

54. *E.g.*, State v. Bartlett, 935 P.2d 1114, 1118 (Mont. 1997), *reh'g denied* (1997).

55. *See* Grissom v. Wainwright, 494 F.2d 30, 32 (5th Cir. 1974).

56. Carriger v. Stewart, 95 F. 3d 755, 763 (9th Cir. 1996), *reh'g en banc granted*, 106 F.3d 1415 (9th Cir.), *vacated on other grounds*, 132 F.3d 463 (9th Cir. 1997), *cert. denied*, 523 U.S. 1133 (1998).

57. Nguyen v. Reynolds, 131 F.3d 1340, 1346 (10th Cir. 1997), *cert. denied*, 525 U.S. 852(1998), *stay denied*, 162 F.3d 600 (10th Cir. 1998).

58. Pedrero v. Wainwright, 590 F. 2d 1383, 1388 (5th Cir. 1979), *cert. denied*, 444 U.S. 943 (1979).

59. Curry v. Estelle, 531 F. 2d 766, 768 (5th Cir. 1976).

60. United States v. Bradshaw, 690 F.2d 704, 712 (9th Cir. 1982), *cert. den.*, 463 U.S. 1210 (1983).

61. Reese v. Wainwright, 600 F. 2d 1085, 1092 (5th Cir. 1979), *cert. denied*, 444 U.S. 983 (1979).

- The presence of severe mental illness,[62]
- A cumulative history of neurological and physiological ailments,[63]
- A history of hospitalization,[64]
- A finding of dangerousness,[65]
- A suicide attempt,[66]
- Borderline intelligence,[67]
- A finding that the defendant requires psychological treatment,[68]
- "Bizarre, volatile, and irrational behavior,"[69]
- Organic brain dysfunction,[70]
- A record of having received medication for "nerves and depression,"[71]
- "Minor defects" in a defendant's cognitive abilities,[72]
- A "diagnosed schizophrenic,"[73]
- A history of paranoid schizophrenia,[74] or
- Having a past record of "aberrational acts."[75]

Also, a significant body of case law has developed holding that an "insane" person may nevertheless be competent to stand trial.[76] On the other hand, a defendant must have "a modicum of intelligence" so as to assist counsel,[77] and must be

62. United States *ex rel.* Cyburt v. Rowe, 638 F.2d 1100, 1103 (7th Cir. 1981).
63. *See* United States v. Sermon, 228 F. Supp. 972, 977 (W.D. Mo. 1964) (fact that defendant was suffering from: (1) chronic brain syndrome, secondary to cerebral arteriosclerosis, (2) arteriosclerotic heart disease, (3) cataracts, (4) osteoarthritis, (5) obesity, and (6) diabetes mellitus did not render him incompetent to stand trial); *see also* State v. Young, 780 P.2d 1233, 1237 (Utah 1989) (defendant suffered from "nervous difficulties"); State v. Caudill, 789 S.W.2d 213 (Mo. Ct. App. 1990) (defendant had history of manic-depressive illness); People v. Ross, 586 N.Y.S.2d 75, 76 (A.D. 1992), *appeal denied,* 589 N.Y.S.2d 861 (1992) (defendant suffered from personality disorder, periods of depression, and "may have been hospitalized on prior occasions"); United States v. Burns, 811 F. Supp. 408, 416 (E.D. Wis. 1993), *aff'd,* 37 F.3d 276 (7th Cir. 1994), *cert. denied,* 515 U.S. 1149 (1995) ("alleged nervous breakdown . . . and subsequent psychiatric treatment").
64. People v. Dominique, 408 N.E.2d 280, 285, 288–89 (Ill. App. 1980); People v. Fowler, 583 N.E.2d 686 (Ill. App. 1991) (defendant had been involuntarily committed); People v. Wheeler, 672 N.Y.S.2d 155 (A.D. 1998) (same).
65. People v. Dominique, 408 N.E. 2d 280, 285, 288–89 (Ill. App. 1980).
66. People v. George, 636 N.E.2d 682 (Ill. App. 1994), *appeal denied,* 631 N.E.2d 713 (Ill. 1994), *cert. denied,* 512 U.S. 1241 (1994).
67. United States v. Murphy, 107 F. 3d 1199, 1203 (6th Cir. 1997).
68. People v. McMillen, 666 N.E. 2d 812, 814 (Ill. App. 1996).
69. Medina v. Singletary, 59 F. 3d 1095, 1107 (11th Cir. 1995), *cert. den.,* 517 U.S. 1247 (1996).
70. United States v. Housh, 89 F. Supp. 2d 1227, 1229–30 (D. Kan. 2000).
71. State v. Mercado, 787 S.W. 2d 848, 852 (Mo. App. 1990).
72. United States v. Liberatore, 846 F. Supp. 569, 577 (N.D. Ohio 1994).
73. State v. Martin, 485 S.E. 2d 352 (N.C. App. 1997).
74. United States v. Calek, 48 F. Supp. 2d 919 (D. Neb. 1999).
75. *See, e.g.,* State v. Messenheimer, 817 S.W.2d 273 (Mo. App. 1991) (defendant had engaged in "abnormal behavior").
76. *See* Note, *supra* note 14, at 677 n.47 (citing cases).
77. *See* Commonwealth v. Blackstone, 472 N.E.2d 1370, 1372 (Mass. App. 1985) ("modicum of rational understanding" is flexible enough concept to accommodate case of defendant

able to "comprehend his own predicament."[78] The Washington Supreme Court has summarized the court's responsibility in this manner:

> The trial judge may make his [competency] determination from many things, including the defendant's appearance, demeanor, conduct, personal and family history, past behavior, medical and psychiatric reports and the statements of counsel.[79]

Thus, in individual cases, courts have focused on evidence that showed a defendant's professed inability to communicate intelligently and assist counsel to be volitional,[80] on the significance of a defendant's refusal to consult with court-appointed counsel,[81] on the significance of conflicts in the expert testimony,[82] and on the "coheren[ce]" of the defendant's responses to the court.[83]

c. Juveniles[84]

In recent years, closer scholarly attention has been paid to the question of the competency of juveniles to stand trial for criminal or quasi-criminal offenses.[85]

---

whose refusal to plead not guilty by reason of insanity is indicative of "grievous detachment from reality"). *See, e.g.,* Noland v. Dixon, 831 F. Supp. 490 (W.D.N.C. 1993) (counsel regarded consultation with defendant as "useless"), *vacated on other grounds,* 53 F.3d 328 (4th Cir. 1995).

78. People v. Jordan, 364 N.Y.S. 2d 474, 477 (1974). *See also,* Bundy v. Dugger, 850 F.2d 1402 (11th Cir. 1988), *cert. denied,* 488 U.S. 1034 (1989); Nowitzke v. State, 572 So. 2d 1346 (Fla. 1990).

79. State v. Johnson, 527 P. 2d 1310, 1312 (Wash 1974) (quoting State v. Dodd, 70 Wash. 2d 513, 424 P.2d 302, 303, *cert. denied,* 387 U.S. 948 (1967)).

80. United States v. Turner, 602 F. Supp. 1295, 1311–13 (S.D.N.Y. 1985).

81. United States v. Pederson, 784 F. 2d 1462, 1464–65 (9th Cir. 1986).

82. Strickland v. Francis, 738 F. 2d 1542, 1551–56 (11th Cir. 1984).

83. State v. Bailey, 627 N.E. 2d 1078, 1084 (Ohio App. 1992), *appeal dismissed as improvidently granted,* 624 N.E. 2d 1062 (Ohio 1994).

84. This section is adapted from 4 PERLIN, *supra* note 8, § 8A-6.1.

85. *See* W. Lawrence Fitch, *Competency to Stand Trial and Criminal Responsibility in the Juvenile Court,* in JUVENILE HOMICIDE: CLINICAL AND FORENSIC ISSUES 145 (D. G. Cornell & E. T. Benedek eds. 1989); *see also* Vance Cowden & Geoffrey McKee, *Competency to Stand Trial in Juvenile Proceedings — Cognitive Maturity and the Attorney-Client Relationship,* 33 J. FAM. L. 629 (1994–95); Kirk Heilbrun et al., *Juvenile Competence to Stand Trial: Issues in Practice,* 20 LAW & HUM. BEHAV. 573 (1996); Geoffrey McKee & Steven Shea, *Competency to Stand Trial in Family Court: Characteristics of Competent and Incompetent Juveniles,* 27 J. AM. ACAD. PSYCHIATRY & L. 65 (1999); Geoffrey McKee, *Competency to Stand Trial in Low-IQ Juveniles,* 19 AM. J. FORENS. PSYCHIATRY 3 (1998); Geoffrey McKee, *Competency to Stand Trial in Preadjudicatory Juveniles and Adults,* 26 J. AM. ACAD. PSYCHIATRY & L. 89 (1998).

For more recent inquiries, *See, e.g.,* Norman Poythress et al., *The Competence-Related Abilities of Adolescent Defendants in Criminal Court,* 30 LAW & HUM. BEHAV. 75 (2006); Jodi Viljoen et al., *Assessing Adolescent Defendants' Adjudicative Competence: Interrater Reliability and Factor Structure of the Fitness Interview Test-Revised,* 33 CRIM. JUST. & BEHAV. 467 (2006); Eileen Ryan & Daniel Murrie, *Competence to Stand Trial and Young Children: Is the Presumption of Competence Valid?* 5 J. FORENS. PSYCHOL. PRAC. 89 (2005); Annette Christy et al., *Juveniles Evaluated Incompetent to Proceed: Characteristics and Quality of Mental Health Professionals' Evaluation,* 35 PROF. PSYCHOL.: RES. & PRAC. 380 (2004).

While a few states preclude consideration of juveniles' competency by prohibiting mental health evaluations prior to the entry of delinquency adjudications,[86] in most jurisdictions the standard for juvenile trial competency is the same as for adult trial competency.[87] In one jurisdiction, however, it has been suggested that, given the inherently reduced ability of juveniles to understand legal proceedings and to cooperate with counsel, the standard for competency in juvenile court might be lower than the applicable adult standard.[88]

Other courts have begun to explore the full range of procedural and substantive issues involved in juvenile commitments. One court, for example, has considered the relationship between a juvenile's mental retardation and the state's ability to transfer his case to adult court,[89] while another has found that, where an incompetent juvenile committed what would have otherwise been an act of juvenile delinquency, the juvenile may be committed only if the act would have constituted a felony had it been committed by an adult.[90] Other courts have found that the dismissal of juvenile delinquency action following an incompetency finding need not be with prejudice,[91] and that the state's children and families department was not statutorily required to treat an incompetent juvenile as an adult for commitment purposes.[92]

---

86. Thomas Grisso et al., *Competency in Juvenile Court,* 10 INT'L J.L. & PSYCHIATRY 1 (1987); Thomas Grisso, *Juvenile Competency to Stand Trial: Questions in an Age of Punitive Reform,* 12 CRIM. JUST. 4 (Fall 1997); *see* Carter v. Florida, 697 So. 2d 529 (Fla. Dist. App. 1997), *reh'g denied* (1997) (defense counsel failed to lay adequate foundation for admission of result of "Grisso Test").

87. Fitch, *supra* note 85, at 150; *see, e.g.,* Smith v. State, 623 So. 2d 369 (Ala. Crim. App. 1992), *cert. quashed* (1993), *cert. denied,* 510 U.S. 1030 (1993); In Interest of S.H., 469 S.E.2d 810 (Ga. App. 1996); *In re* W.A.F., 573 A.2d 1264 (D.C. 1990); S.D.J. v. State, 879 S.W. 2d 370 (Tex. App.), *reh'g denied, writ denied* (1994); for later cases, *see, e.g., In re* Patrick H., 63 Cal. Rptr. 2d 455 (App. 1997); M.D. v. State, 701 So. 2d 58 (Ala. Crim. App. 1997), *reh'g denied* (1997), *cert. denied* (1997); *In re* D.G., 698 N.E.2d 533 (Ohio C.P. 1998); Welfare of D.D.N., 582 N.W.2d 278 (Minn. App. 1998); Golden v. State, 21 S.W.3d 801 (Ark. 2000), *cert. den.,* 531 U.S. 1022 (2000); State v. K.A.W., 1999 WL 987066 (Wash. App. 1999); State v. Settles, 1998 WL 667635, *3 (Ohio App. 1998) (adult competency standard to apply to juveniles, "provided . . . that juveniles are assessed by juvenile rather than adult norms").

88. State in Interest of Causey, 363 So. 2d 472, 476 (La. 1978); *compare* United States v. D.F., 517 U.S. 1231 (1996), *vacating* 63 F.3d 671 (7th Cir. 1995), in light of Ornelas v. United States, 517 U.S. 690 (1996). For further developments in *D.F., see* United States v. D.F., 115 F.3d 413 (7th Cir. 1997) (defendant's confessions were involuntary).

89. K.E.H. v. State, 740 So. 2d 469 (Ala. Crim. App. 1998) (order of transfer remanded so that juvenile court could explain why there were no reasonable grounds to believe juvenile was committable to state department of mental health and mental retardation).

90. *See, e.g.,* Department of Children & Fam. Servs. v. A.A. St. M., 706 So. 2d 367 (Fla. Dist. App. 1998).

91. *In re* Charles B., 978 P.2d 659 (Ariz. App. 1998), *review denied* (1999).

92. State, Dep't of Children & Families v. Morrison, 727 So. 2d 404 (Fla. Dist. App.), *review denied,* 741 So. 2d 1136 (Fla. 1999).

d. Issues of involuntary medication[93]

(1) Historical background[94] One of the most perplexing substantive and procedural problems in the area of competency to stand trial is the question of what has been characterized as "synthetic" or "artificial" competency:[95] whether an incompetent defendant can be medicated against his will so as to make him competent to stand trial. The vast majority of early cases had held that it *was* permissible to medicate criminal defendants so that they meet the threshold standards for competency to stand trial.[96] Courts variously suggested that: (1) the fact that a defendant's competency arises from such medication is of "no legal consequence," since only the defendant's "condition" can be considered;[97] (2) the use of drugs "enhanced, rather than diminished defendant's ability to engage in rational thought and assist counsel at trial";[98] and (3) given the state's interest in bringing an accused to trial, the use of such drugs is thus "fundamental to a scheme of ordered liberty."[99] As the Fifth Circuit noted, the contrary argument "is akin to declaring comatose all those diabetics who, but for periodic insulin injections, would lapse into coma."[100]

Such holdings acknowledged what was perceived as the clinical reality that the administration of drugs "under proper medical supervision has effectively restored many mentally ill citizens to a useful life in which they can function as normally as other citizens not so impaired,"[101] and that to suggest otherwise would "constitute an atavistic repudiation of [such] advances."[102] One major task force study concluded that, when a defendant is medically made competent, the judge and attorneys be told: "(1) that the defendant is appearing under the influence of drugs, and (2) the type of drug administered to the defendant, the dosage, and the effect the drug has on the defendant's demeanor."[103]

---

93. *See generally infra* Chapter 3B.

94. This section is largely adapted from 4 PERLIN, *supra* note 8, § 8A-4.2.

95. *See, e.g.,* State v. Hampton, 218 So. 2d 311, 312 (La. 1969). This concept is discussed in some depth in Thomas Gutheil & Paul Appelbaum, *"Mind Control," "Synthetic Sanity," "Artificial Competence," and Genuine Confusion: Legally Relevant Effects of Antipsychotic Medication,* 12 HOFSTRA L. REV. 77 (1983).

96. *See, e.g.,* State v. Lover, 707 P.2d 1351 (Wash. App. 1985); People v. Hardesty, 362 N.W.2d 787 (Mich. App. 1984); State v. Stacy, 556 S.W.2d 552 (Tenn. Crim. App. 1977); State v. Law, 244 S.E.2d 302 (S.C. 1978); State v. Hayes, 389 A.2d 1379 (N.H. 1978); Craig v. State, 704 S.W.2d 948 (Tex. Ct. App. 1986).

97. *Hampton,* 218 So. 2d at 312.

98. *Hardesty,* 362 N.W.2d at 793; United States v. Buckley, 847 F.2d 991 (1st Cir. 1988), *cert. denied,* 488 U.S. 1015 (1989); Fox v. State, 474 N.W.2d 821 (Minn. 1991); Groover v. State, 574 So. 2d 97 (Fla. 1991).

99. *Lover,* 707 P.2d at 1354 (quoting State v. Maryott, 492 P.2d 239, 243 (Wash. App. 1971) and quoting, in part, Illinois v. Allen, 397 U.S. 337, 347 (1970)).

100. United States v. Hayes, 589 F. 2d 811, 823 (5th Cir. 1979).

101. *Stacy,* 556 S.W.2d at 557–58.

102. People v. Parsons, 371 N.Y.S. 2d 840, 842 (Cty. Ct 1975).

103. GROUP FOR THE ADVANCEMENT OF PSYCHIATRY, MISUSE OF PSYCHIATRY IN THE CRIMINAL COURTS: COMPETENCY TO STAND TRIAL 901 (1974).

On the other hand, a few cases have rejected these approaches, suggesting that it would violate due process to try to convict a defendant who was rendered *incompetent,* either by overmedication[104] or by mismedication,[105] so that he failed to meet the *Dusky* standards.[106]

(2) The Charters *cases and their aftermath*   Some measure of coherence appeared to be brought to this area of the law in the late 1980s. In *United States v. Charters,* the Fourth Circuit, en banc, sharply curtailed the rights of incompetent-to-stand-trial federal detainees to refuse antipsychotic medication.[107] Applying the "professional judgment" standard of *Youngberg v. Romeo,*[108] the court limited its inquiry to whether the drugging decision was made "by an appropriate professional" and allowed for "only one question" to be asked of experts in actions proceeding from medication decisions: "was this decision reached by a process so completely out of professional bounds as to make it explicable only as an arbitrary, nonprofessional one?"[109]

The en banc court vacated an earlier panel decision in the same case, which had provided detainees with significantly greater procedural and substantive due process protections. The panel had premised its conclusion on arguments grounded in the right to privacy, the right to freedom-of-thought process, and the right to freedom from unwanted physical intrusion.[110] In rejecting the panel's reasoning, the court "revealed its apprehensiveness about dealing with underlying social, psychodynamic, and political issues that form the overt and hidden agendas in any right-to-refuse case."[111] Writing about *Charters* 15 years ago, one of the authors of this volume (MLP) had this to say:

104. Whitehead v. Wainwright, 447 F. Supp. 898, 899–901 (M.D. Fla. 1978), *vacated and remanded on other grounds,* 609 F.2d 223 (5th Cir. 1980).

105. *Maryott,* 492 P.2d at 240 (defendant improperly drugged by jailers, not pursuant to court order) (following State v. Murphy, 355 P.2d 323 (Wash. 1960)). Observed the *Maryott* court:

> When mental competence is at issue, the right to offer testimony involves more than mere verbalization. The demeanor in court of one who has raised the issue of his sanity is of probative value to the trier of fact . . . In the instant case, the jury was instructed to give weight to the demeanor of the witnesses and [defendant] testified in his own behalf. [Defendant] claimed to be highly excitable because of his mental condition; yet, the jury saw him as very quiet because he was drugged.

Maryott, 492 P.2d at 242 (citations omitted).

106. *See, e.g.,* State v. Pray, 336 A.2d 174 (Vt. 1975) (error for trial court to fail to inform jury, in case where defendant had raised insanity defense, that defendant was under sedative medication at time of trial).

107. 863 F.2d 302 (4th Cir. 1988) (en banc), cert. denied, 494 U.S. 1016 (1990).

108. 457 U.S. 307, 321 (1982).

109. *Charters,* 863 F. 2d at 313.

110. United States v. Charters, 829 F.2d 479, 490 (4th Cir. 1987), *on reh'g,* 863 F.2d 302 (4th Cir. 1988) (en banc), cert. denied, 494 U.S. 1016 (1990).

111. Michael L. Perlin, *Are Courts Competent to Decide Competency Questions?: Stripping the Facade from United States v. Charters,* 38 KAN. L. REV. 957, 966 (1990).

The en banc opinion incorporated many heuristic devices in its reading of trial testimony: availability, typification, the myth of particularistic proofs, and the vividness effect. Its attempts to "simplify one of the most complex problems facing decisionmakers, assessing mentally disabled individuals' capacity to retain some autonomous decisionmaking power, further reflects the pernicious effect of the heuristic of attribution theory."[112]

Until the late 1990s, *Charters* was the lode star of this area of the law.[113] However, later decisions by the Sixth Circuit, the Illinois Supreme Court, and the Ninth Circuit stressed the significance of the impact of psychotropic medication on the competency-to-stand-trial determination[114] and held that the strict scrutiny standard of substantive due process review applied to this question, finding that the government must prove its case by clear and convincing evidence.[115] Each implicitly rejected the *Charters* methodology, and each seemed to indicate a new willingness to question the methodology used by the en banc Fourth Circuit in *Charters* (thus adding some additional confusion to this area of the law).

The D.C. Circuit subsequently held in *United States v. Weston*[116] (the U.S. Capitol murder case), that the defendant could be medicated against his will in a decision that was clearly influenced by the availability of the so-called "atypical antipsychotics."[117] In an important footnote, the Court noted:

Antipsychotic drugs have progressed since Justice Kennedy discussed their side effects in *Riggins* [*v. Nevada*].[118] There is a new generation of medications having bet-

---

112. Michael L. Perlin, *Pretexts and Mental Disability Law: The Case of Competency*, 47 U. MIAMI L. REV. 625, 66–67 (1993).

113. *See* 4 PERLIN, *supra* note 8, § 8A-4.2c, at 55:

Most post-*Charters* cases have adopted the position of the *en banc Charters* court (*Charters II*), and have limited the scope of an incompetent defendant's right to refuse, endorsing the view that committing "the base-line governmental decision to medicate [to] the appropriate medical personnel of the custodial institution"—subject to judicial review for "arbitrariness"—comported fully with due process, even where the exercise of professional judgment "necessarily involves some interpretation of the disputable 'meaning' of clinical 'facts.'"

114. *See, e.g.,* People v. Kinkead, 695 N.E. 2d 1255 (Ill. 1998); People v. Burton, 703 N.E. 2d 49 (Ill. 1998), *cert. den.,* 526 U.S. 1075 (1999).

115. United States v. Brandon, 158 F. 3d 947 (6th Cir. 1998). *Compare* Kulas v. Valdez, 159 F. 3d 453 (9th Cir. 1998), *cert. den.,* 528 U.S. 1167 (2000) (involuntary administration of antipsychotic medication improper, but, in tort action, treating physician entitled to qualified immunity).

116. 255 F. 3d 873 (D.C. Cir. 2001), *aff'g,* 134 F. Supp. 2d 115 (D.D.C. 2001), *cert. den.,* 534 U.S. 1067(2002).

117. *See* Douglas Mossman, *Unbuckling the "Chemical Straitjacket": The Legal Significance of Recent Advances in the Pharmacological Treatment of Psychosis,* 39 SAN DIEGO L. REV. 1033 (2002).

118. 504 U.S. 127 (1992). In *Riggins,* the Court reinvigorated the right-to-refuse-treatment doctrine in the context of a case involving the criminal trial of a competent-to-stand-trial insanity defense-pleader, holding that a "least intrusive means" or "least restrictive alternative"

ter side effect profiles. See *Weston*, 134 F.Supp.2d at 134 (citing Justice Kennedy's concurrence and writing that "[a]dvances in the primary antipsychotic medications and adjunct therapies make such side effects less likely"); Paul A. Nidich and Jacqueline Collins, *Involuntary Administration of Psychotropic Medication: A Federal Court Update*, 11 No. 4 HEALTH LAWYER 12, 13 (May 1999) ("[I]n light of the progress made in the development of new antipsychotic medications since the Supreme Court's *Riggins* decision in 1992, the courts should revisit this issue with an open mind. . . . [Because of new atypicals,] the fear of side effects should not weigh heavily in the decision whether to treat pretrial detainees or civilly committed persons with antipsychotic medication against their will when that treatment is medically appropriate."). Although the government presently plans to medicate Weston with the older generation of typicals, it could switch to the newer atypicals if side effects from the typicals threaten to impair his right to a fair trial.[119]

On the other hand, there are two more federal appellate cases that have considered the role of atypicals. In *United States v. Gomes*,[120] the Second Circuit held that, as the "heightened scrutiny standard" was appropriate for determining when a nondangerous criminal defendant could be forcibly medicated with antipsychotic drugs for the purpose of rendering him competent, a four-part test needed to be employed in such cases:

> We think that the government must show, and the district court must explicitly find, by clear and convincing evidence (1) that the proposed treatment is medically appropriate, (2) that it is necessary to restore the defendant to trial competence, (3) that the defendant can be fairly tried while under the medication, and (4) that trying the defendant will serve an essential government interest.[121]

The court stressed that the process of medicating a defendant is a "dynamic one," that can be evaluated over the course of treatment "to ascertain, with expert assistance, both its effectiveness and the nature of any side effects."[122] Thus, the court of appeals admonished the district court to "closely monitor the process to ensure that the dosage is properly individualized to the defendant, that it continues to be medically appropriate, and that it does not deprive him of a fair trial or the effective assistance of counsel."[123]

Importantly, in explaining why it adopted this standard, the *Gomes* court looked closely at "recent advances in antipsychotic medication" that "reduce

---

methodology must be used in answering the question of whether such a defendant had the right to refuse the involuntary administration of antipsychotic medications at trial. *See supra* Chapter 3B.

119. *Weston*, 255 F. 3d at 886 n.7.

120. 289 F. 3d 71 (2d Cir. 2002), *vacated*, 539 U.S. 939 (2003), *on remand with orders to vacate*, 69 Fed.Appx. 36 (2d Cir. 2003).

121. *Id*. at 82.

122. *Id*.

123. *Id*.

our concerns that the defendant's health interests and fair trial rights cannot be adequately protected when he is involuntarily medicated to render him competent to stand trial."[124] After carefully considering Justice Kennedy's concurrence in Riggins,[125] the court "first note[d] that significant improvements have been made in antipsychotic medication in the decade since Justice Kennedy expressed his misgivings in Riggins,"[126] stressing the creation of a "new generation of antipsychotic drugs, largely post-dating *Riggins*" with a "more favorable side effect profile."[127] Most of these drugs—the atypicals—"present relatively low risks of the serious side effects associated with conventional drugs such as Mellaril, the drug at issue in Riggins."[128] On this point, the court dismissed Gomes's effort to discount the significance of the atypicals as "not convincing."[129] It concluded by remanding the case for a new hearing in light of its findings.

Then, in another case, decided less than a month prior to *Gomes,* the Eight Circuit, in *United States v. Sell,*[130] considered the same question with virtually the same results, concluding that the government could, subject to limitations, forcibly administer antipsychotic medication for the sole purpose of rendering a pre-trial detainee competent to stand trial, as its interest in restoring defendant's competency so he could be brought to trial was paramount, and as no-less-intrusive means of restoring defendant's competency were available.

(3) the Sell *case*   The Supreme Court spoke on this issue in 2003 in *Sell v. United States,*[131] holding that the federal government may administer antipsychotic drugs involuntarily to render a mentally ill defendant competent to stand trial only if the treatment is medically appropriate, substantially unlikely to have side effects that may undermine the trial's fairness, and necessary to significantly further important governmental trial-related interests.[132]

Charles Sell, formerly a practicing dentist, was charged with several counts of mail fraud, Medicaid fraud, and money laundering in connection with submitting fictitious insurance claims to the federal government for payment.[133] The judge described Sell's behavior at his bail revocation hearing as totally out of control, involving "screaming and shouting," the use of "personal insults" and "racial epithets," and "spitting in the judge's face," and bail was revoked.[134] Sell was subse-

---

124. *Id.* at 83.
125. 504 U.S. at 138–45.
126. *Gomes,* 289 F. 3d at 83.
127. *Id.*
128. *Id.*
129. *Id.*
130. 282 F. 3d 560 (8th Cir. 2002), *vacated & remanded,* 539 U.S. 166 (2003).
131. 539 U.S. 166 (2003).
132. *Id.* at 166.
133. *Id.* at 168.
134. *Id.*

quently indicted for attempting to murder the FBI agent who had arrested him and a former employee who planned to testify against him in the fraud case, and these charges were joined with the fraud charges for trial.[135]

Several months later, Sell was found incompetent to stand trial and ordered hospitalized for up to 4 months to determine whether there was substantial probability that he would attain competency.[136] Two months into the hospitalization the hospital recommended that Sell take antipsychotic medication, and he refused.[137]

After administrative proceedings authorized the hospital's involuntary administration of the medication, Sell obtained a hearing before the same magistrate who had ordered his commitment.[138] The magistrate found that Sell was a danger to himself and others at the hospital, and that "the government has shown in as strong a manner as possible, that anti-psychotic medications are the only way to render the defendant not dangerous and competent to stand trial."[139] He then stayed his order authorizing the involuntary administration of the medication to allow Sell to file an appeal in federal district court.[140]

The district court held that the magistrate's finding of dangerousness was "clearly erroneous," limiting this conclusion to Sell's "dangerousness *at this time* to himself and to those around him *in his institutional context.*"[141] Nevertheless, the court affirmed the magistrate's order, holding that the medication represented the "only viable hope of rendering defendant competent to stand trial" and appeared "necessary to serve the government's compelling interest in obtaining an adjudication of defendant's guilt or innocence of numerous and serious charges."[142] The Eighth Circuit also affirmed, focusing solely on the fraud charges.[143]

The U.S. Supreme Court, per Justice Breyer, vacated the Eighth Circuit's decision and remanded the case for further proceedings. It began by affirming that the Eighth Circuit had jurisdiction to hear Sell's appeal because the district court's involuntary medication order, while not final, was an appealable "collateral order" that conclusively determined a disputed issue of clear constitutional importance.[144] The medication issue was also completely separate from the merits of the case, and effectively unreviewable on appeal from a final judgment because by the time of trial Sell would have undergone the very harm that he sought to avoid.[145]

Reaching the merits, the Court recognized that under *Washington v. Harper*[146]

---

135. *Id.* at 170.
136. *Id.* at 171.
137. *Id.*
138. *Id.* at 172.
139. *Id.* at 173.
140. *Id.*
141. *Id.* at 174 (emphasis in original).
142. *Id.*
143. *Id.*
144. *Id.* at 176.
145. *Id* at 176–77.
146. 494 U.S. 210 (1990).

and *Riggins v. Nevada*[147] Sell had a liberty interest in avoiding the involuntary administration of antipsychotic drugs, and this interest was protected by the Fifth Amendment's due process clause against all but "essential" or "overriding" state interests.[148] The Court held:

> These two cases, *Harper* and *Riggins,* indicate that the Constitution permits the Government involuntarily to administer antipsychotic drugs to a mentally ill defendant facing serious criminal charges in order to render that defendant competent to stand trial, but only if the treatment is medically appropriate, is substantially unlikely to have side effects that may undermine the fairness of the trial, and, taking account of less intrusive alternatives, is necessary significantly to further important governmental trial-related interests.[149]

The Court considered each of these separately. First—using italics to stress the key words—it noted, a court "must find that *important* governmental interests are at stake";[150] bringing an individual to trial accused of a "serious crime" is "important."[151] Second, it added, the court must conclude that "involuntary medication will *significantly further* those concomitant state interests," and must find that administration of the drugs is "substantially likely" to render the defendant competent to stand trial.[152] At the same time, the Court warned, the trial court must find that administration of the drugs is "substantially unlikely to have side effects that will interfere significantly with the defendant's ability to assist counsel in conducting a trial defense, thereby rendering the trial unfair," citing Justice Kennedy's concurrence in Riggins.[153] Third, the trial court must conclude that involuntary medication is "*necessary* to further those interests" and that "any alternative, less intrusive treatments are unlikely to achieve substantially the same results,"[154] citing here the contrasting briefs of Amici American Psychological Association and American Psychiatric Association.[155] Finally, the trial court must conclude that "administration of the drugs is *medically appropriate, that is,* in the patient's best medical interest in light of his medical condition."[156] Here, the court made its only reference to the issue that had been the focus of much attention,

---

147. 504 U.S. 127 (1992).
148. *Sell,* 539 U.S. at 178.
149. *Id.* at 179.
150. *Id.* at 180.
151. *Id.*
152. *Id.* at 181.
153. *Id.; see Riggins,* 504 U.S. at 142–45.
154. *Id.* (emphasis in original).
155. The American Psychological Association argued that nondrug therapies may be effective in restoring psychotic defendants to competence, while the American Psychiatric Association argued, contrarily, that alternative treatments for psychosis were commonly not as effective as medication. *See id.*
156. *Id.* (emphasis added).

both in the circuit decision in *Sell* and in the circuit decisions in *United States v. Gomes:*[157] whether the availability of the new "atypical antipsychotics" would cause a reformulation of the Court's policies:

> The specific kinds of drugs at issue may matter here as elsewhere. Different kinds of antipsychotic drugs may produce different side effects and enjoy different levels of success.[158]

The Court emphasized that the governmental interest under this standard is the interest in rendering the defendant competent to stand trial:

> A court need not consider whether to allow forced medication for that kind of purpose, if forced medication is warranted for a *different* purpose, such as the purposes set out in *Harper* related to the individual's dangerousness, or purposes related to the individual's own interests where refusal to take drugs puts his health gravely at risk. There are often strong reasons for a court to determine whether forced administration of drugs can be justified on these alternative grounds *before* turning to the trial competence question.[159]

The Court stressed that "the inquiry into whether medication is permissible, say, to render an individual nondangerous is usually more 'objective and manageable' than the inquiry into whether medication is permissible to render a defendant competent," and closer to the court's familiar role in assessing dangerousness for the purposes of involuntary civil commitment.[160] If a court can authorize involuntary medication on alternative grounds such as dangerousness "the need to consider authorization on trial competence grounds will likely disappear."[161] If medication cannot be authorized on other grounds, then "the findings underlying such a decision will help to inform expert opinion and judicial decisionmaking in respect to a request to administer drugs for trial competence purposes."[162]

The Court found that, based on the "hypothetical assumption" that the Eighth Circuit was correct in concluding that Sell was not dangerous, that court "was wrong to approve forced medication solely to render Sell competent to stand trial."[163] However, the record suggested that Sell was, in fact, dangerous, and the hospital and the magistrate had approved the forced medication "substantially, if not primarily" on those grounds.[164]

Because the hearing before the magistrate had focused largely on the danger-

157. 289 F. 3d 71 (2d Cir. 2002); *see supra* text accompanying notes 120–29.
158. *Sell,* 539 U.S. at 181.
159. *Id.* at 182 (emphasis in original, citation omitted).
160. *Id.* (quoting *Riggins,* 504 U.S. at 140 (Kennedy, J., concurring)).
161. *Id.* at 183.
162. *Id.*
163. *Id.* at 185.
164. *Id.* at 183.

ousness issues, "the experts did not pose important questions—questions, for example, about trial-related side effects and risks—the answers to which could have helped determine whether forced medication was warranted on trial competence grounds alone."[165] The court invalidated the existing medication order but remanded the case for a determination of whether the order might be justified on grounds unrelated to Sell's competency to stand trial, such as the possibility that Sell might presently pose a danger to himself or others.[166]

Sell will likely prove to be an extraordinarily important decision for several reasons. First, it appears to elevate much of Justice Kennedy's concurring opinion in *Riggins* to majority status. This is important for two separate reasons: First, Justice Kennedy's *Riggins* opinion is relied on at least four times in the course of *Sell*, and this suggests that, in the 11 years after *Riggins* and before *Sell*, the majority of the Court became more comfortable with his position (increasing the burden on the government when it seeks to involuntarily medicate someone in the criminal trial process). Second, Justice Kennedy was the most critical of all the justices of the potential harms of drug side effects, and *Sell* suggests that this is now a position with which a majority of the Court is comfortable.

Second, the language that the Court uses in *Sell* in its harmonization of *Harper* and *Riggins* is significant in many ways. First, it italicizes many phrases: "*important* governmental interests," "*significantly further* concomitant state interests," that involuntary medication is "*necessary* to further those interests," that administration of the drugs is "*medically appropriate.*" That emphasis suggests that the Court wants lower courts to take these issues seriously.

Third, the Court stresses—much more clearly than it did in *Riggins*—the need to engage in a "least restrictive alternative" analysis in every such case. The words *intrusive* and *restrictive* are in the opinion well over a dozen times, and the significance of that use of language should not be underestimated.

Fourth, it is not at all clear what impact *Sell* will have on civil cases (for it bores in on the trial incompetence issue again and again, as that was the focus of the case). However, in its discussion, the court makes clear—albeit in what is dicta—that decisional incompetence and current danger are the only two acceptable overrides in civil cases. It has been 26 years since the Court considered a civil right to refuse case,[167] and thus the Court's endorsement of these factors in this context takes even greater significance.

---

165. *Id.* at 185.
166. *Id.* at 186.
   Justice Scalia, writing for justices O'Connor and Thomas, dissented on the jurisdictional issue, predicting that the majority's application of the collateral order doctrine to this case would allow defendants in Sell's position "to engage in opportunistic behavior" by abruptly ceasing to take their medication part-way through the trial and demanding an interlocutory appeal of a resulting compulsory medication order or otherwise "stopping the proceedings in their tracks." He added that the majority opinion "empowered [Sell] to hold up the trial for months by claiming that review after final judgment 'would come too late' to prevent the violation." *Id.* at 191.
167. *See* Mills v. Rogers, 457 U.S.291 (1982).

Fifth, *Sell* makes clear that the hearing must be a judicial hearing, *not* the sort of bare-bones administrative hearing countenanced in Harper.[168]

e. Quality of assessment

(1) Elements of assessment[169]   Competency evaluations are typically, although perhaps unnecessarily,[170] performed in maximum security hospitals to which defendants have been committed for specified time periods.[171] While slightly more than a third of the states compel this examination to be done on an inpatient basis,[172] about the same number now permit outpatient evaluations as well,[173] often at court clinics located in or near county courthouses.[174] In such cases, although the defendant is not hospitalized, he or she often nevertheless remains incarcerated—for failure to meet bail requirements—pending trial.[175]

Empirical studies[176] have shown that evaluators usually base their decision on a single interview—often lasting less than an hour, and usually completed within a few days of the individual's admission to the maximum security inpatient facility[177]—and that, in the "vast majority of cases," a community-based evaluation would provide a sufficient basis for making competency determinations.[178]

---

168. *See* Paul Appelbaum, *Treating Incompetent Defendants: The Supreme Court's Decision Is a Hard* Sell, 54 PSYCHIATRIC SERVS. 1335, 1336 (2003).

169. This section is largely adapted from 4 PERLIN, *supra* note 8, § 8A-4.1 to 4.1a.

170. *See* Michael L. Perlin, *"For the Misdemeanor Outlaw" The Impact of the ADA on the Institutionalization of Criminal Defendants with Mental Disabilities,* 52 ALABAMA L. REV. 193 (2000).

171. *See* Barbara Weiner, *Mental Disability and the Criminal Law,* in SAMUEL JAN BRAKEL ET AL., THE MENTALLY DISABLED AND THE LAW 693, 744–53 (Table 12.1) (3d ed. 1985). On the question of the validity of a *jailhouse* examination, *see* Hinkle v. Scurr, 677 F.2d 667 (8th Cir. 1982), *cert. den.,* 459 U.S. 1040 (1982).

172. Weiner, *supra* note 171, at 744–53 (Table 12.1).

173. *Id. See* Winick, *supra* note 9, at 930–32 (outpatient evaluations can be done much more quickly and cheaply than inpatient examinations).

174. *See, e.g.,* People v. Parker, 393 Mich. 531, 227 N.W.2d 775 (1975); Weiner, *supra* note 171, at 697.

175. *Id.*

On the question of costs, *see* State, DHRS v. Myers, 696 So. 2d 863 (Fla. Dist. App. 1997), *reh'g & clarification denied* (1997) (county where mentally ill detainee was being held rather than county sheriff or state department of health responsible for cost of detainee's treatment pending trial).

176. *See, e.g.,* Richard Rogers et al., *Fitness Evaluations: A Retrospective Study of Clinical, Criminal, and Sociodemographic Characteristics,* 20 CAN. J. BEHAV. SCI. 192 (1988); Jeffrey Geller et al., *Effect of Evaluation of Competency to Stand Trial on the State Hospital in an Era of Increased Community Services,* 42 HOSP. & COMMUN. PSYCHIATRY 818 (1991); Thomas Grisso, *Pretrial Clinical Evaluations in Criminal Cases: Past Trends and Future Directions,* 23 CRIM. JUST. & BEHAV. 90 (1996).

177. RONALD ROESCH & STEPHEN GOLDING, COMPETENCY TO STAND TRIAL 204 (1980). In State v. Bell, 293 S.C. 391, 360 S.E.2d 706 (1987), *cert. denied,* 484 U.S. 1020 (1988), the court rejected defendant's argument that a competency finding was precluded because the psychologist's testimony was "incomplete or wrong," on the grounds that defense counsel could deal with any such errors of omission or commission on cross-examination.

178. Weiner, *supra* note 171, at 697.

However, other social forces—the use of the competency examination as a means of ensuring the defendant's longer-term removal from the community, desire for trial delays, and use of hospitalization period as a "chip" for subsequent plea bargaining[179]—have served as a fairly strong counterweight to these findings.[180]

Courts have frequently considered both the quality and scope of expert evaluations in this aspect of the proceedings. In one case, the Eleventh Circuit affirmed a habeas corpus grant when the defendant's original expert evaluation focused solely on his proffered delusional compulsion defense; since this evaluation lacked an assessment of his competency to stand trial, it was not an appropriate basis upon which to support a competency finding.[181] And the Tenth Circuit has held that test results from pretrial competency evaluations are not per se inadmissible at trial.[182] Elsewhere, a New Mexico appellate court has ruled that it was not an abuse of discretion for the trial judge to deny the state's motion for an independent evaluation of the defendant by its own expert,[183] and another Tenth Circuit case has found that a state court can find a defendant competent without ordering an evidentiary hearing, even if there is some psychiatric testimony indicating that the defendant is incompetent.[184]

One important issue relating to expert testimony concerns the role of the fact finder. It is clear that a fact finder need not adhere to an expert opinion on incom-

---

179. *Id. See also, e.g.,* Weiner, *supra* note 171, at 696.

180. On the requirements as to the professional training of the evaluator, *see id.* at 698. For a relevant and helpful case on the ability of psychologists to testify at incompetency hearings, *see* People v. Lewis, 393 N.E.2d 1380 (Ill. App. 1979) (overruling People v. Koch, 381 N.E.2d 377 (Ill. App. 1978), and People v. Morthole, 366 N.E.2d 606 (Ill. App. 1977)). *See generally* Michael L. Perlin, *The Legal Status of the Psychologist in the Courtroom,* 5 J. Psychiatry & L. 41 (1977). On the issue of whether or not a particular psychiatrist is qualified to conduct such an examination, *see* People v. Lowe, 109 491 N.Y.S.2d 529 (A.D. 1985); People v. Miller, 562 N.Y.S.2d 300 (A.D. 1990), *appeal denied,* 569 N.Y.S.2d 941 (1991). On the admissibility of testimony by the physician who attended at the defendant's birth (as to the brain damage he might have suffered as a result of a hypoxic episode following premature delivery), *see* State v. Haun, 695 S.W.2d 546 (Tenn. Crim. App. 1985).

Courts have split on the question of whether the defendant has the right to an examination by a psychiatrist of his or her choice. *Compare, e.g.,* United States v. Lincoln, 542 F.2d 746, 749–50 (8th Cir. 1976) (no abuse of discretion to refuse to appoint psychiatrist sought by defense counsel) *with* United States v. Bass, 477 F.2d 723, 725–26 (9th Cir. 1973) (ordinarily desirable to appoint psychiatrist preferred by defendant). *Cf.* Ake v. Oklahoma, 470 U.S. 68 (1985), *discussed extensively* in 4 Perlin, *supra* note 8, § 10-4.2. *See, e.g.,* United States v. Rinchack, 820 F.2d 1557 (11th Cir. 1987) (defendant not entitled to appointment of expert to aid in preparation for competency hearing); *see also* Hill v. Thigpen, 667 F. Supp. 314 (N.D. Miss. 1987), *aff'd in part, rev'd in part on other grounds sub nom.* Hill v. Black, 887 F.2d 513 (5th Cir.), *supplemented,* 891 F.2d 89 (5th Cir. 1989) (failure to appoint expert not erroneous where no serious question presented as to defendant's competency to stand trial).

181. Ford v. Gaither, 953 F.2d 1296 (11th Cir. 1992).

182. United States v. Vazquez-Pulido, 155 F.3d 1213 (10th Cir. 1998), *cert. denied,* 525 U.S. 978 (1998).

183. State v. Garcia, 128 N.M. 721, 998 P.2d 186 (App. 2000).

184. Bryson v. Ward, 187 F.3d 1193, 1203 (10th Cir. 1999), *cert. denied,* 529 U.S. 1058 (2000).

petency if there is a reason to discount it.[185] However, when the expert testimony "clearly and overwhelmingly" points to one conclusion, a jury cannot arbitrarily ignore the experts in favor of lay observations.[186] In one case, the Fifth Circuit set out four factors that could reasonably lead a fact finder to disregard expert testimony on a defendant's mental condition:

1. The correctness or adequacy of the factual assumptions on which the expert testimony is based.
2. Possible bias in the experts' appraisal of the defendant's condition.
3. Inconsistencies in the experts' testimony, or material variations between experts.[187]
4. The relevance and strength of the contrary lay testimony.[188]

On the final subissue, comparing contrary lay testimony, courts must be sure to differentiate between testimony as to the defendant's mental state at the time of offense, often seen as highly prejudicial,[189] and relevant testimony as to the defendant's condition at the time of trial.[190] For lay testimony to be given weight in a competency determination, it is necessary that the witness has had recent, prolonged, and intimate contact with the defendant.[191]

Another issue concerns the quality of expert testimony.[192] In at least one in-

185. Strickland v. Francis, 738 F.2d 1542, 1552 (11th Cir. 1984); White v. Estelle, 669 F.2d 973, 978 (5th Cir. 1982), *cert. denied,* 459 U.S. 1118 (1983); United States v. Makris, 535 F.2d 899, 908 (5th Cir. 1976). On the need for the trial court to make specific fact-findings in a competency determination, *see* Byrd v. State, 719 S.W.2d 237 (Tex. Ct. App. 1986).

186. *Strickland v. Francis, supra* (quoting Brock v. United States, 387 F.2d 2354, 257 (5th Cir. 1967)); *see also* Wallace v. Kemp, 757 F.2d 1102, 1109 (11th Cir. 1985); United States v. Hall, 583 F.2d 1288, 1294 (5th Cir. 1978); State v. Black, 815 S.W.2d 166 (Tenn.), *petit. for appeal overruled,* 1991 WL 167223 (Tenn. 1991); Nunez v. State, 942 S.W.2d 57 (Tex. App. 1997); Mollen v. Mathews, 710 N.Y.S.2d 399 (A.D. 2000).

187. *See, e.g.,* R. L. Goldstein & M. Stone, *When Doctors Disagree: Differing Views on Competency,* 5 Bull. Am. Acad. Psychiatry & L. 90, 95 (1977) (disagreement only in 2.5 percent of group of court-referral cases studied). *See generally* Ronald Roesch, et al., *The Fitness to Stand Trial Interview Test: How Four Professions Rate Videotaped Fitness Interviews,* 7 Int'l J.L. & Psychiatry 115 (1984). For an example, *see* Engle v. Dugger, 576 So. 2d 696 (Fla.), *reh'g denied* (1991).

See also Lagway v. Dallman, 806 F. Supp. 1322, 1338 (N.D. Ohio 1992) (granting writ of habeas corpus where state trial judge "substituted his own psychological expertise for that of the court-appointed expert without any testimony").

188. *Brock,* 387 F.2d at 258. *See Strickland v. Francis,* 738 F.2d at 1552–56 (setting out and applying the *Brock* factors); Bundy v. Dugger, 675 F. Supp. 622, 634 (M.D. Fla. 1987), *aff'd,* 850 F.2d 1402 (11th Cir. 1988), *cert. denied,* 488 U.S. 1034 (1989).

189. *See, e.g.,* Martin v. Estelle, 546 F.2d 177 (5th Cir. 1977), *cert. denied,* 431 U.S. 971 (1977).

190. *Strickland v. Francis,* 738 F.2d at 1554–55.

191. Lokos v. Capps, 625 F.2d 1258, 1267–68 (5th Cir. 1980).

On the right of the court to compel trial counsel to testify at a retrospective competency hearing, *see* People v. Kinder, 512 N.Y.S.2d 597 (A.D. 1987), *appeal denied,* 518 N.Y.S.2d 1042 (1987) (counsel ordered to testify).

192. *See generally* Note, *supra* note 20, at 469–71; *Bundy, supra.*

For subsequent inquiries, *see, e.g.,* Jackson v. Dugger, 547 So. 2d 1197, 1200 (Fla. 1989), *reh'g denied,* (1989) (no requirement that issue of defendant's competency must be reopened be-stance,[193] an intermediate appellate court in Michigan carefully examined this issue in a competency-to-stand-trial inquiry, ruling that it was erroneous for the witness to: (1) express an opinion on the legislature's intent in adopting certain statutory language;[194] (2) quantify (using IQ measurements) "mental retardation," where the legislature had chosen to define it descriptively;[195] and (3) base his expert opinion on "such colloquial and imprecise expressions" as "going bananas" or being "out in left field."[196]

Concerning a third issue, there is a significant body of evidence that suggests that psychiatrists often demand a higher level of competency on the part of defendants than do appellate courts.[197] Dr. McGarry, for example, has suggested that, among less secure mental health professionals, there is a preoccupation with eliciting pathology as a demonstration of one's own expertise; the competence of the examiner may rest on his or her ability to demonstrate incompetency on the part of the defendant.[198]

A fourth issue involves the capacity to detect malingering[199] by the defendant.

---

cause examining psychiatrist "reached a legitimate conclusion based on the symptoms displayed by the defendant but failed to associate those symptoms with another mental deficiency"); United States v. Bennett, 908 F.2d 189, 195 (7th Cir.), *cert. denied*, 498 U.S. 991 (1990) (court's determination that defendant was competent not clearly erroneous where defendant's sole witness conceded that he did not perform any psychological tests on defendant, and that defendant "may have feigned some or all of the symptoms"). In Firo v. State, 878 S.W.2d 254 (Tex. App.), *reh'g overruled, opinion adhered to*, 885 S.W.2d 534 (Tex. App.), *review refused* (1994), the court held that the state's expert's report was inadmissible in a competency hearing as it detailed elements of the charged offense.

193. On the question of the admissibility of psychiatric testimony on the question of competency under the hearsay rule, *see, e.g.*, Hunter v. State, 489 So. 2d 1086, 1087–88 (Miss. 1986).

194. People v. Doan, 366 N.W.2d 593, 595 (Mich. App. 1985).

195. *Id.* at 595–96.

196. *Id.* at 595, 598: "Counsel and the court have a responsibility to make certain that the language used by experts is professional, clear, and within the parameters of the standards set by the law." *See also, e.g.*, Addkison v. State, 608 So. 2d 304, 308 (Miss. 1992) (psychiatrist characterized defendant as "high-end imbecile"); *Buxton, supra* (defense expert misinterpreted legal standard for competency; nonetheless, defendant found competent to stand trial).

197. Michael L. Perlin, *Overview of Rights in the Criminal Process, in* 3 LEGAL RIGHTS OF MENTALLY DISABLED PERSONS 1879, 1885 (Paul Friedman ed. 1979).

198. Louis McGarry, *Demonstration and Research in Competency for Trial and Mental Illness: Review and Preview*, 49 B.U. L. REV. 46, 52–53 (1969). Doctor McGarry's research is analyzed in Jan Schreiber, *Assessing Competency to Stand Trial: A Case Study of Technology Diffusion in Four States*, 6 BULL. AM. ACAD. PSYCHIATRY & L. 439 (1978).

199. Malingering is discussed in this context in Winick, *supra* note 9, at 974–75 n.252. For examples, *see* People v. Torry, 571 N.E.2d 827, *reh'g denied* (Ill. App. 1991), *appeal denied*, 580 N.E.2d 131 (Ill. 1991); Cowan v. State, 579 So. 2d 13 (Ala. Crim. App.), *cert. denied* (1991); United States v. Kokoski, 865 F. Supp. 325 (S.D. W. Va. 1994), *aff'd*, 82 F.3d 411 (4th Cir.), *cert. denied*, 519 U.S. 892 (1996); United States v. Gigante, 1996 WL 497050 (E.D.N.Y. 1996); State v. Robertson, 932 P.2d 1219 (Utah 1997); United States v. Gigante, 925 F. Supp. 967 (E.D.N.Y. 1996), aff'd, 85 F. 3d 83 (2d Cir. 1996).

See *generally* Philip Resnick, *Defrocking the Fraud: The Detection of Malingering*, 30 J. PSYCHIATRY & RELAT. SCI. 93 (1993); Richard Rogers et al., *A Meta-Analysis of Malingering on*

In at least two cases, federal district courts have considered this perennial problem.[200] In *United States v. Zovluck*,[201] the court accepted an expert witnesses' list of common indicators of malingering:

> dramatic acting, special familiarity with textbooks of psychiatry, unusually superior intelligence, professional criminal background, findings incompatible with mental illness, frequent legal manipulation in the past, notoriety, unusually proficient conning ability, impostering, impersonating, etc.[202]

(2) The significance of the Morris-Haroun-Naimark studies   Morris and colleagues have recently published data that call into question one of the baseline assumptions of the entire competency-to-stand-trial process: that clinicians' evaluations of competency are, in fact, reliable. In their paper, *Competency to Stand Trial on Trial,* Morris and two forensic psychiatrists report on research they conducted reviewing how forensic experts implement the legal requirement that a criminal defendant must be competent to stand trial.[203] Using two vignettes (one indicates that the defendant's thinking is impaired, but his pretrial behavior is normal; the other describes a defendant whose pretrial behavior is impaired, but her thinking is not), they found that, in the case of the first vignette, the experts split almost evenly.[204] About half considered the hypothetical defendant competent to stand trial, while the other half did not. In the second, although there was greater agreement, the divergence of expert opinions was still found to be troubling. The data, in their view, raised a "fundamental question" of whether experts really are experts.[205]

---

the MMPI-2, 1 PSYCHOLOG. ASSESSMENT 227 (1994); Douglas Mossman & Kathleen Hart, *Presenting Evidence of Malingering to Courts: Insights from Decision Theory,* 14 BEHAV. SCI. & L. 271 (1996); Richard Rogers & Randall Saleskin, *Beguiled by Bayes: A Re-Analysis of Mossman & Hart's Estimates of Malingering,* 16 BEHAV. SCI. & L. 147 (1998); Richard Rogers et al., *A Comparison of Forensic and Nonforensic Malingerers: A Prototypical Analysis of Explanatory Models,* 22 LAW & HUM. BEHAV. 353 (1998); for the most recent research, *see* Michael Vitacco et al., *An Evaluation of Malingering Screens with Competency to Stand Trial Patients: A Known-Groups Comparison,* 31 LAW & HUM. BEHAV. 249 (2007).

200. *See generally,* Michael L. Perlin, *The Supreme Court, the Mentally Disabled Criminal Defendant, Psychiatric Testimony in Death Penalty Cases, and the Power of Symbolism: Dulling the Ake in Barefoot's Achilles Heel,* 3 N.Y.L. SCH. J. HUM. RTS. 91, 131 n.248 (1985) (quoting Dr. Isaac Ray's (1838 discussion of fear of feigned insanity)). *See* United States v. Zovluck, 425 F. Supp. 719 (S.D.N.Y. 1977); United States v. Turner, 602 F. Supp. 1295 (S.D.N.Y. 1985).

201. 425 F. Supp. 719 (S.D.N.Y. 1977).

202. *Id.,* 425 F. Supp. at 724. For subsequent litigation in this vein, *see* Flugence v. Butler, 848 F.2d 77 (5th Cir. 1988).

On the significance of defendant's cooperation with examining experts, *see* Gilliam v. State, 514 So. 2d 1098, 1100 (Fla. 1987) ("Where a defendant attempts to thwart the process by refusing to cooperate, the court has no duty to order a futile attempt at further examination").

203. Grant H. Morris et al., *Competency to Stand Trial on Trial,* 4 HOUS. J. HEALTH L. & POL'Y 193, 200 (2004).

204. *Id.* at 214.

205. *Id.* at 237.

In his analysis of the Morris article, Prof. John LaFond notes:

> The authors then analyze comments about the two vignettes made by individual evaluators. Some comments about the first vignette suggest that the evaluators too often "played lawyer" in reaching their conclusions, and may need to know about how the clients interacted with their attorney and what the legal defense might be to . . . conduct a thorough evaluation. Comments about the second vignette suggest, among other things, that evaluators gave undue weight to the diagnosis and its severity in reaching their conclusion. Others took treatment needs into account. Simply put, experts infuse their own normative preferences and interpretations of legal standards when determining whether mentally ill defendants are competent to stand trial.[206]

In writing about these findings, one of the authors of this volume (MLP) said this:[207]

> What is the significance of these astounding findings? Let me suggest a few possibilities:
> 1. We have always accepted as conventional wisdom the fact there is high interrater concordance in the assessment of what should be a much more difficult evaluation: whether a defendant is insane (meaning, is he not responsible for his acts because of mental illness which led him to, variously, not know right from wrong, or to be able to appreciate the nature or quality of his act). It would be reasonable to expect greater ambiguity on insanity questions because of several factors: (a) the ambiguity of the tests, (b) the political context of insanity defense evaluations, (c) the greater publicity attached to these cases, and (d) the ultimate implications of the ultimate finding. Yet most studies have consistently demonstrated that the rate of agreement in these cases is remarkably high—often approaching 90 percent. The contrast is startling.
> 2. The competency-to-stand-trial test is often seen as an "easy" or "minimalist" one. Only, it is commonly argued, the most "out of it" criminal defendants will be found IST, in large part because the competency test demands so little mental capacity on the part of the defendant. What, then, to make of the utterly contrary findings in this survey?
> 3. In the years since Bernard Diamond exposed the fallacy of the "impartial expert," scholars for the most part have avoided the dirty little question that was at the core of Diamond's writings in this area: Is there such a thing as a "neutral" or "objective" expert witness? I have always thought that this was a vastly under-discussed question, and perhaps this article will reinvigorate that debate.[208]

---

206. John LaFond, *Foreword: Health Law in the Criminal Justice System*, 4 Hous. J. Health L. & Pol'y 181, 185–86 (2004).

207. Michael L. Perlin, *"Everything's a Little Upside Down, as a Matter of Fact, the Wheels Have Stopped": The Fraudulence of the Incompetency Evaluation Process*, 4 Hous. J. Health L. & Pol'y 239, 244–45 (2004).

208. Perlin, *supra* note 207, at 244–45.

f. Right to counsel[209]

There is no reason to doubt the accuracy of Professor Pizzi's statement: "For practical reasons, the key to the competency issue is the defense attorney."[210]

Problems raised by the possible specter of incompetent counsel involved in cases questioning the competency of a defendant to stand trial are exacerbated by counsel's generally inadequate record in the representation of mentally disabled individuals[211] and its specifically inadequate role in the representation of defendants potentially incompetent to stand trial. A Harvard Medical School study revealed that the *great majority* of defense counsel interviewed were unaware of the common-law criteria for competency to stand trial.[212]

Conversely, few counsel are conversant with psychiatric and psychological principles;[213] the Third Circuit has found, for example, that counsel's failure to contest competency based on *his* observations of the defendant and the presump-

---

209. This section is largely adapted from 4 PERLIN, *supra* note 8, § 8A-4.3.

210. William Pizzi, *Competency to Stand Trial in Federal Courts: Conceptual and Constitutional problems,* 45 U. CHI. L. REV. 21, 27 (1977). *See generally id.* at 57–64. For comprehensive analyses, *see* Rodney Uphoff, *The Role of the Criminal Defense Lawyer in Representing the Mentally Impaired Defendant: Zealous Advocate or Officer of the Court?,* 1988 WIS. L. REV. 65; Christopher Slobogin & Amy Mashburn, *The Criminal Defense Lawyer's Fiduciary Duty to Clients with Mental Diabilities,* 68 FORDHAM L. REV. 1581 (2000); William Geimer, *A Decade of* Strickland's *Tin Horn: Doctrinal and Practical Undermining of the Right to Counsel,* 4 WM. & MARY BILL OF RTS. J. 91 (1995); Josephine Ross, *Autonomy versus a Client's Best Interests: The Defense Lawyer's Dilemma when Mentally Ill Clients Seek to Control Their Defense,* 35 AM. CRIM. L. REV 1343 (1998). *Compare* Engle v. State, 774 P. 2d 1303 (Wyo. 1989), appeal after remand, 821 P. 2d 1285 (Wyo. 1991)(defense counsel's failure to request second psychiatric opinion following filing of competency report did not constitute waiver of right; conviction reversed).

On the right to appellate counsel on issues relating to competency status, *see* Huff v. State, 807 S.W.2d 325 (Tex. Crim. App. 1991). On the interplay between the right to counsel and counsel's right to be notified of a competency examination, *see* People v. Perkins, 562 N.Y.S. 2d 244 (A.D. 1990).

For a recent empirical inquiry, *see* Corey Bayliss & O. Elmer Polk, *Attorneys' Self-Reported Perspectives and Criteria for Requesting Competency Evaluations in Criminal Defense Cases,* 30 CRIM. JUST. REV. 312 (2005).

211. *See, e.g.,* Michael L. Perlin & Robert L. Sadoff, *Ethical Issues in the Representation of Individuals in the Commitment Process,* 45 LAW & CONTEMP. PROBS. 161 (Summer 1982) (hereinafter *Ethical Issues*).

212. LABORATORY OF COMMUNITY PSYCHIATRY, HARVARD MEDICAL SCHOOL, FINAL REPORT, COMPETENCY TO STAND TRIAL AND MENTAL ILLNESS 1-6 (1973)(HARVARD COMPETENCY STUDY). *See* Louis McGarry, *Competency for Trial and Due Process via the State Hospital,* 122 AM. J. PSYCHIATRY 623, 628 (1965) (assistance of counsel "quite rare"). *See generally* Robert J. Golten, *Role of Defense Counsel in the Criminal Commitment Process,* 10 AM. CRIM. L. REV. 385, 386–400 (1972) (enumerating lawyers' responsibilities for ensuring procedural rights in incompetency-to-stand-trial process). On the question of whether a defendant is competent to dismiss his lawyer when the representation is inadequate, *see* Note, *supra* note 14, at 691. *Cf.* People v. Robinson, 582 N.E.2d 1299 (Ill. App. 1991) (stipulation entered into by prosecutor and defense counsel that defendant was fit to stand trial did not violate her due process rights).

213. *See, e.g.,* Michael Perlin, *Fatal Assumption: A Critical Evaluation of the Role of Counsel in Mental Disability Cases,* 16 LAW & HUM. BEHAV. 39 (1992).

tively incompetent defendant's purported wishes to be found competent constituted an "abdication" of his professional obligations.[214] The court noted that counsel, lacking even a "rudimentary understanding of psychiatry," was "wholly unqualified to judge the competency of [his] clients."[215] A lawyer is not entitled to rely merely on his own beliefs about a defendant's mental condition; rather, he must make a reasonable investigation as part of his constitutional duties.[216]

At least one set of commentators has carefully considered the lack of traditional adversary "fit" in defense counsel's representation of the potentially incompetent defendant: The state's medical experts may make their recommendations based on such nonclinical issues as the available bed space at a referral hospital or the perceived litigiousness of the defendant. In addition, defense counsel may have to consider such factors as lack of available bail,[217] conditions of institutionalization at the referral hospital, and the possible iatrogenic or ameliorative impact of psychiatric institutionalization on the defendant, none of which necessarily bears any relationship to the impact of the defendant's purported illness on his capacity to stand trial.[218] On the other hand, if conditions at the referral hospital are perceived as preferable to those in the county jail, and if psychiatric observation serves independent strategic purposes—if the state's case weakens during prolonged confinement, or if plea bargaining possibilities are enhanced—counsel may be influenced by a separate bundle of issues that do not relate to the defendant's competency to stand trial.[219]

The focus of these competing interests was reshaped somewhat by the U.S. Supreme Court case of *Strickland v. Washington*.[220] Under this case, criminal defendants are constitutionally entitled to "reasonably competent counsel."[221] In determining whether counsel is sufficiently inadequate to mandate a reversal of a conviction, the Court established a two-part inquiry:

> A convicted defendant making a claim of ineffective assistance must identify the acts or omissions of counsel that are alleged not to have been the result of reasonable professional judgment. The court must then determine, whether in light of all the circumstances, the identified acts or omissions were outside the range of profes-

---

214. Hull v. Freeman, 932 F.2d 159, 168 (3d Cir. 1991), *overruling on other grounds recognized in* Caswell v. Ryan, 953 F.2d 853 (3d Cir. 1992), *cert. denied*, 504 U.S. 944 (1992).

215. *Id.*

216. Becton v. Barnett, 920 F.2d 1190 (4th Cir. 1990). For sensitive and thoughtful appellate opinions on this question, *see, e.g.,* Bouchillon v. Collins, 907 F.2d 589 (5th Cir. 1990); James v. Singletary, 957 F.2d 1562 (11th Cir. 1992), *on remand*, 995 F.2d 187 (11th Cir. 1993), *cert. denied*, 510 U.S. 896 (1993).

217. *See* Perlin, *supra* note 170.

218. Paul Chernoff & William Schaffer, *Defending the Mentally Ill: Ethical Quicksand*, 10 Am. Crim. L. Rev. 505, 510–19 (1972).

219. *Id.* at 510–19.

220. 466 U.S. 668 (1984). *Strickland* is discussed extensively in 1 Perlin, *supra* note 8, § 2B-11.2 (2d ed. 1998); *see generally* Perlin, *supra* note 200, at 139–64.

221. *Strickland*, 466 U.S. at 687.

sionally competent assistance. In making that determination, the court should keep in mind that counsel's function, as elaborated in prevailing professional norms, is to make the adversarial testing process work in the particular case. At the same time, the court should recognize that counsel is strongly presumed to have rendered adequate assistance and made all significant decisions in the exercise of reasonable professional judgment.[222]

Further, any deficiencies in counsel's performance must be "prejudicial to the defense in order to constitute ineffective assistance under the Constitution."[223] To show such prejudice, a defendant must demonstrate that, but for counsel's unprofessional errors, the result of the proceeding would have been different.[224]

Most post-*Strickland* cases have rejected ineffective assistance of counsel arguments in this context, although there have been several instances in which convictions have been reversed and/or habeas corpus writs granted. Interestingly, in some cases, *Strickland* is not even cited.[225] By way of example, the Montana Supreme Court has held that a defendant was not prejudiced by the absence of counsel at the time of his mental evaluation, where the defendant was offered the opportunity to undergo a second evaluation after counsel was appointed.[226] The finding of lack of prejudice is relied upon as the basis for the vast majority of cases affirming convictions.[227] The reasoning of the Nevada Supreme Court is illustrative:

222. *Id.* at 690.

223. *Id.* at 692.

224. *Id.* at 695–96.

For contemporaneous criticisms of the *Strickland* approach, *see* William Genego, *The Failure of Effective Assistance of Counsel: Performance Standards and Competent Representation*, 22 AM. CRIM. L. REV 181 (1984); Perlin, *supra* note 200, at 157–60; Vivian Berger, *The Supreme Court and Defense Counsel: Old Roads, New Paths: A Dead End?* 86 COLUM. L. REV. 9 (1986). For a later critique, *see* Michael L. Perlin, *"The Executioner's Face Is Always Well-Hidden": The Role of Counsel and the Courts in Determining Who Dies,* 41 N.Y.L. SCH. L. REV. 201 (1996).

225. *See, e.g.,* People v. Fenderson, 510 N.E.2d 479 (Ill. App. 1987), *appeal denied,* 520 N.E.2d 388 (Ill. 1988); People v. Morino, 743 P.2d 49 (Colo. Ct. App.), *cert. denied* (1987); State v. Garrett, 386 S.E.2d 823 (W. Va. 1989); Torres v. Texas, 788 S.W.2d 709 (Tex. Ct. App. 1990); Tyler v. State, 787 S.W.2d 778 (Mo. Ct. App.), *motion for reh'g denied, application for transfer denied* (1990); Garrett v. State, 814 S.W.2d 325 (Mo. Ct. App. 1991); Baird v. State, 906 S.W.2d 746 (Mo. App. 1995), *motion for reh'g and/or transfer denied* (1995), *applic. for transfer denied* (1995); Chambers v. State, 958 S.W.2d 66 (Mo. App. 1997).

226. State v. Bartlett, 282 Mont. 114, 935 P.2d 1114 (1997), *reh'g denied* (1997) (*Strickland* not cited).

227. *See, e.g.,* McCoy v. Lynaugh, 714 F. Supp. 241 (S.D. Tex.), *aff'd,* 874 F.2d 954 (5th Cir. 1989); Rivers v. Turner, 874 F.2d 771 (11th Cir.), *cert. denied,* 493 U.S. 940 (1989); Balfour v. Haws, 892 F.2d 556 (7th Cir. 1989); Dooley v. Petsock, 816 F.2d 885 (3d Cir.), *cert. denied,* 484 U.S. 863 (1987); United States v. Miller, 907 F.2d 994 (10th Cir. 1990); Allsop v. State, 196 Ga. App. 379, 396 S.E.2d 47, *review denied* (1990); People v. Eddmonds, 578 N.E.2d 952, *reh'g denied* (Ill. 1991), *cert. denied,* 503 U.S. 942 (1992); Sanchez v. United States, 921 F. Supp. 56 (D.P.R. 1996); Washington v. Johnson, 90 F.3d 945 (5th Cir. 1996), *cert. denied,* 520 U.S. 1122 (1997); Vogt v. United States, 88 F.3d 587 (8th Cir. 1996); James v. State of Iowa, 100 F.3d 586 (8th Cir. 1996); Hurney v. Class, 551 N.W.2d 577 (S.D. 1996); Miles v. Stainer, 108 F.3d 1109 (9th Cir. 1997), *appeal after remand,* 141 F.3d 1351 (9th Cir. 1998); Morris v. State, 488 S.E.2d 685 (Ga. App. 1997); Johnson v. Singletary, 162 F.3d 630 (11th Cir. 1998),

To state a claim of ineffective assistance of counsel that is sufficient to invalidate a judgment of conviction, petitioner must demonstrate that (1) counsel's performance fell below an objective standard of reasonableness, and (2) counsel's errors were so severe that they rendered the verdict unreliable. (citations omitted) [The defendant] claims that his trial counsel was ineffective for failure to investigate and pursue the possibility that [he] was mentally incompetent to stand trial or an insanity defense at trial due to his traumatic childhood and mental retardation. We conclude this assertion is wholly without merit. The test to determine whether one is mentally competent to stand trial is whether that person "is not of sufficient mentality to be able to understand the nature of the criminal charges against him, and because of that insufficiency, is not able to aid and assist his counsel in the defense interposed upon the trial or against the pronouncement of the judgment thereafter." (Citations omitted) At the evidentiary hearing in this case, both of [defendant's] trial attorneys testified that [he] did not appear to be mentally incompetent, even though they were aware that his intelligence quotient (IQ) was only 68, categorizing [the defendant] as mildly mentally retarded. [Defendant's] primary counsel spoke with him on several occasions, and the attorney never felt the need to investigate whether [he] was competent. He further testified that [the defendant] assisted counsel during the trial, and they spent much time discussing trial strategy without any problems communicating. [Defendant's] second counsel also testified at the hearing that [the defendant] was able to grasp what was going on and could appreciate the gravity of the murder charge. Accordingly, [the defendant] has presented no evidence whatsoever, other than a low IQ, that he was either mentally incompetent to stand trial or that he met the standard for an insanity defense at the time of the murder. Therefore, we conclude that . . . trial counsel cannot be deemed incompetent to have failed to pursue such avenues.[228]

On the other hand, there have been cases in which *Strickland* has led to new trials. In the earliest post-*Strickland*[229] case law developments, one court ruled that

---

reh. and suggested reh. en banc den., 182 F.3d 838 (11th Cir. 1999), *cert. denied,* 528 U.S. 883 (1999); United States v. Boigegrain, 155 F.3d 1181 (10th Cir. 1998), *cert. denied,* 525 U.S. 1083 (1999); Henderson v. State, 977 S.W.2d 508 (Mo. App. 1998); Thomas v. State, 766 So. 2d 860 (Ala. Crim. App. 1998), *reh'g denied* (1998), *aff'd,* 766 So. 2d 975 (Ala. 2000); Harper v. Commonwealth, 978 S.W.2d 311 (Ky. 1998), *reh'g denied* (1998), *cert. den.,* 526 U.S. 1056 (1999); Anderson v. State, 699 N.E.2d 257 (Ind. 1998); Thompson v. Johnson, 7 F. Supp. 2d 848 (S.D. Tex. 1998); Odiaga v. State, 950 P.2d 1254 (Idaho 1997); Funtanilla v. Cambra, 1997 WL 811768 (N.D. Cal. 1997), *aff'd,* 162 F.3d 1168 (9th Cir. 1998), *cert. den.,* 528 U.S. 852 (1999); Huzzie v. State, 512 S.E.2d 5 (Ga. App. 1999); State v. Bryge, 594 N.W.2d 388 (Wis. App. 1999), *aff'd,* 614 N.W.2d 47 (Wis. 2000) (*Strickland* not cited on appeal); Khouri v. State, 1999 WL 710868 (Iowa App. 1999); Woods v. State, 994 S.W.2d 32 (Mo. App. 1999); Spratling v. State, 2000 WL 371017 (Tex. App. 2000); Barnhart v. United States, 2000 WL 1013577 (D.D.C. 2000), *motion to dismiss appeal granted,* 2001 WL 1154546 (D.C. Cir. 2001).
  228. Hill v. State, 953 P. 2d 1077, 1082–83 (Nev. 1998), *cert. den.,* 525 U.S. 1042 (1998).
  229. For a pre-*Strickland* case finding that failure to request a competency hearing where there was evidence "raising a substantial doubt" as to the defendant's competence could constitute ineffective assistance of counsel, *see* Speedy v. Wyrick, 702 F.2d 723, 726 (8th Cir. 1983), *later proceedings,* 748 F.2d 481 (8th Cir. 1984) (*Strickland* not cited). *See also* Crenshaw v. Wolff, 504 F.2d 377 (8th Cir. 1974), *cert. denied,* 420 U.S. 966 (1975). *See also, e.g.,* State v. Brooks, 495 N.E.2d 407 (Ohio 1986); State v. Johnson, 395 N.W.2d 176 (Wis. 1986).

a defendant's guilty plea was involuntarily entered when trial counsel, who had a "doubt" as to her competency to enter it, failed to seek an adjudication on the issue.[230] In a second case, the Florida Supreme Court ordered an evidentiary hearing on counsel's effectiveness where neither a competency-to-stand-trial inquiry nor a psychiatric evaluation was sought. In this case, there was evidence in the record that the defendant had "organic brain damage, [was] mentally retarded, and [had] a lengthy history of abusing certain drugs which have medically proven mentally debilitating side effects," and that the prison officials had administered large doses of Mellaril, "a powerful anti-psychotic drug," to defendant throughout his pretrial and trial incarceration.[231]

Elsewhere, convictions[232] or denial of post-conviction relief[233] have been reversed or grants of writs of habeas corpus affirmed,[234] based on the *Strickland* standard; at least one denial of post-conviction relief was reversed in a case in which *Strickland* was not cited.[235]

g. Sanism and pretextuality[236]

Sanism and pretextuality[237] affect incompetency-to-stand-trial jurisprudence in at least four critical ways: (1) courts resolutely adhere to the conviction that defendants regularly malinger and feign incompetency; (2) courts stubbornly refuse to understand the distinction between incompetency to stand trial and insanity, even though the two statuses involve different concepts, different standards, and different points on the "time line"; (3) courts misunderstand the relationship between incompetency and subsequent commitment and fail to consider the lack of a necessary connection between post-determination institutionalization and

---

230. Hemme v. State, 680 S.W.2d 734, 736–37 (Mo. Ct. App. 1984) (*Strickland* not cited). *See generally infra* Chapter 2B.

231. Groover v. State, 489 So. 2d 15, 17 (Fla. 1986) (*Strickland* not cited), *following remand,* 574 So. 2d 97 (Fla.), *reh'g denied* (1991). On the question of defense counsel's obligations *after* a finding of incompetency to stand trial, *see* Winick & DeMeo, *supra* note 10, at 70–71.

232. *See* Futch v. Dugger, 874 F.2d 1483, 1487 (11th Cir. 1989) (where defendant alleged prison psychologist declared him to be incompetent and that defense counsel knowingly failed to interview psychologist, evidentiary hearing should have been held to investigate question); *see also* State v. Haskins, 407 N.W.2d 309 (Wis. Ct. App. 1987) (counsel failed to raise issue of deaf defendant's competency in spite of his own doubts as to competency, expert opinion as to incompetency, and prior findings of incompetency; new competency hearing ordered on remand); People v. Baldwin, 541 N.E.2d 1315, 1322–23 (Ill. App. 1989) (counsel's failure to present defendant's prior mental health records and decision to proceed to trial prior to investigating defendant's ability to stand trial violated *Strickland*); *see also* Williamson v. Reynolds, 904 F. Supp. 1529 (E.D. Okla. 1995), *aff'd,* 110 F.3d 1508 (10th Cir. 1997) (finding counsel ineffective); *see also Kinkead, supra* (counsel's failure to pursue defendant's right to request competency hearing when defendant is receiving psychotropic drugs does not waive issue).

233. Hull v. Kyler, 190 F.3d 88 (3d Cir. 1999).

234. Barnett v. Hargett, 174 F.3d 1128 (10th Cir. 1999).

235. Hudgins v. Moore, 524 S.E.2d 105 (S.C. 1999).

236. This section is largely adapted from 4 Perlin, *supra* note 8, §§ 8C-1 to 1.4.

237. *See generally* 1 Perlin, *supra* note 8, § 2D-2. On the ways that sanism and pretextuality affect the involuntary civil commitment process, *see id.,* § 2D-2.1.

appropriate treatment, and (4) courts regularly accept patently inadequate expert testimony in incompetency-to-stand-trial cases.[238]

(A) Fear of malingering   Malingering by mentally disabled criminal defendants is statistically rare and is fairly easy to uncover.[239] Yet, in deciding incompetency-to-stand-trial cases, courts continue to focus—in some cases, almost obsessively—on testimony that raises the specter of malingering,[240] notwithstanding other evidence that such feigning is *attempted* in less than 8 percent of all such cases.[241] The fear of such deception has "permeated the American legal system for over a century," notwithstanding the complete lack of evidence that such feigning "has ever been a remotely significant problem of criminal procedure."[242] Again, it is a manifestation of judges' sanism in deciding cases involving criminal defendants with mental disabilities.

238. On the role of stereotyping in this context, *see* People v. Fox, 669 N.Y.S.2d 470, 473 (Cty. Ct. 1997):

> Although the mentally ill have been the victims of stereotypes, the disabilities imposed on them often have reflected that many of the mentally ill do have reduced ability for personal relations, for economic activity, and for political choice. This is not to say that the legal disabilities have precisely fit the actual incapacities of the mentally ill individuals whom the law has burdened, but it is important that the legal disabilities have been related, even if imperfectly, to real inabilities from which many of the mentally ill suffer.

239. Michael L. Perlin, *Unpacking the Myths: The Symbolism Mythology of Insanity Defense Jurisprudence*, 40 CASE W. RES. L. REV. 599, 715–16 nn. 556–58 (1989–90), citing sources; *see* 4 PERLIN, *supra* note 8, § 9C-3.6. *See, e.g.,* David Schretlen & Hal Arkowitz, *A Psychological Test Battery to Detect Prison Inmates Who Fake Insanity or Mental Retardation*, 8 BEHAV. SCI. & L. 75 (1990) (92–95 percent of all subjects correctly classified as either faking or not faking).

240. *See, e.g.,* State v. Evans, 586 N.E.2d 1042 (Ohio 1992), *cert. denied*, 506 U.S. 886 (1992); State v. Sharkey, 821 S.W.2d 544, 546 (Mo. Ct. App. 1991); Blacklock v. State, 820 S.W.2d 882, 884–85 (Tex. Ct. App. 1991), *review refused* (1992); State v. Drobel, 815 P.2d 724, 727 (Utah), *cert. denied*, 836 P.2d 1383 (Utah 1991); Cowan v. State, 579 So. 2d 13, 15 (Ala. Crim. App. 1990), *cert. denied* (Ala. 1991); Farinas v. State, 569 So. 2d 425, 432 (Fla. 1990); People v. Perkins, 562 N.Y.S.2d 244, 245 (A.D. 1990), *appeal denied*, 566 N.E.2d 1179 (N.Y. 1990); Gilbert v. State, 823 S.W.2d 875 (Ark. 1992); People v. Massa, 648 N.E.2d 123 (Ill. App. 1995).

241. Dewey Cornell & Gary Hawk, *Clinical Presentation of Malingerers Diagnosed by Experienced Forensic Psychologists*, 13 LAW & HUM. BEHAV. 375, 381–83 (1989). On the potential role of racial bias in such determinations, *see id.* at 382 (clinicians may overdiagnose malingering in black defendants).

For other research, *see, e.g.,* sources cited *supra* note 199; Richard Rogers et al., *The SIRS as a Measure of Malingering: A Validation Study with a Correctional Sample*, 8 BEHAV. SCI. & L. 85 (1990); R. Michael Bagby et al., *Detection of Dissimulation with the New Generation of Objective Personality Measures*, 8 BEHAV. SCI. & L. 93 (1990); R. Michael Bagby et al., *Detecting Malignancy and Defensive Responding on the MMMP1-2 in a Forensic Inpatient Sample*, 62 J. PERSONALITY ASSESSMENT 191 (1994); John Edens et al., *Utility of the Structured Inventory of Malingered Symptomatology in Identifying Persons Motivated to Malinger Psychopathology*, 27 J. AM. ACAD. PSYCHIATRY & L. 387 (1999).

242. Michael L. Perlin, *The Supreme Court, the Mentally Disabled Criminal Defendant, and Symbolic Values: Random Decisions, Hidden Rationales, or "Doctrinal Abyss"?*, 29 ARIZ. L. REV. 1, 98 (1987); Perlin, *supra* note 239, at 714.

(2) Conflation of standards Trial courts continue to blur the distinction between incompetency to stand trial and insanity.[243] They do this in spite of countless appellate admonitions as to the differences between the two statuses,[244] and in spite of different substantive standards, different behavioral criteria, and obvious temporal differences.[245] Courts ask defendants and experts irrelevant and meaningless questions that bear no relationship to the ultimate question to be decided by the court.[246]

While much of the confusion may stem from *experts'* confusion about the two terms,[247] it is clear that attorneys, trial judges, *and* mental health professionals equally misunderstand the core concepts.[248] The fact that this state of affairs continues—with little or no remediation—suggests that its perpetuation continues to meet sanist aims.[249]

243. *See* 4 PERLIN, *supra* note 8, § 8A-2., at 4 n.11 (citing cases and articles). *See also, e.g.,* State v. Bowman, 681 A.2d 469 (Me. 1996); Justine Dunlap, *What's Competence Got to Do with It: The Right Not to Be Acquitted by Reason of Insanity,* 50 OKLA L. REV. 495 (1997); Thomas Gutheil, *A Confusion of Tongues: Competence, Insanity, Psychiatry, and the Law,* 50 PSYCHIATRIC SERVS. 767 (1999).

244. *See, e.g.,* State v. Spivey, 319 A.2d 461, 470 (N.J. 1974) ("the Court must be careful to distinguish between insanity and incapacity to stand trial"); Aponte v. State, 153 A.2d 665, 670 (N.J.1959) (same); United States v. McEachern, 465 F.2d 833 (5th Cir.), *cert. denied,* 409 U.S. 1043 (1972) ("we note the possible confusion caused by the [trial court's] use of the term 'insanity' when the relevant inquiry is competency to stand trial"). This error is often deemed harmless. *See* Buttrum v. Black, 721 F. Supp. 1268, 1295 (N.D. Ga. 1989), *aff'd,* 908 F.2d 695 (11th Cir.), *reh'g denied,* 916 F.2d 719 (11th Cir. 1990).

245. For the different standards, *compare* 4 PERLIN, *supra* note 8, §§ 8A- 2.2 to 3.16 (incompetency to stand trial), *to id.,* §§ 9A-3 to 9A-3.7 (insanity defense). The relevant time inquiry for trial competency is at the time of the trial; the inquiry for insanity is at the time of the crime.

246. *See, e.g.,* RICHARD ARENS, THE INSANITY DEFENSE 77–79 (1974), reproducing transcripts of competency hearings in which judge merely asks defendants the date, the name of the President, and the Washington Senators' (baseball) standing in the American League, discussed in Michael L. Perlin, *Psychodynamics and the Insanity Defense: "Ordinary Common Sense" and Heuristic Reasoning,* 69 NEB. L. REV. 3, 24 n.95 (1990); Norman Poythress, *Mental Health Expert Testimony: Current Problems,* 5 J. PSYCHIATRY & L. 201, 218 (1977), reporting on a case in which the court asks the forensic psychologist (who had administered the MMPI test to defendant), "Do you believe in free will?" "Do you believe in God?"

247. *See* DEBRA WHITCOMB & RONALD BRANDT, COMPETENCY TO STAND TRIAL 2 (1985); George Dix & Norman Poythress, *Propriety of Medical Dominance of Forensic Mental Health Practice: The Empirical Evidence,* 23 ARIZ. L. REV. 961, 972–74 (1981); David Wexler & Samuel Scoville, *The Administration of Psychiatric Justice: Theory and Practice in Arizona,* 13 ARIZ. L. REV. 1, 65 (1971); Note, *Immediate Appeal of Pretrial Commitment Orders: "It's Now or Never,"* 55 FORD. L. REV. 785, 786 n.8 (1987).

248. ABA CRIMINAL JUSTICE MENTAL HEALTH STANDARDS 159 (1989). For an example of *counsel's* misunderstanding, *see* Kirk v. State, 308 S.E.2d 592, 598 (Ga. App. 1983), *aff'd,* 311 S.E.2d 821 (Ga. 1984) (counsel mistakenly asked for incompetency to stand trial charge in insanity case); Jermyn v. Horn, 1998 WL 754567 (M.D. Pa. 1998), at *23, *aff'd on other grounds,* 266 F.3d 257 (3d Cir. 2001) ("it is important to note that competence to stand trial raises different issues from an insanity defense").

249. Misstatements of the appropriate standard continue. *See* Lafferty v. Cook, 949 F.2d 1546, 1554 (10th Cir. 1991), *cert. denied,* 504 U.S. 911 (1992) (record reveals "unambiguously that the state trial courts evaluation of [defendant's] competency was infected by a mispercep-

(3) Misunderstanding of incompetency commitments   Empirical studies demonstrate that trial judges misunderstand the relationship between incompetency-to-stand-trial findings and subsequent hospital commitment. In a statewide study conducted 4 years after the Supreme Court's decision in *Jackson v. Indiana,*[250] almost half of all judges polled believed that commitment of incompetent criminal defendants to forensic hospitals should be automatic regardless of the severity of the underlying criminal offense or the defendant's present dangerousness.[251] A more recent national study of trial judges revealed that such hospitalization was the judicial intervention of choice in nearly 90 percent of all cases.[252] Even in states that expressly provide for outpatient commitment as an alternative in criminal incompetency cases, judges remain reluctant to employ this mechanism due to their fear that the patient might become violent in an outpatient setting.[253]

Also, there is no necessary correlation between such institutionalization and appropriate treatment. The starkest case is that of Theon Jackson, the appellant in *Jackson v. Indiana.* Jackson was a mentally retarded, deaf-mute individual, incapable of reading, writing, or communicating in any way except through a limited knowledge of sign language, who was indicted on two counts of robbery (apparently both involving purse snatches).[254] Notwithstanding testimony at his competency hearing that it was doubtful that Jackson could ever learn to read or write or become proficient in sign language, and that it would be impossible for him to learn minimal communications skills in an Indiana state institution, Jackson was committed indefinitely to a state *hospital* "until such time as [the state] should certify to the court that the '*defendant is sane.*'"[255]

Although the Supreme Court found for Jackson and struck down such com-

---

tion of the legal requirements set out in *Dusky* [*v. United States*]"), *discussed in* James Cohen, *The Attorney-Client Privilege, Ethical Rules, and the Impaired Criminal Defendant,* 52 U. MIAMI L. REV. 529, 549 (1998).

250. 406 U.S. 715 (1972) (incompetent defendants cannot be automatically permanently housed in maximum security forensic facilities if it is not likely that they will regain their competency to stand trial within the foreseeable future). *See generally* 4 PERLIN, *supra* note 8, § 8A- 5.2.

251. Ronald Roesch & Stephen Golding, *Legal and Judicial Interpretation of Competency to Stand Trial Statutes and Procedures,* 16 CRIMINOLOGY 420, 423–24 (1978). *See* Williams v. State, 964 S.W.2d 747 (Tex. App. 1998), *petit. for discretionary review denied* (1998) (statute setting out issues in making competency determination does not give jury power to consider statutory alternatives for custody and treatment of incompetent defendant).

252. Keri Gould et al., *Criminal Defendants with Trial Disabilities: The Theory and Practice of Competency Assistance* 62 (1992) (unpublished manuscript on file with authors).

253. Note, State v. Gravette: *Is There Justice for Incompetent Defendants in North Carolina?,* 69 N.C. L. REV.1484, 1497 (1991). *See, e.g.,* People v. White, 819 P.2d 1096 (Colo. App.), *reh'g denied* (1991) (finding that state statute does not preclude release on bail of defendant charged with violent crime and found incompetent to stand trial).

On the relationship between the Americans with Disabilities Act and this area of incompetency decisionmaking, *see* 4 PERLIN, *supra* note 8, § 8A-5.4; *see generally,* Perlin, *supra* note 170.

254. *Jackson,* 406 U.S. at 717.

255. *Id.* at 719 (emphasis added).

mitments (that amounted to life sentences without trial),[256] the underlying problem has not been fully ameliorated. Thirteen years after the decision in *Jackson*, Bruce Winick reported that, in almost half the states, *Jackson* remained unimplemented and pre-*Jackson* problems "still persist[ed]."[257] Eight years after Winick reported his findings, Professors Grant Morris and J. Reid Meloy reached precisely the same conclusions.[258]

The commitment of incompetent-to-stand-trial defendants to forensic hospitals often triggers a "shuttle" mechanism: defendants are treated (usually with antipsychotic drugs),[259]temporarily stabilized, returned to court, found competent, and jailed to await trial; at this point, many decompensate and become incompetent once again.[260] This endless cycle has been well documented,[261] but courts have been uniformly silent.[262]

(4) Acceptance of inadequate testimony   Finally, courts regularly accept inadequate testimony in incompetency-to-stand-trial cases.[263] Thus, in *State v. Pruitt*,

256. *Id.* at 730–38.

257. Winick, *supra* note 9, at 940. *Compare* State v. Werner, 796 P.2d 610, 612–13 (N.M. Ct. App.), *cert. denied* (1990) (no error to treat dangerous patients committed pursuant to *Jackson* differently from civil patients).

258. Grant Morris & J. Reid Meloy, *Out of Mind? Out of Sight: the Uncivil Commitment of Permanently Incompetent Criminal Defendants*, 27 U.C. DAVIS L. REV. 1, 3 (1993).

259. *See* 4 PERLIN, *supra* note 8, § 8A-4.2.

260. Note, *supra* note 253, at 1498; *see* Bruce Winick, *Incompetency to Stand Trial: An Assessment of Costs and Benefits, and a Proposal for Reform*, 39 RUTGERS L. REV. 243, 248–49 (1987); Winick, *supra* note 9, at 931–35.

261. *See, e.g.,* Ellen Wertlieb, *Individuals with Disabilities in the Criminal Justice System: A Review of the Literature*, 18 CRIM. JUST. & BEHAV. 332, 337 (1991), discussing United States v. Juarez, 540 F. Supp. 1288 (W.D. Tex. 1982) (mentally retarded incompetent-to-stand-trial defendant not treated for over 3 years due to jurisdictional dispute between state and federal institutions). For a more recent case, *see, e.g.,* State *ex rel.* Hager v. Marten, 594 N.W.2d 791 (Wis. 1999) (defendant's 5-month incarceration without incompetency evaluation did not violate time periods for such evaluations).

262. *See, e.g.,* United States v. Deters, 143 F.3d 577 (10th Cir. 1998) (order that defendant be confined for purpose of psychiatric evaluation affirmed).

263. WHITCOMB & BRANDT, *supra* note 247, at 2 (experts' reports often "empty and meaningless"). For a review of such deficiencies, *see id.* at 1, reporting on findings in Ingo Keilitz, "Mental Health Examination in Criminal Justice Settings: Organization, Administration, and Program Evaluation" (1981) (courts often fail to provide reasons for evaluation requests; courts often fail to screen out unwarranted evaluation requests; no agreement between justice and mental health systems as to purpose of evaluation; evaluation report frequently delayed at great length). On the ways that courts all too often rubber stamp psychiatric testimony, *see* Alison Barnes, *Beyond Guardianship Reform: A Reevaluation of Autonomy and Beneficence for a System of Principled Decision-Making in Long Term Care*, 41 EMORY L.J. 633, 688 (1992), and *see id.* n.288 (citing Dale Albers & Richard Pasewark, *Involuntary Hospitalization: Surrender at the Courthouse*, 2 AM. J. COMMUN. PSYCHOL. 287 (1974); Perlin, *supra* note 111). For a prototypical case, *see, e.g.,* White v. State, 414 S.E.2d 328 (Ga. App. 1992).

By way of example, the MacArthur Competence Assessment Tool-Criminal Adjudication (MacCAT-CA) has only been referred to in *seven* reported cases as of the writing of this book

the sole expert witness testified in conclusionary terms that the defendant "suffered no mental disease or defect, and . . . understood the respective roles of the cast of characters at the trial, and the nature of the charges against him," yet never indicated what it was that the defendant "actually understood."[264] While the conviction in *Pruitt* was reversed on other grounds, a majority of the court was satisfied that this testimony was sufficient upon which to base a competency finding.[265] In *Hensley v. State,* the court found no abuse of discretion on the incompetency-to-stand-trial question, when the defendant was able to deny the crime and name the alleged victim, in spite of the uncontested fact finding that the defendant's "testimony and actions at the competency hearing were not generally meaningful."[266]

Elsewhere, notwithstanding defendant's history of hospitalization, his attempted suicide and subsequent drug overdose and his contemporaneous use of prescribed antipsychotic medications and suicidal ideation, no bona fide doubt was raised as to his fitness to stand trial, and the court's decision not to conduct a competency hearing was not error.[267] These and other similar cases[268] suggest that the most minimal testimony will satisfy courts in such incompetency-to-stand-trial inquiries.[269]

(see Westlaw, ALLCASES database, last searched June 19, 2007). On the use of this instrument, *see, e.g.,* Debra Pinels et al., *Practical Application of the MacArthur Competence Assessment Tool-Criminal Adjudication (MacCAT-CA) in a Public Sector Forensic Setting,* 34 J. AM. ACAD. PSYCHIATRY & L. 179 (2006); Patricia Zapf & Jodi Viljoen, *Issues and Considerations Regarding the Use of Assessment Instruments in the Evaluation of Competency to Stand Trial,* 21 BEHAV. SCI. & L. 351 (2003); Patricia Zapf & Ronald Roesch, *An Investigation of the Construct of Competence: A Comparison of the FIT, the MacCAT-CA, and the MacCAT-T,* 29 LAW & HUM. BEHAV. 229 (2005); Randy Otto et al., *Psychometric Properties of the MacArthur Competence Assessment Tool-Criminal Adjudication (MacCAT-CA),* 10 PSYCHOL. ASSESSMENT 435 (1998); NORMAN POYTHRESS ET AL., ADJUDICATIVE COMPETENCE: THE MACARTHUR STUDIES (2002); Thomas Grisso, *Competence to Stand Trial,* in EVALUATING COMPETENCIES: FORENSIC ASSESSMENTS AND INSTRUMENTS 69 (Thomas Grisso ed. 2003).

264. 480 N.E.2d 499, 504 (Ohio App. 1984). The witness also admitted that, while he had been aware that the defendant was evaluated by mental health professionals at a VA hospital, he did not have copies of those records, admitting further that, depending on the content of those records, his opinion might have been different. *Id.*

265. *Id.* at 509 (Markus, J., concurring).

266. 575 N.E.2d 1053, 1055 (Ind. App. 1991), *trans. denied* (1992).

267. People v. Lopez, 576 N.E.2d 246, 247–48 (Ill. App. 1991), *appeal denied,* 580 N.E.2d 127 (Ill. 1991).

268. *See, e.g.,* Rollins v. Leonardo, 938 F.2d 380 (2d Cir. 1991), *cert. denied,* 502 U.S. 1062 (1992) (defendant was escapee from psychiatric hospital at time he was tried for offense); United States v. Caicedo, 937 F.2d 1227, 1232 (7th Cir. 1991) (although trial counsel stated that he did not know if defendant could cooperate with him in the preparation of a defense, he stated that defendant was *"perfectly competent"*) (emphasis in opinion); United States v. Prince, 938 F.2d 1092 (10th Cir.), *cert. denied,* 502 U.S. 961 (1991) (no abuse of discretion in refusal to hold competency hearing where defendant exposed himself and urinated in courtroom); Watts v. Singletary, 87 F.3d 1282 (11th Cir. 1996), *suggestion for reh'g en banc denied,* 102 F.3d 1119 (11th Cir. 1996), *cert. denied,* 520 U.S. 1267 (1997)(defendant failed to establish bona fide doubt as to competency notwithstanding fact he slept through approximately 70 percent of court proceedings).

269. On one court's dismissive attitude toward a defendant taking the drug Prozac for depression, *see* United States v. Grimes, 173 F.3d 634 (7th Cir. 1999). On the relationship be-

2. The Disposition of Cases of Persons Found Incompetent to Stand Trial[270]

a. Historical background

Traditionally, a finding of incompetency to stand trial (IST) led to either a long-term or, in many cases, a permanent commitment to maximum security wings of state psychiatric hospitals.[271] Thus, Dr. Louis McGarry's findings that, in Massachusetts, more incompetent defendants left Bridgewater Hospital—the facility to which persons diagnosed with IST were regularly committed—by dying than by all other avenues combined[272] has never been challenged. The anecdotal stories of incompetent defendants institutionalized for half a century awaiting trial[273] were by no means atypical but rather demonstrated that lawyers' objections to the then-prevalent system were neither "idle conjecture"[274] nor "mere theoretical objection[s]."[275]

Even in the cases of defendants not facing a constructive life sentence, the IST

---

tween a defendant's cognitive understanding of competency proceedings and what the court characterized as "rote learning" (through a forensic Competency Restoration Program), *see* United States v. Duhon, 104 F. Supp. 2d 663, 671–76 (W.D. La. 2000) (defendant's lack of cognitive understanding compelled finding of continued incompetence to stand trial).

Researchers and scholars have begun to turn their attention to many of the issues raised in this section. *See, e.g.,* Janet Warren et al., *Forensic Mental Health Clinical Evaluation: An Analysis of Interstate and Intersystemic Differences,* 21 Law & Hum. Behav. 377 (1997); Jennifer Skeem et al., *Logic and Reliability of Evaluations of Competence to Stand Trial,* 22 Law & Hum. Behav. 519 (1998); Norman Poythress et al., *Client Abilities to Assist Counsel and Make Decisions in Criminal Cases: Findings from Three Studies,* 18 Law & Hum. Behav. 437 (1997); Julio Arboleda-Flores et al., *An Evaluation of Legal Outcomes Following Pretrial Forensic Assessment* 39 Can. J. Psychiatry161 (1994); S. Plotnick et al., *Is There Bias in the Evaluation of Competency to Stand Trial,* 21 Int'l J. L. & Psychiatry 291 (1998); Elisa Robbins et al., *Competency to Stand Trial: A Study of Actual Practice in Two States,* 25 J. Am. Acad. Psychiatry & L. 469 (1997).

270. This section is largely adapted from 4 Perlin, *supra* note 8, §§ 8A-5.1 to 5.3.

271. A 1968 survey article summarized the issues clearly:

Incompetents are generally confined in hospitals for the criminally insane, which, it is fair to say, are usually the poorest available facilities. The defendant is held in stricter custody with fewer privileges than if he were confined in a prison or ordinary mental hospital. He receives little treatment, usually less than if he had been civilly committed to a mental institution. . . .

Gerald Bennett, *Competency to Stand Trial: A Call for Reform,* 59 J. Crim. L., Criminology & Pol Sci. 569, 571 (1968) (footnotes omitted). *See, e.g., Brief of Donald McEwan, Petitioner Pro Se,* in Joseph Katz et al., Psychoanalysis, Psychiatry and Law 700 (1967) (comparing conditions in hospital for the criminally insane and in state prison).

272. Louis McGarry, *The Fate of Psychotic Offenders Referred for Trial,* 127 Am. J. Psychiatry 1181 (1971).

273. *See, e.g.,* Bruce Ennis, Prisoners of Psychiatry ch. 3 (1972) (discussing United States *ex rel.* von Wolfersdorf v. Johnston, 317 F. Supp. 66 (S.D.N.Y. 1970) (22 years)); Engelberg, *Pretrial Criminal Commitment to Mental Institutions: The Procedure in Massachusetts and Suggested Reform,* 17 Cath. U. L. Rev. 163 (1967) (63 years).

274. James Gobert, *Competency to Stand Trial: A Pre- and Post-Jackson Analysis,* 40 Tenn. L. Rev. 659, 663 n.26 (1973).

275. *Id.* at 664 (discussing *United States ex rel. von Wolfersdorf, supra*).

determination was fraught with other perils due to the problems of delay, disappearing witnesses, increased frustration and anxiety,[276] and greater stigmatization, all of which combined to "impose added liabilities" upon the IST defendant,[277] especially since an incompetency commitment "arguably decrease[d] a defendant's chances for a favorable recovery."[278] Notwithstanding these clinical and empirical realities, if defense counsel had a "bona fide doubt" as to his client's competency,[279] he was still obligated to raise this doubt to the court's attention.[280]

b. Jackson v. Indiana

In *Jackson v. Indiana,* the Supreme Court held that the long-term, indeterminate commitment of an individual, based solely on his incompetence to stand trial, violates the Constitution.[281]

The defendant in *Jackson* was a person with mental retardation who was also deaf and mute, incapable of reading, writing, or communicating in any way except for a limited knowledge of sign language.[282] A Mississippi native, he had never attended a school of any kind until he moved to Indiana with his family at age 24.[283] He had been indicted on two counts of robbery (apparently purse snatches), involving less than $10.[284] After pleading not guilty, Jackson was examined by two state doctors who agreed that he was unable to understand the nature of the charges against him or participate in his defense.[285] One of the witnesses stated that it was doubtful that he would ever learn to read or write or become proficient in sign language, and suggested that his "prognosis appear[ed] rather dim."[286] An interpreter testified that Indiana had no facilities that could "help someone as badly off as Jackson to learn minimal communications skills."[287]

Based on this testimony, the trial judge ordered the defendant committed to the state department of mental health "until such time as that Department should certify to the court that the 'defendant is sane.'"[288] Counsel then filed a motion for a new trial, contending there was no evidence that the defendant was "insane" or that "he would ever attain a status which the court might regard as 'sane' in the sense of competency to stand trial," arguing that the commitment amounted to

---

276. McGarry, *supra* note 272, at 53, 56; Gobert, *supra* note 274, at 663.
277. Bennett, *supra* note 271, at 572.
278. Gobert, *supra* note 274, at 663.
279. *See* Pate v. Robinson, 383 U.S. 375 (1966).
280. The potential ethical paradoxes are raised in Gobert, *supra* note 274, at 666–67.
281. 406 U.S. 715, 720 (1972).
282. *Id.* at 717.
283. *Id.,* petition for certiorari at 21 (app.).
284. *Id.* at 717.
285. *Id.* at 718–19.
286. *Id.* at 719.
287. *Id.*
288. *Id.*

a "life sentence" without conviction, and that such a sentence was proscribed by the due process, equal protection, and cruel and unusual punishment clauses of the Constitution.[289]

The Supreme Court found (1) that it is a violation of the equal protection clause to subject an incompetent-to-stand-trial (IST) defendant to a more lenient commitment standard and to a more stringent standard of release than generally applicable to those who have never been charged with offenses, "thus condemning him in effect to permanent institutionalization,"[290] and (2) that it is a violation of the due process clause to commit an individual for more than the "reasonable period of time" necessary to determine "whether there is a substantial chance of his attaining the capacity to stand trial in the foreseeable future."[291]

If it were to be determined that the defendant would *not* regain his competence within such a "foreseeable time," then the state "must either institute the customary civil commitment proceeding that would be required to commit indefinitely any other citizen, or release the defendant."[292] Further, even if it were determined that the defendant "probably soon will be able to stand trial," his continued commitment "must be justified by progress toward that goal."[293] While the Court did not set a finite time limit on the "reasonable length of time" in which such a determination should be made, it noted that Jackson's 3 1/2-year period of confinement "sufficiently establishe[d] the lack of a substantial probability that he will ever be able to participate fully in a trial."[294]

However, the Court declined to dismiss the charges against Jackson, characterizing this issue as "not sufficiently ripe for ultimate decision."[295] *First,* the court indicated that, based on the record before it, it could not rule on Jackson's criminal responsibility at the time of the alleged offenses.[296] *Second,* since Jackson never presented a speedy trial argument squarely to the state courts, the court declined to determine whether dismissal of the charges could be premised on that ground.[297] *Third,* the court stated that both courts and commentators had noted the "desirability of permitting some proceedings to go forward despite the defendant's incompetency,"[298] and that nothing in its prior incompetency-to-stand-trial decisions precluded states from allowing, "at a minimum, an incompetent defendant to raise certain defenses such as insufficiency of the indictment, or make certain pretrial motions through counsel."[299]

289. *Id.*
290. *Id.* at 730.
291. *Id.* at 733.
292. *Id.* at 738.
293. *Id.*
294. *Id.* at 738–39.
295. *Id.*
296. *Id.*
297. *Id.* at 740.
298. *Id.* at 740–41.
299. *Id.* at 741, and n.31.

C. Post-Jackson developments

While *Jackson* has certainly "minimiz[ed] the [previous] gross abuse of incompetency commitment,"[300] significant implementation and enforcement gaps remain. At least one apparent gap in the *Jackson* decision remains as a result of the U.S. Supreme Court's failure to specify the "reasonable period" of time during which criminal charges can be left open while a defendant is pending trial as incompetent to stand trial (IST).[301] As noted earlier, as of 1985, about half of the jurisdictions still statutorily permitted indefinite hospitalization based solely on a finding of continuing incompetency to stand trial,[302] often in the "worst institution in the state."[303] When the 1985 research was repeated in 1993, there was virtually no significant change,[304] nor was there any significant change found when the research was reviewed in 2000.[305]

In some jurisdictions, the hospitalization of incompetent defendants has been permitted for specified periods—ranging from 6 months to 5 years[306]—or for such period limited to determining the likelihood of recovery of competency,[307] or for the maximum period or a percentage of the maximum period that the defendant could have served had he been convicted and given the maximum sentence allowed.[308] There seems no reason to question Barbara Weiner's observation that both the longer time periods and the time periods calculated on the basis of the sentence equivalent "are difficult to square with the *Jackson* rationale,"[309] or Winick's claim that "the problem of lengthy hospitalization still persists."[310]

According to Professors Grant Morris and J. Reid Meloy:

> What is the reasonable period of time necessary to evaluate the incompetent defendant's condition and to predict whether he or she will become competent in the near future? Although more than twenty years have passed since the Court decided *Jackson,* this question has not been answered by the statutes of thirty states and the District of Columbia. Of this number, twenty-three jurisdictions do not address the issue at all. Eight states address the issue but do not specify the length of the evaluation detention period. Typically, these statutes merely parrot the Jackson language allowing the incompetent defendant's detention for a "reasonable" period. Of the

---

300. Winick, *supra* note 9, at 940.

301. *See, e.g.,* Gobert, *supra* note 274, at 683–84.

302. Weiner, *supra* note 171, at 693.

303. Winick, *supra* note 9, at 942.

304. *See* Morris & Meloy, *supra* note 258, and see *id.* at 9: "Many states still have not implemented *Jackson.*"

305. *See* Perlin, *supra* note 170, at 204–05.

306. *Compare* WASH. REV. CODE ANN. § 10.77.090(4) (1980) (90 days) *with* OR. REV. STAT. § 161.370(3) (1983) (maximum sentence of 5 years). *But see* Jackson v. Indiana, 406 U.S. 715, 738–39 (1972) (3½ years sufficient time for defendant such as Jackson).

307. *See, e.g.,* Wyo. Stat. Ann. § 7-11-303(g) (1977).

308. *See, e.g.,* La. Code Crim. Proc. § 648(A), (B) (maximum).

309. Weiner, *supra* note 171, at 704.

310. Winick, *supra* note 9, at 941.

twenty states that specify the length of the detention period, ninety days is the most frequent period specified, with the shortest period being thirty days and the longest being twelve months . . .

Is the court that ordered the incompetent defendant's treatment statutorily obligated to periodically review the defendant's progress toward attaining competence? Although more than 20 years have passed since the court decided *Jackson,* the question has not been answered by the statutes of 32 states and the District of Columbia. Of this number, 20 jurisdictions do not address the issue at all. Thirteen states mandate a clinical review of the defendant's condition but do not require a court hearing. In 4 of the 13 states, the frequency of clinical review is not specified. In the 10 states that do specify frequency of clinical review, a 90-day interval is most typically mandated.

Of the 18 states whose statutes mandate judicial oversight, 8 states require a hearing at the end of 90 days and subsequent hearings after an additional 90 days or some lengthier period of time. The statutes of six states mandate an initial court review after 6 months. Maine requires a court review after 30 days, the shortest period specified. California requires a court review after 18 months, the longest period specified.[311]

B. COMPETENCY TO PLEAD GUILTY[312]

1. Introduction

Prior to 1993, there were two distinct lines of competency-to-plead-guilty cases: those that held that the standard for competency to plead guilty was the same as the standard for competency to stand trial, and those that held that the standard for pleading guilty was a more stringent one.[313] In 1993, the Supreme Court resolved this dispute by holding, in *Godinez v. Moran,*[314] that a unitary standard was constitutionally appropriate. Subsequently, a series of post-*Godinez* cases has explored collateral issues that were not before the Court in that case.[315]

2. Historical Background

Professors Ellis and Luckasson appropriately characterized the issue of assessing the competence of guilty pleas entered by mentally disabled defendants as pre-

---

311. *See* Morris & Meloy, *supra* note 258, at 9–12.
312. This section is largely adapted from 4 PERLIN, *supra* note 8, §§ 8B-2 to 2.3.
313. *See generally,* Michael L. Perlin, *"Dignity Was the First to Leave":* Godinez v. Moran, *Colin Ferguson, and the Trial of Mentally Disabled Criminal Defendants,* 14 BEHAV. SCI. & L. 61 (1996).
314. 509 U.S. 389 (1993).
315. *See infra* Chapter 2D–2G; *see generally,* Michael L. Perlin, *Beyond Dusky and Godinez: Competency Before and After Trial,* 21 BEHAV. SCI. & L. 297 (2003).

senting "one of the most difficult doctrinal and practical problems faced by the criminal justice system,"[316] a difficulty reflected in the "sharply divided"[317] case law that has developed in this area.[318]

It had been generally recognized that the standard for competence to plead guilty was higher than for other sorts of consent or waiver in the criminal context.[319] However, courts split on the significant question[320] of whether the standard to plead guilty is the same as, higher than, or otherwise different from, the traditional standard for assessing competence to stand trial: whether the defendant has "sufficient present ability to consult with his lawyer with a reasonable degree of understanding—and whether he has a rational as well as factual understanding of the proceedings against him."[321]

The majority view held that there is no substantial difference, and that the same test applies in assessing the validity of a guilty plea.[322] This position was

316. James Ellis & Ruth Luckasson, *Mentally Retarded Criminal Defendants,* 53 GEO. WASH. L. REV. 414, 460 (1985). Although they focus solely on defendants with mental *retardation,* similar, although not identical, problems are raised in cases of defendants with mental *illness.* For an example of an opinion dealing, in this context, with a defendant with mental retardation, *see* People v. Van Ostran, 168 Ill. App. 3d 517, 522 N.E.2d 851 (1988).

317. Ellis & Luckasson, *supra* note 316, at 460.

318. *See, e.g.,* Flugence v. Butler, 848 F.2d 77 (5th Cir. 1988); Williams v. Coughlin, 664 F. Supp. 665 (E.D.N.Y. 1987), *on reconsideration,* 1987 WL 15289 (E.D.N.Y. 1987); People v. Wishon, 163 Ill. App. 3d 852, 516 N.E.2d 1011 (1987) (all upholding competency findings); State v. Bishop, 162 Ariz. 103, 781 P.2d 581 (1989); People v. Daubman, 190 Ill. App. 3d 684, 546 N.E.2d 1079 (1989); State v. Romers, 159 Ariz. 271, 766 P.2d 623 (Ct. App. 1988) (defendant not competent to enter plea).

319. Ellis & Luckasson, *supra* note 316, at 461. *See, e.g.,* United States v. Young, 355 F. Supp. 103, 111 (E.D. Pa. 1973) (contrasting standard for guilty plea with waiver of *Miranda* rights). The issues in question are discussed carefully in United States v. Buckley, 847 F.2d 991, 998–99 (1st Cir. 1988), *cert. denied,* 488 U.S. 1015 (1989).

320. *See* Ellis & Luckasson, *supra* note 316, at 460–61, for a discussion of the heightened significance of the guilty plea in the contemporary administration of criminal justice systems. *See, e.g.,* Albert Alschuler, *The Changing Plea-Bargaining Debate,* 69 CALIF. L. REV. 652 (1981); Hans Zeisl, *The Offer That Cannot Be Refused,* in FRANKLIN E. ZIMRING & RICHARD S. FRASE, THE CRIMINAL JUSTICE SYSTEM: MATERIALS ON THE ADMINISTRATION AND REFORM OF THE CRIMINAL LAW 558 (1980).

321. *See* United States v. Greene, 722 F. Supp. 1221 (E.D. Pa. 1989). On the question of the use of a "substituted judgment" theory in the case of a defendant adjudged permanently incompetent to plead guilty, *see* Commonwealth v. DelVerde, 398 Mass. 288, 496 N.E.2d 1357 (1986)(rejecting doctrine). For subsequent developments, *see* Commonwealth v. DelVerde, 401 Mass. 447, 517 N.E.2d 159 (1988)(commitment of defendant to maximum security hospital supported by evidence). The earlier *DelVerde* opinion is discussed in Note, 21 SUFFOLK L. REV. 308 (1987).

322. *See, e.g.,* Malinauskas v. United States, 505 F.2d 649 (5th Cir. 1974); Stinson v. Wainwright, 710 F.2d 743 (11th Cir.), *cert. denied,* 464 U.S. 984 (1983); United States *ex rel.* McGough v. Hewitt, 528 F.2d 339 (3d Cir. 1975); Williams v. Bordenkircher, 696 F.2d 464 (6th Cir.), *cert. denied,* 461 U.S. 916 (1983); People v. Turner, 443 N.E.2d 1167 (Ill. App. 1982); State *ex rel.* Kessick v. Bordenkircher, 294 S.E.2d 134 (W. Va. 1982); State *ex rel.* Wilson v. Hedrick, 379 S.E.2d 493 (W. Va. 1989); Chickakly v. United States, 926 F.2d 624 (7th Cir. 1991); Treadwell v. Lockhart, 948 F.2d 453 (8th Cir. 1991). Cases are collected in Bruce J. Winick & Terry L. DeMeo, *Competency to Stand Trial in Florida,* 35 U. MIAMI L. REV. 31, 71 n.236 (1980).

challenged, however, by a series of cases involving defendants with both mental illness[323] and mental retardation,[324] and that suggested a separate test: "A defendant is not competent to plead guilty if a mental [disability] has substantially impaired his ability to make a reasoned choice among the alternatives presented to him and to understand the consequences of his plea."[325] Such a test has been employed by those courts that find it necessary for judges to "assess a defendant's competency *with specific reference to the gravity of the decisions* with which the defendant is faced."[326]

Professors Ellis and Luckasson point out that the difference in approach is particularly important in cases involving mentally retarded individuals, given the real possibility that their comprehension of the procedures involved is "substantially impaired,"[327] coupled with the well-documented efforts of many mentally retarded individuals to "hide and deny their disabilities and to 'pass' as normal."[328] While this alternative test is thus "particularly attractive," it is also "troubling," since, "if a defendant is so retarded that he is incompetent to stand trial, he is denied the opportunity to reduce his sentence through effective plea bargaining—an opportunity available to all other defendants."[329]

Instead, the authors urge, the approach suggested by the ABA Mental Health Standards[330] was a "better" one:[331] while the Standards concede that there may be defendants competent to stand trial, but whose disability makes it impossible to plead at an acceptable level of competence, special information must be presented to the trial court to trigger the use of a separate test,[332] thus establish-

---

323. *See, e.g.,* Seiling v. Eyman, 478 F.2d 211 (9th Cir. 1973); Steinsvik v. Vinzant, 640 F.2d 949 (9th Cir. 1981); State v. Walton, 228 N.W.2d 21 (Iowa 1975). *Seiling* and its progeny are discussed in Peter Silten & Richard Tullis, *Mental Competency in Criminal Proceedings,* 28 HASTINGS L. J. 1053, 1073 (1977) ("*Seiling* is open to serious question"), and Note, *Mental Competency: The Ninth Circuit's Analysis,* 8 GOLDEN GATE U.L. REV. 87 (1977) (generally applauding separate test).

324. The lead case was United States v. Masthers, 539 F.2d 721 (D.C. Cir. 1976). *Masthers* is discussed critically in Note, *Competence to Plead Guilty and the Retarded Defendant: United States v. Masthers* 9 CONN. L. REV. 176 (1976).

325. *Seiling,* 478 F.2d at 215 (quoting Schoeller v. Dunbar, 423 F.2d 1183, 1194 (9th Cir. 1970), *cert. denied,* 400 U.S. 834 (1970) (Hufstedler, J., dissenting)).

326. *Seiling,* 478 F.2d at 215 (emphasis added). Professor Slovenko appears to applaud this distinction. Ralph Slovenko, *The Developing Law on Competency to Stand Trial,* 5 J. PSYCHIATRY & L. 165, 187 (1977).

327. *Masthers,* 539 F.2d at 730 (Hastie, J., concurring). *Compare* United States *ex rel.* Butler v. Bara, 757 F. Supp. 210 (S.D.N.Y. 1990) (defendant's bare assertion of low I.Q. insufficient to place into question claim that he was incompetent to have entered guilty plea), *to* United States v. Hoskie, 950 F.2d 1388 (9th Cir. 1991) (no showing that defendant with 62 I.Q. was competent to stand trial).

328. Ellis & Luckasson, *supra* note 316, at 462–63 n.271 (discussing ROBERT EDGERTON, THE CLOAK OF COMPETENCE: STIGMA IN THE LIVES OF THE MENTALLY RETARDED 144–71 (1967)).

329. Ellis & Luckasson, *supra* note 316, at 464.

330. *See* ABA CRIMINAL JUSTICE MENTAL HEALTH STANDARDS (1984) (STANDARDS).

331. Ellis & Luckasson, *supra* note 316, at 464.

332. *See id.* at 463 (discussing STANDARDS, *supra* note 19, § 7-5.1 (1984), and *id.,* Commentary at 291–95).

ing a "rebuttable presumption that a defendant who meets the test for standing trial will also be competent to plead."[333] Such an inquiry would "produce a small group of defendants who are denied access to plea bargaining,"[334] but in these cases, the judge should take into account the defendant's incompetence to plead "and reduce the sentence to approximate that which the defendant might have received had he been able to engage in effective plea bargaining."[335]

Although this appears to be a reasonable compromise, two problems are left unresolved: first, defense counsel's generally conceded inability to understand mental retardation, its causes, and its symptoms;[336] and, second, the well-documented tendency of trial judges to sentence mentally retarded offenders to lengthier terms of imprisonment than nonretarded offenders.[337] If the effects of these forces could be mediated, then the ABA's recommendation might be seen as a more appropriate palliative for a particularly intractable problem.[338]

3. Other Procedural Issues

Several other pre-*Godinez* cases assessed a variety of procedural issues in this context, including the right of a habeas petitioner to a hearing on the issue of his competency to plead guilty,[339] the obligation on a trial judge to hold, *sua sponte,* a competency hearing prior to accepting defendant's guilty plea,[340] and the interplay between a defendant's competency to plead guilty and the requirements of FED. R. CRIM. PROC. 11.[341]

---

333. Ellis & Luckasson, *supra* note 316, at 463.

334. *Id.* at 464.

335. *Id.*

336. *See* 4 PERLIN, *supra* note 8, § 8A-6.5.

337. *See id.,* § 11-4.2. *See* Weiner, *supra* note 171, at 737 (adult retarded offenders incarcerated for average of 6.9 years as compared to 3.9 years for the nonretarded). Interestingly, Ellis and Luckasson themselves note that persons with mental retardation are more likely to serve longer sentences than other offenders. Ellis & Luckasson, *supra* note 316, at 479–80. *See also* Weiner, *supra* at n.38 (offenders with mental retardation confess more easily than other offenders).

338. *Cf.* Winick, *supra* note 9, at 972 n.247 (characterizing debate over dual standards as "artificial" and "too abstract").

339. *See* Smith v. Freeman, 892 F.2d 331 (3d Cir. 1989) (granting hearing); Anderson v. United States, 948 F.2d 704 (11th Cir. 1991) (same); Tiller v. Esposito, 911 F.2d 575 (11th Cir. 1990); *compare* Hernandez-Hernandez v. United States, 904 F.2d 758, 763–64 (1st Cir. 1990) (defendant's motion to vacate guilty plea denied where claim not raised at trial; no evidence that "gross miscarriage of justice" would occur).

On the question of the special procedural problems raised by federal habeas corpus challenges to state court guilty pleas, *see, e.g.,* Bolius v. Wainwright, 597 F.2d 986 (5th Cir. 1979); Spikes v. United States, 633 F.2d 144 (9th Cir. 1980).

340. *See* United States v. Collins, 949 F.2d 921 (7th Cir. 1991) (no such obligation exists unless defendant's acts trigger reasonable doubt).

341. *See* Rivers v. United States, 923 F. Supp. 92 (W.D. Va. 1996), *aff'd,* 101 F.3d 696 (4th Cir. 1996) (defendant out of time to raise claim flowing from 1977 conviction).

4. The *Godinez* Decision

The Supreme Court ended the controversy over the question of the two standards in assessing guilty pleas under the federal constitution[342] by holding, in *Godinez v. Moran*,[343] that the standard for pleading guilty was no higher than for standing trial.[344] In earlier proceedings, the Ninth Circuit Court of Appeals had reversed a district court denial of Moran's application for a writ of habeas corpus, concluding that the trial record should have led the trial court to "entertain a good faith doubt about [Moran's] competency to make a voluntary, knowing, and intelligent waiver," and that waiver of constitutional rights required a "higher level of mental functioning than that required to stand trial," a level it characterized as "the capacity for 'reasoned choice.'"[345]

The Supreme Court reversed, per Justice Thomas, rejecting the notion that competence to plead guilty must be measured by a higher (or even different) standard from that used in incompetency-to-stand-trial cases.[346] It reasoned that a defendant who was found competent to stand trial would have to make a variety of decisions requiring choices: whether to testify, whether to seek a jury trial, whether to cross-examine his accusers, and, in some cases, whether to raise an affirmative defense.[347] While the decision to plead guilty is a "profound one," "it is no more complicated than the sum total of decisions that a defendant may be called upon to make during the course of a trial."[348] Finally, the court reaffirmed that any waiver of constitutional rights must be "knowing and voluntary."[349]

It concluded on this point:

> Requiring that a criminal defendant be competent has a modest aim: It seeks to ensure that he has the capacity to understand the proceedings and to assist counsel. While psychiatrists and scholars may find it useful to classify the various kinds and degrees of competence, and while States are free to adopt competency standards that are more elaborate than the *Dusky* formulation, the Due Process Clause does not impose these additional requirements.[350]

---

342. *See* 4 PERLIN, *supra* note 8, § 8B-2.1.

343. 509 U.S. 389 (1993).

344. After Moran was found competent to stand trial, he discharged his counsel and pled guilty (explaining that he wanted to prevent the presentation of mitigating evidence, *see* 4 PERLIN, *supra* note 8, § 12-3.3, at his sentencing). *Id.* at 392. The court accepted his guilty plea, finding that it had been "freely and voluntarily" given. *Id.* at 393. He was subsequently sentenced to death. *Id.*

345. Moran v. Godinez, 972 F. 2d 263, 265–67 (9th Cir. 1992), *rev'd*, 509 U.S. 389 (1993). For subsequent developments, *see* Moran v. McDaniel, 80 F.3d 1261 (9th Cir. 1996) (denying writ of habeas corpus after subsequent resentencing to death).

346. *Godinez,* 509 U.S. at 390.

347. *Id.* at 398.

348. *Id.*

349. *Id.* at 400, quoting Parke v. Raley, 506 U.S. 20, 29 (1992).

350. *Godinez,* 509 U.S. at 403, citing, in a *cf.,* Medina v. California, 505 U.S. 437 (1992), *see* 4 PERLIN, *supra* note 8, § 8A-3.1b.

Justices Kennedy and Scalia concurred, noting their concern with those aspects of the opinion that compared the decisions made by a defendant who pleads guilty with those made by one who goes to trial, and expressing their "serious doubts" that there would be a heightened competency standard under the due process clause if these decisions were *not* equivalent.[351] Justice Blackmun dissented (for himself and Justice Stevens), focusing squarely on what he saw as the likely potential that Moran's decision to plead guilty was the product of "medication and mental illness."[352] He reviewed the expert testimony as to the defendant's state of depression, a colloquy between the defendant and the trial judge in which the court was informed that the defendant was being given medication, the trial judge's failure to inquire further and discover the psychoactive properties of the drugs in question, the defendant's subsequent testimony as to the "numbing" effect of the drugs, and the "mechanical character" and "ambiguity" of the defendant's answers to the court's questions at the plea stage.[353]

On the question of the multiple meanings of competency, Justice Blackmun added:

> [T]he majority cannot isolate the term "competent" and apply it in a vacuum, divorced from its specific context. A person who is "competent" to play basketball is not thereby "competent" to play the violin. The majority's monolithic approach to competency is true to neither life nor the law. Competency for one purpose does not necessarily translate to competency for another purpose.[354]

He concluded:

> To try, convict and punish one so helpless to defend himself contravenes fundamental principles of fairness and impugns the integrity of our criminal justice system. I cannot condone the decision to accept, without further inquiry, the self-destructive "choice" of a person who was so deeply medicated and who might well have been severely mentally ill.[355]

351. *Godinez*, 509 U.S. at 403 (emphasis added).

352. *Id.* at 410.

353. *Id.* at 410–11. *See also id.* at 411 ("such drugs often possess side effects that may 'compromise the right of a medicated criminal defendant to receive a fair trial . . . by rendering him unable or unwilling to assist counsel,'" quoting Riggins v. Nevada, 504 U.S. 127, 142 (1992) (Kennedy, J., concurring)).

For a pre-*Godinez* case, *see* Price v. Wainwright, 759 F.2d 1549 (11th Cir. 1985) (discussing impact of medication on defendant's competency to enter guilty plea).

354. *Godinez*, 509 U.S. at 413, citing Richard Bonnie, *The Competence of Criminal Defendant: A Theoretical Reformulation,* 10 Behav. Sci. & L. 291, 299 (1992); Ronald Roesch & Stephen Golding, Competency to Stand Trial 10–13 (1980).

For a post-*Godinez* case addressing this precise point, *See, e.g.,* People v. Randle, 661 N.E.2d 370, 376 (Ill. App. 1995), *reh'g denied* (1996), *appeal denied,* 667 N.E.2d 1061 (Ill. 1996) ("Fitness speaks only to a person's ability to function within the context of the trial; it does not refer to sanity or competence in other areas," quoting People v. Coleman, 660 N.E.2d 919, 928 (Ill. 1995), *reh'g denied* (1996), *cert. denied,* 519 U.S. 827 (1996)).

355. *Godinez*, 509 U.S. at 414. On remand, the Ninth Circuit affirmed the trial court's denial of Moran's habeas petition, finding that his guilty plea entry was voluntary and intelligent. Mo-

Justice Blackmun's dissent in *Godinez* is a powerful document that speaks simultaneously to the empirical realities of the criminal trial process—the impact of mental illness and medication on a defendant's capacity for reasoned choice, and perhaps most importantly, the role of pretextuality in the incompetency-to-stand-trial process.[356] He rejects the formulistic approach of Justice Thomas's majority opinion, weighs the pertinent social science evidence, and demonstrates how the trial record reflects the "ambiguity" of the controlling colloquy between counsel and the trial judge.[357]

The underlying tensions of the case are even further exacerbated because the defendant had been sentenced to death. The Supreme Court has considered the relationship between mental illness and the competency to be executed,[358] the relationship between mental retardation and the competency to be executed,[359] and has—as of yet[360]—declined to consider on the merits the constitutionality of medicating a defendant so as to make him competent to be executed.[361] The decision in *Godinez*—virtually guaranteeing less-searching inquiries in cases involving defendants of questionable competency—will likely complicate even further this area of mental disability law jurisprudence.[362]

---

ran v. Godinez, 40 F.3d 1567 (9th Cir.), *amended on denial of reh'g*, 57 F.3d 690 (9th Cir. 1994), *but see id.* at 1577 (Pregerson, J., dissenting). In a subsequent opinion, the Ninth Circuit found that a reasonable trial judge should have entertained a good faith doubt as to the defendant's competence during his change-of-plea hearing, and that the failure to hold a competency hearing was a due process violation, but also found that this violation was cured by a retrospective competency hearing, and that the defendant's waivers were voluntary and intelligent. Moran v. Godinez, 57 F.3d 690 (9th Cir. 1995), *but see id.* at 700 (Pregerson, J., dissenting).

356. *See generally,* Michael L. Perlin, *Pretexts and Mental Disability Law: The Case of Competency,* 47 U. MIAMI L. REV. 625 (1993).

357. For the first empirical examinations of this question, *see* Douglas Mossman & Neal W. Dunseith, Jr., *"A Fool for a Client": Print Portrayals of 49 Pro Se Criminal Defendants,* 29 J. AM. ACAD. PSYCHIATRY L. 408 (2001), and Erica Hashimoto, *Defending the Right of Self-representation: An Empirical Look at the Pro Se Felony Defendant ,* 85 N.C. L. REV. 423 (2007), the latter article concluding that the vast majority of pro se felony defendants—nearly 80%—did not display outward signs of mental illness.

358. *See* Ford v. Wainwright, 477 U.S. 399 (1986); *see infra* Chapter 2 H.

359. *See* Atkins v. Virginia, 536 U.S. 304 (2002), *see infra* Chapter 2 H.

360. *See* Panetti v. Quarterman, 127 S. Ct. 2842 (2007) (declining to specifically answer this question).

361. *See infra* Chapter 2 H.

362. For scholarly interpretations of *Godinez, see* Alan Felthous, *The Right to Represent Oneself Incompetently: Competency to Waive Counsel and Conduct One's Own Defense Before and After Godinez,* 18 MENT. & PHYS. DIS. L. REP. 105 (1994); Bruce Winick, *Criminal Law: Reforming Incompetency to Stand Trial and Plead Guilty: A Restated Proposal and a Response to Professor Bonnie,* 85 J. CRIM. L. & CRIMINOLOGY 571 (1995); Grisso, *supra* note 176, 23 CRIM. JUS. & BEHAV. 90 (1996); David Shapiro, *Ethical Dilemmas for the Mental Health Professional: Issues Raised by Recent Supreme Court Decisions,* 34 CAL. W. L. REV. 177 (1997); Christopher Slobogin & Amy Mashburn, *The Criminal Defense Lawyer's Fiduciary Duty to Clients with Mental Diabilities,* 68 FORDHAM L. REV. 1581 (2000); Martin Sabelli & Stacey Leyton, *Train Wrecks and Freeway Crashes: An Argument for Fairness and Against Self-Representation in the Criminal Justice System,* 91 J. CRIM. L. & CRIMINOLOGY 161 (2000).

5. Post-*Godinez* Developments

Most post-*Godinez* cases have affirmed convictions, reinstated convictions, or de-nied writs of habeas corpus,[363] although several have reversed convictions in cases in which there was reasonable doubt about a defendant's competence,[364] where an incorrect competency standard was presented,[365] or where the plea colloquy was inadequate in a case involving a defendant with mild mental retardation.[366]

Several cases have explored the relationship between the administration of psy-chotropic medication and a defendant's competency to enter a guilty plea, finding in one instance that, notwithstanding defendant's claim that the drugs "influ-enced" him at the time of his plea, he failed to show that there was a requisite "fair and just" reason to allow him to withdraw it;[367] in another, that the use of

---

363. *E.g.,* United States v. Day, 998 F.2d 622, 627 (8th Cir. 1993), *cert. denied,* 511 U.S. 1130 (1994) (rejecting defendant's claim that the court should have conducted a competency hearing prior to allowing him to proceed pro se); *see also, e.g.,* DeVille v. Whitley, 21 F.3d 654 (5th Cir.), *cert. denied,* 513 U.S. 968 (1994); Krawczuk v. State, 634 So. 2d 1070 (Fla.), *reh'g denied, cert. denied,* 513 U.S. 881 (1994); Weisberg v. State of Minn., 29 F.3d 1271 (8th Cir. 1994), *cert. denied,* 513 U.S. 1126 (1995); Nachtigall v. Class, 48 F.3d 1076 (8th Cir. 1995); People v. Woods, 931 P.2d 530 (Colo. App. 1996), *reh'g denied* (1996); United States v. Lebron, 76 F.3d 29 (1st Cir. 1996), *cert. denied,* 518 U.S. 1011 (1996); Gosier v. Welborn, 175 F.3d 504 (7th Cir. 1999), *cert. denied,* 528 U.S. 1006 (1999); Commonwealth v. Robbins, 431 Mass. 442, 727 N.E.2d 1157 (2000); United States v. Neeley, 189 F.3d 670 (7th Cir. 1999), *reh'g & reconsideration en banc denied* (1999), *cert. denied,* 528 U.S. 1190 (2000); Miranda-Gonzalez v. United States, 181 F.3d 164 (1st Cir. 1999); Magee v. State, 752 So. 2d 1100 (Miss. App. 1999); State v. Harper, 922 P.2d 383 (Idaho 1996); State v. Walton, 738 So. 2d 36 (La. App.), *writ denied,* 748 So. 2d 434 (La. 1999); State v. Wilson, 31 S.W. 3d 189 (Tenn. Crim. App. 2000); People v. Lawley, 38 P.3d 461 (Cal. 2002), *cert. denied,* 537 U.S. 1073 (2002) (same); People v. Koontz, 46 P.3d 335 (Cal. 2002) (same); Jermyn v. Horn, 266 F.3d 257 (3d Cir. 2001) (trial court did not err in refusing to allow defendant to represent himself); People v. Howzie, 102 Cal. Rptr. 2d 887 (2001) (same); Gall v. Parker, 213 F.3d 265 (6th Cir. 2000) (same); McCoin v. State, 56 S.W.3d 609 (Tex. App. 2001) (same).

364. *E.g.,* Miles v. Stainer, 108 F.3d 1109 (9th Cir 1997), *appeal after remand,* 141 F.3d 1351 (9th Cir. 1998) (court's failure to ask defendant whether he had been taking psychotropic medication before his entering guilty plea raised reasonable doubt about defendant's compe-tence); United States v. Graves, 98 F.3d 258 (7th Cir. 1996) (trial court had reasonable cause to believe defendant was incompetent to plead guilty).

See also, e.g., United States v. Giron-Reyes, 234 F.3d 78 (1st Cir. 2000) (district court re-quired to hold second competency hearing before accepting guilty plea after defendant's com-petency was certified as restored); Warren v. Lewis, 206 F. Supp. 2d 917 (M.D.Tenn. 2002) (trial court required to hold competency hearing); State v. Marshall, 27 P.3d 192 (Wash. 2001) (en banc) (same); Shafer v. Bowersox, 168 F. Supp. 2d 1055 (E.D. Mo. 2001) (defendant's guilty plea was not made knowingly, intelligently, and voluntarily); Matter of Fleming, 16 P.3d 610 (Wash. 2001) (en banc) (trial counsel ineffective in failing to apprise court that defen-dant's competency to plead guilty was in question). See also Commonwealth v. Conaghan, 740 N.E.2d 956 (Mass. 2000) (ordering competency evaluation of defendant seeking to withdraw guilty plea 4 years after it was entered); People v. Shanklin, 814 N.E.2d 139 (Ill. App. 2004); Deere v. Woodford, 339 F.3d 1084 (9th Cir. 2003).

365. State v. Bolin, 713 N.E. 2d 1092 (Ohio App. 1998).

366. State v. Thompson, 708 A. 2d 192 (Vt. 1998).

367. State v. Sarette, 589 A. 2d 125, 128–29 (N.H. 1991). *Compare* Schenck v. State, 662 So. 2d 998 (Fla. Dist. App. 1995) (Patiente, J., dissenting) (criticizing trial court for not in-

such drugs did not render the plea involuntary;[368] in another, that the defendant's unsupported statement that his guilty plea was involuntary because he had taken medication was insufficient to raise question to invoke certification discretion,[369] and in another, that the fact that defendant was taking psychotropic medication near the time he had pleaded guilty might have obligated the court to conduct a competency hearing.[370]

C. COMPETENCY TO WAIVE COUNSEL[371]

As with competency-to-plead-guilty law,[372] competency-to-waive-counsel law can be divided into three sections: the case law that developed prior to the Supreme Court's 1993 decision in *Godinez v. Moran*,[373] the decision in *Godinez*,

---

quiring into drugs defendant was taking, his mental condition, or presence of hallucinations) (*Godinez* not cited).

368. Long v. Iowa, 920 F. 2d 4,6 (8th Cir. 1990); *see also,* State v. Green, 943 P.2d 929 (Idaho 1997) (plea valid; *Godinez* not cited); Thomas v. Senkowski, 968 F. Supp. 953 (S.D.N.Y. 1997) (same) *but see* Miles, 108 F.3d at 1112–13 (state court's failure to inquire prior to accepting guilty plea as to whether prisoner was taking antipsychotic medication raised reasonable doubt as to defendant's competence); People v. Jamison, 756 N.E.2d 788 (Ill. 2001) (same); Thirkield v. Pitcher, 199 F. Supp. 2d 637 (E.D. Mich. 2002) (same); United States v. General, 278 F.3d 389 (4th Cir. 2002) (same); Hastings v. Yukins, 194 F. Supp. 2d 659 (E.D. Mich. 2002) (plea valid, citing Godinez), Dalton v. Commonwealth 2003 WL 22747884 (Ky. App. 2003) (psychiatric medication did not hinder guilty plea) (Godinez not cited); Means v. State, 103 P.3d 25 (Nev. 2004).

369. State v. Blue, 644 A. 2d 859 (Conn. App. 1994), *cert. denied,* 644 A.2d 919 (Conn. 1994).

370. People v. McKay, 668 N.E. 2d 580 (Ill. App. 1996), *appeal denied,* 675 N.E.2d 637 (Ill. 1996).

For other cases on the same issue, *See, e.g.,* Freeman v. McBride, 843 F. Supp. 452 (N.D. Ind.), *aff'd,* 16 F.3d 1225 (7th Cir. 1992) (defendant competent to enter guilty plea even though he was taking drug Thorazine at time of competency hearing); Garzee v. State, 126 Idaho 396, 883 P.2d 1088 (App. 1994) (defendant's cognitive abilities to enter plea not impaired by administration of antipsychotic medications); Carey v. United States, 50 F.3d 1097, 1099 (1st Cir. 1995), *reh'g & suggestion for en banc denied* (1995) (district court not required to ask defendant about prescription drug use during guilty plea colloquy; record reflected defendant in "complete command of his facilities"); Miles v. Stainer, 108 F.3d 1109, 1112–13 (9th Cir. 1997), *appeal after remand,* 141 F.3d 1351 (9th Cir. 1998) (state court's failure to inquire prior to accepting guilty plea as to whether prisoner was taking antipsychotic medication raised reasonable doubt as to defendant's competence); United States v. Damon, 191 F.3d 561 (4th Cir. 1999), *on remand,* 17 Fed. Appx. 198 (4th Cir. 2001), *cert. den.,* 534 U.S. 1170 (2002) (district court was required, at plea colloquy, to make inquiry into effect defendant's medication had on his ability to make a voluntary plea).

On the relationship between involuntary medication and competence to proceed in general, *see* Robert Schopp, *Involuntary Treatment and Competence to Proceed in the Criminal Process: Capital and Noncapital Cases,* 24 BEHAV. SCI. & L. 495 (2006); *compare* Christopher Slobogin, *Competency on the Criminal Context: An Analysis of Robert Schopp's Views,* 24 BEHAV. SCI. & L. 529 (2006).

371. This section is largely adapted from 4 PERLIN, *supra* note 8, §§ 8B-3.1 (2d ed. 2002).

372. *See supra* Chapter 2B.

373. 509 U.S. 389 (1993).

and post-*Godinez* case law. In addition, the Supreme Court has also considered the question of the right to waive counsel at the appellate stage of criminal proceedings.[374]

1. Historical Background[375]

A significant amount of case law has developed over the question of the level of competency required for a defendant to waive representation by counsel.[376] Since the U.S. Supreme Court's ruling in *Faretta v. California*,[377] that a defendant has a federal constitutional right to represent himself if he voluntarily elects to do so, courts have focused on the question of whether a defendant has "the *mental capacity to waive the right to counsel* with a realization of the probable risks and consequences of his action."[378]

To meet such a standard, it is not necessary that the defendant be *technically* competent to represent himself,[379] but only that he be "free of mental disorder which would so impair his free will that his decision to waive counsel would not be voluntary."[380] In fact, neither bizarre statements and actions,[381] mere eccentric behavior,[382] nor a finding that the defendant had been diagnosed as having paranoid schizophrenia[383] have been found in specific cases to be enough to establish lack of capacity to represent oneself.[384]

On the other hand, waiver of counsel should be "carefully scrutinized,"[385] and

374. Martinez v. Court of Appeal of Cal., 528 U.S. 152 (2000).

375. This section is largely adapted from 4 PERLIN, *supra* note 8, § 8B-3.1a.

376. *See, e.g.,* Felde v. Blackburn, 795 F.2d 400 (5th Cir. 1986), for later proceedings, see 817 F. 2d 281 (5th Cir. 1987), *reh. den.*, 820 F. 2d 1223 (5th Cir. 1987), *cert. den.*, 484 U.S. 873 (1987); People v. Burnett, 234 Cal. Rptr. 67 (App. 1987), *abrogated by*, State v. Hightower, 49 Cal. Rptr. 2d 40 (App. 1996); State v. Hahn, 726 P. 2d 25 (Wash. 1986).

377. 422 U.S. 806, 835 (1975). *See, e.g.,* Note, *Faretta v. California and the Pro Se Defense: The Constitutional Right of Self Representation*, 25 AM. U.L. REV. 897 (1976); Richard Chused, *Faretta and the Personal Defense: The Role of a Represented Defendant in Trial Tactics*, 65 CALIF. L. REV. 636 (1977).

378. People v. Clark, 213 Cal. Rptr. 837, 840 (App. 1985), *rev. den.* (1985) (emphasis in original). *See generally* Robert Miller & Leonard Kaplan, *Representation by Counsel: Right or Obligation?* 10 BEHAV. SCI & L. 395 (1992).

379. *Clark*, 213 Cal. Rptr. at 840.

380. Curry v. Superior Court of Fresno County, 141 Cal. Rptr. 884, 888 (App. 1977) (citing Peter R. Silten & Richard Tullis, *Mental Competency in Criminal Proceedings*, 28 HASTINGS L.J. 1053, 1066 (1977).

381. People v. Miller, 167 Cal. Rptr. 816, 880 (App. 1980).

382. *Curry*, 141 Cal. Rptr. at 888.

383. State v. Evans, 610 P.2d 35 (Ariz. 1980).

384. *Clark*, 213 Cal. Rptr. at 841. *See also, e.g.,* People v. Powell, 225 Cal. Rptr. 703 (App. 1986) (not abuse of discretion for court to find, after *Faretta* inquiry, that defendant had capacity to waive counsel in post-insanity acquittal commitment hearing); *see also,* State v. Drobel, 815 P.2d 724 (Utah App. 1991), *cert. den.*, 836 P. 2d 1383 (Utah 1991).

385. People v. Kessler, 447 N.E.2d 495, 499 (Ill. App. 1983) (citing People v. Heral, 342 N.E.2d 34 (Ill. 1976)).

the record must reflect that "the accused was offered counsel and knowingly and intelligently refused the offer."[386] In a searching decision, a New Jersey intermediate appellate court has considered the full range of underlying issues:

> Without the guiding hand of counsel, a defendant may lose his freedom because he does not know how to establish his innocence. . . . Trained counsel is also necessary to vindicate fundamental rights that receive protection from rules of procedure and exclusionary principles. . . . Where the doctrine supporting these rights "has any complexities the untrained defendant is in no position to defend himself."

These considerations militate strongly in favor of exercising great caution in determining whether a proposed waiver of counsel satisfies constitutional standards. Within the context of the potential pitfalls of self-representation, it has been said that "the court must make certain by direct inquiry on the record that defendant is aware of 'the nature of the charges, the statutory offenses included with them, the range of allowable punishments thereunder, possible defenses to the charges and circumstances in mitigation thereof, and all other facts essential to a broad understanding of the whole matter.'"[387]

The court is required to conduct "more than a routine inquiry when making that determination."[388] Thus, at least several courts[389] have found that the standard for self-representation is a higher one than the standard for competency to stand trial,[390] since "literacy and a basic understanding over and above the competence to stand trial may be required."[391] As the Wisconsin Supreme Court has observed:

> Surely a defendant who, while mentally competent to be tried, is simply incapable of effective communication or, because of less than average intellectual powers, is

386. *Kessler,* 447 N.E. 2d at 499 (citing People v. Williams, 421 N.E.2d 551 (Ill. App. 1981)); *see also* People v. Moore, 513 N.E.2d 24, *appeal denied,* 517 N.E.2d 1092 (Ill. App. 1987); Cerkella v. Florida, 588 So. 2d 1058 (Fla. Dist. App. 1991).

387. State v. Slattery, 571 A.2d 1314, 1320–21 (N.J. App. Div. 1990) (citations omitted) (defendant functioned at "low average" range of intelligence).

388. *Kessler,* 447 N.E. 2d at 499 (citing People v. Feliciano, 417 N.E.2d 824 (Ill. App. 1981)). *See also, e.g.,* United States v. Purnett, 910 F.2d 51 (2d Cir. 1990) (defendant entitled to new trial where trial court accepted waiver of counsel before making determination of defendant's competency).

389. *But see, e.g., Curry, supra;* People v. Reason, 372 N.Y.S.2d 614 (1975). *Reason* is criticized in Silten & Tullis, *supra* note 380, at 1070.

390. *See, e.g.,* United States *ex rel.* Konigsberg v. Vincent, 526 F.2d 131 (2d Cir. 1975); State v. Kolocotronis, 436 P.2d 774 (Wash. 1968); Pickens v. State, 292 N.W.2d 601 (Wis. 1980); State v. Harding, 670 P.2d 383, 391 (Ariz. 1983). *See also* Johnson v. State, 507 A.2d 1134, 1141 (Md. App. 1986) (finding of competency to stand trial does not automatically lead to a conclusion that an accused is also competent to waive right to counsel). *Pickens* is cited with approval in State v. Mott, 784 P.2d 278, 284 (Ariz. 1989).

391. *Pickens,* 292 N.W.2d at 611 (citing *Faretta,* 422 U.S. at 835).

unable to attain the minimal understanding necessary to present a defense, is not to be allowed "to go to jail under his own banner.". . .[392]

2. *Godinez v. Moran*

In *Godinez v. Moran*,[393] the Supreme Court ruled that, under federal constitutional law, the standard for waiving counsel is the same as for being found competent to stand trial.[394] It found there was "no reason" to believe that the decision to waive counsel requires an "appreciably higher level of mental functioning than the decision to waive other constitutional rights."[395]

It rejected the defendant's arguments that a self-representing defendant must have "greater powers of comprehension, judgment and reason, than would be necessary to stand trial with the aid of an attorney,"[396] concluding that this rested on a "flawed premise: the competence that is required of a defendant seeking to waive his right to counsel is the competence to *waive the right,* not the competence to represent himself."[397] Relying on its decision in *Faretta,* it found that a defendant's ability to represent himself "has no bearing upon his competence to choose self-representation."[398]

Justice Blackmun dissented, concluding on this point:

> A finding that a defendant is competent to stand trial establishes only that he is capable of aiding his attorney in making the critical decisions required at trial or in plea negotiations. The reliability or even relevance of such a finding vanishes when its basic premise—that counsel will be present—ceases to exist. The question is no longer whether the defendant can proceed with an attorney but whether he can proceed alone and uncounselled.[399]

---

392. *Pickens,* 292 N.W.2d at 611 (quoting United States v. Denno, 348 F.2d 12, 15 (2d Cir. 1965). *See also Powell,* 225 Cal. Rptr. at 711–12. *But see* State v. Williams, 621 P.2d 423, 427 (Kan. 1980) (trial court not required to hold further hearings as to defendant's continued competency to represent himself after he had broken a door and window subsequent to beginning of trial).

393. 509 U.S. 389 (1993).

394. *Godinez,* 509 U.S. at 398. On remand, the Ninth Circuit affirmed the trial court's denial of Moran's habeas petition, finding that his guilty plea entry was voluntary and intelligent. Moran v. Godinez, 40 F.3d 1567 (9th Cir.), *amended on denial of reh'g,* 57 F.3d 690 (9th Cir. 1994), *but see id.* at 1577 (Pregerson, J., dissenting). In a subsequent opinion, the Ninth Circuit found that a reasonable trial judge should have entertained a good faith doubt as to the defendant's competence during his change-of-plea hearing, and that the failure to hold a competency hearing was a due process violation, but also found that this violation was cured by a retrospective competency hearing, and that the defendant's waivers were voluntary and intelligent. Moran v. Godinez, 57 F.3d 690 (9th Cir. 1995), *but see id.* at 700 (Pregerson, J., dissenting). *See supra* note 355.

395. *Godinez,* 509 U.S. at 398.

396. *Id.,* citing Silten & Tullis, *supra* note 380, at 1968.

397. *Godinez,* 509 U.S. at 399 (emphasis in original).

398. *Id.*

399. *Godinez,* 509 U.S. at 411–12.

For scholarly considerations of this aspect of *Godinez, see, e.g.,* Stacey Giulianti, *The Right*

At least one federal judge has endorsed Justice Blackmun's "thoughtful dissent,"[400] concluding:

That this result [allowing for the waiver of counsel in case of "unstable" defendant "prone to paranoid delusions," *see id.*] is constitutionally permissible is deeply disturbing and ultimately "impugns the integrity of our criminal justice system." *Godinez,* 509 U.S. at 417 (Blackmun J., dissenting).[401]

3. Post-*Godinez* Developments

Post-*Godinez* case law has been mixed. The majority of cases have affirmed convictions,[402] but several have required remands,[403] at least one of which relied on *state* constitutional law as the basis of its decision.[404] Several cases

---

to Proceed Pro Se at Competency Hearings: Practical Solutions to a Constitutional Catch-22, 47 U. MIAMI L. REV. 883 (1993); Randall Bateman, *Federal and State Perspectives on a Criminal Defendant's Right to Self-Representation,* 20 J. CONTEMP. L. 77 (1994); John Quinn, *"Attitudinal" Decision Making in the Federal Courts: A Study of Constitutional Self-Representation Claims,* 33 SAN DIEGO L. REV. 701 (1996); Jennifer Corinis, *A Reasoned Standard for Competency to Waive Counsel After* Godinez v. Moran, 80 B.U. L. REV. 265 (2000); Sabelli & Leyton *supra* note 362.

On the relationship between a defendant's purportedly delusional refusal to enter an insanity defense and his competency to waive counsel, *see* Christopher Cheatham & Thomas Litwack, *Professionals' Attitudes Regarding a New York Defendant Who Delusionally Refuses a Viable, Counsel-Recommended Insanity Defense Should Be Found Competent or Incompetent to Stand Trial,* 31 J. L. & PSYCHIATRY 433 (2003).

400. *See* Gov't of Virgin Islands v. Charles, 72 F.3d 401, 411 (3d Cir. 1995) (Lewis, J., concurring).

401. *Id.* at 413. And *see id.* at 411:

This case presents us with a window through which to view the real-world effects of [*Godinez*], and it is not a pretty sight.

402. *E.g.,* Thanos v. State, 332 Md. 511, 632 A.2d 768 (App. 1993) (dismissing defendant's appeal); State v. Wise 879 S.W.2d 494 (Mo. 1994), *cert. denied,* 513 U.S. 1093 (1995) (no error to allow defendant to represent himself); Wilkins v. Delo, 886 F. Supp. 1503 (W.D. Mo. 1995) (finding that petitioner intelligently and voluntarily waived right to counsel not entitled to presumption of correctness); United States v. Schmidt, 105 F.3d 82 (2d Cir.), *cert. denied,* 522 U.S. 846 (1997) (trial court conducted adequate inquiry as to defendant's ability to waive counsel knowingly and intelligently); Simpson v. State, 517 S.E. 2d 830 (Ga. App. 1999) (trial court not required to make a sua sponte inquiry into pro se defendant's competency to stand trial); Collier v. State, 959 S.W.2d 621 (Tex. Crim. App. 1997), *reh'g denied* (1998), *cert. denied,* 525 U.S. 929 (1998) (defendant's decision to waive counsel was voluntary); State v. Wolf, 237 Conn. 633, 678 A.2d 1369 (1996) (defendant competent to represent himself); State v. Day, 233 Conn. 813, 661 A.2d 539 (1995) (defendant competent to waive counsel).

403. *E.g.,* State v. Thornblad, 513 N.W.2d 260 (Minn. App. 1994), *appeal after remand,* 1995 WL 46205 (Minn. App.), *review denied* (1995) (reversible error where court refused to allow competent-to-stand-trial defendant to represent himself); People v. Nauton, 34 Cal. Rptr. 2d 861 (Cal. App. 1994) (same); United States v. Cash, 47 F.3d 1083 (11th Cir. 1995) (trial court's colloquy with defendant insufficient to determine validity of waiver of right to counsel); State v. Pollard, 657 A.2d 185 (Vt. 1995) (defendant did not waive right to counsel competently and intelligently); State v. Rater, 568 N.W.2d 655 (Iowa 1997) (lack of sufficient inquiry

have applied *Godinez* to the situation of so-called "hybrid representation,"[405] and often, *Godinez* is not even cited in decisions affirming convictions,[406] reversing them,[407] and to other collateral questions that arise in waiver situations.[408]

One case, by way of example, has found that a defendant's decision to represent himself at trial precluded any relief that might be based on ineffective assistance of counsel.[409] Yet another—while affirming the defendant's conviction—explored the implications of inconsistent positions taken by the govern-

---

by court rendered defendant's waiver invalid); Wilkins v. Bowersox, 933 F. Supp. 1496 (W.D. Mo. 1996), *aff'd,* 145 F.3d 1006 (8th Cir. 1998), *reh'g & suggestion for reh'g en banc denied* (8th Cir. 1998) (defendant not competent to represent himself); United States v. Zedner, 193 F. 3d 562 (2d Cir. 1999) (trial court had substantial reason to doubt defendant's competence, and thus was required to appoint counsel to represent him at competency hearing); State v. Chamley, 568 N.W.2d 607 (S.D. 1997) (defendant had right to proceed pro se).

See also, United States v. Joseph, 333 F.3d 587 (5th Cir. 2003) (evidence as a whole, including opinion of court-appointed evaluator and observations by various law enforcement agents, supported determination that defendant was competent and waiver of counsel on morning of trial was knowingly and intelligently made); Fahy v. Horn, 2003 WL 22017231 (E.D. Pa. 2003) (Court interprets *Godinez* as asking two distinct questions: competency to waive right and whether waiver is knowing and voluntary; defendant possessed competency regarding both).

404. State v. Klessig, 564 N.W.2d 716, 723–24 (Wis. 1997).

405. Dunn v. State, 693 So. 2d 1333 (Miss. 1997) (defendant who received hybrid representation not deprived of his right to counsel). *Compare* State v. Bartlett, 898 P.2d 98 (Mont. 1995) (standby counsel's motion for mental examination should have been granted as matter of right); Sherwood v. State, 717 N.E. 2d 131 (Ind. 1999) (trial court's imposition of hybrid representation scheme over defendant's valid waiver of counsel denied him actual control of his defense and thus violated his Sixth Amendment rights). *See also,* State v. Arguelles, 63 P.3d 731 (Utah 2003) (defendant was competent to waive counsel in death penalty case in spite of being a "death penalty volunteer" where standby counsel voiced no concerns about competency).

406. *E.g.,* State v. Reed, 503 S.E.2d 747 (S.C. 1998), *reh'g denied* (1998) (waiver knowing and voluntary, *Godinez* not cited); State v. Cornell, 878 P.2d 1352 (Ariz. 1994) (acceptance of defendant's waiver of counsel without ordering competency hearing did not violate defendant's due process rights; *Godinez* not cited); Visage v. State, 664 So. 2d 1101 (Fla. Dist. App. 1995), *review granted,* 671 So. 2d 789 (1996), *jurisdiction discharged,* 679 So. 2d 735 (Fla. 1996), *reh'g den.,* (1996) (no abuse of discretion where trial court denied defendant right to represent himself; *Godinez* not cited).

407. Howard v. State, 701 So. 2d 274 (Miss. 1997) (defendant's waiver of right to counsel not voluntary; *Godinez* not cited); People v. Newton, 671 N.Y.S.2d 601 (Sup. 1998), *discussed in* Alden, *Waiver of Counsel Void for Incapacity,* N.Y.L.J. (Mar. 5, 1998), at 1 (*Godinez* not cited).

408. People v. Fitzpatrick, 77 Cal. Rptr. 2d 634 (App. 1998), *review denied* (1998) (revocation of defendant's right to self-representation justified by determination that defendant was deliberately delaying trial; *Godinez* not cited); State v. Thomas, 484 S.E.2d 368 (N.C. 1997) (error to appoint counsel to litigate question of defendant's capacity to waive counsel; *Godinez* not cited).

409. Commonwealth v. Appel, 689 A.2d 891 (Pa. 1997), *rearg. denied* (1997), *habeas corpus conditionally granted,* 1998 WL 323805 (E.D. Pa. 1999), *aff'd,* 250 F. 3d 203 (3d Cir. 2001) (*Godinez* not cited).

ment on the defendant's competence (arguing that she was *not* incompetent to waive counsel in a criminal case while arguing, in a subsequent proceeding, that she suffered from a serious mental disease).[410] And, the California Supreme Court has found that the determination that a defendant was not competent to waive counsel did not necessarily show error in finding him competent to stand trial,[411] Elsewhere, the Idaho Supreme Court has ruled that an inpatient evaluation was not necessary before allowing a defendant to plead guilty,[412] when the South Dakota Supreme Court rejected a defendant's claim that his mental retardation should have allowed him to withdraw a previously entered guilty plea,[413] and the Connecticut Supreme Court has held that the trial court's improper denial of a capital defendant's request for a hearing on his competency to stand trial did not violate due process, because in accepting defendant's guilty plea the court had implicitly found him competent to stand trial.[414]

On the other hand, the District of Columbia Court of Appeals has reversed a conviction when the trial court allowed the defendant to represent herself at a competency-to-stand trial hearing.[415] Elsewhere, the Ninth Circuit reversed one conviction when a jury trial waiver was accepted without inquiry when there was reason to suspect defendant's mental instability,[416] and another in which the government failed to prove that the defendant's waiver of trial counsel was knowing and intelligent.[417] And, at least one court has considered the paradox of a potentially incompetent defendant waiving his right to asserting the incompetency status, concluding that it was "doubtful" whether defendant could waive the status of competence to stand trial because it is contradictory to argue that a defendant may be incompetent and yet knowingly and intelligently waive his right to have the court determine capacity.[418]

---

410. United States v. Schmidt, 105 F.3d 82 (2d Cir. 1997), *cert. denied,* 522 U.S. 846 (1997) (conflict in positions did not require reversal of defendant's convictions; *Godinez* not cited).

411. People v. Welch, 85 Cal. Rptr. 2d 203 (1999), *cert. denied,* 528 U.S. 1154 (2000).

412. State v. Harper, 922 P.2d 383 (Idaho 1996).

413. State v. Bailey, 546 N.W.2d 387 (S.Dak. 1996).

414. State v. Johnson, 751 A.2d 298 (Conn. 1999).

415. United States v. Klat, 59 F. Supp. 2d 47 (D.D.C. 1999), *aff'd,* 213 F.3d 697 (D.C. Cir. 2000).

416. United States v. Christensen, 18 F.3d 822 (9th Cir. 1994).

417. United States v. Mohawk, 20 F.3d 1480 (9th Cir. 1994); *see also,* United States v. Arlt, 41 F.3d 516, 520 (9th Cir. 1994) (citing *Mohawk* approvingly on the necessary elements of a judge's inquiry before accepting a counsel waiver), *appeal after remand,* 85 F.3d 638 (9th Cir. 1996).

418. State v. Carmouche, 872 So. 2d 1020 (La. 2002).

After the manuscript for this book was submitted, the Supreme Court granted certoriari on the important question of whether a state may adopt a higher standard for measuring compe-

4. Right of Self-Representation on Appeal[419]

The Supreme Court has since declined to extend the constitutional right of self-representation to the appellate process, concluding that the history relied upon in *Faretta* was inapplicable to that process.[420] *Godinez* is not cited in the Court's opinion.

Martinez has been the subject of remarkably little judicial construction. In one case, the Arkansas Supreme Court ruled that, although *Martinez* left to the state appellate courts the discretion to allow a layperson to proceed *pro se* on appeal, "it also recognized that representation by trained appellate counsel is of distinct benefit to the appellant as well as the court," thus concluding that appellant, who was represented by counsel qualified to represent defendants in capital cases, had not demonstrated that there was any good cause to permit him to serve as cocounsel or to file a supplemental *pro se* brief.[421]

D. OTHER CRIMINAL COMPETENCIES[422]

Introduction

In Justice Kennedy's concurrence in *Godinez v. Moran*,[423] he focused on the impact of *Godinez's* unitary standard on cases involving *other* aspects of the criminal competency inquiry. Writing for himself and for Justice Scalia, Justice Kennedy asserted "The Due Process Clause does not mandate different standards of competency at various stages of or for different decisions made during the criminal proceedings."[424] Although he did not further define "criminal June 19, 2007 proceedings," this immediately followed his interpretation of the universality of the *Dusky* standard in "other" competency cases: "That standard is applicable from the time of arraignment through the return of a verdict."[425]

In this subchapter, we will explore the criminal competency standard in matters *other than* trial, guilty pleas, and counsel waivers: pretrial process issues, trial process issues, posttrial process issues, and others. It must be kept in mind that each of the pretrial process issues precedes the "time of arraignment" referred to by Justice Kennedy, and each of the posttrial process issues follows the "time of verdict" in the same opinion.

---

tency to represent oneself at trial than for assessing competency to stand trial. *See* Indiana v. Edwards, 128 U.S. 741, 2007 WL 2361185 (2007).

419. This section is adapted from 4 PERLIN, *supra* note 8, § 8B-3.1d.

420. Martinez v. Court of Appeal of Cal., *supra* note 374.

421. Fudge v. Stone, 19 S.W.3d 22, 22 (Ark. 2000).

422. This subchapter is largely adapted from Perlin, *supra* note 315.

423. 509 U.S. 389 (1993).

424. Godinez, 509 U.S. at 404 (Kennedy, J., concurring) (emphasis added).

425. *Id.* at 403.

1. Pretrial Process Issues

a. Confessions law

There is a robust body of case law dealing with confession questions. Since 1960, it has appeared clear that a confession is inadmissible if the defendant was mentally incompetent at the time it was given.[426] Since the U.S. Supreme Court's decision in *Miranda v. Arizona,*[427] the prosecution has been prohibited from using any custodial statements unless the defendant has waived his right to silence by a voluntary, knowing, and intelligent waiver.[428] Whether a waiver is knowingly and intelligently made depends on the specific facts and circumstances of each case, including the background, experience, and conduct of the accused.[429] The state bears the burden of proving that the waiver was so knowingly and intelligently made.[430]

Courts must employ "special care" in the evaluation of confessions of individuals with mental disabilities,[431] and, while mental deficiency "of itself"[432] does not render a confession involuntary, it is a "relevant factor"[433] that must be considered in the "totality of circumstances."[434] Neither subnormal intelligence,[435] "lack of education and illiteracy,"[436] nor "previous incidents of mental instability"[437] are "necessarily dispositive" of the issue of mental competence at the time the confession is given.[438]

---

426. *See* Blackburn v. Alabama, 361 U.S. 199 (1960). Such a confession is proscribed as not being the product of "a rational intellect and free will." *Id.,* at 208. *See, e.g.,* Kimbell v. State, 252 Ga. 65, 311 S.E.2d 465 (1984). *But see* Colorado v. Connelly, 479 U.S. 157 (1986) (coercive police activity a necessary predicate to finding of involuntariness of confession, even in the case of defendant with mental disabilities). For a full discussion of *Connelley, see* 4 PERLIN, *supra* note 8, §§10-3.3 to 3.3d, at 406–21 (2d ed. 2002).

427. 384 U.S. 436 (1966).

428. *Id.* at 444.

429. Edwards v. Arizona, 451 U.S. 477 (1981). *Cf. Connelly, supra.*

430. Miranda, 384 U.S., at 436.

431. *See, e.g.,* People v. Simmons, 326 N.E.2d 383 (Ill. 1975); People v. Turner, 306 N.E.2d 27 (Ill. 1973).

432. People v. Redmon, 468 N.E.2d 1310, 1314 (Ill. App. 1984) (quoting Turner, 306 N.E.2d, at 30).

433. *See* State v. Smith, 370 N.W.2d 827, 830 (Wis. 1985).

434. Redmon, 468 N.E.2d at 1315 (quoting Turner, 306 N.E.2d at 30). *Cf.* Connelly, 479 U.S. at 169–170 (notions of "free will" have no place in Constitutional analysis of confession's admissibility).

435. *See* State v. Jenkins, 268 S.E.2d 458 (N.C. 1980).

436. State v. Osborne, 330 S.E.2d 447, 448 (Ga. App. 1985).

437. *See* State v. Vickers, 291 S.E.2d 599 (N.C. 1982).

438. State v. Simpson, 334 S.E.2d 53, 59 (N.C. 1985). *Cf.* State v. Sergent, 621 P.2d 209, 211–212 (Wash. App. 1980) ("The combination of the defendant's incompetency, his mental illness, the medication he was taking, and his adverse reactions to those drugs, his attempt at plea bargaining and his waiver of fundamental constitutional rights without the assistance of his attorney, compel us to find that his statement to [the police officer] was involuntary"). For a practical guide to experts in determining whether an adult is competent to waive her or his *Miranda* rights, *see* Daniel Greenfield & Philip Witt, *Evaluation Adult Miranda Waiver Competency,* 33 J. PSYCHIATRY & L. 471 (2005). For an empirical investigation of the compe-

Generally, a statement has been found to be inadmissible where "the mental subnormality [sic] is so great that an accused is incapable of understanding the meaning and effect of his confessions,"[439] or where defendant's mental illness is combined with other circumstances so that it is not the "product of an essentially free and unconstrained choice by the maker."[440] However, this is old news. Other important pretrial questions have been the subject of virtually no scholarly attention: matters involving searches and seizures, lineups, and preliminary hearings. Generally, with respect to these and other pretrial process rights, courts have declined to establish a separate standard for determining the competency of a criminal defendant to participate at a suppression or other pretrial hearing, generally ruling that the "bona fide doubt" procedural standard of *Pate v. Robinson* is similarly applicable.[441]

b. Search and seizure

At least two cases have explored the relationship between competency to consent and a subsequent police search and seizure.[442] In one, a federal district court ruled that mental competency is relevant to any inquiry in determining voluntariness of a consent.[443] In the other, the Fourth Circuit rejected a defendant's similar argument, on the basis that the defendant cited "no authority for the proposition that such incompetency renders consent to the search invalid."[444] Also, a New York trial court has ruled that defense counsel was not entitled to waive an incompe-

---

tence of *juveniles* to so waive their rights, *see* Jodi Viljoen & Ronald Roesch, *Competence to Waive Interrogation Rights and Adjudicative Competence in Adolescent Defendants: Cognitive Development, Attorney Contact and Psychological Symptoms,* 29 LAW & HUM. BEHAV. 723 (2005).

439. Casias v. State, 452 S.W.2d 483, 488 (Tex. Crim. App. 1970).

440. Jackson v. United States, 404 A.2d 911, 923 (D.C. App. 1979) (quoting Culombe v. Connecticut, 367 U.S. 568, 602 (1961)).

441. United States ex rel. Phillips v. Lane, 580 F. Supp. 839, 843 (N.D. Ill. 1984) (citing cases). *See also* People v. Vallen, 488 N.Y.S.2d 994, 997 (Sup. Ct. 1985) ("The criminal process does not proceed in . . . piecemeal and independent stages, but . . . all stages of a criminal proceeding are interdependent and intertwined").

442. On a defendant's competency to consent to a police search, *see* James Wulach, *Psychological Evaluation of the Consent to Search,* 18 J. PSYCHIATRY & L. 319 (1990). On the role of consent in the area of search and seizure law in this context generally, *see* Russell Galloway, *Basic Fourth Amendment Analysis,* 32 SANTA CLARA L. REV. 737, 760–61 (1992), citing in part Schneckloth v. Bustamonte, 412 U.S. 218 (1973):

> Searches are permitted without probable cause or particularized justification if based on voluntary consent of a person with authority over the place searched or a person whom the police reasonably believe possesses such authority. To determine whether consent is voluntary, the Court uses a "totality of the circumstances" test focusing on such factors as the competence and mental condition of the person who consented, whether she knew of the right to refuse, whether she cooperated or resisted, whether she was in custody when she consented, and whether the police made a "claim of authority" to search or engaged in other coercive conduct.

443. United States v. Ocampo, 492 F. Supp. 1211 (E.D.N.Y. 1980).

444. United States v. Flannery, 879 F.2d 863 1989 WL 79731, *4 (4th Cir. 1989).

tent defendant's right to be present at a suppression hearing.[445] Note, however, that all of these cases were decided prior to *Godinez*.

c. Lineups

One case has held that an incompetent criminal suspect could be required to participate in a prearraignment lineup.[446] The court in this case cited Justice Kennedy's *Godinez* concurrence and concluded that it was "unclear" whether the Dusky standard applied to prearraignment matters.[447]

d. Preliminary hearing

One case has held that if an information[448] is dismissed due to defendant's incompetence at the preliminary hearing stage, the defendant is entitled to another preliminary hearing once competence is restored.[449] *Godinez* was not cited in this case.

e. Diversion to mental health courts

Scholars have begun to investigate the prevalence of incompetence in that cohort of defendants identified as potentially divertable to mental health courts.[450]

2. Other Trial Process Issues

Introduction

Other cases have considered the relationship between a defendant's competency and such issues as jury waiver, evidentiary objections, and statements to the media. Yet others have considered the implications of juror incompetency and witness incompetency.[451]

a. Jury waivers

Courts have split on jury waiver questions. The Ninth Circuit has ruled that a waiver should not have been accepted without further inquiry as to defendant's

---

445. *See* People v. Matthews, 585 N.Y.S.2d 948 (Sup. Ct. 1992).

446. *See* Matter of Harris, 627 N.Y.S. 2d 207 (Sup. Ct. 1995), and *see id.* at 209–11 (explaining the significance of this inquiry).

447. *Id.* at 209.

448. California has long proceeded in criminal cases by the use of an "information" rather than an indictment. See Hurtado v. California, 110 U.S. 516 (1884).

449. People v. Duncan, 93 Cal. Rptr. 2d 173 (App. 2000), reh'g denied (2000).

450. *See* Kenneth Stafford & Dustin Wygant, *The Role of Competency to Stand Trial in Mental Health Courts,* 23 Behav. Sci. & L. 245 (2005) (majority of defendants in this cohort found to be incompetent to stand trial). On mental health courts in general, *see* Norman Poythress et al., *Perceived Coercion and Procedural Justice in the Broward Mental Health Court,* 25 Int'l J. L. & Psychiatry 517 (2002); Henry Steadman et al., *From Referral to Disposition: Case Processing in Seven Mental Health Courts,* 23 Behav. Sci. & L. 215 (2005).

451. Of course, *Godinez* is not facially relevant to either of these issues.

mental state,[452] noting that the defendant "must be competent to waive the jury right, and the waiver must in fact be voluntary, knowing, and intelligent."[453] According to the Ninth Circuit, this requirement of *Godinez* spoke to more than simply a competency determination:

> Whereas competency goes to a defendant's capacity in general, "[t]he purpose of the 'knowing and voluntary' inquiry, by contrast, is to determine whether the defendant actually does understand the significance and consequences of a particular decision."
>
> The Court has called this inquiry a "serious and weighty responsibility." *Johnson v. Zerbst,* 304 U.S. 458, 465 . . . (1938). We now hold that district courts may not discharge this responsibility in cases where they have reason to suspect a defendant may suffer from mental or emotional instability without an in-depth colloquy which reasonably assures the court that under the particular facts of the case, the signed waiver was voluntarily, knowingly, and intelligently made.[454]

On the other hand, another court has ruled that a defendant's due process rights were not violated when jury selection proceeded while defendant was undergoing psychological evaluation for purposes of determining competency to stand trial, a case in which no finding of incompetency had ever been made.[455] In addition, one pre-*Godinez* court has required a separate finding that a defendant—found to be competent to stand trial—was also competent to waive a jury trial.[456]

b. Evidentiary objections

On the question of the impact of a defendant's incompetence on the admissibility into evidence of several letters he wrote at the time he had been found incompetent to stand trial, a Virginia appellate court has ruled that such incompetence did not preclude admission into evidence.[457] Another court has ruled, contrarily, that it was reversible error to use the deposition testimony of the victim in a criminal case that was taken at the time when the defendant was incompetent.[458]

c. Statements to the media

Yet another court has concluded that finding the defendant incompetent to stand trial compelled the conclusion that he was also incompetent to waive other rights

---

452. United States v. Christensen, 18 F.3d 822 (9th Cir. 1994).

453. *Id.,* at 824, citing *Godinez,* 509 U.S., at 399–400.

454. *Id.,* at 826, also quoting *Godinez,* 509 U.S., at 401 n.12.

455. Brown v. Doe, 803 F. Supp. 932 (S.D.N.Y. 1992), *aff'd,* 2 F.3d 1236 (2d Cir. 1993), *cert. denied,* 510 U.S. 1125 (1994).

456. State v. Cameron, 704 P.2d 1355 (Ariz. 1985); *see also* Coronado v. Lefevre, 748 F. Supp. 131 (S.D.N.Y. 1990) (same standard to determine competency to waive jury trial as competency to stand trial); compare Harringer v. State, 566 So. 2d 893 (Fla. Dist. Ct. App. 1990) (no evidence presented that defendant was competent to waive jury trial).

457. *See* Jones v. Commonwealth, 526 S.E.2d 281 (Va. App. 2000).

458. Williams v. State, 685 N.E.2d 730 (Ind. App. 1997).

relating to the prosecution (in this case, speaking publicly to the media about the alleged crime).[459]

d. Competency of jurors

At least one court has ruled that there was no error requiring reversal of a conviction where a juror related his "reactive psychosis" experience to other jurors.[460] Here, the court reasoned:

> While jurors may not receive information from an outside source nor act as expert witnesses in the jury room, they are entitled to rely on and to relate their own common sense and life experiences during deliberations. Here the record reveals only the statement quoted above without any indication that the jury was improperly pressured to apply this juror's personal experience to the case at hand.[461]

e. Competency of witness to testify

Many cases have considered the procedures to be employed in determining whether a witness is competent to testify. The lead case of *Sinclair v. Wainwright*[462] set out the controlling legal standards:

> Turning then to the merits of appellant's due process claim, it may be noted "that a [person with mental disability] may be allowed to testify if he is able to [comprehend] the obligation of an oath and give a correct account of matters he has seen or heard . . ." (Shuler v. Wainwright, 491 F.2d 1213 (5th Cir. 1974)). But if a patient in a mental institution is offered as a witness, an opposing party may challenge competency, whereupon it becomes the duty of the court to make such an examination as will satisfy the court of the competency of the proposed witness. (Id. at 1223–24). And if the challenged testimony is crucial, critical, or highly significant, failure to conduct an appropriate competency hearing implicates due process concerns of fundamental fairness [citation omitted]. This is not to say "that every allusion as to incompetency of a witness [is to] be exhaustively explored by the trial judge, particularly where all other evidence substantiates competency." United States v. Crosby, 462 F.2d 1201, 1203 n. 5 (D.C. Cir. 1972). But in the present situation, as in Crosby, id. at 1203, we believe a "red flag" of material impact on competency was flying. [The potential witness] was offered as an eyewitness to many of the critical aspects of the state's case against Sinclair. He had been declared incompetent to stand trial by the judge who was trying Sinclair. Only by a reasonable exploration of all the facts and circumstances could the trial judge exercise sound discretion concerning the competency of the witness. The findings of the court with respect to competency should have been made to appear on the record. The record reflects no searching exploration and no stated reasons for overruling appellant's competency objections.

459. Mann v. State's Attorney for Montgomery County, 468 A.2d 124, 129 (Md. 1983).
460. *See* State v. Lindeken, 799 P.2d 23 (Ariz. App.), *review denied* (1990).
461. *Id.,* at 406 (defendant convicted of manslaughter; insanity defense rejected).
462. 814 F.2d 1516 (11th Cir. 1987).

In such circumstances, we are obliged to remand for a determination on the record of the competency of the witness . . .[463]

At least one of *Sinclair's* assertions—its reliance on *Shuler* for the proposition that "If a patient in a mental institution is offered as a witness, an opposing party may challenge competency, whereupon it becomes the duty of the court to make such an examination as will satisfy the court of the competency of the proposed witness"[464]—is seriously flawed. As a matter of law, incompetency cannot be presumed as a result of either mental illness or institutionalization.[465] Furthermore, there is "no necessary relationship between mental illness and incompetency that renders [the mentally ill persons] unable to provide informed consent to medical treatment."[466] Yet, it is clear that courts will continue to, *sub silentio,* follow this doctrine, especially in criminal cases.[467]

---

463. *Id.* at 1522–23.

For earlier case law, see Shuler v. Wainwright, 491 F.2d 1213 (5th Cir. 1974); Hills v. Henderson, 529F.2d 397 (5th Cir.), *cert. denied,* 429 U.S. 850 (1976); United States v. Crosby, 462 F.2d 1201 (D.C. Cir.1972). For later cases, see, e.g., Hughes v. State, 546 N.E.2d 1203 (Ind. 1989); Ambles v. State, 383 S.E.2d 555(Ga. 1989); Commonwealth v. Fayerweather, 546 N.E.2d 345 (Mass. 1989); State v. Dumaine, 783 P.2d1184 (Ariz. 1989); Gilpin v. McCormick, 921 F.2d 928 (9th Cir. 1990); Nelson v. Farrey, 874 F.2d 1222(7th Cir. 1989), *cert. denied,* 493 U.S. 1042 (1990); State v. Olivo, 589 A.2d 597 (N.J. 1991); United States v. Pryce, 938 F.2d 1343 (D.C. Cir. 1991); State in Interest of B.G., 589 A.2d 637 (App. Div. 1991); People v. Rainge, 570 N.E.2d 431, *reh'g denied* (Ill. App. 1991); Simmons v. State, 683 So. 2d 1101 (Fla. Dist.App. 1996), *reh'g denied* (1997); State v. Blasius, 559 A.2d 1116 (Conn. 1989); State v. Danforth, 573N.W.2d 369 (Minn. App. 1997), *review denied* (1998), *appeal after remand,* 1999 WL 262143 (1999); Gilstrap v. State, 945 S.W.2d 192 (Tex. App. 1997), *petit. for discretionary review denied* (1997); State v. Henries, 704 A.2d 24 (App. Div. 1997); Schutz v. State, 957 S.W.2d 52 (Tex. Crim. App. 1997); Commonwealth v. Lloyd, 702 N.E.2d 395 (Mass. App. Ct. 1998); State v. Ballos, 602 N.W.2d 117 (Wis. App. 1999), *review denied,* 609 N.W.2d 473 (Wis. 2000); State v. Dillon, 1999 WL 148370 (Ohio App.1999); State v. Washington, 506 S.E.2d 283 (N.C. App. 1998), *review denied* (1999), *appeal dismissed* (1999); United States v. Gonzalez-Maldonado, 115 F.3d 9 (1st Cir. 1997); People v. Stephenson, 555 N.E.2d 802 (Ill. App. 1990).

On whether the prosecution must disclose the medical record of a government witness, *see* Drew v. United States, 46 F.3d 823 (8th Cir. 1995), *cert. denied,* 516 U.S. 817 (1995) (failure to disclose was immaterial; no due process deprivation). On the question of the state's obligation to turn over witness statements at competency hearings, *see* People v. McPhee, 614 N.Y.S.2d 884 (Sup. 1994) (state compelled to turn over statements); State v. Bruno, 673 A.2d 1117 (Conn. 1996) (trial court properly denied defendant's motion for in camera inspection of witnesses' psychiatric records); cf. State v. Israel, 963 P.2d 897 (Wash. App. 1998), *review denied,* 972 P.2d 465 (Wash. 1998) (no compelling reasons to justify psychological examination of alleged co-conspirator). *See generally* Note, *The Mentally Deficient Witness: The Death of Incompetency,* 14 LAW & PSYCHOL. REV.107 (1990).

464. Sinclair, 514 F.2d, at 1522, quoting Shuler, 491 F.2d, at 1223–24.

465. In re Labelle, 728 P.2d 138, 146 (Wash. 1986).

466. Davis v. Hubbard, 506 F. Supp. 915, 935 (N.D. Ohio 1980); Michael L. Perlin, *Competency, Deinstitutionalization, and Homelessness: A Story of Marginalization,* 28 HOUS. L. REV. 63, 113–114 (1991); Bruce J. Winick, *Competency to Consent to Treatment: The Distinction Between Assent and Objection,* 28 HOUS. L. REV. 15 (1991).

467. *See also, e.g.,* Meyers v. Commonwealth, 87 S.W.3d 243 (Ky. 2002) (reversing conviction and holding that statements codefendant/witness made during competency evaluations

3. After Trial

Introduction

Cases have considered the impact of competency on virtually every posttrial stage, including motions for new trials, sentencing, probation hearings, parole revocation hearings, conditional release hearings, participation in post-conviction relief proceedings, and appeals. Again, the application of the *Godinez* unitary standard to post-conviction proceedings has never been considered by the Supreme Court.[468]

a. New trial motions

At least one case has held that a defendant has a right to be competent at a motion for a new trial.[469]

b. Sentencing

It is black-letter law that a court may not sentence an incompetent defendant.[470] In the case of a defendant who becomes incompetent between the time of the guilty verdict and the time of sentence, most state statutes provide for the same test to be

---

were admissible on issue of memory and for impeachment purposes after codefendant became a witness); United States v. Love, 329 F.3d 981 (8th Cir. 2003) (reversing conviction where defendant was not granted access to mental health records of sole witness, who had schizophrenia and short- and long-term memory impairment); Brown v. United States, 766 A.2d 530 (D.C. Cir. 2001) (reversing convictions and holding that defendants were entitled to elicit testimony from victim's psychiatrist on the impact of mental illness on her reliability as a witness); State v. Calliham, 55 P.3d 573 (Utah 2002) (affirming murder conviction and finding no abuse of discretion in trial judge's failure to order psychological examination of witness); United States v. Alperin, 128 F. Supp. 2d 1251 (N.D. Cal. 2001) (defendant entitled to in camera review of mental health records of victim, holding as a matter of first impression that possibility of imprisoning an innocent person is a harm sufficiently compelling to justify an exception to privilege).

468. Also, to the best of our knowledge, an issue discussed by the Supreme Court in Drope v. Missouri, 420 U.S. 162 (1975), has never been considered in this context: can (or *must*) the question of competency here be raised by the prosecutor or the judge, or only by defense counsel? See Michael L. Perlin, *"For the Misdemeanor Outlaw": The Impact of the ADA on the Institutionalization of Criminal Defendants with Mental Disabilities,* 52 Ala. L. Rev. 193 198 n.33 (2000) (discussing *Drope* in this context).

469. See Williams v. Turpin, 87 F.3d 1204 (11th Cir. 1996). Interestingly, neither *Dusky* nor *Drope* nor *Godinez* was cited in this case.

470. See Winick & DeMeo, *supra* note 10, and cases cited at *id.* n.242. For a recent Canadian study, *see* Allan Manson, *Fitness to Be Sentenced: A Historical, Comparative, and Practical Review,* 29 Int'l J. L. & Psychiatry 262 (2006).

See, e.g., United States v. Collins, 949 F.2d 921 (7th Cir. 1991); State v. Phelps, 600 N.E.2d 329 (Ohio App. 1991), jurisdictional motion overruled, 583 N.E.2d 971 (Ohio 1992); Stover v. State, 621 N.E.2d (Ind. App. 1993); Calloway v. State, 651 So. 2d 752 (Fla. Dist. App. 1995); compare People v. Hall, 541 N.E.2d1369, 1375–76 (Ill. App. 1989) (defendant's "cognitive difficulties" did not raise bona fide doubt of fitness so as to entitle him to presentencing fitness examination); People v. Sanchez, 662 N.E.2d 1199 (Ill. 1996), *reh'g denied* (1996), *cert. denied,* 483 U.S. 1010 (1996) (no error where trial judge failed to conduct fitness hearing prior to sentencing hearing); State v. Lott, 671 So. 2d 1182 (La. App. 1996) (defendant competent at time of sentencing); see also Gilbert v. State, 951 P.2d 98 (Okla. Crim. App. 1997), *reh'g*

employed as is used when determining a defendant's competency to stand trial,[471] with "the emphasis on the defendant's capacity to tell his attorney about factors that would mitigate his sentence or would refute aggravating circumstances brought up by the prosecution, as well as on his understanding of the punishment."[472] Also, at least one court has held that a psychiatric competency-to-stand-trial evaluation cannot be ordered after a defendant is sentenced.[473]

c. Probation hearings

Some attention is now being paid to the relationship between competency and probation revocation matters.[474] If a reasonable doubt arises as to a defendant's competence to participate in a probation hearing,[475] the court must hold a separate hearing to determine the defendant's competence to participate.[476] However,

---

denied (1998), post-conviction relief denied, 955 P.2d 727 (Okla. Crim. App.), cert. denied, 525 U.S. 890 (1998); People v. Dewer, 663 N.Y.S.2d 425 (A.D. 1997), appeal denied, 670 N.Y.S.2d 406 (1998); People v. Walker, 685 N.E.2d 997 (Ill. App. 1997); United States v. Hinton, 218 F.3d 910 (8th Cir. 2000); People v. Kilgore, 992 P.2d 661 (Colo. App. 1999), reh'g denied (1999), cert. denied (2000); State v. Tilden, 988S.W.2d 568 (Mo. App. 1999); Reed v. Texas, 14 S.W.3d 438 (Tex. App. 2000), petit. for discretionary review refused (2001); State v. Fish, 759 So. 2d 937 (La. App. 2000); Woods v. State, 994 S.W.2d 32 (Mo. App. 1999); United States v. Gigante, 1997 WL 782355 (E.D.N.Y. 1997), supplemented, 996 F. Supp. 194(E.D.N.Y. 1998) (defendant competent to be sentenced).

United States v. Sanchez, 38 F. Supp. 2d 355, 366 (D.N.J. 1999) has cited Godinez (using a "cf. also" reference) on the competency-to-be-sentenced question, on the "modest aim" of a competency inquiry:("seek[ing] to ensure that [the defendant] had the capacity to understand the proceedings and to assist counsel").

On the relationship between a defendant's "episodes" at sentencing and his competency to stand trial, see People v. Sandham, 673 N.E. 2d 1032 (Ill. 1996) (competency hearing required).

471. See Weiner, supra note 171, at 705–706. See generally, Weissman, Determinative Sentencing and Psychiatric Evidence: A Due Process Examination, 27 St. Louis U.L.J. 347 (1983).

472. Weiner, supra note 171 at 706. See, e.g., Wojtowicz v. United States, 550 F.2d 786 (2d Cir.), cert. denied, 431 U.S. 972 (1977) (defendant entitled to evidentiary hearing as to competency at time of sentencing based on allegations that he had attempted to commit suicide on eve of sentencing); Pate v. Commonwealth, 769 S.W.2d 46 (Ky. 1989) (competency hearing not required); United States v. Pellerito, 878 F.2d 1535 (1st Cir. 1989), appeal after remand sub nom.; United States v. Rivera-Martinez, 931 F.2d 148, cert. denied, 502 U.S. 862 (1991) (examination required to determine competency at time of sentencing); State v. Drga, 916 P. 2d 739 (Mont. 1996) (resumption of proceedings following commitment to mental health facility without determining that defendant had regained his fitness to stand trial invalidated conviction and sentence).

473. State v. Tokar, 918 S.W.2d 753 (Mo. 1996), cert. den., 519 U.S. 933 (1996).

474. See State v. Lockwood, 632 A.2d 655 (Vt. 1993) (no competency hearing required prior to commencement of probation revocation hearing); see also Merle v. United States, 683 A.2d 755 (D.C. 1996) (mental illness not a defense to probation violation); Guzman v. State, 923 S.W.2d 792 (Tex. App. 1996) (defendant competent at time of probation revocation hearing); compare State v. Singleton, 472 S.E.2d 640 (S.C. App. 1996) (trial court abused its discretion in not ordering competency examination in probation revocation proceeding).

475. See, e.g., Sailer v. Gunn, 548 F.2d 271, 274 (9th Cir. 1977); Soria v. State, 1997 WL 61491 (Tex. App. 1997); State ex rel. Vanderbeke v. Endicott, 563 N.W.2d 883 (Wis. 1997);

in at least one case, the court has held that such a hearing is only to be required when there is evidence of "recent severe mental illness, or at least moderate mental retardation or *truly* bizarre acts by the defendant."[477]

d. Parole revocation hearings
Courts are beginning to consider the relationship between competency and parole revocation hearings; generally, it has been held that the court must hold a separate hearing to determine the defendant's competence to participate.[478]

e. Conditional release hearings
In cases involving conditional release or community supervision, the court must hold a separate hearing to determine the defendant's competence to participate.[479]

f. Participation in post-conviction relief proceedings
Courts have begun to consider the question of a defendant's competency to participate in post-conviction proceedings,[480] and have generally found that trial competency standards apply at this stage.[481] In *O'Rourke v. Endell,* the court focused on that aspect of *Godinez* that discussed the standards for waiver, stressing that the purpose of the "knowing and voluntary" inquiry "is to determine whether

---

State ex rel. Juergens v. Cundiff, 939 S.W.2d 381 (Mo. 1997); Metzgar v. State, 741 So. 2d 1181 (Fla. Dist. App. 1999). *Godinez* is cited in none of the post-1993 cases in this cohort.

476. See Winick & DeMeo, *supra* note 49, at 73; compare State v. Qualls, 552 N.E.2d 957 (Ohio App. 1988) (Issue of competency to participate in probation revocation proceeding may be raised by court or defendant; decision as to whether to hold competency hearing vested in trial court's sound discretion).

477. Eddie v. State, 100 S.W. 3d 437 (Tex. App. 2003) (emphasis added). *See also,* Harrison v. State, 905 S.W. 2d 858 (Ala. Crim. App. 2005) (defendant not entitled to psychiatric evaluation to determine mental competency at probation revocation hearing).

478. See Winick & DeMeo, *supra* note 470, at 73; *compare* Qualls, *supra* (issue of competency to participate in probation revocation proceeding may be raised by court or defendant; decision as to whether to hold competency hearing vested in trial court's sound discretion), to People ex rel. Newcomb v. Metz, 409 N.Y.S.2d 554 (A.D. 1978) (absent statutory authority to contrary, interests of fundamental fairness mandated a consideration of parolee's mental competency during parole revocation process; a determination of that question, however, is not a condition precedent to parole revocation proceeding, but merely a factor to be considered in mitigation of, or as an excuse for, charged violations of parole).

479. United States v. Woods, 944 F. Supp. 778 (D. Minn. 1996) (conditional release); Rice v. State, 991 S.W.2d 953 (Tex. App. 1999), *reh'g overruled* (1999), *petit. for discretionary review refused* (1999) (community supervision). *Godinez* is cited in neither case.

480. See State v. Debra A.E., 523 N.W.2d 727 (Wis. 1994) (setting out standards to be employed in cases in which the defendant is unable to assist counsel or to make decisions committed by law to defendant with reasonable degree of rational understanding).

481. Carter v. State, 706 So. 2d 873 (Fla. 1997), *reh'g denied* (1998); Sanchez-Velasco v. State, 702 So. 2d 224 (Fla. 1997); O'Rourke v. Endell, 153 F.3d 560 (8th Cir. 1998), *reh'g & suggestion for reh'g en banc denied* (8th Cir. 1998), *cert. denied,* 525 U.S. 1148 (1999); Matheney v. State, 688 N.E.2d 883 (Ind. 1997), *reh'g denied* (1998); People v. Johnson, 730 N.E.2d 1107 (Ill. 2000); House v. State, 754 So. 2d 1147 (Miss. 1999), *reh'g denied* (2000); Hundley v. State, 1999 WL 668723 (Tenn. Crim. App. 1999).

the defendant actually does understand the significance and consequences of a particular decision and whether the decision is uncoerced."[482] In *Carter v. State,* a death penalty case, the court underscored that competency hearings are required "only after a capital defendant shows there are specific factual matters at issue that require the defendant to independently consult with counsel."[483]

In *Rohan v. Woodford,*[484] the court found that the petitioner had the right to be competent for post-conviction proceedings, and that he was entitled to a stay in proceedings until found competent, and that refusing to stay proceedings pending restoration of competence denied the defendant his statutory right to assistance of counsel, whether or not counsel can identify with precision the information that was sought. In an especially thoughtful and scholarly opinion, the court stressed the "unique position of the defendant,"[485] in potentially assisting counsel at a habeas hearing :

> At least some of the claims in Gates's [the defendant] petition could potentially benefit from his assistance. His principal contention, for example, is that he was incompetent to stand trial and that his trial counsel were constitutionally ineffective for failing to pursue a competency hearing. Like most ineffective assistance claims, this one depends in large measure on facts outside the record. See Massaro v. United States, U.S., 123 S. Ct. 1690, 1694 (2003). To prevail, Rohan [trial court's appointed "best friend"] would likely have to show Gates was incompetent at trial. If Gates were competent today, he could provide information to bolster that claim. His own testimony about his former state of incompetence, for example, would (to the extent credited by the court) support his position. He could also direct counsel to circumstantial evidence of his incompetence at the time.

Gates's private knowledge could also be relevant to his trial counsel's deficiency in failing to pursue a competency hearing. Whether trial counsel were constitutionally ineffective may depend on their interactions with Gates. The more obvious his incompetence at the time, the more likely that they were deficient for failing to recognize it. Unless Gates can offer his side of the story, we can rely only on trial counsel's version of events.[486]

---

482. *O'Rourke,* 153 F.3d, at 567–68.

483. *Carter,* 706 So. 2d, at 875.

An extensive study of death row inmates in Mississippi raised "grave concerns regarding the self-representation competency" of this cohort. *See* Mark Cunningham & Mark Vigen, *Without Appointed Counsel in Capital Postconviction Proceedings: The Self-Representation Competency of Mississippi Death Row Inmates,* 26 CRIM. JUST. & BEHAV. 293 (1999). This study, however, has never been cited in a reported case (last searched: June 19, 2007). *See also,* Clive A. Stafford Smith & Rémy Voisin Starns, *Folly by Fiat: Pretending that Death Row Inmates Can Represent Themselves in State Capital Post-Conviction Proceedings,* 45 LOY. L. REV. 55 (1999) (same).

484. 334 F.3d 803 (9th Cir. 2003).

485. *Id.* at 818.

486. *Id.*

g. Appeals[487]

At least one court has held that, if there is a bona fide question as to a defendant's competence, he does not waive his right to file an appeal.[488] On the other hand, at least four state supreme and appellate courts have held that a defendant's appeal could proceed even if the defendant had become incompetent, as the appellate record contained only legal issues, and counsel did not need to rely on the defendant to determine which issues were worth pursuing.[489]

4. Other Miscellaneous Procedural Matters

Other cases have explored questions of a defendant's competence to be extradited,[490] and the application of *Godinez* to questions of waiver of counsel in the involuntary civil commitment hearing of a federal prisoner.[491] In this last setting, the Eighth Circuit rejected the defendant's argument that his commitment to a mental health facility demonstrated his inability to waive counsel as "unpersuas[ive]":

> Whether an individual possesses sufficient capacity to knowingly waive his right to counsel is no longer distinct from the question of his competency to stand trial [citing to *Godinez*]. The mere fact that Veltman needed "custody for care or treatment in a suitable facility" does not mean he lacked sufficient capacity to decide to proceed pro se. . . . The purpose of the waiver doctrine "is to determine whether the defendant actually does understand the significance and consequences of a particular decision and whether the decision [to proceed unassisted] is uncoerced" [citing to *Godinez*]. After carefully reviewing the record, we affirm the district court's determination that Veltman possessed sufficient mental capacity to waive his statutory right to counsel. . . .[492]

---

487. On the question of a defendant's right to waive counsel on appeal, *see supra* Chapter 2 C 4.

488. People v. McKay, 668 N.E.2d 580 (Ill. App. 1996), *appeal denied*, 675 N.E.2d 637 (Ill. 1996). *See also* Gentzen v. State, 689 So. 2d 1178 (Fla. Dist. App. 1997), *reh'g denied* (1997) (court lacked jurisdiction to consider appeal filed by defendant who had been found to be incompetent to proceed in criminal case). *Compare* State v. Currier, 649 A.2d 246 (Vt. 1994) (dismissal of appeal inappropriate where record did not indicate whether waiver was knowing and intelligent).

489. People v. Kelly, 822 P.2d 385, 413–15 (Cal. 1992), *reh'g denied* (1992), *cert. denied*, 506 U.S. 881 (1992); State v. White, 815 P.2d 869, 878 (Ariz. 1991); Dugar v. Whitley, 615 So. 2d 1334 (La. 1993); Florescu v. State, 623 S.E. 2d 147 (Ga. App. 2005).

490. *In re Hinnant*, 678 N.E.2d 1314 (Mass. 1997) (defendant must be competent for rendition of extradition to proceed), discussed in Eric Loeffler, *In re Hinnant: The Relevance of Competence in Interstate Extradition Proceedings*, 25 New Eng. J. Crim. & Civ. Confinement 469 (1999); Lopez-Smith v. Hood, 121 F.3d 1322 (9th Cir. 1997) (affirming denial of defendant's petition for writ of habeas corpus); Oliver v. Barrett, 269 Ga. 512, 500 S.E.2d 908 (1998) (extradition proper). *See also, e.g.,* Pruett v. Barry, 696 P.2d 789 (Colo. 1985); Jones v. Warmuth, 272 S.E.2d 446 (W. Va. 1980); People v. Kent, 507 N.Y.S.2d 353 (Sup. Ct. 1986).

491. United States v. Veltman, 9 F.3d 718 (8th Cir. 1993), *cert. denied*, 511 U.S. 1044 (1994); *see* 1 Perlin, supra note 8, § 2C-4.2a, at 317–18 (2d ed. 1998).

492. Veltman, 9 F. 3d, at 722.

5. Conclusion

The lack of commentary about the cases in this important (yet largely hidden) area of the law is surprising. The failure of most of the cases to carefully consider the relevant precedents (and analogous developments in other jurisdictions) is even more surprising. And this is, to some extent, curious, given the significance of this inquiry at every juncture of the criminal process.

There is no question that competency considerations at other stages of pretrial, trial, and post-trial proceedings will grow in importance in the coming years. Although *Godinez* established a unitary test for competency to plead guilty and to waive counsel, again, collateral competency questions permeate the entire criminal trial process. It is a matter to which closer attention must be paid.

E. IMPACT OF INCOMPETENCY FINDING ON ABILITY TO ENTER INSANITY PLEA[493]

Several cases have considered the significance of an incompetency finding on a defendant's ability to enter a plea of not guilty by reason of insanity, holding that due process prohibits any determination of sanity until such time as the defendant is restored to competency.[494] Another case has held that a statute permitting an incompetent defendant to offer a defense on the merits, but not one based on mental illness, did not violate the defendant's equal protection rights.[495] As an incompetent defendant is definitionally unable to participate in his defense, it could not be assured that any adjudication resulting from an insanity trial would "represent a fair and just determination of the mental element of the offense placed in issue by the insanity plea."[496]

On the other hand, the fact that a defendant had previously been found to

---

493. This subchapter is largely adapted from Perlin, *supra* note 315.

For a clinical perspective on this issue, *see* William Johnson et al., *The Relationship of Competency to Stand Trial and Criminal Responsibility,* 17 CRIM. JUST. & BEHAV. 169 (1990).

494. *See* Coolbroth v. District Ct. of 17th Judicial Dist., 766 P.2d 670 (Colo. 1988); United States v. Evans, 704 F. Supp. 81 (E.D. Pa. 1989); *see also* State v. Werner, 796 P.2d 610 (N.M. 1990), *cert. den.* (1990).

Compare People v. Angeletakis, 7 Cal. Rptr. 2d 377, *review denied* (Cal. App. 1992), *cert. denied,* 507 U.S. 926 (1993) (affirming denial of motion of insanity acquittee for proceedings to consider his competency to stand trial on the question of an extension of his post-insanity acquittal commitment). *Coolbroth* is discussed in this context in Justine Dunlap, *What's Competence Got to Do With It: The Right Not to Be Acquitted by Reason of Insanity,* 50 OKLA. L. REV. 495, 506 n.89 (1997).

495. Spero v. Commonwealth, 678 N.E.2d 435 (Mass. 1997).

496. Coolbroth, 766 P.2d at 673. *See also* Evans, 704 F. Supp. at 84 ("futile" to attempt to conduct meaningful insanity evaluation as long as defendant remains "overtly psychotic"). *See generally* R.J. Mackay & Gerry Kearns, *The Trial of the Facts and Unfitness to Plead,* 1997 CRIM. L. REV. 644.

On the relationship between a defendant's purportedly delusional refusal to enter an insanity defense and his competency to waive counsel, *see* Cheatham & Litwack, *Professionals' Attitudes*

be insane does not render him subsequently incompetent to proceed to trial per se on another charge.[497] Yet another case has found that a defendant who elects to represent himself at trial can also waive pleading the insanity defense.[498] Interestingly, in this case, the Utah Supreme Court used *Godinez* to find for the defendant:

> Therefore, Woodland should not be required to display a heightened level of competency to waive his right to a particular defense. See *Godinez* . . . (holding that competency standard for standing trial is same as standard for determining competency to waive right to counsel). The trial court correctly concluded that Woodland knowingly and voluntarily waived his right to assert a mental illness defense.[499]

F. IMPACT OF INCOMPETENCY FINDING ON ABILITY TO ENTER GUILTY BUT MENTALLY ILL PLEA[500]

At least one case has held that a guilty but mentally ill conviction[501] would be invalid where the defendant's competence had not been re-evaluated before trial.[502]

G. IMPACT OF INCOMPETENCY ON THE TRIAL OF A DEFENDANT AS A SEXUALLY VIOLENT PREDATOR[503]

A few cases have begun to consider the impact of a defendant's incompetence on Sexually Violent Predator Act (SVPA) commitment, with courts splitting on whether the defendant has the same right to be competent for these purposes as

---

Regarding a New York Defendant Who Delusionally Refuses a Viable, Counsel-Recommended Insanity Defense Should Be Found Competent or Incompetent to Stand Trial, 31 J. L. & Psychiatry 433 (2003). *See supra* note 399.

497. People v. Blehm, 791 P.2d 1177, 1181 (Colo. Ct. App. 1989), *aff'd*, 817 P.2d 988 (Colo. 1991).

498. State v. Woodland, 945 P.2d 665 (Utah 1997). On a defendant's right to not plead insanity, *see* 4 Michael L. Perlin, Mental Disability Law: Civil and Criminal, 9A-8, at 241–45 (2d ed. 2002). *Compare* State v. Martinez, 651 A.2d 1189 (R.I. 1994) (Standards for competency to stand trial and competency to testify as witness are distinct from standard for criminal responsibility).

499. Woodland, 945 P.2d at 670–71.

500. This subchapter is largely adapted from Perlin, supra note 315.

501. *See* 4 Perlin, *supra* note 8, §§ 9A-3.7, at 169–79.

502. *See* People v. Harris, 460 N.W.2d 239 (Mich. App. 1990).

503. This subchapter is largely adapted from Perlin, supra note 315.

for criminal proceedings.[504] Scholars have just begun to write about the implications of this question.[505]

H. COMPETENCY TO BE EXECUTED

1. Introduction

One of the most difficult problems in criminal procedure law involves the question of whether persons with mental disabilities can be subject to execution. Two radically different bodies of case law have developed in this area: one on the question of defendants with mental illness,[506] and one on the question of defendants with mental retardation.[507] A recent U.S. Supreme Court decision ensures that the question of how competency to be executed must be determined will remain the focus of intense scrutiny,[508] although, interestingly, the Court, in the same decision, side-stepped the difficult issues related to whether the state could involuntarily medicate an individual for the purpose of making him competent to be executed.[509]

This subchapter proceeds in this manner. First, we consider the historical roots of the prohibition on the execution of the "currently insane." Next, we examine the Supreme Court case law as it applies to persons with mental illness. Then, we consider it as it applies to persons with mental retardation. After that, we discuss the specific issues raised around the question of whether a currently incompetent person can be involuntarily medicated so as to make him competent to be executed. Finally, we will look briefly at the issue of a defendant's competency to waive his right to habeas corpus review of his death sentence.

2. Persons with Mental Illness[510]

Dr. Paul Appelbaum, in regarding the question of the constitutional appropriateness of standards and procedures required to determine whether a death row prisoner with mental illness is competent to be executed, aptly characterized it as

---

504. *Compare* Commitment of Smith, 600 N.W.2d 258 (Wis. App. 1999) (defendant has same right to be competent during SVPA proceedings as in any criminal proceeding) to State v. Ransleben, 144 P.3d 397 (Wash. App. 2006) (defendant's right to counsel did not include implied right to be competent during proceeding); *see generally* 1 PERLIN, *supra* note 5, § 2A-3.3, at 75–92.

505. *See, e.g.,* Alan Abrams et al., *The Case for a Threshold of Competency in Sexually Violent Predator Civil Commitment Proceedings,* 28 AM. J. FORENS. PSYCHIATRY (2007) (in press).

506. *See infra* Chapter 2 H 2.

507. *See infra* Chapter 2 H 3.

508. *See* Panetti v. Quarterman, 127 S. Ct. 2842 (2007), *reversing* Panetti v. Dretke, 448 F. 3d 815 (5th Cir. 2006).

509. *See generally,* MICHAEL L. PERLIN & HENRY A. DLUGACZ, MENTAL HEALTH ISSUES IN JAILS AND PRISONS: CASES AND MATERIALS, Chapter 10B (in press) (2008).

510. This section is largely adapted from 4 PERLIN, *supra* note 8, §§12-4.1 to1e.

"one of the more perplexing issues in criminal justice today."[511] While, in *Ford v. Wainwright*,[512] the Supreme Court finally gave a partial answer, to some extent the conundrum perceived by Dr. Appelbaum still exists.[513] Examination of the *Ford* opinion in its historical context should, however, reveal some helpful clues to understanding both the depth of the Supreme Court's true position on this matter, and the expected impact of the *Ford* case.

The issue of executing "the insane"[514] is one that has plagued the legal system for centuries.[515] In their seminal study,[516] professors Hazard and Louisell examined arguments made by Blackstone,[517] Hale,[518] and Coke,[519] specifically opposing such execution, and looked also at the writings of St. Thomas Aquinas[520] and Shakespeare[521] for the religious and cultural roots of the doctrine.[522] In his classic treatise on *Insanity and the Criminal Law,* Dr. William White focused over 60 years ago on the "general feeling of abhorrence against executing a person who is insane."[523]

Although the Supreme Court had rejected, as recently as 1950, the argument that there was a due process right to a preexecution judicial sanity determination,[524] that decision predated by 12 years the court's incorporation of the Eighth Amendment's prohibition against cruel and unusual punishment to be applied to the states,[525] and the court had not considered the argument again since that time.

---

511. Paul Appelbaum, *Competence to be Executed: Another Conundrum for Mental Health Professionals,* 37 Hosp. & Commun. Psychiatry 682 (1986).

512. 477 U.S. 399 (1986).

513. Appelbaum, *supra* note 511, at 682.

514. On the question of the competency of persons with mental *retardation* to be executed, *see infra* Chapter 2 H (3).

515. For a helpful overview, *see* Jonathan Entin, *Psychiatry, Insanity, and the Death Penalty: A Note on Implementing Supreme Court Decisions,* 79 Crim. L. & Criminology 218 (1988).

516. Geoffrey Hazard & David Louisell, *Death, the State, and the Insane: Stay of Execution,* 9 UCLA L. Rev. 381 (1962).

517. *Id.* at 383–84 (citing Blackstone, Commentaries *395–*96 (13th ed. 1800)).

518. Hazard & Louisell, *supra* note 516 at 383 (citing 1 Hale, Pleas of the Crown 34–35 (1736)).

519. Hazard & Louisell, *supra* note 516 at 384–85 (citing Coke, Third Institute 6 (1797)).

520. Hazard & Louisell, *supra* note 516 at 387 (citing Aquinas, Summa Theologica, First Part, *Treatise on the Angels,* ques. 64, art. 2, objection, reply to second objection; Aquinas, Summa Contra Gentiles, bk. 3, ch. 146).

521. Hazard & Louisell, *supra* note 516 at 387–88 (citing and quoting Shakespeare, *Hamlet,* act. III, sc. iii, lines 72–96).

522. *See also* Barbara Ward, *Competency for Execution: Problems in Law and Psychiatry,* 14 Fla. St. U.L. Rev. 35, 49–57 (1986). Traditional arguments are collected in Solesbee v. Balkcom, 339 U.S. 9, 17–19 (1950) (Frankfurter, J., dissenting).

523. William White, Insanity and the Criminal Law 245 (1923) (da Capo 1981 reprint).

524. *Solesbee,* 339 U.S. at 12.

525. Robinson v. California, 370 U.S. 660 (1962).
Substantive constitutional protections of the Bill of Rights are only made applicable against the actions of the states when those sections are found to have been "incorporated" into the

In short, while the slate was not a clean one when certiorari was granted in *Ford*, neither was there much in the way of binding precedent for the court to uphold, distinguish, or overrule.

Given the significance of capital punishment in contemporary American political debates,[526] it should be no surprise that the conundrum[527] raised by Dr. Appelbaum has begun, again, to assume greater significance as an issue to be confronted both by forensic psychiatrists and the law. This has become especially important in the post-Hinckley[528] universe, in which insanity defense statutes[529]—seen traditionally (albeit incorrectly)[530] as "an impenetrable bulwark to prevent execution of the insane"[531]—have narrowed,[532] and in which some states have even "abolished" the insanity defense.[533] What can be expected, simply, is that more offenders with mental illness[534] will be represented in prison,[535] and that a significant number of death row inmates will suffer serious mental disorder.[536]

Fourteenth Amendment's Due Process clause. *See, e.g.,* Peter J. Rubin, *Square Pegs and Round Holes: Substantive Due Process, Procedural Due Process, and the Bill of Rights,* 103 COLUM. L. REV. 833(2003).

526. *See* Michael L. Perlin, *The Supreme Court, The Mentally Disabled Criminal Defendant, Psychiatric Testimony in Death Penalty Cases, and the Power of Symbolism: Dulling the Ake in Barefoot's Achilles Heel,* 3 N.Y.L. SCH. HUM. RIGHTS ANN. 91, 97 (1985) (hereinafter *Barefoot's Ake*). *See supra* note 200.

527. Appelbaum, *supra* note 311, at 682.

528. *See, e.g.,* MICHAEL L. PERLIN, THE JURISPRUDENCE OF THE INSANITY DEFENSE 138–42 (1994).

529. For an analysis of the tactical problems confronted by counsel for mentally ill defendants facing the death penalty on the question of whether to interpose the insanity defense, *see* Welsh White, *The Psychiatric Examination and the Fifth Amendment Privilege in Capital Cases,* 74 J. CRIM. L. & CRIMINOLOGY 943, 989–90 (1983).

530. *See Barefoot's Ake, supra* note 526, at 96 n.31, and *see especially* G. SCOTT, THE HISTORY OF CAPITAL PUNISHMENT 105–08 (1950).

531. *Barefoot's Ake, supra* note 526, at 96. *See, e.g.,* sources cited *id.* at nn.27–30. Chief Justice Burger has made it clear that, in his view, the prohibition of imprisoning and executing the insane is rooted strictly in the past. *See* Warren Burger, *Psychiatrists, Lawyers and the Courts,* FED. PROB. 3, 5 (1964):

> I have little doubt that *in times past, especially prior to the mid-1800's,* a great many people were found guilty and condemned either to lengthy imprisonment or even to death when their wrongful conduct was, *by present day standards and knowledge,* attributable to a true lack of recognition of wrong or true lack of capacity to control behavior. (emphasis added).

532. *See, e.g.,* 18 U.S.C. § 20(a) (1984).

533. *See, e.g.,* 4 PERLIN, *supra* note 8, §9A-6 (discussing abolition jurisdictions).

534. *See,* for a survey, Henry Steadman, et al., *Mentally Disordered Offenders: A National Survey of Patients and Facilities,* 6 L. & HUM. BEHAV. 31 (1982).

535. *See generally,* PERLIN & DLUGACZ, *supra* note 509.

536. It has been estimated that "as many as fifty percent of Florida's death row inmates become intermittently insane." Ward, *supra* note 17, at 42. *See generally* Dorothy Lewis, et al., *Psychiatric and Psychoeducational Characteristics of 15 Death Row Inmates in the United States,* 143 AM. J. PSYCHIATRY 838 (1986).

The issues involved in psychiatric participation in capital punishment decision-making[537] raise a series of intractable[538] operational problems for mental health professionals: the responsibility of psychiatrists to appropriately construe the key terms in operative statutes (such as the Florida law that prohibited execution if the defendant did not have "the mental capacity to understand the nature of the death penalty");[539] assessment of the appropriate standard of proof;[540] reliability

537. The general ethical issues relating to medical participation in execution by lethal injection were raised 25 years ago by Dr. William Curran and an associate who argued that such involvement—"by intentional, careful, skillful injection of a medically prepared substance into the veins of the prisoner," William Curran and Ward Casscells, *The Ethics of Medical Participation in Capital Punishment by Intravenous Drug Injection,* 302 NEW ENG. J. MED. 226, 228 (1980) (hereinafter Curran)—seemed to constitute a "grievous expansion of medical condonation of and participation in capital punishment." *Id. See also Strange Bedfellows: Death Penalty and Medicine,* 248 J.A.M.A. 518 (1982).

Drawing on declarations of the International Conference for the Abolition of Torture, *id.,* citing *Final Report, Amnesty International Conference for the Abolition of Torture* (Paris), Dec. 10–11, 1973, and the 29th World Medical Assembly of the World Medical Association (the so-called Declaration of Tokyo) (Curran, *supra,* at 228, citing 22 WORLD MED. J. 87 (1975)), the authors concluded that a medical professional who "orders or prepares a chemical substance to kill a prisoner under sentence of death would be in direct violation, Curran, *supra,* at 229, of these accords. Similarly, they suggested that it would be ethically improper for physicians to monitor the condemned prisoner's condition during the drug administration and to carry on this action to pronounce his death when heartbeat and respiration were found to be absent." Curran, *supra,* at 229.

They concluded by urging that medical professionals should "examine seriously the issues presented by this new method of capital punishment." *Id.* at 230: "The line should be drawn here. The medical profession in the United States should formally condemn all forms of medical participation in this method of capital punishment." *Id.*

See generally, Bruce Arrigo & Jeffrey Tasca, *Right to Refuse Treatment, Competency to be Executed, and Therapeutic Jurisprudence: Toward A Systematic Analysis,* 24 L. & PSYCHOL. REV. I (1999); Alfred Freedman & Abraham Halpern, *The Psychiatrist's Dilemma: A Conflict of Roles in Legal Executions,* 33 AUSTRALIAN & N.Z. J. PSYCHIATRY 629 (1999); Alfred M. Freedman & Abraham L. Halpern, *The Erosion of Ethics and Morality in Medicine: Physician Participation in Legal Executions in the United States,* 41 N.Y.L. SCH. L. REV. 169 (1996); Richard Showalter, *Psychiatric Participation in Capital Sentencing Procedures,* 13 INT'L J. L. & PSYCHIATRY 261 (1990); Alfred M. Freedman & Abraham L. Halpern, *The Psychiatrist's Dilemma: a Conflict of Roles in Legal Executions,* 33 AUSTL. & N.Z. J. PSYCHIATRY 629, 629 (Oct. 1999); Douglas Mossman, *Assessing and Restoring Competency to Be Executed: Should Psychiatrists Participate?,* 5 BEHAV. SCI. & L. 397 (1987); Richard Bonnie, *Dilemmas in Administering the Death Penalty: Conscientious Abstention, Professional Ethics, and the Needs of the Legal System,* 14 LAW & HUM. BEHAV. 67 (1990) (Bonnie I); Stanley Brodsky, *Professional Ethics and Professional Morality in the Assessment of Competence for Execution: A Reply to Bonnie,* 14 LAW & HUM. BEHAV. 91 (1990); Richard Bonnie, *Grounds for Professional Abstention in Capital Cases: A Reply to Brodsky,* 14 LAW & HUM. BEHAV. 99 (1990) (Bonnie II).

538. Ward, *supra* note 23, at 100. *See also* Note, *Medical Ethics and Competency to Be Executed,* 96 YALE L.J. 167, 173–79 (1986) (hereinafter Yale Note). *See id.* at 184 (characterizing dilemma as "insoluble").

539. FLA. STAT. ANN. § 922.07(3) (1986 Supp.).

540. Michael Radelet & George Barnard, *Ethics and the Psychiatric Determination of Competency to Be Executed,* 14 BULL. AM. ACAD. PSYCHIATRY & L. 37, 43 (1986).

of diagnoses; and possibility of regression between evaluation and execution.[541] They also raise core ethical problems that have not yet been resolved.

The Supreme Court's decision to hear *Ford v. Wainwright*[542] suggested some recognition of the depth of the problem and appeared to promise a relatively broad-based solution, since Florida's "competency-to-be-executed" law[543] was similar in critical aspects to the statutes enacted in over a half dozen other states.[544]

Alvin Ford was convicted in 1974 of murdering a police officer during an attempted robbery,[545] and sentenced to death.[546] While there was no suggestion that he was incompetent at the time of the offense, his trial, or his sentencing,[547] he began to manifest behavioral changes in 1982, nearly 8 years after his conviction.[548] He developed delusions[549] and hallucinations,[550] and his letters—focusing on the local activities of the Ku Klux Klan[551]—revealed "an increasingly pervasive delusion that he had become the target of a complex conspiracy, involving the Klan and assorted others, designed to force him to commit suicide."[552]

Counsel requested that a psychiatrist continue to see Ford and recommend appropriate treatment.[553] After 14 months of evaluation and interviews, the treating psychiatrist concluded that the defendant suffered from "a severe, uncontrollable

---

541. Radelet & Barnard, *supra* note 540, at 43. *See also* Hazard & Louisell, *supra* note 516 at 400.

542. 477 U.S. 399 (1986).

543. FLA. STAT. ANN. § 922.07 (1985).

544. *See* Ward, *supra* note 523, at 75 n.231. For a survey of all state laws, *see id.* at 101–107 (Appendix).

545. Ford v. State, 374 So. 2d 496, 497 (Fla. 1979), *cert. denied*, 445 U.S. 972 (1980).

546. *Ford*, 477 U.S. at 401.

547. *Id.* at 402.

548. *Id.*

549. "Delusions" are false beliefs or wrong judgments held with convictions despite incontrovertible evidence to the contrary.

550. "Hallucinations" are the apparent, often strong, subjective perceptions of an object or event when no such situation is present.

551. *Ford*, 477 U.S. at 402.

552. *Id.*:

He believed that the prison guards, part of the conspiracy, had been killing people and putting the bodies in the concrete enclosures used for beds. Later, he began to believe that his women relatives were being tortured and sexually abused somewhere in the prison. This notion developed into a delusion that the people who were tormenting him at the prison had taken members of Ford's family hostage. The hostage delusion took firm hold and expanded, until Ford was reporting that 135 of his friends and family were being held hostage in the prison, and that only he could help them. By "day 287" of the "hostage crisis," the list of hostages had expanded to include "senators, Senator Kennedy, and many other leaders." App., 53. In a letter to the Attorney General of Florida, written in 1983, Ford appeared to assume authority for the "crisis," claiming to have fired a number of prison officials. He began to refer to himself as "Pope John Paul, III," and reported having appointed nine new justices to the Florida Supreme Court. *Id.* at 59.

553. *Id.*

mental disease which closely resembles 'Paranoid Schizophrenia With Suicide Potential'"—a "major mental disorder . . . severe enough to substantially affect [defendant's] present ability to assist in the defense of his life."[554]

Ford's lawyer then invoked Florida procedures governing the determination of competency of an inmate sentenced to death.[555] In accordance with the statute, the governor appointed three psychiatrists to evaluate whether the defendant had "the mental capacity to understand the nature of the death penalty and the reasons why it was imposed upon him."[556] After a single 30-minute meeting, each psychiatrist reported separately to the governor. While each produced a different diagnosis,[557] all found him to have sufficient capacity to be executed under state law.[558]

The governor subsequently, and "without explanation," signed Ford's death warrant.[559] After the state courts rejected Ford's application for a *de novo* hearing to determine competency,[560] he applied for a writ of habeas corpus in federal court, seeking an evidentiary hearing on his sanity, "proffering the conflicting findings of the Governor-appointed commission and subsequent challenges to their methods by other psychiatrists."[561]

After the district court denied the petition without a hearing, the Eleventh Circuit granted a certificate of probable cause and stayed the defendant's execution,[562] and the Supreme Court rejected the State's application to vacate the stay.[563] A divided panel of the Eleventh Circuit affirmed the district court's denial of the writ,[564] and the Supreme Court granted certiorari "to resolve the important issue whether the Eighth Amendment prohibits the execution of the insane and, if so, whether the District Court should have held a hearing on [defendant's] claim."[565]

A fractured Supreme Court reversed, and remanded for a new trial. In the only portion of any of the four separate opinions to command a majority of the

---

554. *Id.* at 402–03. Ford subsequently refused to see the psychiatrist again, believing that the psychiatrist had now joined the conspiracy against him. *Id.* at 403. Later, Ford "regressed further into nearly complete incomprehensibility, speaking only in a code characterized by intermittent use of the word 'one,' making statements such as 'Hands one, face one. Mafia one. God one, father one. Pope one. Pope one. Leader one." [App.] at 72. *Ford,* 477 U.S. at 403.

555. FLA. STAT. ANN. § 922.07 (West 1985).

556. FLA. STAT. ANN. § 922.07(2) (West 1985).

557. *Ford,* 477 U.S. at 404. One psychiatrist diagnosed Ford as suffering from "psychosis with paranoia"; a second as "psychotic"; and a third as having a "severe adaptational disorder." *Id.* All three, however, found that he had enough "cognitive" functioning to know "fully well what can happen to him." *Id.*

558. *Id.*

559. *Id.*

560. *Id.*

561. *Id.*

562. Ford v. Strickland, 734 F.2d 538 (11th Cir. 1984).

563. Wainwright v. Ford, 467 U.S. 1220 (1984).

564. 752 F.2d 526 (11th Cir. 1985).

565. *Ford,* 477 U.S. at 405.

Court,[566] Justice Marshall concluded that the Eighth Amendment did prohibit the imposition of the death penalty on an insane prisoner.[567]

First, he pointed out that, since the Court decided *Solesbee v. Balkcom*[568] in 1950, its Eighth Amendment jurisprudence had "evolved substantially,"[569] and that its ban on "cruel and unusual punishment embraces, at a minimum, those modes or acts of punishment that had been considered cruel and unusual at the time that the Bill of Rights was adopted,"[570] and recognizes the "evolving standards of decency that mark the progress of a maturing society."[571] In coming to its determination, the Court must take into account "objective evidence of contemporary values before determining whether a particular punishment comports with the fundamental human dignity that the Amendment protects."[572]

The opinion traced the common-law development of the doctrine barring execution of the insane,[573] noting that, while the reasons for the rule were not precisely clear, "it is plain the law is so."[574] It concluded that there was "virtually no authority condoning the execution of the insane at English common law,"[575] and that "this solid proscription was carried to America."[576]

This "ancestral legacy" has not "outlived its time," the court added.[577] No state currently permits execution of the insane,[578] and it is "clear that the ancient and humane limitation upon the State's ability to execute its sentences has as firm a hold upon the jurisprudence of today as it had centuries ago in England":[579]

> The various reasons put forth in support of the common-law restriction have no less logical, moral, and practical force than they did when first voiced. For today,

566. On the question of what procedures were appropriate to satisfy the Constitution, three other Justices joined Justice Marshall. *Id.* at 401. Justice Powell concurred on that issue, and wrote separately. *Id.* at 418. Justice O'Connor (for herself and Justice White) concurred in part and dissented in part. *Id.* at 427. Justice Rehnquist (for himself and the Chief Justice) dissented. *Id.* at 431.

567. *Id.* at 405–10.

568. 339 U.S. 9 (1950).

569. *Ford*, 477 U.S. at 405.

570. *Id.* at 405–06 (citing, inter alia, Solem v. Helm, 463 U.S. 277, 285–86 (1983) (Burger, C. J., dissenting)).

571. *Ford*, 477 U.S. at 406 (citing Trop v. Dulles, 356 U.S. 86, 101 (1958) (plurality opinion)).

572. *Ford*, 477 U.S. at 406 (citing Coker v. Georgia, 433 U.S. 584, 597 (1977) (plurality opinion)).

573. *Ford*, 477 U.S. at 406–07.

574. *Ford*, 477 U.S. at 408 (quoting Hawles, *Remarks on the Trial of Mr. Charles Bateman*, 11 How. St. Tr. 474, 477 (1685)).

575. *Ford*, 477 U.S. at 408.

576. *Id.*: "[I]t was early observed that 'the judge is bound' to stay the execution upon insanity of the prisoner." *Id.* (citing 1 CHITTY, A PRACTICAL TREATISE ON THE CRIMINAL LAW *761 (5th Am. ed. 1847), and 1 WHARTON, A TREATISE ON CRIMINAL LAW § 59 (8th ed. 1880)).

577. *Ford*, 477 U.S. at 408.

578. *Id. See id.* at 408–09 n.2 (listing statutes).

579. *Id.* at 409.

no less than before, we may seriously question the retributive value of executing a person who has no comprehension of why he has been singled out and stripped of his fundamental right to life. See Note, The Eighth Amendment and the Execution of the Presently Incompetent, 32 Stan. L. Rev. 765, 777 n.58 (1980). Similarly, the natural abhorrence civilized societies feel at killing one who has no capacity to come to grips with his own conscience or deity is still vivid today. And the intuition that such an execution simply offends humanity is evidently shared across the Nation. Faced with such wide-spread evidence of a restriction upon sovereign power, this Court is compelled to conclude that the Eighth Amendment prohibits a State from carrying out a sentence of death upon a prisoner who is insane. Whether its aim be to protect the condemned from fear and pain without comfort or understanding, or to protect the dignity of society itself from the barbarity of exacting mindless vengeance, the restriction finds enforcement in the Eighth Amendment.[580]

On the question of what procedures were appropriate in such a case, the Court was sufficiently fragmented that no opinion commanded a majority of justices. In a four-Justice opinion, Justice Marshall concluded that, under the federal habeas corpus statute[581] and *Townsend v. Sain*,[582] a *de novo* evidentiary hearing on Ford's sanity was required, unless "the state-court trier of fact has after a full hearing reliably found the relevant facts."[583] Further, if some sort of state judgment were rendered, the habeas statute compels federal courts to hold an evidentiary hearing if state procedures were inadequate,[584] or insufficient,[585] or if the applicant did not receive a "full, fair and adequate hearing" in state court.[586]

In cases such as the one before the Court—where fact-finding procedures must "aspire to a heightened standard of reliability"[587]—the ascertainment of a prisoner's sanity "as a lawful predicate to execution calls for no less stringent standards than those demanded in any other aspect of a capital proceeding,"[588] a standard particularly demanding in light of the reality that "the present state of the mental sciences is at best a hazardous guess however conscientious."[589] Under this analysis, Florida's procedures failed to pass muster. The state procedure was "wholly within the executive branch, *ex parte,* and provides the exclusive means

580. *Id.* at 409–10.
581. 28 U.S.C. § 2254.
582. 372 U.S. 293 (1963).
583. *Id.* at 312–13.
584. 28 U.S.C. § 2254(d)(2).
585. 28 U.S.C. § 2254(d)(3).
586. 28 U.S.C. § 2254(d)(6).
587. *Ford,* 477 U.S. at 411.
588. *Id.* at 411–12.
589. *Solesbee,* 339 U.S. at 23 (Frankfurter, J., dissenting). *See also* O'Connor v. Donaldson, 422 U.S. 563, 584 (1975) (Burger, C.J., concurring) ("there are many forms of mental illness that are not understood"); Addington v. Texas, 441 U.S. 418, 429 (1979) ("Given the lack of certainty and the fallibility of psychiatric diagnosis, there is a serious question as to whether a state could ever prove beyond a reasonable doubt that an individual is both mentally ill and likely to be dangerous").

of determining sanity."[590] That this "most cursory form of procedural review[591] fails to achieve even the minimal level of reliability required for the protection of any constitutional interest, and thus falls short of adequacy under *Townsend,* is self-evident."[592]

There were three significant deficiencies in the Florida procedures. First, state practice failed to allow any material relevant to the ultimate decision to be submitted on behalf of the prisoner,[593] in contravention of Court doctrine that the fact finder must have before it "all possible relevant information about the individual defendant whose fate it must determine."[594] Any procedure that precludes the prisoner or his or her counsel from presenting material relevant to his or her sanity or bars consideration of such material by the fact finder is "necessarily inadequate."[595]

On this point, Justice Marshall cited to and quoted from his opinion for the court in *Ake v. Oklahoma,*[596] holding that, because "'psychiatrists disagree widely and frequently on what constitutes mental illness [and] on the appropriate diagnosis to be attached to given behavior and symptoms,'[597] the fact finder must resolve differences in opinion within the psychiatric profession 'on the basis of the evidence offered by each party'[598] when a defendant's sanity is at issue in a criminal trial."[599] The same holds true, he concluded, after conviction:

> [W]ithout any adversarial assistance from the prisoner's representative—especially when the psychiatric opinion he proffers is based on much more extensive evaluation than the state-appointed commission—the factfinder loses the substantial benefit of potentially probative information. The result is a much greater likelihood of an erroneous decision.[600]

Second, under Florida law, the defendant had no opportunity to challenge or impeach the opinion of the state-appointed experts through cross-examination,[601]

---

590. *Ford,* 477 U.S. at 412.

591. The Governor's office had refused to inform the defendant's counsel whether his submission of written materials (including psychiatric reports of experts who examined Ford "at great length") would be considered. *Id.* at 413.

592. *Id.*

593. *Id.*

594. *Id.* (quoting *Jurek v. Texas,* 428 U.S. 262, 276 (1976) (plurality opinion)).

595. *Ford,* 477 U.S. at 414.

596. 470 U.S. 68 (1985). *See, e.g.,* 4 PERLIN, *supra* note 5, §10-4.2.

597. *Ford,* 477 U.S. at 414 (quoting *Ake,* 470 U.S. at 81).

598. *Ford,* 477 U.S. at 414 (quoting *Ake,* 470 U.S. at 81).

599. *Ford,* 477 U.S. at 414.

600. *Id.* at 414.

601. *Id.* at 415:

> "[C]ross-examination . . . is beyond any doubt the greatest legal engine ever invented for the discovery of the truth." 5 J. Wigmore, *Evidence* § 1367 (Chadbourn rev. 1974). Cross-examination of the psychiatrists, or perhaps a less formal equivalent, would contribute markedly to the process of seeking truth in sanity disputes by bringing to light the bases

thus creating a "significant possibility that the ultimate decision made in reliance on those experts will be distorted."[602] Third, and "[p]erhaps the most striking defect," was the placement of the decision entirely in the executive branch: "The commander of the State's corps of prosecutors[603] cannot be said to have the neutrality that is necessary for reliability in the factfinding proceeding."[604] "In no other circumstance of which we are aware," Justice Marshall concluded on this point, "is the vindication of a constitutional right entrusted to the unreviewable discretion of an administrative tribunal."[605]

The opinion thus left it to the state to develop appropriate procedures "to enforce the constitutional restriction upon its execution of sentences,"[606] noting that it was not suggesting that "only a full trial on the issue of sanity will suffice to protect the federal interests."[607] The lodestar of any such procedures, however, "must be the overriding dual imperative of providing redress for those with substantial claims and of encouraging accuracy in the factfinding determination."[608] Because the state's procedures failed to provide adequate assurance of accuracy to satisfy the *Townsend* doctrine, the defendant was thus entitled under the habeas corpus statute to a *de novo* evidentiary hearing on the question of his competence to be executed.[609]

---

for each expert's beliefs, the precise factors underlying those beliefs, any history of error or caprice of the examiner, any personal bias with respect to the issue of capital punishment, the expert's degree of certainty about his or her own conclusions, and the precise meaning of ambiguous words used in the report.

602. *Id. See also id.* at n.3:

The adequacy of the fact-finding procedures is further called into question by the cursory nature of the underlying psychiatric examination itself. While this Court does not purport to set substantive guidelines for the development of expert psychiatric opinion, *cf.* Barefoot v. Estelle, 463 U.S. 880, 903 (1983) (parallel citations omitted), we can say that the goal of reliability is unlikely to be served by a single group interview, with no provisions for the exercise of the psychiatrists' professional judgment regarding the possible need for different or more comprehensive evaluative techniques. The inconsistency and vagueness of the conclusions reached by the three examining psychiatrists in this case attest to the dubious value of such an examination.

603. *See* Fla. Stat. Ann. § 922.07 (West 1985).
On the issue of dual loyalties in general, *see* Jerome Shestack, *Psychiatry and the Dilemma of Dual Loyalties,* in Medical, Moral and Legal Issues in Mental Health Care 7 (Frank Ayd, ed. 1974); Loren Roth, *To Respect Persons, Families, and Communities: Some Problems in the Ethics of Mental Health Care,* 40 Psychiatry Digest 17 (1979). On this issue in the context of other competency inquiries, *see supra* Chapter 1C.
604. *Ford,* 477 U.S. at 416.
605. *Id.*
606. *Id.* at 416–17. *See also id.* at 417 n.4.
607. *Id.* at 416.
608. *Id.* at 417.
609. *Id.* at 417–18. Subsequently, the Florida Supreme Court promulgated an emergency rule in response to the *Ford* decision, *see In re* Emergency Amendment to Florida Rules of Criminal Procedure, 497 So. 2d 643 (Fla. 1986), promulgating Fla. R. Crim. P. § 3.811 (and *see* Martin v. Wainwright, 497 So. 2d 872 (Fla. 1986), *cert. denied,* 481 U.S. 1033 (1987),

Justice Powell concurred, joining fully in the majority's opinion on the substantive Eighth Amendment issue,[610] but differing substantially from Justice Marshall's opinion on the issue of the appropriate procedures that states must follow pursuant to the *habeas* statute.[611] Further, Justice Powell considered an issue not addressed by the court: the meaning of *insanity* in the context of the case before it.[612]

First, after considering the common-law justifications for barring execution of the insane, Justice Powell concluded that the Eighth Amendment should only bar the execution of those "who are unaware of the punishment they are about to suffer and why they are to suffer it,"[613] a category into which Ford "plainly fit"[614] on capital trials and sentencing proceedings.[615]

Second, since the defendant's competency to stand trial was never seriously in question, the state could presume that the defendant remained sane at the time

---

directing counsel to follow rule's procedures). That rule was later replaced by FLA. R. CRIM. P. §§ 3.811–3.812 (1988), promulgated in *In re* Amendments to Florida Rules of Criminal Procedure, 518 So. 2d 256 (Fla. 1987).

Under the replacement rule, execution of the insane—defined as one who "lacks the mental capacity to understand the fact of the impending execution and the reason for it," FLA. R. CRIM. P. § 3.811(b)—is prohibited, *id.* at (a). No motion for a stay of execution based on insanity will be heard until the Governor holds "appropriate proceedings" under state statute, *id.* at (c); after a finding by the Governor that the prisoner is "sane to be executed," the prisoner's counsel may move for a stay and hearing, *id.* at (d). Among the papers to be filed with the motion request are all expert reports that had previously been submitted to the Governor, *id.* at (d)(3), along with "such other evidentiary materials and written submissions including reports of experts," *id.* at (d)(4). If the hearing judge "has reasonable grounds to believe" that the prisoner is insane, he shall order a stay, and may order further proceedings. *Id.* at (e).

The court hearing is not to be a review of the Governor's determination, but is a *de novo* hearing. FLA. R. CRIM. P. § 3.812(a). At such a hearing, the court may (1) require the prisoner's presence, (2) appoint up to three neutral examining experts, and (3) "[e]nter such other orders as may be appropriate to effectuate a speedy and just resolution of the issues raised." *Id.* at (c). The court may admit other evidence it deems relevant at such a hearing, and is not to be strictly bound by the rules of evidence. *Id.* at (e). After the hearing, if the court finds "by clear and convincing evidence" that the prisoner is insane, it shall enter an order continuing the stay of execution; otherwise, the stay should be set aside. *Id.* at (f).

For later changes, *see In re* Amendments to the Florida Rules of Criminal Procedure, 606 So. 2d 227 (Fla. 1992) (rules of evidence inapplicable to such proceedings).

610. *Ford,* 477 U.S. at 418. (Powell, J., concurring).

611. *Id.*

612. *Id. Cf.* Mezer & Rheingold, *Mental Capacity and Incompetency: A Psychological Problem,* 119 AM. J. PSYCHIATRY 827, 828 (1962) (identifying varying competency standards governing eleven separate areas of the law). *See generally supra* Chapter 1.

613. *Ford,* 477 U.S. at 422.

614. *Id. Compare* Rector v. Bryant, 501 U.S. 1239, 1239 (1991) (Marshall, J., dissenting from denial of *certiorari*), criticizing court's decision to deny *certiorari* in case presenting question of whether a prisoner whose mental incapacity renders him unable to recognize or communicate facts that would make his sentence unlawful or unjust is nonetheless competent to be executed. For further proceedings, *see* Rector v. Clinton, 308 Ark. 104, 823 S.W.2d 829 (1992).

615. *Id.* He noted that "some defendants may lose their mental facilities and never regain them, and thus avoid execution altogether." *Id.* at n.5.

sentence was to be carried out, and thus might require "a substantial threshold showing of insanity merely to trigger the hearing process."[616]

Third, the sanity issue here was not like the basic "historical fact" issues at trial or sentencing; rather, it called for a "basically subjective judgment,"[617] depending substantially on "expert analysis in a discipline fraught with 'subtleties and nuances.'"[618] In such cases, "ordinary adversarial procedures—complete with live testimony, cross-examination, and oral argument by counsel—are not necessarily the best means of arriving at sound, consistent judgments as to a defendant's sanity."[619]

In short, he concluded that constitutionally acceptable procedures "may be far less formal than a trial."[620] In addition to provision by the state of an impartial officer or board to receive evidence and argument from defense counsel, including expert psychiatric evidence that might differ from the state's own evaluation, the state "should have substantial leeway to determine what process best balances the various interests at stake."[621] Because the defendant's "viable" Eighth Amendment claim was not fairly adjudicated, he therefore was entitled to a habeas hearing in federal court, Justice Powell concluded, and he thus joined the court's judgment.[622]

Writing for herself and Justice White, Justice O'Connor concurred in part and dissented in part. While she agreed fully with Justice Rehnquist's two-Justice dissent that the Eighth Amendment did not create a substantive right not to be executed while insane (and she thus did not join in the Court's opinion or reasoning),[623] she found further that it was "inescapable" that Florida state law provided a protected liberty interest in not being executed while incompetent.[624]

As Florida did not provide "even those minimal procedural protections required by due process,"[625] she would have vacated the judgment and remanded for a state court hearing in a manner "consistent with the requirements of the Due Process Clause."[626] She emphasized, however, that, in her view, the federal court should have no role "whatever in the substantive determination of a defendant's competency to be executed."[627]

Relying on the Court's decision in *Hewitt v. Helms*,[628] that liberty interests may stem from either the due process clause or state law, she read applicable, man-

---

616. *Id.* at 426. In a "*cf.*" reference, he cited to *Ake,* 470 U.S. at 82–83.

617. *Id.* at 426 (citing *Addington, supra,* with a "*cf.*" reference to Barefoot v. Estelle, 463 U.S. 880 (1983)); *see generally* 4 PERLIN, *supra* note 8, §§ 12-2 to 2.2.

618. *Ford,* 477 U.S. at 426 (quoting *Addington,* 441 U.S. at 430).

619. *Ford,* 477 U.S. at 426 (citing, in a "*cf.*" reference, Parham v. J.R., 442 U.S. 584, 609 (1979)).

620. *Ford,* 477 U.S. at 427.

621. *Id.*

622. *Id.*

623. *Id.* at 427 (O'Connor, J., concurring in part and dissenting in part).

624. *Id.*

625. *Id.*

626. *Id.*

627. *Id.* at 427–28.

628. 459 U.S. 460, 466 (1983).

datory Florida statutes[629] as creating a protected liberty expectation that "state conduct injurious to an individual will not occur 'absent specified substantive predicates.'"[630] This was so even when the same statute specified certain procedures to be followed;[631] "regardless of the procedures the State deems adequate for determining the preconditions to adverse official action, federal law defines the kind of process a State must afford prior to depriving an individual of a protected liberty or property interest."[632]

Due process demands in this sort of case are "minimal," she concluded,[633] noting that "substantial caution" was warranted "before reading the Due Process Clause to mandate anything like the full panoply of trial-type procedures."[634] This was so for several reasons: (1) after a valid conviction, the demands of due process are "reduced accordingly;"[635] (2) the potential for false claims and deliberate delay in this context is "obviously enormous;"[636] and (3) by definition, the defendant's protected interest can "*never* be conclusively and finally determined . . . until the very moment of execution."[637] Even given the "broad latitude"[638] that she would give the states in this area, Justice O'Connor concluded that one aspect of Florida's procedure—failure to consider the defendant's written submissions[639]—violated the "fundamental requisite" of due process, entitling an individual an opportunity to be heard, and thus rendered it constitutionally deficient.[640]

Thus, Justice O'Connor would have ordered the Eleventh Circuit to return the case to Florida "so that it might assess [defendant's] competency in a manner that accords with the command of the Fourteenth Amendment."[641] She reiterated that the "only federal question presented in cases such as this is whether the State's positive law has created a liberty interest and whether its procedures are adequate to protect that interest from artificial deprivation." If those procedures are adequate, then, "a federal court has no authority to second guess a state's substantive competency determination."[642]

---

629. FLA. STAT. ANN. § 922.07(3) (West 1985).

630. *Ford*, 477 U.S. at 428 (O'Connor, J., concurring in part and dissenting in part) (quoting, in part, *Hewitt*, 459 U.S. at 471–72).

631. *Ford*, 477 U.S. at 428.

632. *Id.* (citing Cleveland Bd. of Educ. v. Loudermill, 470 U.S. 532, 541 (1985)).

633. *Ford*, 477 U.S. at 429 (O'Connor, J., concurring in part and dissenting in part).

634. *Id.*

635. *Id.,* (citing Meachum v. Fano, 427 U.S. 215, 224 (1976)).

636. *See* Nobles v. Georgia, 168 U.S. 398, 405–06 (1897). *Cf.* Joseph Rodriguez, Laura LeWinn, & Michael L. Perlin, *The Insanity Defense Under Siege: Legislative Assaults and Legal Rejoinders,* 14 RUTGERS L.J. 397, 404 (1983)(no question as to presence of serious mental illness in 138 of 141 successful insanity defense cases studied).

637. *Ford*, 477 U.S. at 429 (O'Connor, J., concurring in part and dissenting in part) (emphasis in original).

638. *Id.*

639. *Id.* at 429–30. *See* Goode v. Wainwright, 448 So. 2d 999, 1101 (Fla. 1984) (describing governor's "publicly announced policy of excluding all advocacy on the part of the condemned from the process of determining whether a person under a sentence of death is insane").

640. *Ford*, 477 U.S. at 430 (O'Connor, J., concurring in part and dissenting in part).

641. *Id.*

642. *Id.* at 430–31.

Finally, Justice Rehnquist dissented on behalf of himself and the Chief Justice.[643] In his view, the Florida procedures were "fully consistent with the 'common-law heritage' and current practice on which the Court purports to rely,"[644] and, in their reliance on executive branch procedures, they were "faithful to both traditional and modern practice."[645] Further, he saw no reason to abandon *Solesbee,* which had sanctioned procedures vesting decision-making in "the solemn responsibility of a state's highest executive with authority to invoke the aid of the most skillful class of experts on the crucial questions involved."[646] He concluded that Florida law did not grant the defendant the sort of entitlement "that gives rise to the procedural protections for which he contends."[647]

To create a constitutional right to a judicial determination of sanity prior to execution "needlessly complicates and postpones still further any finality in this area of the law,"[648] in an area where yet another adjudication "offers an invitation to those who have nothing to lose by accepting it to advance entirely spurious claims of insanity."[649] He concluded:

> Since no State sanctions execution of the insane, the real battle being fought in this case is over what procedures must accompany the inquiry into sanity. The Court reaches the result it does by examining the common law, creating a constitutional right that no State seeks to violate, and then concluding that the common-law procedures are inadequate to protect the newly created but common-law based right. I find it unnecessary to "constitutionalize" the already uniform view that the insane should not be executed, and inappropriate to "selectively incorporate" the common-law practice. I therefore dissent.[650]

Ford v. Wainwright was both a curious and difficult opinion,[651] and one reflecting much of the ambiguity and ambivalence permeating this subject matter.[652] To some extent, *Ford* served as a paradigm of the Supreme Court's confu-

---

643. *Id.* at 431 (Rehnquist, J., dissenting).
644. *Id.*
645. *Id.*
646. *Id.* at 432.
647. *Id.* at 434.
648. *Id.* at 435.
649. *Id.*:

A claim of insanity may be made at any time before sentence, and, once rejected, may be used again; a prisoner found sane two days before execution might claim to have lost his sanity the next day thus necessitating another judicial determination of his sanity and presumably another stay of execution.

650. *Id.*
651. For commentaries on *Ford, see, e.g.,* Yale Note, *supra* note 538; *The Supreme Court, 1985 Term,* 100 HARV. L. REV. 100 (1986) (hereinafter *1985 Term*); Salguero, *Medical Ethics and Competency to Be Executed,* 96 YALE L.J. 167 (1986); Showalter, *supra* note 537; Mossman, *supra* note 537; Bonnie I & Bonnie II, *supra* note 537; Brodsky, *supra* note 537.
652. *See Barefoot's Ake, supra* note 21, at 167–69. An analysis of *Ford* sees it as "sanctioning a double paradox: condemned prisoners are killed if they are sane, but spared if they are insane;

sion and, to some extent, its use of rationalization as a means of dealing with many of the cases it has decided in the past several decades dealing with criminal defendants with serious mental illness.[653]

First, the difficulty that is always faced in the application of a plurality opinion[654] is increased when the states have enacted such a wide range of statutory vehicles for making the critical determination,[655] and when it is truly not clear what sort of procedures a state need enact to meet *Ford's* standards.[656]

---

insane prisoners are cured in order that they may be killed." *1985 Term, supra* note 651, at 106 (footnote omitted).

The American Bar Association amended its Criminal Justice Mental Health Standards in line with *Ford:*

(a) Convicts who have been sentenced to death should not be executed if they are currently mentally incompetent. If it is determined that a condemned convict is currently incompetent, execution should be stayed.

(b) A convict is incompetent to be executed if, as a result of mental illness or retardation, the convict cannot understand the nature of the pending proceedings, what he or she was tried for, the reason for the punishment, or the nature of the punishment. A convict is also incompetent if, as a result of mental illness or mental retardation, the convict lacks sufficient capacity to recognize or understand any fact which might exist which would make the punishment unjust or unlawful, or lacks the ability to convey such information to counsel or to the court.

Standard 7-.5.6.

653. *See generally,* Perlin, supra note 242, 29 at 78–98.

654. On the meaning and interpretation of plurality decisions by the Supreme Court, and their implication for the judicial process, *see, e.g.,* John Davis & William Reynolds, *Juridical Cripples: Plurality Opinions in the Supreme Court,* 1974 DUKE L.J. 59; Note, *The Precedential Value of Supreme Court Plurality Opinions,* 80 COLUM. L. REV. 756 (1980) (hereinafter Columbia Note); Note, *Plurality Decisions and Judicial Decisionmaking,* 94 HARV. L. REV. 1127 (1981) (hereinafter Harvard Note).

Where multiple opinions appear to be of "varying scope or breadth," Columbia Note, *supra,* at 760, the Court has indicated that the opinion concurring in the judgment on the "narrowest grounds" represents the highest common denominator of majority agreement and should thus be considered authoritative for future cases. *Id.* at 761. *See* Gregg v. Georgia, 428 U.S. 153, 169 n.15 (1976) (plurality opinion). *See, e.g.,* Vitek v. Jones, 445 U.S. 480, 497 (1980) (on question of scope of right to assistance available to prisoner prior to prison-mental hospital transfer, Justice Powell's separate one-justice opinion becomes judgment of the Court). *See also* Columbia Note, *supra,* at 767 (lower courts look for guidance to "the alignment of the Justices and the extent of agreement, the compatibility of different lines of reasoning, the persuasiveness of the various rationales, and the relative stature of the opinion writers"). Interestingly, another commentator has noted that, among the areas in which plurality opinions "consistently occur," are cases involving the death penalty and various constitutional criminal procedure questions. Harvard Note, *supra,* at 1137 n.66.

The *Gregg* "narrowest grounds" standard has been interpreted as "referring to the ground that is most nearly confined to the precise fact situation before the Court, rather than to a ground that states more general rules." United States v. Martino, 664 F.2d 860, 872–73 (2d Cir. 1981). *But see, e.g.,* Catterson v. Caso, 472 F. Supp. 833, 836 (E.D.N.Y. 1979) (holding of concurring Justices viewed as holding of the court).

655. *See, e.g.,* Ward, *supra* note 522, at 72–76. *But see* Harris v. State, 499 N.E.2d 723 (Ind. 1986) (imposition of death penalty in case of defendant found guilty but mentally ill does not constitute cruel and unusual punishment; *Ford* distinguished). For an early interpretation of *Ford* in another jurisdiction, *see, e.g.,* Evans v. McCotter, 805 F.2d 1210 (5th Cir. 1986) (no fact question presented as to whether defendant was insane within meaning of *Ford*).

656. For a possible array of options, *see* Yale Note, *supra* note 538, at 184–86.

Second, there were significant inconsistencies between the positions articulated in the various *Ford* opinions and positions with which the Court appeared to be entirely comfortable in the past:

1. Justice Powell's position that the *only* question is not "*whether* but *when*"[657] ignored the possibility that organic brain damage, for instance, could make a once competent-to-be-executed defendant become *irreversibly* incompetent, or that, in a state that has abolished the insanity defense, it is not beyond the realm of possibility that a defendant like the petitioner in *Jackson v. Indiana*[658] might face execution.[659]

2. His reliance on *Parham v. J.R.*[660] for the proposition that the protections of the adversary process in proceedings to determine the appropriateness of medical decisions "may well be more illusory than real"[661] was astonishing when applied to a death penalty case. *Parham* countenanced looser procedural safeguards in the juvenile commitment context, in part, because of the assumption that "natural bonds of affection lead parents to act in the best interests of their children."[662] Certainly, no one would suggest that such a benign motive propels state action in a capital punishment case.[663]

3. At its base, Justice Rehnquist's dissent—cosigned by Chief Justice Burger—saw little purpose for "constitutionalizing" the competency-to-be executed procedures, since he viewed the problem as basically a trivial one: no state sanctions execution of "the insane," so why "needlessly complicate[] and postpone[] still further any finality in this area of the law"?[664] This was a far cry from the Chief Justice Burger's familiar position in *O'Connor v. Donaldson*,[665] that there can be "little responsible debate regarding 'the uncertainty of diagnosis in this field and the tentativeness of professional judgment.'"[666]

4. Both Justice Rehnquist's and Justice O'Connor's opinions remained obsessed with the fear that defendants will raise "false"[667] or "spurious claims"[668] in desperate attempts to stave off execution. This fear—a *doppelganger* of the public's

657. *Ford,* 477 U.S. at 425 (Powell, J., concurring).

658. 406 U.S. 715, 726 (1972) ("There is nothing in the record that even points to any possibility that Jackson's present condition can be remedied at any future time"). *See generally supra* Chapter 2A.

659. *See, e.g.,* People *ex rel.* Myers v. Briggs, 46 Ill. 2d 281, 263 N.E.2d 109 (1970) (defendant indicted for murder in case "virtually indistinguishable" from the clinical and procedural facts of *Jackson; see* 406 U.S. at 735–36).

660. 442 U.S. 584 (1979).

661. *Id.* at 609, *quoted in Ford,* 477 U.S. at 526 (Powell, J., concurring).

662. *Parham,* 442 U.S. at 618 (citing 1 BLACKSTONE, COMMENTARIES *447, 2 KENT, COMMENTARIES ON AMERICAN LAW *190).

663. *See 1985 Term, supra* note 146, characterizing Justice Powell's opinion as "foggy."

664. *Ford,* 477 U.S. at 435 (Rehnquist, J., dissenting).

665. 422 U.S. 563, 584 (1975) (Burger, C. J., concurring).

666. *Id.,* (quoting, in part, Greenwood v. United States, 350 U.S. 366, 375 (1956)).

667. *Ford,* 477 U.S. at 429 (O'Connor, J., concurring in part and dissenting in part).

668. *Id.* at 435 (Rehnquist, J., dissenting).

"swift and vociferous . . . outrage"[669] over what it perceives as "abusive"[670] insanity acquittals, thus allowing "guilty" defendants to "beat the rap"[671]—was dispatched more than adequately almost 150 years ago by Dr. Isaac Ray, the father of American forensic psychiatry:

> The supposed insurmountable difficulty of distinguishing between feigned and real insanity has conduced, probably more than all other causes together, to bind the legal profession to the most rigid construction and application of the common law relative to this disease, and is always put forward in objection to the more humane doctrines.[672]

On the other hand, at least one inevitable outcome of *Ford* has been that more clinicians became aware of the problems involved and began to stake out the competing positions outlined by Radelet and Barnard, Ward, and Appelbaum, as a step toward, perhaps, "achieving consensus within the professions."[673] A study of the aftermath of the *Ford* case glumly concluded that, despite the decision in that litigation, "it remains all but impossible" for defense counsel to prove that a death row client is incompetent to be executed.[674]

Subsequent to *Ford,* courts have split in their assessment of whether individual defendants were competent to be executed under the standards set out in that case.[675]

---

669. *See* INGO KEILITZ & JUNIUS FULTON, THE INSANITY DEFENSE AND ITS ALTERNATIVES: A GUIDE FOR POLICYMAKERS (1984).

670. *See* Michael L. Perlin, *"The Things We Do for Love": John Hinckley's Trial and the Future of the Insanity Defense in the Federal Courts,* 30 N.Y.L. SCH. L. REV. 857, 859 (1985) (Book Review of LINCOLN CAPLAN, THE INSANITY DEFENSE AND THE TRIAL OF JOHN W. HINCKLEY, JR. (1984)), and see sources cited *id.* nn.6–7.

671. *Id.* at 860.

672. ISAAC RAY, A TREATISE ON THE MEDICAL JURISPRUDENCE OF INSANITY § 247, at 243 (Overholser, ed., 1962 ed.).

673. Appelbaum, *supra* note 511, at 683. *See also* Yale Note, *supra* note 538, at 186:

> The states have enacted and implemented competency to be executed statutes that pose an irreconcilable ethical conflict for the medical profession. Based on an analysis of the relevant medical ethics and state interests, this Note contends that the state must accommodate the ethical integrity of the medical profession. This proposal is not revolutionary. The state has traditionally respected and upheld the ethical integrity of various professions. It must now do so in the context of medical treatment of the insane condemned, because to do so otherwise results in the anathema of making "one learned profession the very agent of an attack upon the ethical foundations of another."(footnotes omitted) (quoting, in part, Derr, *Why Food and Fluids Can Never Be Denied,* 16 HASTINGS CENTER REP. 28, 30 (Feb. 1986)).

Cf. 1985 Term, supra note 651, at 107 ("With *Ford,* the Court approves an arrangement in which psychiatrists clear the tortured minds of capital prisoners so that the state can fill their bodies with electricity").

674. *See* Michael Radelet & Kent Miller, *The Aftermath of* Ford v. Wainwright, 10 BEHAV. SCI. & L. 339 (1992).

675. *Compare, e.g.,* Rector v. Lockhart, 727 F. Supp. 1285 (E.D. Ark. 1990), *aff'd,* 923 F.2d 570 (8th Cir.), *cert. denied,* 501 U.S. 1239 (1991), *further proceedings sub nom.* Rector v. Clin-

As with other important areas of criminal procedure, the question of whether a defendant was "malingering" remains an important question in this context.[676] Other cases decided on related questions reveal a continued failure on the part of many courts to authentically implement the *Ford* decision.[677]

The Supreme Court has subsequently ruled that a petitioner's *Ford*-based claim that he was incompetent to be executed, that was raised for the second time after his initial claim was dismissed by the district court as premature, was not a "second or successive" application under the Antiterrorism and Effective Death Penalty Act,[678] affirming a decision below, and allowing the prisoner to raise a *Ford* claim in federal court.[679]

---

ton, 823 S.W.2d 829 (Ark. 1992). Shaw v. Armontrout, 900 F.2d 123 (8th Cir. 1990), *aff'd*, 971 F.2d 181 (8th Cir. 1992), *cert. denied*, 507 U.S. 927 (1993); State v. Harris, 789 P.2d 60 (Wash. 1990); Granviel v. Lynaugh, 881 F.2d 185 (5th Cir. 1989), *cert. denied*, 495 U.S. 963 (1990); Singleton v. Endell, 870 S.W.2d 742 (Ark. 1994), *cert. denied*, 513 U.S. 960 (1994); Magwood v. State, 689 So. 2d 959 (Ala. Crim. App. 1996), *reh'g denied* (1996), *cert. denied* (1996), *cert. den.*, 522 U.S. 836 (1997); *In re* Personal Restraint of Benn, 952 P.2d 116 (Wash. 1998) (same); Johnson v. Cabana, 818 F.2d 333 (5th Cir.), *cert. denied*, 481 U.S. 1061 (1987) (defendant competent to be executed); Medina v. State, 690 So. 2d 1241 (Fla. 1997), *cert. denied*, 520 U.S. 1151 (1997) (same); Commonwealth v. Jermyn, 709 A.2d 849 (Pa. 1998), *habeas corpus granted in part*, 1998 WL 754567 (M.D. Pa. 1998) (same); Moody v. Johnson, 139 F.3d 477 (5th Cir.), *cert. denied*, 515 U.S. 1126 (1998) (same); *In re* Heidnik, 720 A.2d 1016 (Pa. 1998), *rearg. denied* (1998) (same); Billiot v. State, 655 So. 2d 1 (Miss. 1995), *reh'g denied* (1995), *cert. denied*, 516 U.S. 1095 (1996); Singleton v. State, 437 S.E.2d 53 (S.C. 1993), *to* Martin v. Dugger, 686 F. Supp. 1523 (S.D. Fla. 1988), *aff'd*, 891 F.2d 807 (11th Cir.), *reh'g denied*, 898 F.2d 160 (11th Cir. 1989), *cert. denied*, 498 U.S. 881 (1990) (hearing required to determine defendant's competency to be executed); Billiot v. State, 515 So. 2d 1234 (Miss. 1987) (same); *Ex parte* Jordan, 758 S.W.2d 250 (Tex. Crim. App. 1988) (execution stayed pending defendant's regaining competency); State v. Harris, *supra*, 789 P.2d at 73–75 (Utter, J., dissenting) (trial court used incorrect definition of competency, thus failing to comply with due process protections of *Ford*).

676. *See* Boggs v. State, 667 So. 2d 765, 766 n.3 (Fla. 1996) (discussing press report of trial judge's beliefs that defendant was "faking mental illness to avoid execution"). *Compare* Coe v. State, 17 S.W.3d 193 (Tenn. 2000) (defendant not entitled to additional time to counter state's theory that he was malingering).

677. *See, e.g.*, Cuevas v. Collins, 932 F.2d 1078, 1084 (5th Cir. 1991) (hearing not required unless defendant "so deranged that he is unaware that he is about to be put to death"); Garrett v. Collins, 951 F.2d 57 (5th Cir. 1992), *cert. den.*, 502 U.S. 1083 (1992) (defendant's belief that his dead aunt would protect him from effects of toxic agents used during execution did not preclude imposition of death penalty on grounds of incompetency); Shaw v. Delo, 762 F. Supp. 853 (E.D. Mo. 1991), *aff'd*, 971 F. 2d 181 (8th Cir. 1992), *cert. den.*, 507 U.S. 927 (1993) (funds for investigative and expert services to support incompetency claim were not necessary).

On the question of whether a trial court can exclude the death penalty as a possible punishment because of a defendant's mental illness, *see* Commonwealth v. Ryan, 5 S.W.3d 113 (Ky. 1999), *reh'g denied* (1999) (finding that court lacked authority to do so).

678. 28 U.S.C. §§ 2244, 2244(b)(3).

679. Stewart v. Martinez-Villareal, 523 U.S. 637 (1998). *Compare* Nguyen v. Gibson, 162 F.3d 600 (10th Cir. 1998) (claim of incompetency to be executed deemed to be successor habeas petition).

a. *The significance of* Panetti

The Supreme Court subsequently reinforced its ruling in *Ford* in its 2007 decision in *Panetti v. Quarterman*.[680] Panetti, who had been convicted of capital murder in the slayings of his estranged wife's parents, had been hospitalized numerous times for serious psychiatric disorders.[681] Notwithstanding his "bizarre," "scary", and "trancelike" behavior,[682] he was found competent to stand trial and competent to waive counsel.[683] He was convicted (the jury rejecting his insanity defense), and was sentenced to death.[684] After his direct appeals and initial petition of habeas corpus were rejected, Panetti filed a subsequent habeas writ petition, alleging that he did not understand the reasons for his pending execution.[685] This petition was rejected, the court concluding that the test for competency to be executed "requires the petitioner know no more than the fact of his impending execution and the factual predicate for the execution."[686] The Fifth Circuit affirmed,[687] and the Supreme Court granted certiorari.[688]

The Court reversed in a 5-4 decision,[689] and in the course of its opinion,[690] significantly elaborated on its *Ford* opinion in two dimensions: As to the procedures that are to be afforded to a defendant seeking to assert a *Ford* claim, and as to the substance of the *Ford* standard.

On the first matter, it found error in the trial court's failure to provide the defendant an adequate opportunity to submit expert evidence in response to the report filed by the court-appointed experts,[691] thus depriving him of his "constitutionally adequate opportunity to be heard."[692] The fact-finding procedures on which the trial court relied, it concluded, were "'not adequate for reaching reasonably correct results' or, at a minimum, resulted in a process that appeared to be 'seriously inadequate for the ascertainment of the truth.'"[693]

On the second, it carefully elaborated on—and clarified—*Ford*. It reviewed

---

680. 127 S. Ct. 2842 (2007).

681. *Id.* at 2848.

682. *Id.* at 2849.

683. *Id.; see supra* Chapter 3 C.

684. *Panetti,* 127 S. Ct. at 2849.

685. *Id.*

686. Panetti v. Dretke, 401 F. Supp. 705, 711 (W.D. Tex. 2004).

687. Panetti v. Dretke, 448 F. 3d 815 (5th Cir. 2006).

688. Panetti v. Quarterman, 127 S. Ct. 852 (2007).

689. Justice Kennedy wrote the majority opinion.

690. In a jurisdictional ruling of great importance to death penalty litigation, the Court also found that the defendant's claim was not barred by federal legislation that generally prohibited "successive" habeas corpus applications. *See* Panetti v. Quarterman, 127 S. Ct. 2842, 2852–55 (2007). The significance of this portion of the opinion is beyond the scope of the book.

691. *Id.* at 2587.

692. *Id.* at 2858.

693. *Id.* at 2859, quoting, in part, *Ford,* 477 U.S., at 423–24(Powell, J., concurring in part and concurring in judgment) (internal quotation marks omitted).

the testimony that demonstrated the defendant's "fixed delusion" system,[694] and quoted with approval expert testimony that had pointed out that "an unmedicated individual suffering from schizophrenia can 'at times' hold an ordinary conversation and that 'it depends [whether the discussion concerns the individual's] fixed delusional system.'"[695] Here, it rejected the appellate court's interpretation of the *Ford* standard—that competency to be executed depends only on three findings: that the prisoner is aware he committed the murders, that he is going to be executed, and that he is aware of the reasons the State has given for his execution.[696] This narrow test, the Supreme Court concluded, unconstitutionally foreclosed the defendant from establishing incompetency by the means that Panetti sought to employ in the case at bar: by making a showing that his mental illness "obstruct[ed] a *rational understanding* of the State's reason for his execution."[697] The Fifth Circuit had squarely confronted this issue, and had found that "awareness" was "not necessarily synonymous with 'rational understanding;'"[698] the Supreme Court rejected this position, finding that it was "too restrictive to afford a prisoner the protections granted by the Eighth Amendment."[699]

In this case, the Court found, the Fifth Circuit improperly treated a prisoner's delusional belief system "as irrelevant if the prisoner knows that the State has identified his crimes as the reason for his execution."[700] Nowhere, the Court continued, did *Ford* indicate that "delusions are irrelevant to 'comprehen[sion]' or 'aware [ness]' if they so impair the prisoner's concept of reality that he cannot reach a rational understanding of the reason for the execution."[701] If anything, the Court continued, "the *Ford* majority suggests the opposite."[702]

After quoting the "simply offends humanity" language from Ford,[703] the Court

---

694. *Panetti*, 127 S. Ct. at 2859. *See id*:

Four expert witnesses testified on petitioner's behalf in the District Court proceedings. One explained that petitioner's mental problems are indicative of "schizo-affective disorder," resulting in a "genuine delusion" involving his understanding of the reason for his execution. According to the expert, this delusion has recast petitioner's execution as "part of spiritual warfare . . . between the demons and the forces of the darkness and God and the angels and the forces of light." As a result, the expert explained, although petitioner claims to understand "that the state is saying that [it wishes] to execute him for [his] murder[s]," he believes in earnest that the stated reason is a "sham" and the State in truth wants to execute him "to stop him from preaching." Petitioner's other expert witnesses reached similar conclusions concerning the strength and sincerity of this "fixed delusion."

(Citations to record omitted).
695. *Id.* at 2860.
696. *Id.*, quoting *Panetti*, 448 F. 3d at 819.
697. *Panetti*, 127 S. Ct. at 2860.
698. *Panetti*, 448 F. 3d at 817–18.
699. *Panetti*, 127 S. Ct. at 2860.
700. *Id.* at 2861.
701. *Id.*
702. *Id.*
703. 477 U.S. at 407–08; see *supra* text accompanying note 580.

focused on the reasons why executing an insane person "serves no retributive purpose":[704]

> [I]t might be said that capital punishment is imposed because it has the potential to make the offender recognize at last the gravity of his crime and to allow the community as a whole, including the surviving family and friends of the victim, to affirm its own judgment that the culpability of the prisoner is so serious that the ultimate penalty must be sought and imposed. The potential for a prisoner's recognition of the severity of the offense and the objective of community vindication are called in question, however, if the prisoner's mental state is so distorted by a mental illness that his awareness of the crime and punishment has little or no relation to the understanding of those concepts shared by the community as a whole. This problem is not necessarily overcome once the test set forth by the Court of Appeals is met. And under a similar logic the other rationales set forth by *Ford* fail to align with the distinctions drawn by the Court of Appeals.[705]

There was no support in *Ford* ("or anywhere else"), the Court added, for the proposition that "a prisoner is automatically foreclosed from demonstrating incompetency once a court has found he can identify the stated reason for his execution."[706] Although it conceded that concepts such as "rational understanding" could be difficult to define, and that some might fail to be punished on account of "reasons other than those stemming from a severe mental illness," it concluded, on this point: "The beginning of doubt about competence in a case like petitioner's is not a misanthropic personality or an amoral character. It is a psychotic disorder."[707] In this case, it again underlined, it was the prisoner's "severe, documented mental illness that is the source of gross delusions preventing him from comprehending the meaning and purpose of the punishment to which he has been sentenced."[708]

After coming to this conclusion, the Court added that it was not attempting to set out a rule to govern all competency determinations, and then remanded so that the "underpinnings of petitioner's claims [could] be explained and evaluated in further detail on remand."[709] Among the questions it sought to be explored in greater depth was "the extent to which severe delusions may render a subject's perception of reality so distorted that he should be deemed incompetent," citing here to an aspect of the amicus brief by the American Psychological Association that had discussed ways in which mental health experts can inform competency determinations.[710]

Justice Thomas dissented.[711] He found that Panetti's submissions to the trial

704. *Id.* at 408.
705. *Panetti*, 127 S. Ct. at 2861.
706. *Id.* at 2862.
707. *Id.*
708. *Id.*
709. *Id.* at 2863.
710. *Id.*
711. Joining him in this dissent were the Chief Justice, and Justices Scalia and Alito.

court on the competency question were "meager,"[712] and that there was "nothing in the record to suggest that Panetti would have submitted any additional evidence had he been given another opportunity to do so,"[713] criticizing the majority's opinion as a "half-baked holding" that "thrust[s] already muddled *Ford* determinations into . . . disarray."[714]

Although *Panetti* chose not to consider the following issue on which much attention had been focused—the question of medicating defendants so as to make them competent to be executed[715]—it will remain an enormously significant opinion with regard to the underlying issues for at least two reasons: the fact that it fleshes out the constitutionally adequate procedural standards for making a determination on execution competency (by demanding that defendants have the opportunity to submit adequate expert evidence to respond to evidence on competency "solicited by the state court" as part of the defendant's "constitutionally adequate opportunity to be heard"),[716] and the fact that it clarifies the *Ford* substantive test to demand that the prisoner possess a "rational understanding"[717] of the reasons he is to be executed. Moreover, there are several other aspects of *Panetti* that need further consideration.

Although the Court does not state this directly, it was clear that, in the Fifth Circuit at least (the federal circuit that includes Texas, the state in which Panetti was convicted), the *Ford* test was no test at all. Panetti's lawyers told this to the court in their petition for *certiorari*:

> Two decades have passed since this Court decided *Ford,* and the Fifth Circuit has yet to find a *single* death row inmate incompetent to be executed. During this same period, the State of Texas has executed 360 people.[718]

In other areas of the law, the Supreme Court has considered the (lack of) value of a "paper" remedy that had never been invoked.[719] Although this aspect of Panetti's *certiorari* petition is never directly addressed in the majority's opinion, it is certainly reasonable to speculate that this sorry track record might have had some impact on the Court's thinking.

In explaining its decision, the Court stressed that, in a case in which a prisoner's mental state "is so distorted by a mental illness" that he does not share with "the community as a whole" an understanding of the concepts of crime and

---

712. *Id.* at 2870.
713. *Id.* at 2872.
714. *Id.* at 2873.
715. *See infra* Chapter 3 H 4.
716. *Id.* at 2858.
717. *Id.* at 2860.
718. Panetti v. Quarterman, 2006 WL 3880284, *26 (2006) (appellant's petition for certiorari).
719. *See* Perlin, *supra* note 112, at 634 (1993), discussing Fuentes v. Shevin, 407 U.S. 67, 85 n.14 (1972) (provision of a discovery mechanism not invoked by a single defendant in a 442-case sample).

punishment, the objective "of community vindication [is] called in question."[720] For years, scholars have been tentatively exploring the relationship between therapeutic jurisprudence[721] and the implications of the execution of persons with severe mental disabilities.[722] Here, the Court frontally considers the implications of this dilemma, and it can be safely forecast that more attention will be paid to this specific issue in the coming years.

The Court clarifies that it is limiting its decision to individuals with "severe mental illness," as opposed to those with a "misanthropic personality disorder."[723] The question of whether a personality disorder might be the basis for an insanity defense has plagued the courts for years,[724] and it can be expected that this aspect of the Court's opinion will provoke significant new future case law and scholarship.

The Court's opinion, finally, expands the role of the expert witness in competency determinations. First, its procedural prong tells us that the trial court's failure to allow the defendant to introduce evidence on this question was a failure of constitutional dimensions. Second, its conclusion's citation to the American Psychological Association's amicus brief (that had discussed the ways that experts can inform competency determinations) tells us that a majority of this Court (albeit a bare majority) is comfortable with (and responsive to) a greater role for mental health experts in judicial proceedings. We cannot underestimate the significance of this attitude.

---

720. *Panetti*, 127 S. Ct. at 2861.

721. *See supra* Chapter 1 A.

722. *See, e.g.*, David B. Wexler & Bruce J. Winick, *Therapeutic Jurisprudence as a New Approach to Mental Health Law Policy Analysis and Research*, 45 U. Miami L. Rev. 979, 992–97 (1991); Bruce J. Winick, *Competency To Be Executed: A Therapeutic Jurisprudence Perspective*, 10 Behav. Sci. & L. 317, 328–37 (1992); Arrigo & Tasca, *supra* note 537 at 43–46 (1999); Robert L. Sadoff, *Therapeutic Jurisprudence: A View from a Forensic Psychiatrist*, 10 N.Y.L. Sch. J. Hum. Rts. 825, 827 (1993). See also, Michael L. Perlin, *"The Executioner's Face Is Always Well-Hidden"* : *The Role of Counsel and the Courts in Determining Who Dies*, 41 N.Y.L. Sch. L. Rev. 201, 234 (1996); Michael L. Perlin, *A Law of Healing*, 68 U. Cin. L. Rev. 407, 432 (2000).

723. *Panetti*, 127 S. Ct. at 2862.

724. *Compare, e.g.*, United States v. Salava, 978 F.2d 320 (7th Cir. 1992) (rejecting a government argument that expert testimony on the insanity defense should be excluded because the diagnosis did not qualify as "severe" for purposes of 18 U.S.C. § 17; instead accepting the expert's opinion that the defendant's diagnosis of antisocial and paranoid personality disorder were severe), to Beiswenger v. Psychiatric Sec. Review Bd., 84 P.3d 180 (Or. Ct. App. 2004) (because legislature intended to exclude personality disorders such as sexual conduct disorders and substance abuse from the definition of "mental disease or defect" under the insanity defense, personality disorders also should not be treated as mental diseases or defects when considering the continued commitment of insanity acquittees). *See generally*, Bruce Winick, *Ambiguities in the Legal Meaning and Significance of Mental Illness*, 1 Psychol. Pub. Pol'y & L. 534 (1995) (discussing the implications of Foucha v. Louisiana, 504 U.S. 71 (1992), on this question (in *Foucha*, the Supreme Court ruled that due process barred the retention of a nonmentally ill insanity acquittee in a mental hospital).

3. Persons with Mental Retardation

While *Ford v. Wainwright*[725] clarified the question of the constitutionality of executing persons with mental illness, it did not answer the collateral and equally important issue of the constitutionality of executing individuals who have mental retardation. Three years later, in *Penry v. Lynaugh,*[726] the Supreme Court approached the question from a significantly different perspective, and reached a strikingly different conclusion.[727]

There, it initially rejected the argument that defendant's mental retardation barred capital punishment.[728] Although she conceded that the execution of the "profoundly or severely retarded" might violate the Eighth Amendment, Justice O'Connor suggested that such persons were unlikely to be convicted or face that penalty in light of "the protections afforded by the insanity defense today"[729]—an observation astonishing either in its naivete or its cynicism.[730]

It further dismissed Penry's argument that there was an "emerging national consensus" against execution of the retarded, noting that only one state had legislatively banned such executions, and rejecting Penry's evidence on this point of public opinion surveys as an "insufficient basis" upon which to ground an Eighth Amendment prohibition.[731]

On the question of whether such punishment was disproportionate, Justice O'Connor[732] rejected Penry's argument that individuals with mental retardation do not have the same degree of culpability, as they do not have the same "judgment, perspective and control as persons of normal intelligence."[733] On the record before the court, she could not conclude that *all* mentally retarded persons—"by virtue of their mental retardation alone, and apart from any individualized consideration of their personal responsibility—invariably lack the cognitive, volitional, and moral capacity to act with the degree of culpability associated with the death penalty."[734] Further, she rejected the concept that there was a baseline "mental age" beneath which one could not be executed, arguing that this sort of a bright-

---

725. 477 U.S. 399 (1986).

726. 492 U.S. 302 (1989).

727. For pre-*Penry* cases dealing with this population, *see* Bell v. Lynaugh, 858 F.2d 978 (5th Cir. 1988), *cert. denied*, 492 U.S. 925 (1989) (mentally retarded individuals subject to death penalty); State v. Jones, 378 S.E.2d 594 (S.C. 1989), *cert. denied*, 494 U.S. 1060 (1990) (same); Brogdon v. Butler, 824 F.2d 338 (5th Cir. 1987) (same).

728. *Penry,* 492 U.S. at 336.

729. *Id.,* at 3333.

730. *See generally,* Perlin, *supra* note 722.

731. *Id.* at 334. *See generally* V. Stephen Cohen, *Exempting the Mentally Retarded from the Death Penalty: A Comment on Florida's Proposed Legislation,* 19 FLA. ST. U. L. REV. 457 (1991).

732. This aspect of Justice O'Connor's opinion was not joined in by any other member of the court. The remainder of the opinion reflected a majority.

733. *Id.* at 338.

734. *Id.*

line test might have a "disempowering effect" on the mentally retarded if applied in other areas of the law (such as contracts or domestic relations).[735] She thus concluded that, while mental retardation might "lessen" a defendant's culpability, the Eighth Amendment did not preclude the execution of *any* mentally retarded person.[736]

In partial dissent,[737] Justice Brennan (for himself and for Justice Marshall)[738] stated that he would ban capital punishment in the case of any mentally retarded offender who "thus lack[ed] the full degree of responsibility for [his] crimes that is a predicate for the constitutional imposition of the death penalty."[739]

The ambiguity of the *Ford* and *Penry* opinions was substantially resolved some 13 years after *Penry* when the Supreme Court decided *Atkins v. Virginia*[740] in 2002, bringing some initial closure to this question. In *Atkins,* the Supreme Court held that the execution of people with mental retardation violated the Eighth Amendment's prohibition against cruel and unusual punishment, thus effectively overruling *Penry.*[741]

The opening paragraph of Justice Stevens' majority opinion provides important signposts as to the development of the case:

> Those mentally retarded persons who meet the law's requirements for criminal responsibility should be tried and punished when they commit crimes. Because of their disabilities in areas of reasoning, judgment, and control of their impulses, however, they do not act with the level of moral culpability that characterizes the most serious adult criminal conduct. Moreover, their impairments can jeopardize the reliability and fairness of capital proceedings against mentally retarded defendants. Presumably for these reasons, in the 13 years since we decided *Penry,* the American public, legislators, scholars, and judges have deliberated over the question whether the death penalty should ever be imposed on a mentally retarded criminal. The consensus reflected in those deliberations informs our answer to the question presented by this case: whether such executions are "cruel and unusual punishments" prohibited by the Eighth Amendment to the Federal Constitution.[742]

---

735. *Id.* at 338–40. This assertion of Justice O'Connor has been used to buttress a decision upholding the admissibility of a confession of a person with mental retardation (*see generally* 4 PERLIN, *supra* note 8, §§ 10-3 *et seq*). *See* United States v. Macklin, 900 F.2d 948, 952–53 (6th Cir. 1990), *cert. den.,* 498 U.S. 840 (1990).

736. *Id.* at 340.

737. Justices Brennan and Marshall joined in those aspects of the majority's opinion that dealt with the question of mitigation. *Id.* at 341.

738. Justice Stevens also partially dissented (for himself and Justice Blackmun), concluding that executions of the mentally retarded are unconstitutional. *Id.* at 349.

739. *Id.* at 341 (Brennan, J., concurring in part and dissenting in part).

740. 536 U.S. 304 (2002).

741. This section is largely adapted from Michael L. Perlin, *Recent Criminal Legal Decisions: Implications for Forensic Mental Health Experts,* in FORENSIC PSYCHOLOGY: ADVANCED TOPICS 333 (Alan Goldstein ed. 2006); *see also,* Michael L. Perlin, *"Life Is in Mirrors, Death Disappears":* Giving Life to Atkins, 33 N. MEX. L. REV. 315 (2003).

742. *Id.* at 306.

In coming to its decision, the court underscored its position that "it suggests that some characteristics of mental retardation undermine the strength of the procedural protections that our capital jurisprudence steadfastly guards."[743] Mental retardation, the court found, involves "not only subaverage intellectual functioning, but also significant limitations in adaptive skills such as communication, self-care, and self-direction that became manifest before age 18."[744] It continued in the same vein:

> Mentally retarded persons frequently know the difference between right and wrong and are competent to stand trial. Because of their impairments, however, by definition they have *diminished capacities* to understand and process information, to communicate, to abstract from mistakes and learn from experience, to engage in logical reasoning, to control impulses, and to understand the reactions of others.
>
> There is no evidence that they are more likely to engage in criminal conduct than others, but there is abundant evidence that they often act on impulse rather than pursuant to a premeditated plan, and that in group settings they are followers rather than leaders. Their deficiencies do not warrant an exemption from criminal sanctions, but they do diminish their personal culpability.[745]

In light of these deficiencies, the Court found that its death penalty jurisprudence provided two reasons "consistent with the legislative consensus that the mentally retarded should be categorically excluded from execution."[746] First, there is a serious question as to whether either justification that has been recognized as a basis for the death penalty applies to mentally retarded offenders. *Gregg v. Georgia*[747] identified "retribution and deterrence of capital crimes by prospective offenders" as the social purposes served by the death penalty.[748] Unless the imposition of the death penalty on a mentally retarded person "measurably contributes to one or both of these goals, it 'is nothing more than the purposeless and needless imposition of pain and suffering,' and hence an unconstitutional punishment."[749]

On the question of retribution, the Court reasoned that, in light of its precedents in this area:[750]

> If the culpability of the average murderer is insufficient to justify the most extreme sanction available to the State, the lesser culpability of the mentally retarded offender surely does not merit that form of retribution. Thus, pursuant to our narrow-

---

743. *Id.* at 317.
744. *Id.* at 318.
745. *Id.* (Emphasis added).
746. *Id.*
747. 428 U.S. 153 (1976).
748. *Id.* at 183.
749. *Atkins,* 536 U.S. at 319, quoting Enmund v. Florida, 458 U.S. 782, 798 (1982).
750. *E.g.,* Godfrey v. Georgia, 446 U.S. 420, 433 (1980), vacating death sentence because petitioner's crimes did not reflect "a consciousness materially more 'depraved' than that of any person guilty of murder."

ing jurisprudence, which seeks to ensure that only the most deserving of execution are put to death, an exclusion for the mentally retarded is appropriate.[751]

On the question of deterrence, the Court again looked at earlier cases for a restatement of the proposition that "capital punishment can serve as a deterrent only when murder is the result of premeditation and deliberation,"[752] and pointed out that "Exempting the mentally retarded from that punishment will not affect the 'cold calculus that precedes the decision' of other potential murderers," that sort of calculus being "at the opposite end of the spectrum from behavior of mentally retarded offenders."[753] Deterrence, the Court noted, is predicated upon the notion that the increased severity of the punishment will inhibit criminal actors from carrying out murderous conduct. "Yet it is the same cognitive and behavioral impairments that make these defendants less morally culpable—for example, the diminished ability to understand and process information, to learn from experience, to engage in logical reasoning, or to control impulses—that also make it less likely that they can process the information of the possibility of execution as a penalty and, as a result, control their conduct based upon that information."[754] Nor will exempting persons with mental retardation from execution lessen the deterrent effect of the death penalty with respect to nonretarded offenders, the Court added. "Such individuals are unprotected by the exemption and will continue to face the threat of execution. Thus, executing the mentally retarded will not measurably further the goal of deterrence."[755]

The reduced capacity of mentally retarded offenders provided an additional justification for a categorical rule making such offenders ineligible for the death penalty.[756] The Court noted that there was an "enhanced" risk of improperly imposed death penalty in cases involving defendants with mental retardation because of the possibility of false confessions, as well as "the lesser ability of mentally retarded defendants to make a persuasive showing of mitigation in the face of prosecutorial evidence of one or more aggravating factors."[757] The Court also stressed several additional interrelated issues: the difficulties that persons with mental retardation may have in providing meaningful assistance to their counsel, their status as "typically poor witnesses," and the ways that their demeanor "may create an unwarranted impression of lack of remorse for their crimes."[758]

Here, the Court acknowledged an important difficulty: "reliance on mental retardation as a mitigating factor can be a two-edged sword that may enhance the likelihood that the aggravating factor of future dangerousness will be found by the jury," raising the specter that "mentally retarded defendants in the aggregate face a special risk of wrongful execution."[759] It thus concluded:

751. *Atkins,* 536 U.S. at 319.
752. *Enmund,* 458 at 799.
753. *Atkins,* 536 U.S. at 320, citing, in part, *Gregg,* 428 U.S. at 186.
754. *Id.*
755. *Id.*
756. *Id.* at 320.
757. *Id.*
758. *Id.* at 321.
759. *Id.*

Construing and applying the Eighth Amendment in the light of our "evolving standards of decency," we therefore conclude that such punishment is excessive and that the Constitution "places a substantive restriction on the State's power to take the life" of a mentally retarded offender.[760]

There were two dissents. Dissenting for himself, Justice Thomas, and Justice Scalia, the Chief Justice criticized that part of the majority's methodology that had relied upon public opinion polls, the views of professional and religious organizations, and the status of the death penalty in other nations as part of the basis for its decision.[761] Justice Scalia also dissented (for himself, the Chief Justice, and Justice Thomas), noting, "Seldom has an opinion of this Court rested so obviously upon nothing but the personal views of its members."[762]

On the deterrence issue, Justice Scalia concluded that "the deterrent effect of a penalty is adequately vindicated if it successfully deters many, but not all, of the target class."[763] Again, he rejected what he characterized as the majority's "flabby" argument that persons with mental retardation faced a "special risk" for wrongful execution (suggesting that "just plain stupid. . . , inarticulate . . . or even ugly people" might face a similar risk, but that, if this were in fact so, it was not an issue that came within the ambit of the Eighth Amendment).[764]

Finally, he expressed his "fear of faking":

> One need only read the definitions of mental retardation adopted by the American Association of Mental Retardation and the American Psychiatric Association to realize that the symptoms of this condition can readily be feigned. And. . . . the capital defendant who feigns mental retardation risks nothing at all.[765]

"Nothing has changed," he concluded, in the nearly 300 years since Hale wrote his *Pleas of the Crown:*

> [Determination of a person's incapacity] is a matter of great difficulty, partly from the easiness of counterfeiting this disability . . . and partly from the variety of the degrees of this infirmity, whereof some are sufficient, and some are insufficient to excuse persons in capital offenses.[766]

a. Issues for experts after Atkins

One of the critical issues that remains in the aftermath of *Atkins* is its impact on expert witnesses. The expert's role in almost any case involving a defendant with

---

760. *Id.* at 321, quoting, in part, *Ford,* 477 U.S. at 305.
761. *Id.* at 322–25.
762. *Id.* at 338.
763. *Id.*
764. *Id.* at 352.
765. *Id.* at 354.
766. *Id.*

a mental disability charged with crime is significant. But, in death penalty cases in which the question as to death-eligibility is whether the defendant can be categorized in a way that comports with a specific disabling condition, the role of the expert is perhaps greater than in virtually any other area of criminal law.

What are some of the factors that the expert must consider? "Speech, language and memory impairments, physical and motor disabilities, IQ examinations and other tests require a professional evaluation and assessment by various mental health experts."[767] Such experts should be able to convey to the jury "the effects that mental retardation has on behavior and decision-making, explain the vulnerable and suggestible nature of a mentally retarded individual, and educate juries about the full spectrum of mental retardation, irrespective of the defendant's appearance or demeanor," and must be able to "state their findings in plain, comprehensible language and common sense terms used by the average person."[768] Also, the expert must be willing and able to "consult school records, placement records, psychoeducational reports, individualized education plans, interviews with parents and teachers if possible, vocational, employment, and military records, criminal records, prison records, and probation and state agency records."[769]

Most importantly, the post-*Atkins* expert must have the ability to contextualize the meaning of IQ scores and functional abilities for fact finders. *Atkins* endorses a definition of mental retardation that subsumes "subaverage intellectual functioning [and] significant limitations in adaptive skills such as communication, self-care, and self-direction that became manifest before age 18."[770] There is no question that, in assessing who is "subaverage," the defendant's IQ score will be of critical, perhaps dispositive, importance in determining death eligibility. This is inherently problematic, for multiple "real life" reasons.

The difference between an IQ score of 68 (and thus within the definition of "mentally retarded") and a score of 72 (and thus outside that definition) is often statistically and functionally meaningless. Already, some post-*Atkins* decisions and many post-*Atkins* statutes have talismanically focused on the 70 IQ cutoff as a precise eligibility number.[771] Given the accepted and well-known error of measurement of 5%,[772] the arbitrariness of using a unitary cutoff score,[773] the subjec-

---

767. Shruti S. B. Desai, *Effective Capital Representation of the Mentally Retarded Defendant,* 13 CAP. DEF. J. 251, 268 (2001).

768. *Id.,* quoting John H. Blume & Pamela Blume Leonard, *Principles of Developing and Presenting Mental Health Evidence in Criminal Cases,* 24 CHAMPION 63, 67 (2000).

769. John Fabian, *Death Penalty Mitigation and the Role of the Forensic Psychologist,* 27 LAW & PSYCHOL. REV. 73, 114 (2003), citing Denis W. Keyes et al., *Mitigating Mental Retardation in Capital Cases: Finding the "Invisible" Defendant,* 22 MENT. & PHYS. DISABILITY L. REP. 529, 533–35 (1998).

770. *Atkins,* 536 U.S. at 318.

771. *See* Douglas Mossman, *Atkins v. Virginia: A Psychiatric Can of Worms,* 33 N.M. L. REV. 255, 268–69 (2003), discussing Murphy v. State, 54 P.3d 556, 568 (Okla. Crim. App. 2002), and State v. Lott, 779 N.E.2d 1011, 1014 (Ohio 2002).

772. *Id.* at 269.

773. Note, *Implementing Atkins,* 116 HARV. L. REV. 2565, 2573–74 (2003).

tivity in scoring,[774] the phenomenon known as the "Flynn effect" (document-ing a worldwide rise in IQ scores),[775] the "slipperiness" of quantifying "adaptive skills,"[776] experts are in the untenable position of working in a legal environment that presumes a dyadic universe (retarded/not retarded) that does not exist else-where. Cases such as *Walters v. Johnson*[777] and *State v. Kelly*[778]—that refer to the WAIS test as the "gold standard" of testing—inevitably make the enterprise more difficult.

The expert must understand that courts—often following the direct orders of state statute—will seek to limit their testimony to nothing more than numbers. In response, the expert must be ready to (1) explain the limitations of *any* numerical cutoff, and (2) contextualize the score in light of the defendant's adaptive and functional abilities.

Experts must also acknowledge that they will be working with a wide range of lawyers, from the very best to the very worst. In no area of the law is this range more puzzling and more confounding than in death penalty litigation: some de-fendants are represented by death penalty specialists whose entire careers are de-voted to this difficult work; others are represented by the "bottom of the barrel,"[779] a universe whose profound ineptitude has led some scholars to conclude that the most important variable in determining which defendants are to be put to death is the quality of the defendant's trial lawyer.[780] Such lawyers were characterized some 30 years ago by Judge David Bazelon as "walking violations of the Sixth Amendment."[781] That characterization, unfortunately, has not worn thin.

Even if the defendant is fortunate enough to *not* be assigned such counsel, the expert may still find that counsel is, nonetheless, poorly informed about mental disabilities. The lawyer may not understand what mental retardation *is*. The law-yer may not know the difference between mental retardation and mental illness. The lawyer may rely solely on visual stereotypes of mental retardation (e.g., is the defendant rocking? Drooling?).[782] He may rely on one piece of evidence of "nor-mal" behavior as a sufficient basis upon which to reject retardation. He may mis-interpret a defendant's obliging, confirmatory response to questions as evidence of the defendant's average (or better than average) intelligence. And the lawyer may have no idea—in the cases of defendants whose retardation falls just outside

---

774. Mossman, *supra* note 771, at 269.

775. *See generally,* James Flynn, *The Hidden History of IQ and Special Education: Can the Problems Be Solved?* 6 Psychol., Pub. Pol'y & L. 191 (2000).

776. Note, *supra* note 773, at 2575–76.

777. Walters v. Johnson, 269 F. Supp. 2d 692, 695 (W.D. Va. 2003).

778. State v. Kelly, 2002 WL 31730874, *11 (Tenn. Ct. Crim. App. 2002).

779. Stephanie Saul, *When Death Is the Penalty: Attorneys for Poor Defendants Often Lack Experience and Skill,* N.Y. Newsday, Nov. 25, 1991, at 8.

780. Stephen B. Bright, *Death By Lottery—Procedural Bar of Constitutional Claims in Capi-tal Cases Due to Inadequate Representation of Indigent Defendants,* 92 W. Va. L. Rev. 679, 695 (1990).

781. David L. Bazelon, *The Defective Assistance of Counsel,* 42 U. Cin. L. Rev. 1, 2 (1973).

782. Keyes, *supra* note 769, at 536.

the numerical cutoff range (in those jurisdictions using such cutoffs)—how to develop mitigation evidence based on the client's mental state.[783]

The revolution embedded in the *Atkins* decision will be meaningless unless expert witnesses understand its full meaning, take seriously both the demands it places on them, as well as the pervasiveness of bias in this area, and unless they seriously consider their need to be connected with counsel throughout the entire enterprise. Their expertise in making an assessment of the existence or absence of mental retardation is lost on the process if counsel does not appreciate how to develop the testimony, anticipate and deal with challenges to it, and ensure that the expert's findings can be taken into proper account by the fact finder. In this new and critical area of death penalty jurisprudence, the potential for both inadequate representation and inadequate expert assistance is great; consultation and close collaboration is imperative.

b. Atkins *and sanism*

In considering the real world impact of *Atkins,* it is necessary to assess the degree to which juror sanism will affect and infect judicial decision-making. In an earlier paper, one of the authors (MLP) said this:

> A review of case law, controlled behavioral research and "real life" research not only casts grave doubt on its validity, but tends to reveal the opposite: that jurors generally distrust mental disability evidence, that they see it as a mitigating factor only in a handful of circumscribed situations (most of which are far removed from the typical scenario in a death penalty case), that lawyers representing capital defendants are intensely skeptical of jurors' ability to correctly construe such evidence, and that jurors actually impose certain preconceived schemas in such cases that, paradoxically, result in outcomes where the most mentally disabled persons (those regularly receiving doses of powerful antipsychotic medications) are treated the most harshly, and that jurors tend to over-impose the death penalty on severely mentally disabled defendants.

Why is this? I argue that it results from a combination of important factors: jurors' use of cognitive simplifying devices (heuristics) in which vivid, negative experiences overwhelm rational data (and a death penalty case is a fertile environment for such cognitive distortions) and which reify their sanist attitudes, courts' pretextuality in deciding cases involving mentally disabled criminal defendants, and courts' teleological decision-making in reviewing such cases.[784]

Again, jurors' focus on visual cues and clues (e.g., is the defendant drooling?)[785]

---

783. *See generally,* Fabian, *supra* note 769.

784. Michael L. Perlin, *The Sanist Lives of Jurors in Death Penalty Cases: The Puzzling Role of "Mitigating" Mental Disability Evidence,* 8 NOTRE DAME J.L., ETHICS & PUB. POL'Y 239, 241–42 (1994).

785. *See id.* at 265("[T]he public has always demanded that mentally ill defendants comport with its visual images of 'craziness.'").

the judiciary's obsessive preoccupation with the possibility of malingering, and the possibility that mental retardation may be used as an aggravating (rather than mitigating) factor at the penalty phase (to determine whether capital punishment should be imposed) all counsel us to be extraordinarily vigilant in our efforts to eradicate sanism in such cases.

4. The Use of Medication to Make a Death Row Inmate Competent to Be Executed

One question that was not addressed directly in *Ford v. Wainwright*,[786] in *Penry v. Lynaugh*,[787] or in *Atkins v. Virginia*,[788] was whether a state could involuntarily medicate an individual under a death sentence so as to make him competent to be executed.[789] The Supreme Court granted certiorari in *Perry v. Louisiana*[790] (presenting this precise question), thus making it appear that this gap would be resolved. However the Court declined to rule on the merits, remanding the case, instead, to the Louisiana Supreme Court for reconsideration[791] in light of the decision in *Washington v. Harper*.[792]

On remand, the Louisiana Supreme Court found, under *state* constitutional law,[793] that the state was prohibited from medicating Perry to make him competent to be executed.[794] Concluded the court:

> For centuries no jurisdiction has approved the execution of the insane. The state's attempt to circumvent this well-settled prohibition by forcibly medicating an insane prisoner with antipsychotic drugs violates his rights under our state constitution. . . . First, it violates his right to privacy or personhood. Such involuntary medication requires the unjustified invasion of his brain and body with discomforting, potentially dangerous and painful drugs, the seizure of control of his mind and thoughts, and the usurpation of his right to make decisions regarding his health or medical treatment. Furthermore, implementation of the state's plan to medicate forcibly and execute the insane prisoner would constitute cruel, excessive and unusual punishment. This particular application of the death penalty fails to measurably contribute

---

786. 477 U.S. 399 (1986).

787. 492 U.S. 302 (1989).

788. 536 U.S. 304 (2002).

789. On refusal of medication generally, *see* 2 PERLIN, *supra* note 8, §§ 3B-1 et seq (2d ed. 1999). On prisoners' right to refuse medication, *see id.,* § 3B-8.2; *see generally* Washington v. Harper, 494 U.S. 210 (1990). *See infra* Chapter 3B.

790. 494 U.S. 1015 (1990).

791. 498 U.S. 38 (1990), *reh'g denied,* 498 U.S. 1075 (1991).

792. 494 U.S. 210 (1990).

793. A state can always provide more rights to a criminal defendant under its constitution than are afforded to the defendant under the U.S. Constitution, but can never afford fewer. See, e.g., ERWIN CHEMERINSKY ET AL., FEDERAL JURISDICTION § 10.5, at 707 (4th ed. 2003) ("State constitutions can provide more rights than exist under the United States Constitution, but the state court must make it clear that the decision is based on the state constitution.").

794. State v. Perry, 610 So. 2d 746 (La. 1992).

to the social goals of capital punishment. Carrying out this punitive scheme would add severity and indignity to the prisoner's punishment beyond that required for the mere extinguishment of life. This type of punitive treatment system is not accepted anywhere in contemporary society and is apt to be administered erroneously, arbitrarily or capriciously.[795]

This decision was not re-appealed to the Supreme Court (no doubt because of its state constitutional law basis).

While the Supreme Court's disposition of *Perry* did not clarify the underlying issues,[796] it appeared inevitable that this question would arise again in the future, thus giving the Court, if it so chose, a second chance to weigh the competing values. Yet, for 15 years this did not happen, and the only relevant developments were in the lower federal courts and the state courts.

By way of examples, the South Carolina Supreme Court relied upon the Louisiana Supreme Court's decision in *Perry* to support its conclusion that medicating a defendant to make him competent to be executed would violate the South Carolina *state* constitution.[797] On the other hand, in *Singleton v. Norris*,[798] the Arkansas Supreme Court ruled that the state had the burden to administer antipsychotic medication as long as a prisoner was alive and was a potential danger either to himself or to others, and that the collateral effect of the involuntary medication—rendering him competent to understand the nature and reason for his execution—did not violate due process. The Supreme Court subsequently denied certiorari.[799]

Later, in the *Singleton* litigation, Singleton filed a petition for a writ of habeas corpus seeking a stay of execution. Denial of the writ was affirmed by the Eighth Circuit, which held that neither due process nor the Eighth Amendment prevented the state from executing an inmate who has regained competency as the result of forced medication that is part of "appropriate medical care."[800]

Turning to the substantive question, the Court noted that it was guided by both *Harper* and *Ford* and that its task was to weigh the State's interest in carrying out a lawfully imposed sentence against Singleton's interest in refusing medication. The Court found that Singleton "prefers to take the medication rather than be in an unmedicated and psychotic state" and that he suffered no substantial

795. *Id.* at 747–48.
796. On the right of defendants awaiting trial or at trial to refuse the involuntary administration of antipsychotic medication, *see* Riggins v. Nevada, 504 U.S. 127 (1992), discussed in 2 PERLIN, *supra* note 8, § 3B-8.3.
797. Singleton v. State, 437 S.E.2d 53, 60–62 (S.C. 1993).
798. 338 Ark. 135, 992 S.W.2d 768 (1999).
799. *See* 528 U.S. 1084 (2000). *Singleton* is criticized in Rebecca A. Miller-Rice, *The "Insane" Contradiction of Singleton v. Norris: Forced Medication in a Death Row Inmate's Medical Interest Which Happens to Facilitate His Execution*, 22 U. ARK. LITTLE ROCK L. REV. 659 (2000), and in Kelly Gabos, *The Perils of Singleton v. Norris: Ethics and Beyond*, 32 AM. J. L. & MED. 117 (2006).
800. 319 F.3d 1018 (8th Cir. 2003), *cert den.*, 540 U.S. 832 (2003).

side effects.[801] It held that as a result, the State's interest in carrying out its lawfully imposed sentence was the "superior one."[802] The Court went on to note that Singleton had proposed no less intrusive means of insuring his competence and never argued that he was not competent with the medication—other than to put forth what the Court termed his "artificial competence theory."[803]

The Court then turned to what it deemed the "core of the dispute," namely "whether the antipsychotic medication is medically appropriate for Singleton's treatment."[804] The Court found Singleton to have "implicitly conceded" that the treatment was in his short-term medical interest.[805] In addressing his central claims, the Court reasoned:

> Singleton's argument regarding his long-term medical interest boils down to an assertion that execution is not in his medical interest. Eligibility for execution is the only unwanted consequence of the medication. The due process interests in life and liberty that Singleton asserts have been foreclosed by the lawfully imposed sentence of execution and the Harper procedure. In the circumstances presented in this case, the best medical interests of the prisoner must be determined without regard to whether there is a pending date of execution. Thus, we hold that the mandatory medication regime, valid under the pendency of a stay of execution, does not become unconstitutional under *Harper* when an execution date is set.[806]

The Court also rejected Singleton's claim, based on *State v. Perry*, that the Eighth Amendment prohibited execution of one who is made "artificially competent":

> Closely related to his due process argument, Singleton also claims that the Eighth Amendment forbids the execution of a prisoner who is "artificially competent." Singleton relies principally on a case construing an analogous provision in the Louisiana Constitution. State v. Perry, 610 So. 2d 746 (La. 1992). . . . We note, however, that the *Perry* court accepted the view of "best medical interests" that we have rejected. 610 So. 2d at 766. The court also found Perry's medication was ordered solely for purposes of punishment and not for legitimate reasons of prison security or medical need. 610 So. 2d at 757. We decline to undertake a difficult and unnecessary inquiry into the State's motives in circumstance [*sic*] where it has a duty to provide medical care.[807]

Citing *Estelle v. Gamble*,[808] for the proposition that the government has an obligation to provide medical care to those whom it incarcerates, the Court reasoned that "any additional motive or effect is irrelevant." It concluded:

801. 319 F.3d at 1025.
802. *Id.*
803. *Id.*
804. *Id.*
805. *Id.* at 1026.
806. *Id.*
807. *Id.* at 1027.
808. 429 U.S. 97, 103 (1976).

Ford prohibits only the execution of a prisoner who is unaware of the punishment he is about to receive and why he is to receive it. A State does not violate the Eighth Amendment as interpreted by Ford when it executes a prisoner who became incompetent during his long stay on death row but who subsequently regained competency through appropriate medical care.[809]

In a dissenting opinion, Judge Heaney stated:

I believe that to execute a man who is severely deranged without treatment, and arguably incompetent when treated, is the pinnacle of what Justice Marshall called "the barbarity of exacting mindless vengeance."[810]

Judge Heaney went on to cite facts from the record that indicated that even in a medicated state, Singleton appeared not to fully or rationally comprehend death or the nature of his sentence. After noting examples of Singleton's beliefs regarding death, including the belief that his victim was not truly dead and that a person can be executed by correctional officers and then have his breathing "started up again" by judges, he turned to a discussion of "synthetic" sanity:

Singleton's case is exemplary of the unpredictable result antipsychotic treatment has on mentally ill prisoners. . . . Based on the medical history in this case, I am left with no alternative but to conclude that drug-induced sanity is not the same as true sanity. Singleton is not "cured"; his insanity is merely muted, at times, by the powerful drugs he is forced to take. Underneath this mask of stability, he remains insane. Ford's prohibition on executing the insane should apply with no less force to Singleton than to untreated prisoners.[811]

Finally, noting the impact of the majority's ruling not only on mentally ill prisoners but on the integrity of the medical profession, the dissent concluded:

I would hold that the State may continue to medicate Singleton, voluntarily or involuntarily, if it is necessary to protect him or others and is in his best medical interest, but it may not execute him. I continue to believe that the appropriate remedy is for the district court to enter a permanent stay of execution.[812]

Several years later, in *Panetti v. Dretke,*[813] the Fifth Circuit found that a medicated defendant was competent to be executed. There, it affirmed a decision of

809. *Singleton,* 319 F. 3d at 1030, citing *Ford,* 429 U.S. at 103.
810. *Id.,* citing Ford. v. Wainwright, 477 U.S. 399, 410 (1986).
811. *Id.* at 1034.
812. *Id.* at 1037.
  The U.S. Supreme Court denied certiorari, *see* 540 U.S. 832 (2003), and after more than 20 years on death row, Singleton was executed in January of 2004.
813. 448 F. 3d 815 (5th Cir. 2006).

the district court that had found that the defendant suffered from schizoaffective disorder, and had a "delusional belief system in which he viewed himself as
being persecuted for his religious activities and beliefs," believing that the State
is "in league with the forces of evil to prevent him from preaching the Gospel."
Nonetheless, as the defendant was aware that he was to be executed, that he had
committed the murders for which he was convicted and sentenced to death, and
that the "State's stated reason for executing him is that he committed two murders," the district court held that Panetti was competent to be executed.[814] The
Supreme Court subsequently granted certoriari and ultimately reversed, holding
that the defendant was denied the constitutional procedures to which he was
entitled under *Ford*.[815] The decision, however, did not discuss the issue of involuntary medication, so this question remains unresolved.

5. Competency to Waive Right to Federal Habeas Corpus Review[816]

At virtually the same time that the Supreme Court held that jury discretion
was a necessary element of a constitutionally valid capital sentencing statutory
scheme,[817] it also held that a death row prisoner could knowingly and intelligently waive further post-conviction review,[818] thus reaffirming its classic test set
out nearly 4 decades earlier in *Johnson v. Zerbst:*[819] in order to allow waiver of a
federally guaranteed right, the court must be convinced that the waiver decision
is made intelligently and competently.[820]

The issue of competence becomes central to a waiver determination, particu-

---

814. *Id.* at 817.

815. Panetti v. Quarterman, 127 S.Ct. 2842 (2007).

816. This section is generally adapted from 4 PERLIN, *supra* note 8, §12-5.

817. *See* Gregg v. Georgia, 428 U.S. 153 (1976).

818. "The Court is convinced that Gary Mark Gilmore made a knowing and intelligent
waiver of any and all federal rights he might have asserted after the Utah trial court's sentence
was imposed." Gilmore v. Utah, 429 U.S. 1012, 1013 (1976). For later cases on this question,
see, e.g., Vargas v. Lambert, 159 F.3d 1161 (9th Cir.), *stay vacated,* 525 U.S. 925 (1998) (mother
had standing to seek stay of execution to allow for hearing on prisoner's current competency);
O'Rourke v. Endell, 153 F.3d 560 (8th Cir. 1998), *reh'g & suggestion for reh'g en banc denied*
(1998), *cert. denied,* 525 U.S. 1148 (1999) (state court denied defendant due process when it
failed to appoint attorney to argue that defendant lacked competency to waive appeal in post-
conviction proceedings).

819. 304 U.S. 458 (1938).

820. *Id.* at 465. *Johnson* characterized waiver as an "intentional relinquishment or abandonment of a known right or privilege." *Id.* at 464. For a helpful, if somewhat dated, overview of the
issue of waiver in general, *see* Comment, *Criminal Waiver: The Requirements of Personal Participation, Competence and Legitimate State Interest,* 54 CALIF. L. REV. 1262 (1966). For subsequent
perspectives, *see* Julie Levinsohn Milner, *Dignity or Death Row? Are Death Row Rights to Die
Diminished? A Comparison of the Right to Die for the Terminally Ill and the Terminally Sentenced,* 24
NEW ENG. J. CRIM. & CIV. CONFINEMENT 281 (1998); Matthew Norman, *Standards and Procedures for Determining Whether a Defendant Is Competent to Make the Ultimate Choice—Death:
Ohio's New Precedent for Death Row "Volunteers,"* 13 J.L. & HEALTH 103 (1998–99).

larly because of the procedural posture in which the challenge is framed. Often, a third party will seek to obtain post-conviction review on behalf of or as next friend of a prisoner who refuses to seek review for himself,[821] and the prisoner's competency thus becomes pivotal in determining whether or not a third party will have standing to proceed.[822] Given the general "standing" doctrine in federal courts—if one refuses to assert his or her constitutional rights, barring incapacity or lack of access to the courts, no one else may raise them for the individual[823]—if a prisoner, sentenced to death, is found competent to "knowingly and intelligently" waive habeas relief (or any other post-conviction remedy), he may do so, and third parties may not seek further review for him.[824]

A court's inquiry into mental competency is specific to the time when a defendant has chosen to relinquish his post-conviction rights.[825] Acknowledging the critical importance of such procedures, because of the "obviously irreversible nature of the death penalty,"[826] courts thus demand some level of psychiatric and psychological scrutiny prior to making their determination on this question.[827]

The Supreme Court set out the test for determination of mental incompetence when a prisoner chose to forego further appeals in the capital punishment case of *Rees v. Peyton*.[828] There, after the district court's rejection of Rees' federal habeas claims was affirmed by the Fourth Circuit,[829] a petition for *certiorari* was filed in the Supreme Court.[830] Rees instructed his counsel to withdraw the petition and abandon further legal proceedings;[831] his counsel, however, was unwilling to withdraw the petition absent a psychiatric evaluation.[832]

In a brief and unanimous *per curiam* opinion, the Court determined that it was

---

821. *See* Tim Kaine, *Capital Punishment and the Waiver of Sentence Review*, 18 HARV. C.R.-C.L.L. REV. 483, 492 (1983).

822. *See generally, e.g.,* Richard Strafer, *Volunteering for Execution: Competency, Voluntariness and the Propriety of Third Party Intervention*, 74 J. CRIM. L. & CRIMINOLOGY 860 (1983).

823. *See* Kaine, *supra* note 821, at 493 n.41.

824. On the issue of "volunteering" for executions in general, *see* Strafer, *supra* note 822, at 911–12.

825. *See* Demosthenes v. Baal, 495 U.S. 731 (1990) (state court finding that inmate was competent to waive his right to pursue post-conviction relief was binding on federal habeas court).

826. Hays v. Murphy, 663 F.2d 1004, 1013 (10th Cir. 1981) (quoting Evans v. Bennett, 440 U.S. 1301, 1306 (1979)).

827. In *Hays,* 663 F.2d at 1005, the court noted that sufficient evidence of mental impairment had been presented earlier in the proceedings to require careful examination and evaluation. The limited observations made of defendant by experts were shown by the record to have been insufficient to determine the critical questions involved, and the case was thus remanded for further proceedings.

828. 384 U.S. 312 (1966).

829. Rees v. Peyton, 225 F. Supp. 507 (E.D. Va. 1964), *aff'd,* 341 F.2d 859 (4th Cir. 1965), *cert. den.,* 516 U.S. 802 (1995).

830. *Rees,* 384 U.S. at 313.

831. *Id.*

832. *Id.*

ultimately its reponsibility to determine the question as to whether Rees would be allowed to withdraw his petition, and that, in the resolution of that determination, Rees' mental competence was "of prime importance."[833] It was necessary to consider whether Rees had "the capacity to appreciate his position and make a rational choice with respect to continuing or abandoning further litigation or on the other hand whether he is suffering from a mental disease, disorder, or defect which may substantially affect his capacity in the premises."[834]

The Rees test[835] has been interpreted as an application of three questions:

1. Is the person suffering from a mental disease or defect?
2. If the person is suffering from a mental disease or defect, does that disease or defect prevent him from understanding his legal position and the options available to him?
3. If the person is suffering from a mental disease or defect that does not prevent him from understanding his legal position and the options available to him, does that disease or defect, nevertheless, prevent him from making a rational choice among his options?[836]

If the court answers the first question in the negative, it need not go further.[837] Likewise, where a defendant was found competent by three examining psychiatrists to plead guilty to a series of felony charges (including murder), and no further psychiatric testimony of incompetence was submitted, the evidence was deemed insufficient to grant petitioners standing to proceed as "next friends."[838] *Some* minimum showing of incompetence must appear before a competency hearing is deemed necessary.[839]

---

833. *Id.*

834. *Id.* at 314.

The *Rees* test is criticized in Franz v. State, 754 S.W. 2d 839, 843 (Ark. 1988), and in Strafer, *supra* note 822.

835. *Rees* remained pending in the Supreme Court for 30 years. See Rees v. Sup't, Virginia State Penitentiary, 516 U.S. 802 (1995) (denying *certiorari*). The earlier history of the *Rees* case is discussed in Rumbaugh v. Procunier, 753 F.2d 393, 398 n.1 (5th Cir.), *cert. denied,* 473 U.S. 919 (1985), and *id., 753* F.2d at 403 n.1 (Goldberg, J., dissenting).

836. *Rumbaugh,* 753 F.2d at 398.

837. *Id.*

838. *See, e.g.,* Lenhard v. Wolf, 603 F.2d 91, 93 (9th Cir. 1979).

839. *Id.* at 95. *Rumbaugh* has been cited as providing "appropriate judicial guidance" in Streetman v. Lynaugh, 674 F. Supp. 229, 236 (E.D. Tex. 1987).

For subsequent litigation, *see* Lonchar v. Zant, 978 F.2d 637 (11th Cir. 1992), *cert. denied,* 507 U.S. 956 (1993) (defendant's sister lacked standing to petition court for writ of habeas corpus as defendant's next friend); *In re* Cockrum, 867 F. Supp. 494 (E.D. Tex. 1994) (appointed counsel sufficiently dedicated to defendant's best interest for purposes of being appointed as "next friend" for purposes of pursuing habeas corpus writ); Calambro v. Second Judicial Dist. Ct., 114 Nev. 106, 964 P.2d 794 (1998) (because defendant was competent, petitioner-mother lacked standing to file "next friend" petition); *In re* Heidnik, 112 F.3d 105 (3d Cir. 1997) (daughter met burden of establishing defendant's inability to prosecute action on his own).

The second threshold finding—that the defendant's understanding has been compromised by mental disease or defect—is predominantly answered by the testimony of the mental health experts involved.[840] To this extent, one court granted a stay of execution pending a competency hearing following allegations that the post-conviction maintenance of defendant on antidepression and antianxiety drugs had rendered him "unable to appreciate, realize or reconsider the impact of his decision to forego further judicial relief."[841] In granting a stay, the district court explicitly instructed that sufficient time be allowed before examination to permit the effects of the drugs impairing the defendant's judgment to abate.[842]

The final question—whether the mental impairment prevented the defendant from making a rational choice in foregoing subsequent available remedies—is the most difficult one. Various reasons have been suggested to justify a death row prisoner's decision to give up his remaining appeals: "depression over the lengthy appeals process, despair over abysmal prison conditions on death row, desire to spare one's family from continuing anguish."[843] Whether any decision refusing to forestall death can be characterized as "rational" presents a difficult ethical and philosophical issue that the courts will ultimately have to resolve.[844]

In a later attempt to resolve this issue, one district court clearly defaulted to a decision based on the defendant's "understanding":[845]

> In order to find that [defendant's] decision is rational, this court need not agree that [his] decision is the "correct" one or the "best" one; the question is only whether or not his decision is based on a rational understanding of the circumstances before him.[846]

---

840. *See, e.g., Rumbaugh,* 753 F.2d at 399–400.

841. Groseclose *ex rel.* Harries v. Dutton, 589 F. Supp. 362, 363 (M.D. Tenn. 1984).

842. *Id.* at 366.

843. Kaine, *supra* note 776, at 490.

844. On the burden of proof issue, *compare* Groseclose *ex rel.* Harries v. Dutton, 594 F. Supp. 949, 953 (M.D. Tenn. 1984) (petitioner bears risk of non-persuasion on competency) *with* Smith by and through Smith v. Armontrout, 632 F. Supp. 503, 515 (W.D. Mo. 1986), *aff'd,* 812 F.2d 1050 (8th Cir. 1987) (state bears burden of persuasion).

845. *Smith by and through Smith,* 632 F. Supp. at 509.

846. *Id.* Subsequently, the court reasoned that, while a false sign of helplessness is a sign of a mentally disturbed individual, the defendant's state of hopelessness was a reasonable assessment of his situation. It thus concluded that, while the deplorable conditions on death row undoubtedly had some effect on the defendant, they did not render his decision involuntary. *Id.* at 515.

Although the court found the defendant to suffer from severe mental disorders, it further found that he was sufficiently competent to forego further review of his capital murder conviction and death sentence. *Id.* at 514.

For earlier proceedings in the same aspect of this litigation, *see* Smith by and through Smith v. Armontrout, 604 F. Supp. 840 (W.D. Mo. 1985). For subsequent proceedings, *see* Smith v. Armontrout, 692 F. Supp. 1079 (W.D. Mo.), *appeal dismissed,* 857 F.2d 1228, *supplemented,* 865 F.2d 1502 (8th Cir. 1988); *see also id.* 888 F.2d 530 (8th Cir. 1989).

A marginally more insightful analysis was sketched out by the Fifth Circuit in *Rumbaugh v. Procunier,*[847] in which the court initially acknowledged the existence of mental disease that "does not impair the cognitive function but impacts only on the volitional, the person's ability to make a rational choice among available options."[848] There, the Court of Appeals affirmed a trial court decision holding that the defendant possessed the requisite mental competence to waive federal habeas review.[849] The Court appeared to rely on expert testimony[850] that found the defendant to be mentally ill but nonetheless able to "have a rational understanding of [his] current situation or logical understanding of [his] current situation."[851] His decision was thus the "product of a reasonable assessment of the legal and medical facts and a reasoned thought process, albeit one that we would disagree with."[852]

In a stinging dissent,[853] Judge Goldberg attempted to clarify the meaning of *Rees'* use of the phrase "rational choice."[854] According to his opinion, "rational choice" requires that the actor has been shown to choose means that relate logically to his ends, and that the ends of his actions are his ends.[855] By erroneously equating "rational" with "logical," the majority—in Judge Goldberg's view—

847. 753 F.2d 393 (5th Cir. 1985).

848. *Id.* at 399. *See id.* at n.2, and *Smith by and through Smith,* 604 F. Supp. at 842 (citing cases).

849. Rumbaugh v. Estelle, 558 F. Supp. 651 (N.D. Tex. 1983), *aff'd sub nom.* Rumbaugh v. Procunier, 753 F.2d 395 (5th Cir. 1985).

850. For the internal conflict in expert testimony, *see Rumbaugh,* 753 F.2d at 399–400. On the question of the authority to appoint an expert in such a case, *see Smith by and through Smith,* 604 F. Supp. at 843–45.

851. *Rumbaugh,* 753 F.2d at 400.

852. *Id.* at 402:

It appears that Charles Rumbaugh is able to feed relevant facts into a rational decision-making process and come to a reasoned decision; that one of the facts fed into the process is that Rumbaugh is mentally ill, he has severe depression, with no hope of successful treatment which would reduce his current mental discomfort to a tolerable level or enable him to exist in the general prison population or the outside world if his appeals were successful; that Rumbaugh's assessment of his legal and medical situations, and the options available to him, are reasonable. . . .

853. *Id.* at 403 (Goldberg, J., dissenting): "With all due respect to my brethren, I am incredulous that anyone could fairly read the record as establishing this person's competency to waive next-friend collateral review of his conviction and sentence."

854. *Id.* at 404.

855. *Id. See also* Rumbaugh v. McCotter, 473 U.S. 919, 920 (1985) (Marshall, J., dissenting from denial of *certiorari*):

The choice the courts below describe is a choice of a desperate man seeking to use the State's machinery of death as a tool of suicide. It is no more rational than the tragic choices of those driven to suicide by their tormented inner lives in a myriad of contexts. . . . [T]his was not the sort of free and uncoerced "rational" choice that we required in *Rees.*

disregarded the substantial evidence that the defendant's state of depression diminished his capacity for free and voluntary choice.[856]

He concluded:

> The troubled life of Charles Rumbaugh presents an abundance of moral questions that people of thought have debated without satisfactory resolve since antiquity. If it invites hubris to dictate death, on this we cannot pass. But we must at least acknowledge in ourselves the inability to understand in full the workings of the human mind. Where we must pretend to such capacity, however, we should grant ourselves and those who suffer most from our mistakes the benefit of an admittedly grave doubt. To look askance when a next-friend could tell us how a condemned's conviction or sentence falls outside the precious safeguards of the Constitution is to place the burdens of our own flawed knowledge on the one we chose to kill. The failure to rise to this self-appointed level of responsibility is resplendent with neither truth nor justice. It seems, unfortunately, to be the American way.[857]

6. Conclusion

The question of competency in a criminal context continues to be an important one, both with regard to the number of cases in which this status is raised, the scope of type of cases in which it is raised, and the practical implications of adopting one standard or another in any of the subareas of the law discussed in this chapter. It is a question to which the United States Supreme Court has returned on many occasions, and will return again.[858]

The case law in this area is far from coherent, but some of the more recent decisions do reflect more nuanced decision-making (by way of example, the Supreme Court cases of *Sell v. United States*[859] and *Panetti v. Quarterman*[860]). Also, scholars have begun to consider the deeper textures of the underlying issues much more carefully and thoughtfully.[861]

856. *Id. See also Groseclose ex rel. Harries*, 594 F. Supp. at 951, permitting criminal defendant to proceed as a party plaintiff asserting lack of voluntariness in waiving post-conviction remedies due to allegedly inhumane prison conditions.

857. *Rumbaugh*, 753 F.2d at 415–16 (Goldberg, J., dissenting). *See also, e.g.*, Strafer, *supra* note 274, at 912:

> As long as we are willing to grant the State [the] awesome power [of capital punishment], the torturous environment of death rows across the country and the various suicidal dysfunctions often attendant to prisoners guilty of murder must not be casually ignored in the name of consent and free will, as if the prisoner were waiving nothing more than the right to a jury trial for petit larceny. . . .

858. *See* Indiana v. Edwards, 128 U.S. 741, 2007 WL 2361185 (2007) (granting *certiorai* on the question of whether States may adopt a higher standard for measuring competency to represent oneself at trial than for measuring competency to stand trial). *See supra* note 418.

859. 539 U.S. 166 (2003). *See supra* text at notes 131–68.

860. 127 S. Ct. 2842 (2007). *See supra* text at notes 680–724.

861. *See, e.g.*, Morris et al, *supra* note 30.

Yet, this is still an area of the law that is rife with sanist actions[862] and pretextual decisionmaking.[863] Several years ago, one of us (MLP) wrote this about the court process in these cases:

> The abdication on the part of lawyers (leaving it to mental health professionals to develop their own competence assessment standards with little assistance) and on the part of judges (refusing to independently assess clinical testimony), the failure of most clinicians to use standardized and validated tests, the lack of meaningful dialogue between the lawyer and the evaluator, are all symptoms of the same malignancy: the corrosive impact of sanism on the legal process.[864]

It is the hope of the authors that the publication of this volume helps, if only modestly, to remediate this situation.

862. *See, e.g.,* Perlin, *supra* note 207.
863. Perlin, *supra* note 112.
864. Perlin, *supra* note 207, at 252 (footnotes omitted).

3

Competency and the Institutionalization of Persons by Reason of Mental Disability

A. INVOLUNTARY CIVIL COMMITMENT

1. Introduction

The civil commitment process, through which individuals are confined to psychiatric hospitals against their will via state action, affects more people than any other similar intersection of the legal and mental health systems.[1] This chapter explores the connection between civil commitment and competence. This connection arises in three primary ways: (1) when lack of competence is a statutory prerequisite for a valid involuntary civil commitment (i.e., when a hospital wishes to confine someone against his or her will and must, according to law, show that the person has a serious or severe mental condition that represents a danger to self or others,[2] or to put it differently, lacks competence to function independently in a way that is safe to the self and others, or lacks the willingness or capacity to voluntarily submit to treatment); (2) when a person wishes to be voluntarily admitted to a hospital but must be competent to do so (i.e., must have some basic level of understanding of the admission decision and its ramifications); (3) following a finding of civil commitment, the degree to which the person retains or is denied the presumption of competence to make decisions as to treatment and/or conditions of confinement.

---

1. Joseph D. Bloom, *Thirty-Five Years of Working with Civil Commitment Statutes,* 32 J. AM. ACAD. PSYCHIATRY LAW 430 (2004).
2. JOHN PARRY & ERIC Y. DROGIN, MENTAL DISABILITY LAW, EVIDENCE AND TESTIMONY 298 (2007).

2. Background

Most adult members of society who are not under the jurisdiction of the criminal justice system may come and go freely, limited primarily by their desires, obligations, and means. They are presumed to be competent to make decisions.[3] They may decide what to eat for breakfast in the morning, whom they will marry, or whether they elect to take a particular medication suggested by their physician. This is not entirely so for people subject to involuntary civil commitment.

In the past, involuntary commitment extinguished many of the basic civil rights afforded most citizens, including any presumption of competence to make autonomous decisions the person may have enjoyed prior to commitment.[4] This was not generally viewed as improper, but rather was seen as a natural outgrowth of the responsibility of the sovereign to protect a person incapable of self care, or *parens patraie*. The other, although initially secondary, justification employed was the inherent power of the state to protect society from those whose uncontrollable behavior threatened other members of society.[5]

Seen in this light, the decision to remove someone from society and place that person in a psychiatric hospital was characterized as a strictly medical determination to be made by a physician, perhaps guided by the wishes of the person's family.[6] In this schema there was little perceived need for judicial oversight and even less for procedural protections, legal representation, or due process of law. Any person subject to involuntary civil commitment was, by virtue of that involuntary commitment, considered incompetent to engage in meaningful decision-making.[7] Adhering to the "hands-off" doctrine, courts routinely held that the inner workings of psychiatric hospitals were "beyond the ken of the court," and best left to hospital superintendents.[8] Following this doctrine, courts routinely declined to hold evidentiary hearings concerning the conditions of institutions such as psychiatric hospitals or corrections facilities, thus creating a barrier between the constitution and the inside of the institution. In fact, as recently as 1960 the Iowa Supreme Court held in *Prochaska v. Brineger*[9] that the Fourteenth Amendment's due process clause was not implicated by the involuntary civil commitment process.[10]

It was not until the 1970s that U.S. courts—perhaps spurred on by the civil

---

3. Of course the other major exception to this is those under guardianship orders; *see infra* Chapter 4 D.

4. *See, e.g.,* Lessard v. Schmidt, 349 F. Supp. 1078 (E.D. Wis. 1972).

5. *See, e.g.,* Ralph Slovenko, *Commentary: Reviewing Civil Commitment Laws*, 18 Psychiatric Times 10 (2000).

6. *Id.*

7. *See, e.g.,* 1 Michael L. Perlin, Mental Disability Law: Civil and Criminal §§ 2A-2.1a to 2.1b (2d ed. 1999).

8. *See, e.g.,* Banning v. Looney, 213 F.2d 771 (10th Cir. 1954).

9. 102 N.W.2d 870,872 (Iowa 1960).

10. *Id.*

rights movement[11]—would begin to seriously consider cases challenging commitment to a hospital. When they did, some pioneering judges began to rule that the wholesale removal of the legal indicia of adulthood—for example, the right to be compensated for work, to vote, to make treatment decisions, to move about freely—violated the constitution.[12] Further, some clinicians began to understand that the earlier approach was psychologically destructive, as it undercut the emotional strengths and social supports that promote recovery and sound management of mental illness, creating in their stead, dependence, regression, and isolation.[13]

Courts in this era began to analyze the underlying issues more closely. In the process, they started to reject two previously little-questioned assumptions: (1) that mental illness in and of itself was a sufficient reason to involuntarily confine a person to a hospital[14] and (2) that all people who did require involuntary hospitalization unfailingly lacked the capacity to make any decisions for themselves.[15] Over time, this led to increased judicial oversight of commitment proceedings as well as to a growing emphasis on procedural protections for those who were subjected to them, taking the decision-making power out of the sole discretion of physicians. This swing of the pendulum did not go unchallenged, so that now some argue that the process has become too legalistic, losing sight of the original focus on providing the patient with needed medical and protective intervention.[16]

3. Legal Developments

As previously noted, as recently as the 1960s courts held that constitutional protections simply did not apply to confinement in a psychiatric hospital.[17] At that time, there were few hearings prior to involuntary commitment, and those that were held lacked procedural due process. State statutes governing commitment generally failed to spell out the basis for commitment or define key terms such as *mental illness*. Certainly, there was no judicial determination or review of decisions, no specification regarding the treatment that was required or whether the needed treatment was in fact obtainable in the institution where the person was to be confined. Additionally, there was no right to counsel in the proceedings that did take place. In fact, few outsiders of any kind were involved in the matter.

11. *See* 1 Perlin, *supra* note 7, §1-2.1.

12. *See infra* Chapter 3 D 4.

13. *See, e.g.,* Michael Perlin et al., *Therapeutic Jurisprudence and the Civil Rights of Institutionalized Mentally Disabled Persons: Hopeless Oxymoron or Path to Redemption?,* 1 Pyschol Pub. Pol'y & L. 80 (1995).

14. The most important of these being O'Connor v . Donaldson, 422 U.S. 563 (1975); *see generally,* 1 Perlin, *supra* note 7, §2A-4.4.d.

15. *Id.*

16. *See, e.g.,* Bruce J. Winick, Civil Commitment: A Therapeutic Jurisprudence Model (2005)

17. *Prochaska, supra* note 9.

The United States Supreme Court first rejected the notion that the Constitution effectively stopped "at the institution's walls" in the 1972 case of *Jackson v. Indiana,*[18] a case involving an involuntary civil commitment of a defendant found incompetent to stand trial.[19] The heart of the holding in *Jackson* was that, at minimum, the due process clause of the Constitution required that the "nature and duration" of commitment bear some "reasonable relation" to the purpose for which the individual was committed.[20] For the first time, the Supreme Court held that the due process clause applied to a civil hospital commitment. This is important because, contrary to the teachings of the "hands-off doctrine," it also demonstrated that the Court would not decline to examine this type of case simply because it involved issues related to the services available within a psychiatric institution.

Importantly, Justice Blackmun—in his unanimous opinion for the Court—stated that, considering the number of persons subject to commitment proceedings, "it is perhaps remarkable that the substantive constitutional limitations on this power have not been more frequently litigated."[21] This signaled to the bar that it would not be futile to bring cases challenging the constitutionality of various aspects of commitment.

Increased judicial scrutiny of the civil commitment process continued in the period following *Jackson.* Just 3 years later, in *O'Connor v. Donaldson,*[22] the Supreme Court held, for the first time, that people with mental illness subjected to civil commitment retained a constitutional "right to liberty."[23] The court went on to hold that a state cannot constitutionally confine "without more," a nondangerous individual who is capable of surviving safely in freedom by himself, and that the mere presence of mental illness was not a sufficient basis for involuntary commitment.[24] *O'Connor* thus established the principle that a psychiatric diagnosis was constitutionally insufficient as the sole basis to justify civil commitment, that something "more" was required. The court's formulation implied that the additional factor, beyond mental illness, that was required to pass constitutional muster (the"more") was dangerousness. Thus, by 1975, it was clear that mental illness by itself was not a good enough reason to keep someone in a hospital, and that some showing of dangerousness to self or others was required.

If cases such as *O'Connor* taught that a person subject to involuntary civil commitment had a right to liberty subject to certain limiting factors such as danger-

---

18. *Jackson* 406 U.S. 715 (1972).

19. *See supra* Chapter 2 A 2 b.

20. *Jackson* 406 U.S. at 738.

21. *Id.* at 737.

22. 422 U.S. 562 (1975).

23. *Id.* at 575–76. *O'Connor* began as primarily a right-to-treatment case but, as the appeals process progressed, transmuted into a civil commitment case; *see* 1 PERLIN, *supra* note 7, § 2A-4.4d, at 144–46.

24. *O'Connor,* 422 U.S. at 576.

ousness (substantive due process), it was left to subsequent courts to elaborate the mechanisms and procedures by which that right would be protected (procedural due process). Without *procedural* due process, *substantive* due process rights have little practical meaning in the real world. While variations abounded, courts dealing with this question of how to effectuate the right to liberty in the civil commitment context fell into two broad categories: (1) those that saw a civil commitment proceeding as primarily an inquiry into what was best for the patient, thus engendering great deference to the opinions of clinicians and family members, and (2) those that viewed the proceeding as a potential infringement on the subject's freedom, with the concomitant emphasis on legal protections and zealous advocacy.

French v. Blackburn[25] is a leading example of a case promoting the notion that civil commitment proceedings are essentially for the benefit of those subject to them, and consequently, a court could tolerate less rigorous procedural due process protections. The judge in *French* noted the "humanitarian purposes"[26] of the proceeding and emphasized the notion of "deference to qualified medical opinion. . . ."[27] Viewed through this lens, rigid adherence to due process requirements to, for example, notify the person subject to the proceeding of a list of witnesses who would be testifying against him, was not required "[i]n light of the nature of the proceedings. . . ." In fact, a natural outgrowth of this treatment-centered perspective is the view that affording a person subject to possible involuntary hospitalization extensive procedural due process rights in the context of an adversarial proceeding interferes with clinicians' efforts to provide needed treatment.

Other courts, however, took what was eventually to become the prevailing view—that civil commitment proceedings put their subject at peril for a "massive curtailment of liberty,"[28] and that, as a result, due process required many if not all of the procedural protections afforded a criminal defendant. The leading example of this approach was the seminal case from the federal district court in Wisconsin, *Lessard v. Schmidt.*[29] This was an important decision because it applied almost the full range of protections developed in the criminal trial process to the involuntary commitment process, including right to counsel, privilege against

---

25. 428 F. Supp. 1351 (M.D.N.C. 1977).
26. *Id*. at 1355.
27. *Id*.
28. *Vitek v. Jones,* 445 U.S. 480 (1980):

We have recognized that for the ordinary citizen, commitment to a mental hospital produces "a massive curtailment of liberty," and in consequence "requires due process protection." The loss of liberty produced by an involuntary commitment is more than a loss of freedom from confinement. It is indisputable that commitment to a mental hospital "can engender adverse social consequences to the individual" and that "[w]hether we label this phenomena 'stigma' or choose to call it something else . . . we recognize that it can occur and that it can have a very significant impact on the individual." Also, "[a]mong the historic liberties" protected by the Due Process Clause is the "right to be free from, and to obtain judicial relief for, unjustified intrusions on personal security."

29. 349 F. Supp. 1078 (E.D. Wis. 1972).

self-incrimination, and strict adherence to the rules of evidence. The primary exception, interestingly, was the right to trial by jury.[30] In stark contrast to the *French* court's emphasis on the humanitarian purpose of civil commitment proceedings as a justification for lax procedures, *Lessard* quoted Justice Brandeis, who said: "Experience should teach us to be most on our guard to protect liberty when the government's purposes are beneficent. . . . The greatest dangers to liberty lurk in insidious encroachment by men of zeal, well-meaning but without understanding."[31]

These early cases established the baseline principles: that constitutional protections were implicated by the civil commitment process, that mental illness per se was a constitutionally insufficient ground to confine a person to a hospital (the implication being that a showing of dangerousness was required), and that some set of meaningful procedures was required to protect these rights. In the decades that followed, courts struggled with new questions raised by these holdings. Many courts struck down civil commitment statutes, particularly in states that did not modernize their statutes to incorporate the teachings of *Jackson, O'Connor,* and *Lessard.*[32]

Courts began by building the basic rationale to constitutionally permit involuntary confinement in a hospital. Two primary justifications emerged: *parens patriae* and *police power. Parens patriae* refers to the state's right to act on behalf of those incapable of protecting their own welfare, while *police power* refers to the sovereign's inherent duty to protect society in general.[33] These ideas have been distilled into the now famous inquiry in this area of law: "Is the patient dangerous to self or others?"

Deceptively straightforward, these concepts are really quite difficult to define and put into practice. A person who is actively attempting to commit suicide is clearly a "danger to self," but what about a person who inappropriately approaches strangers on a busy street (thus raising the possibility that one of them

---

30. The court did not find that the constitution demanded a right to a jury trial in such cases, although some state commitment statutes do now provide this right. See, e.g., N.Y. Ment. Hygiene L.§§9.33 & 9.35.

The standard of proof by which the proponent of involuntary commitment must prove that the legal standard is met is an other important issue which arose once courts began to grapple with the legal mechanisms for effectuating an involuntarily committed person's substantive due process rights. *See, e.g.,* Addington v. Texas, 441 U.S. 418 (1979) (constitutionally mandated minimum standard of proof was clear and convincing evidence). To some extent, this "compromise decision" reflected the court's unwillingness to (1) on one hand, equate commitment entirely with a criminal conviction notwithstanding that they both involved deprivations of liberty, or, on the other (2), give unbridled deference to predictions of dangerousness made by psychiatric experts. *See* 1 Perlin, *supra* note 7, § 2C-5.1a.

31. *Lessard,* quoting *Olmstead v. United States,* 277 U.S. 438, 479 (1928) (Brandeis, J., dissenting).

32. In contrast, some states revised their statutes. Those amended civil commitment statutes generally withstood constitutional challenge. *See generally,* 1 Perlin, *supra* note 7, § 2A-5.

33. Gary Melton et al., Psychological Evaluations for the Courts 308–309 (2d ed. 1999) (Melton).

will hurt him), or the person who deliberately puts herself in confrontational situations with the police, raising the likelihood that she will be shot? Or, what of a person who, by choice, lives on the street rather than seeking shelter from cold weather?[34] In applying this "dangerous to self"(or *parens patriae*) standard, what are courts to make of an individual who is stabilized and nondangerous within the confines of the structured hospital environment, but who, according to hospital staff, almost certainly will cease to take medication and become dangerous upon release?[35]

Likewise, a person actively seeking to harm another might clearly be labeled a "danger to others," but what about the person who destroys property—is danger to property sufficient to justify civil commitment?[36] Are overt actions undertaken to harm others required to meet this dangerousness standard, or will thoughts of harming others suffice? If acts are required, how recent and how overt must they be?

Perhaps even more fundamental are the vexing questions of how do we define mental illness, and can anyone predict dangerous behavior? Are professionals better than laypeople at doing so? What are acceptable means of assessing dangerousness in the context of court testimony? Are people really "dangerous" or "not dangerous," or is a more appropriate inquiry one of degree, context, and time frame?

We will explore each of these complex questions in the following section.

4. Dangerousness

Troublesome to civil commitment law are both the legal definition and the clinical assessment of "dangerousness." Statutory and case law definitions of dangerousness vary from jurisdiction to jurisdiction. In both arenas, what might appear to be definitive law actually reflects idiosyncratic interpretations by trial-level finders of law hearing individual cases.[37] Clinical approaches to both the definition and assessment of dangerousness also vary widely, ranging from cursory clinical

---

34. *See, e.g., in re* Boggs, 136 Misc.2d 1082 (N.Y. Sup. Ct. 1987), *rev'd* 523 N.Y.S.2d 71 (A.D. 1987), *appeal dismissed as moot*, 70 N.Y.2d 981 (1988), *motion for reargument den.*, 71 N.Y. 2d 994 (N.Y. 1988).

35. *See, e.g., In the Matter of Seltzer v. Hogue* 594 N.Y.S. 2d 781 (A.D. 1993).

This question implicates the complex issue of insight into one's illness as well as the fact that, in reality, the outcome of many civil commitment hearings outcome turns on the degree to which the judge is convinced that a person will continue to voluntarily and reliably continue to take medication following release. A person who evinces "insight" into his or her illness and the need to regularly take medication to control symptoms has a better chance of being discharged than does a person without insight or willingness to submit to ongoing medication.

36. Suzuki v. Yuen, 617 F.2d 173 (9th Cir. 1980).

37. Indeed, trial courts frequently ignore or misinterpret Supreme Court precedents in this area. *See, e.g.*, Michael L. Perlin, *Morality and Pretextuality, Psychiatry and Law: of "Ordinary Common Sense," Heuristic Reasoning, and Cognitive Dissonance*, 19 BULL. AM. ACAD. PSYCHIATRY & L. 131 (1991).

impression to precise assessment of both static and variable risk factors assessed by means of standardized assessment instruments.[38]

a. Case law

Lessard v. Schmidt was also important for its tightly drawn definition of dangerousness, a definition that paved the way for challenges to older civil commitment statutes.[39] The *Lessard* court held that commitment must be based upon dangerousness, and a finding of dangerousness could only be justified "upon a finding of a recent overt act, attempt or threat to do substantial harm to oneself or another."[40] Further, the danger to oneself entailed, inter alia, an "immediate danger at the time of the hearing of doing further harm to his or herself."[41] While not all of the cases in the years following *Lessard* subscribed to its "overt act" requirement,[42] the case was groundbreaking and remains relevant today for the proposition that a finding of dangerousness requires some specific proof beyond a diagnosis or vague impression on the part of the hospital staff that the person in question may be dangerous to some unknown object, to some unquantifiable degree, at some unspecified point in the future.

With this groundwork laid, other courts attempted to refine the dangerousness standard. The next major conceptual step forward was the 1975 New Jersey state Supreme Court decision in *State v. Krol*.[43] This case was somewhat atypical, as it arose out of a challenge to the commitment of a criminal defendant following a finding of not guilty by reason of insanity, rather than, as was more commonly the case, out of a constitutional attack on the state's overall commitment schema. In holding that the statute under which Krol was confined was unconstitutional on both equal protection and due process grounds, the *Krol* court rejected facile equations of mental illness, past criminal conduct, or socially undesirably behavior with current or future dangerousness.[44] Rather, the *Krol* court held, a court

---

38. Both judicial decisions and professional associations representing psychiatrists have expressed uncertainty about the ability of experts to predict dangerousness. In a recent formulation, the Fifth Circuit held that expert testimony in federal death penalty sentencing hearings on future dangerousness was not subject to the admissibility standards of *Daubert v. Merrell Dow Pharmaceuticals,* 509 U.S. 579 (1993). It noted that, as the Court had held in Barefoot v. Estelle, 463 U.S. 880 (1983), that a layperson could reasonably sensibly determine future dangerousness, it was not sensible to challenge the general reliability of expert testimony regarding assessment in this area. The proper inquiry, the Court held, was whether expert evidence would be probative in assisting jurors in their assessment of the defendant's future dangerousness. United States v. Fields, 483 F.3d 313 (5th Cir. 2007).

39. Lessard v. Schmidt, 349 F. Supp. 1078 (E.D. Wis. 1972). *See* 1 PERLIN, *supra* note 7, § 2A-4.4a, at 131 ("*Lessard* was the forerunner of a generation of involuntary civil commitment cases").

40. *Lessard,* 349 F. Supp. at 1093.

41. *Id.* at 1093 n.24

42. *See* 1 PERLIN, *supra* note 7, § 2A-4.5.

43. 68 N.J. 236, 344 A.2d 289 (1975). *See generally,* 1 PERLIN, *supra* note 7, §2A-4.4b.

44. *Krol,* 344 A.2d at 301–02. *But see Jones v. United States,* 463 U.S. 354 (1983), in which the United States Supreme Court accepted the assumption that involvement in the criminal jus-

must make a finding of a "substantial risk of dangerous conduct within the reasonably foreseeable future."[45]

Such an analysis required that a court evaluate several fundamental factors: the magnitude, likelihood, and seriousness of the risk of dangerousness involved.[46] Simply put, a court ordering involuntary civil commitment had to make an individualized assessment of the person's current condition and context to evaluate what degree of risk was present to whom at what point in time. This sophisticated analysis, by its nature, required a judge to reject the "all or nothing" approach with its implicit reliance on the category of "mental patient" or "criminal" in favor of a more nuanced schema placing dangerousness along a continuum in terms of imminence, degree, and context. Any perceived risk of dangerousness had to be weighed against the deprivation of liberty that involuntary commitment entailed.

Meaningful adherence to the *Krol* court's teaching would require the transformation of civil commitment hearings from brief, somewhat pro forma exercises, into complex, challenging, and potentially time-consuming proceedings.[47] Further, meaningful application of the standard announced in *Krol* required adequate assistance of competent counsel for the person at risk for involuntary commitment.[48]

Although not all subsequent cases followed rationales evident in *Lessard* and *Krol,* these two cases defined the contours of the debate as to the meaning of dangerousness in the civil commitment context. One substantive split in authority arising out of this debate involved the question of whether an "overt act" was required to sustain a commitment.[49] While some courts maintained that the constitution required such a showing,[50] a distinct line of cases declined to adopt this standard.[51] Some, for example, concluded that a recent overt act was not required

---

tice system by virtue of an insanity plea was indicative of dangerousness regardless of the nature of the offense (appellant had been charged with attempted petty larceny [shoplifting]).

45. *Krol,* 344 A. 2d at 302.

46. *Id.*

47. *See, e.g.,* Parham v. J. R., 442 U.S. 584, 609 n.17 (1979) , citing Dale Albers & Richard Pasewark, *Involuntary Hospitalization: Surrender at the Courthouse,* 2 AM. J. COMMUNITY PSYCHOLOGY 287, 288 (1974) (mean hearing time for 21 of 300 consecutive commitment cases was 9.2 minutes); Dorothy Miller & Michael Schwartz, *County Lunacy Commission Hearings: Some Observations of Commitments to a State Mental Hospital,* 14 SOCIAL PROB. 26 (1966) (mean time for hearings was 3.8 minutes); Thomas Scheff, *The Societal Reaction to Deviance: Ascriptive Elements in the Psychiatric Screening of Mental Patients in a Midwestern State,* 11 SOCIAL PROBS. 401, 408 (1964) (averaging 9.2 minutes). *Compare* Michael L. Perlin, *An Invitation to the Dance: An Empirical Response to Chief Justice Warren Burger's "Time-Consuming Procedural Minuets" Theory in Parham v. J.R.,* 9 BULL. AM. ACAD. PSYCHIATRY & L. 149 (1981) (criticizing *Parham*).

48. On the question of competence of counsel in involuntary civil commitment cases in general, *see In re* the Mental Health of K.G.F., 29 P.3d 485 (Mont. 2001).

49. 1 PERLIN, *supra* note 40, § 2A-4.5, at 152–55.

50. *See, e.g., Lessard, supra.*

51. *See* 1 PERLIN, *supra* note 7, §2A-4.5, at 155–56.

to sustain a commitment in cases where, unlike *Lessard,* expert testimony was available to the court indicating a reasonable likelihood that the person would represent a danger to himself or others.[52] Some courts expressed the opinion that the determination of whether such as act was in fact a predicate to a valid commitment was best left to the legislative forum.[53] To the extent that states revised their statutes in the intervening years, the trend has been away from this requirement, toward more general definitions of dangerousness.

5. Ability to Care for Self

When discussing the "danger to self" rationale for commitment, a recent, serious suicide attempt can be considered to meet the requirement for "recent overt act." However, many behaviors or lifestyle choices a person may make could be considered detrimental (dangerous?) when measured against some abstract ideal. As anyone examining the parent-child relationship will attest, value judgements surely attach to the determination of whether a particular choice is good or bad, harmful or beneficial. Most could likely agree that a decision to commit suicide is harmful and correctly evokes the state's *parens patriae power;*[54] conversely, a decision, for example, not to continue with a graduate school education, while perhaps viewed by some as detrimental to a person's long-term success and well-being, would clearly not implicate such power and must be distinguished from the former example. The difficulty comes in deciding where along such a spectrum of self-harm a given behavior falls, and at what point the state has the right, duty, or obligation to abridge personal autonomy. Such a range of scenarios cannot be properly aggregated into one uniform standard of inquiry.

Prior to the 1970s and the wave of cases described earlier in this chapter challenging many of the previously held assumptions regarding civil commitments, the notion was uncritically accepted and broadly interpreted that the state might be acting in the best interests of the mentally ill by involuntarily confining them to hospitals. Thus, findings that there was a need to protect the person's general welfare or that an individual was in need of care and treatment were sufficient to justify commitment.[55] This broad view of the state's power to commit was consistent with a lack of emphasis on the individual rights for such people, as well as an unquestioned reliance on the medical model that viewed them as sick and in need of care, as determined by their physician. This was true despite the lack of

52. United States *ex rel.* Mathew v. Nelson 461 F. Supp. 707, 712 (N.D. Ill. 1978). Note that this approach places much faith in the ability of a psychiatric expert to predict future *dangerousness,* but at the same time implicitly questions the predictive value of a *recent overt act.*

53. *See, e.g., Project Release v. Prevost,* 722 F.2s 960, 974 (2d Cir. 1983).

54. But, even with regard to this example, note that suicide is considered a potentially acceptable choice of a competent individual in some instances. *See* Oregon's Death with Dignity Act (ORE. REV. STAT. § 127.800–995, and *Gonzalez v. Oregon,* 546 U.S. 243 (2006)).

55. *See* 1 PERLIN, *supra* note 7, §2A-4.6b at 159–65.

adequate treatment available in many public institutions and conditions that were in many cases simply inhumane.[56]

Like the hands-off doctrine in general,[57] this laissez-faire approach to commitment was rejected by a number of courts during the 1970s. These courts tended to reject a best-interest of the patient (as determined by the treating physician) analysis in favor of a legal- and rights-based framework. Even today, most states do not impose a capacity criterion on *a parens patriae* commitment.[58] *State ex rel. Hawks v. Lazaro*,[59] a 1974 decision by the West Virginia Supreme Court, was an early case striking down a commitment statute that permitted, inter alia, commitment based upon a showing that the person needed custody, care, or treatment in a hospital.[60] The court found a standard based upon the state simply substituting its own judgment as to what was desirable or wise to be unconstitutional. However, the court did sanction commitment based upon a person being passively dangerous.[61] Someone could be committed involuntarily upon a showing that "by sheer inactivity he will permit himself to die either of starvation or lack of care."[62] The *Lazaro* court thus provided a model for courts choosing to recognize that some behavior that was not active or aggressive could indeed be construed as dangerous, within a constitutional framework of involuntary commitment, while at the same time rejecting the notion that a person could be confined for behavior deemed merely not in his best interest as determined by the state acting through a hospital physician.

Other courts during this era were similarly skeptical about overly broad applications of the *parens patriae* power. A good example is *Colyar v. Third Judicial District Court*,[63] in which the court essentially held that a hospital's good intentions and desire to be of assistance did not negate the constitutional protections afforded the subject of civil commitment.[64] Rather, the state had to show a "compelling state interest to justify its action."[65] The court clarified its rationale by noting that a mentally ill person who did not provide for her basic needs could pose a danger to herself not because she had mental illness that interfered with procurement of psychiatric treatment, but rather because the illness did not per-

---

56. *Cf. O'Connor v. Donaldson*, 422 U.S. 563 (1975), *Wyatt v. Stickney*, 325 F. Supp. 781 (M.D. Ala. 1971).

57. *See* Banning v. Looney, 213 F.2d 771 (10th Cir. 1954), and *supra* text accompanying notes 8–10.

58. *See* MELTON, *supra* note 33, at 308. *Compare* DEL. CODE ANN. 16 § 5001 (1) (mental illness is that which "renders such person unable to make responsible decisions with respect to his hospitalization"); KAN. STAT. ANN § 59-2902 (h) (a mentally ill person "lack capacity to make an informed decision concerning treatment").

59. 202 S.E.2d 109 (W.Va. 1974).

60. *Id.*, and *see* 1 PERLIN, *supra* note 7, § 2A-4.6b, at 160.

61. *Lazaro*, 202 S.E. 2d at 123.

62. *Id.*

63. 469 F. Supp. 424 (D.Utah 1979).

64. *Id.* at 429, and *see* 1 PERLIN, *supra* note 7, § 2A-4.6b, at 162.

65. *Id.* at 430.

mit her to care for herself.[66] While caring for oneself may include seeking medical attention, in this formulation it is not the desire to avoid psychiatric treatment, nor is it mental illness per se that justifies the commitment. Rather, the commitment is justified based upon the inability to make reasoned decisions about care and the danger posed by a failure to care for basic needs.[67]

The approach taken by courts, as in all of the areas described in this chapter, is subject to variations in approach (swings of the pendulum), influenced by changes in political climate, high-profile media events, and the reactions of staff charged with implementing innovations. Seen from this perspective, it should not be surprising that some courts and legislatures reacted against this shift toward individual rights and what they perceived to be cramped applications of the state's *parens patriae* power. Contributing to this reaction may have been the increasingly visible homeless population on our nation's streets, along with the perception that the emphasis on protecting the rights of the mentally ill had resulted in the premature release of people from psychiatric hospitals.[68] Just as courts imposed dangerousness as a threshold finding to justify commitment, some courts began to further refine the circumstances encompassed by this concept. The competing tensions reflected in these cases are (1) the effort to avoid pathologizing poverty and homelessness, and (2) the concern that elevating individual rights to liberty, might result in individual suffering and the exacerbation of vexing social problems.

New York provides an important example of the emergence of this tension and its resolution. While dangerousness is required by both statute and case law as a basis for commitment,[69] more recent cases have expanded the definition of this term. For example, in the case of *In the Matter of Selzer v. Hogue,*[70] the court held that a person diagnosed with organic brain disorder, schizophrenia, and chronic substance abuse required involuntary commitment in a hospital. Although his current condition was not acute, the court held that Hogue was indeed dangerous because of his history of mental illness and dangerousness and, importantly, because his treatment history revealed that when he was released he would "invariably"[71] deteriorate, engage in substance abuse, and become dangerous to both himself and others. Thus, the court found that this pattern of behavior—release, substance abuse, exacerbation of mental illness, dangerous behavior—which was seen as an inevitable cycle, was found to be sufficient grounds for continued retention.

A New York court of the same era similarly broadly interpreted the dangerous-

66. *Id.* at 431.

67. This decoupling of commitment criteria from desire to resist treatment is critical to the discussion of right to refuse treatment *infra* Chapter 3 C.

68. *See, e.g.,* Thomas Gutheil, *In Search of True Freedom: Drug Refusal, Involuntary Medication, and "Rotting with Your Rights On,"* 137 Am. J. Psychiatry 327 (1980).

69. *See, e.g.,* N.Y. Ment. Hygiene L. §9.27, *Scopes v. Shah,* 398 N.Y.S.2d 911 (A.D. 1977).

70. 594 N.Y.S.2d 781 (A.D. 1993).

71. *Id.* at 785.

ness requirement in the case of *Boggs v. New York City Health and Hospitals Corp.*[72] This case involved highly contested litigation surrounding the commitment of a 40-year-old woman, known as Billy Boggs, who lived on a sidewalk located on the East Side of Manhattan. She was found to pose a danger to herself, and over her objection, she was hospitalized. At trial, expert testimony was adduced that Boggs did not represent a danger of serious harm to herself or others.[73] In upholding her commitment, however, the court relied heavily on what was perceived as her lack of capacity to understand her need for food, clothing, or shelter. The court justified her continued retention on the basis of Ms. Boggs' neglect and refusal to care for herself—as a result of her mental illness—to the extent that she presented a harm to her own well-being.[74]

These two cases illustrate a trend toward more expansive interpretations of the dangerousness standard. These factors—lack of ability to care for basic needs outside of the hospital, and inability to continue with treatment following release (based on lack of insight and past patterns of behavior in the community)—are routinely used to justify involuntary commitment in New York at the present time.

6. Gravely Disabled

In what is really a more precise term for this expanded definition of dangerousness to self, justified by the *parens patriae* power, all states have some version of the "gravely disabled" category of commitment.[75] In some jurisdictions this has emerged directly through case law; in others, by case law interpreting the state's commitment statute, and in still others, de facto through a statutory definition of dangerousness that is broadened to encompass it. California was the first state to codify this concept in statute,[76] providing for the involuntary commitment of a person who "as a result of a mental disorder, is unable to provide his basic personal needs for food, clothing and shelter."[77] These provisions are generally upheld as constitutional.[78] Even *O'Connor*—the landmark case that established that

---

72. 522 N.Y.S.2d 407 (N.Y. Sup. Ct. 1987), *rev'd* 523 N.Y.S.2d 71 (A.D. 1987), *appeal dismissed as moot*, 70 N.Y.2d 981 (1988), *motion for reargument den.*, 71 N.Y. 2d 994 (N.Y. 1988).

73. *Boggs*, 522 N.Y.S. 2d at 412.

74. *Boggs*, 523 N.Y.S.2d at 72. See Tanya Marie Luhrmann, *"The Street Will Drive You Crazy": Why Homeless Psychotic Women in the Institutional Circuit in the United States Often Say No to Offer of Help*, Am J Psychiatry AiA:1-6, published in advance, December 17, 2007. This article notes that refusals of help among this cohort are produced not only by a lack of insight, but also "from the local culture's ascription of meaning to being 'crazy.'" The author suggests that, given this insight, offers of help may be more accepted if the explicit diagnosis is downplayed. *Id.* at 1.

75. Melton, *supra* note 33, at 309.

76. *See* 1 Perlin, *supra* note 7, § 2A-4.7.

77. Cal. Welf. & Inst. Code § 5008(h)(1) 1997.

78. *See, e.g.,* Doe v. Galinot 486 F.Supp. (C.D. Cal. 1979), *aff'd*, 657 F.2d 1017 (9th Cir., 1981).

the due process clause of the U.S. Constitution was implicated by an involuntary commitment—noted that the state may not constitutionally confine "without more" a nondangerous individual who *is capable of surviving safely in freedom by himself.*[79] Judicial scrutiny of this standard has since tended to focus on the appropriateness of its application rather than the standard itself.[80] Perhaps even more so than other areas of inquiry, the assessment of one as gravely disabled and/or unable to care for one's basic needs is both highly fact- and context-dependent. Additionally, for this inquiry to be conducted in a meaningful fashion, there must be an assessment of not only the person's diagnosis and mental status but a functional assessment of the person's situation in the community. Such inquiry, when done thoroughly, addresses in detail the issues that must be analyzed by the court in order to make a refined judgment of the justifiability of involuntary commitment.

More recently, the Alaska Supreme Court in *Wetherhorn v. Alaska Psychiatric Institute*[81]—one of the most important decisions in this area—addressed the meaning of the gravely disabled standard. The Alaska commitment statute permits the hospital to ". . . commit the respondent to a treatment facility for not more than thirty days if it finds, by clear and convincing evidence, that the respondent is mentally ill and as a result is likely to cause harm to the respondent or others or is gravely disabled."[82] In this case, Wetherhorn was found to be gravely disabled. The court interpreted this standard strictly, stating:

> We furthermore agree with the Supreme Court of Washington that "[i]t is not enough to show that care and treatment of an individual's mental illness would be preferred or beneficial or even in his best interests." Indeed, AS 47.30.730 does require more than a best interests determination. For example, it requires that the petition for commitment "allege that the evaluation staff has considered but has not found that there are any less restrictive alternatives available" [citation omitted] and "allege with respect to a gravely disabled respondent that there is reason to believe that the respondent's mental condition could be improved by the course of treatment sought." As further protection, the statute directs the court to make its findings by "clear and convincing" evidence.[83]

Wetherhorn provides significant protections to those seeking to challenge involuntary commitments. While accepting the gravely disabled concept, it strongly upholds the clear and convincing standard of evidence and breathes life into the less restrictive alternative doctrine.[84]

---

79. *See O'Connor, supra* 56.
80. *See* 1 PERLIN, *supra* note 7, §2A-4.7 at 171.
81. 156 P.3d 371 (Alaska 2007).
82. ALASKA STAT. ANN. § 47.30.700.
83. *Wetherhorn,* 156 P. 3d at 378.
84. It also raises probing questions: By way of example, think of two people with identical mental health disabilities. One has health insurance that makes available ongoing treatment and an adequate dwelling near a supportive, involved family. The other has no health insurance or

B. COMPETENCY AND THE RIGHT
TO REFUSE TREATMENT

1. Introduction

> Every human being of adult years and sound mind has a right to determine what shall be done with his own body; and a surgeon who performs an operation without his patient's consent, commits an assault, for which he is liable in damages. (Citations omitted) This is true except in cases of emergency where the patient is unconscious and where it is necessary to operate before consent can be obtained.[85]

While both the law and relevant science have evolved in the 94 years since Justice Cardozo wrote those words, they still eloquently reflect the fundamental principles that undergird the right to resist unwanted treatment. Whether finding its basis in traditional common law tort principles, as did Cardozo—if you touch me without my consent you have committed an assault—or, as this section will explore, in constitutional protections such as the right to due process of law, right to privacy, or freedom of thought, the basic principles appear relatively straightforward: Those who are competent to make treatment decisions, including those committed to a psychiatric hospital, have a qualified right to refuse unwanted treatment except in an emergency situation.[86]

Broadly speaking, in the modern era this right stems from general informed consent doctrine and from state and federal constitutional rights.[87] The law presumes competence to make treatment decisions for most people, the primary exceptions being children, the elderly, and those with a mental disability.[88] Unfortunately, these seemingly direct pronouncements have proven to be troublesome in their application, leading some commentators to consider this one of the most controversial aspects of this area of law.[89] Courts looking specifically at the right to refuse unwanted medications for involuntarily committed patients in psychiatric hospitals developed opposing structures for analyzing these issues: Essentially, they either sought to protect the individual from unwanted medication absent specific showings, subject to rigorous analysis under an expanded due process model, or, seeing the proceeding regarding forced medication as a step in the process of providing the person with needed treatment, they provided

---

means to pay for needed treatment, plans to live temporarily with a friend but will likely reside in a public homeless shelter, and has had no contact with his foster family for the past 10 years. His plans following discharge are to "find a doctor, and continue with treatment." Are they in fact on equal footing in making their case for release? Should they be?

85. *Schloendorff v. The Society of the New York Hospital*, 105 N.E. 92 (N.Y. 1914).

86. *See, e.g.,* Mills v. Rogers, 457 U.S. 291 (1982).

87. *See infra* Chapter 4 A 1.

88. *See, e.g.,* GARY MELTON ET AL., *supra* note 33, PSYCHOLOGICAL EVALUATIONS FOR THE COURTS: A HANDBOOK FOR MENTAL HEALTH PROFESSIONALS AND LAWYERS 347 (2nd ed. 1999).

89. *See, e.g., id.* at 345–46.

limited due process protections under cramped readings of the Constitution's due process clause.[90]

As we will discuss subsequently, the Supreme Court missed two major opportunities to clarify the legal standard when it sidestepped two important "right to refuse" civil litigation cases during the 1980s.[91] In some instances, state courts moved in to fill the void.[92] In addition to the lack of broad doctrinal direction, courts have provided little guidance to clinicians attempting to assess competence in this area.[93] This section will outline the historical development of the right to refuse treatment and the underlying legal principles—both state and federal—focusing first on the right to refuse unwanted psychotropic medications, and then on other treatments. It will then explore the application of these legal principles to courtroom proceedings.

2. Psychotropic Medications

The development of this area of law closely parallels advances in the creation of psychotropic medications used in the treatment of mental disorders. In the 1950s, the French anesthesiologist and surgeon, Henri Leborit, discovered Thorazine, the first antipsychotic medication, by chance as he searched for medications to assist in the performance of his surgical practice. Noticing the calming effect this medication had on his surgery patients, Leborit considered that Thorazine might have a similar effect on psychiatric patients.[94] Thus began the modern era of treatment of mental disabilities with medications. The development of psychotropic medications led to major advancements in the treatment of psychiatric disorders. For the first time, treatment outside of a hospital was a potentially obtainable goal for those with major psychiatric disorders. For many people, psychiatric symptoms such as hallucinations and delusions were reduced through the use of these medications, and some stayed in the hospital for shorter periods of time and experienced longer periods of functioning in the community between hospitalizations.[95]

The promise of successful medical treatment for serious psychiatric conditions was now available, where once there was little. As is often the case with apparent panaceas for complex medical, social, and emotional difficulties, an initial wave of euphoria was followed by a strong dose of reality. It quickly became clear

---

90. Henry Dlugacz, *Riggins v. Nevada:* Towards a Unified Standard For a Prisoner's Right to Refuse Medication? 17 LAW & PSYCHOL. REV. 41, 42 (1993).

91. *Id.* at 46.

92. *See infra* Chapter 3 B 8.

93. MELTON ET AL., *supra* note 33, at 347.

94. Henri Laborit et al., *Un Nouveau Stabilisateur Vegetatif, Le 4560 Rp.* 60 PRESSE MED. 206 (1952).

95. *See, e.g.,* 2 MICHAEL L. PERLIN, MENTAL DISABILITY LAW: CIVIL AND CRIMINAL §3B-2, at 158 (2d ed. 1999).

that, notwithstanding the dramatic benefits these medications obtained for some people, not all were helped by them, and even those who were helped were put at risk for potentially serious side effects.[96] Additionally, as is not uncommon in institutional settings with insufficient staffing, the sedating effects of these medications were at times used, not for the treatment and benefit of the patients, but rather to make life easier for staff—or, even worse, to punish patients.[97]

Concern over side effects animated much of the judicial involvement in this area. No medication is without some risk of producing side effects.[98] For patients using older psychotropic medications, the incidence of side effects has been noted to be in the range of 24% to 56%.[99] Side effects may include tardive dyskinesia, characterized by unwanted bodily movements, tongue thrusting, and drooling.[100] Other potential side effects include the rare but potentially fatal and underreported neuroleptic malignant syndrome.[101] Newer, so-called second-generation medications thus far appear to have a much lower side effect profile, at least for these particular side effects, but as experience with their use increases, so has concern about other, potentially dangerous side effects such as weight gain and diabetes.[102]

In short, the major advancement of medication created a new set of complexities and concerns that have played out in court cases throughout the 1970s and 1980s. Advocates representing patients who are seeking to resist psychotropic medications have battled hospitals and physicians seeking to provide these potentially beneficial treatments, sometimes against the will of the patient.

3. Early Cases

During the 1970s, there developed a mutually reinforcing interplay among court decisions involving prisoners and people institutionalized in psychiatric hospitals. In the typical scenario, prisoners would gain a particular institutional right and then patient advocates would seek an analogous right on behalf of the institutional mental health patients. Surely, went the reasoning, if a court had granted convicts this right, then simple justice demanded that a resident of a psychiatric

96. *Id.* at 158–64, and sources cited at nn.10–23.

97. Davis v. Hubbard, 506 F. Supp. (N.D. Ohio 1980).

98. *See, e.g.,* JERROLD G. BERNSTEIN, CLINICAL PHARMACOLOGY 168 (2d ed. 1984).

99. *Id.* at165, 168.

100. Donald J. Kemma, *Current Status of Institutionalized Mental Health Patients' Right to Refuse Psychotropic Drugs,* 6 J. LEGAL MED. 107, 111–112 (1985).

101. Harrison G. Pope et al., *Frequency and Presentation of Neuroleptic Malignant Syndrome in a Large Psychiatric Hospital,* 143 AM. J. PSYCHIATRY 1227 (1986).

102. *See, e.g.,* American Diabetes Association et al., *Consensus Development Conference on Antipsychotic Drugs and Obesity and Diabetes,* 27 DIABETES CARE 596 (2004) ; Karen A. Graham et al., *Effect of Olanzapine on Body Composition and Energy Expenditure in Adults with First-episode Psychosis.* 162 AM. J. PSYCHIATRY 118 (2005); Laurent Holzer et al., *Quetiapine-Induced Weight Gain and Escitalopram.* 162 AM. J. PSYCHIATRY 201 (2005). For the most recent research on these medications see T. Scott Stroup et al., *Effectiveness of Olanzapine, Quetiapine, and Risperidone in Patients with Chronic Schizophrenia after Discontinuing Perphenazine: A CATIE Study,* 164 AM. J. PSYCHIATRY 415 (2007).

hospital, who after all had done no wrong, should be afforded at minimum the same baseline protection.

It is not surprising, then, that many of the precursor cases in this area of institutional rights came from the correctional context. In *Mackey v. Procunier,*[103] for example, the general practice of administering medication only meant to be prescribed to an anaesthetized patient to a fully conscious prisoner was held, by the Ninth Circuit Court of Appeals, to "raise serious constitutional questions respecting cruel and unusual punishment or impermissible tinkering with the mental process."[104] While the pronouncement regarding cruel and unusual punishment, an Eighth Amendment concern echoed in *Knecht v. Gillman,*[105] would pertain primarily to prisoners as opposed to civilly committed patients, the concern noted by the *Boyd* court about "tinkering" with the thought process was a clear forerunner of an early line of cases viewing the unwanted administration of psychotropic medications as implicating the First Amendment's protection of freedom of thought and expression.[106] Other early cases examined Fourth Amendment, as well as right to privacy and ultimately due process rationales, to support the right to refuse treatment.[107]

The two most important federal constitutional cases attempting to effectuate this bourgeoning right to refuse treatment were *Rogers v. Okin*[108] and *Rennie v. Klein,*[109] two cases with torturous paths through the trial and appeals processes of the federal courts. Both of these cases afforded the Supreme Court opportunities to clarify the constitutional standard for the right to refuse treatment in the civil context, opportunities the Court chose to sidestep in favor of remands to the lower court. As a result, federal courts were left with little clear, practical guidance for handling these cases.

4. *Rennie:* The District Court

Rennie involved a highly intelligent[110] former pilot and flight instructor who was hospitalized for treatment of schizophrenia at Ancora Psychiatric Hospital in

---

103. 477 F.2d 877 (9th Cir. 1973).

104. *Id.* at 877.

105. 488 F.2d 1136 (8th Cir. 1973).

106. *See, e.g.,* Scott v. Plante, 532 F.2d 939 (3d Cir. 1976), regarding the civil context application of this notion. This case also emphasized procedural due process rights as the patient in question had never been adjudicated incompetent.

107. *See, e.g.,* Rochin v. California, 342 U.S. 165 (1952), for the underlying rationales.

108. 478 F. Supp. 1342 (D. Mass. 1979), *modified,* 634 F.2d 650 (1st Cir. 1980), *vacated and remanded sub nom.* Mills v. Rogers, 457 U.S. 291 (1982), *on state court certification sub nom* Rogers v. Comm'r Dep't of Mental Health, 458 N.E.2d (Mass. 1983), *on remand,* 738 F.2d 1 (1st Cir. 1984).

109. 462 F. Supp. 1131 (D.N.J. 1978), *modified on other grounds,* 476 F. Supp. 1294 (D.N.J. 1979), *vacated and remanded on other grounds,* 458 U.S. 1119 (1982), *aff'd on reh'g,* 720 F.2d 266 (3d Cir. 1983).

110. *Rennie,* 462 F. Supp. at 1135.

New Jersey. While the original theory of Rennie's case against the institution involved numerous claims, the case was narrowed to a right-to-refuse-treatment case involving the hospital's desire to medicate Rennie, against his will, with psychotropic medications, primarily Prolixin. Rennie sought to enjoin the hospital from administrating medication to him absent an emergency.[111] In stark contrast to the passive stance earlier courts had adopted pursuant to the "hands-off" doctrine,[112] Federal Judge Stanley S. Brotman held 14 days of hearings and heard testimony from numerous witnesses.[113]

While acknowledging that psychotropic medications were "widely accepted"[114] in the practice of psychiatry, the court made a finding of fact that "all psychotropic drugs cause dysfunctions of the central nervous system called extrapyramidal symptoms, as well as other side effects."[115] The district court held that an involuntarily committed patient had, absent an emergency, a constitutional right, growing out of the right to privacy, to refuse medication absent an emergency.[116] The balance between these admittedly strong interests—treatment of schizophrenia and avoidance of serious side effects—called for, the court ruled, a personal decision that should be made by the patient unless a strong state interest intervened.[117]

Of course, like other constitutional rights, the *Rennie* court did not consider this right to refuse medication to be absolute. The court reasoned that a three-part inquiry was required to determine whether this right obtained in any given instance: (1) Was the patient dangerous? (2) Was the patient competent to make a decision concerning drug refusal, and (3) Was a less restrictive alternative to medication available?[118] The most germane for our purposes is the question of competence to make a treatment decision, where the court found that mental illness did not equate with a finding of lack of competence.[119] However, Judge Brotman did acknowledge that a finder of fact would have to examine the degree to which the underlying mental illness formed the basis for the wish to refuse medication.[120] In this way, the *Rennie* court, while at the same time upholding a strong right to refuse treatment, foreshadowed later concerns that a right to refuse treatment could become nothing more than a denial of adequate treatment to a person lacking the competence to make a reasoned decision.

Having established that a constitutional due process interest did indeed attach to the question of forced medication, the *Rennie* court established a remedy that included, again absent an emergency, a right to a due process hearing prior to the

---

111. *Id.* at 1134.
112. *See supra* Chapter 3 A 5.
113. *Id.*
114. *Id.*
115. *Id.* at 1137–38.
116. *Id.* at 1144.
117. *Id.* at 1145.
118. *Id.* at 1145–46.
119. *Id.* at 1145.
120. *Id.* at 1146.

administration of medication over objection. This hearing was to include rights to be a part of the decision-making process, to legal representation, and to an independent psychiatrist.[121] While aspects of this decision did not withstand the appeals process, *Rennie* remains one of the twin pillars of cases grappling with the complex series of issues to be considered in this area, raising such important issues as medication side effects and the degree to which the Constitution requires extensive procedural due process protections prior to the unwanted administration of medication.

5. *Rogers:* The District Court

Shortly after *Rennie,* the district court in Massachusetts decided *Rogers v. Okin*.[122] A complex case, *Rogers* sought, among other things, to end unwanted medication practices based upon First, Fourth, Eighth, Ninth, and Fourteenth Amendment theories.[123] Following 72 days of trial, the district court found that the constitutional right to privacy protected medication decision-making; the court enjoined the hospital from forcibly medicating patients absent an emergency.[124]

Like the district court in *Rennie,* the *Rogers* court placed emphasis on the competency determination. The court declared that it would presume competence of institutionalized patients to make treatment decision in nonemergency circumstances.[125] This was so, the court held, notwithstanding the likelihood that such patients may suffer from "some impairment in their relationship to reality [because they are] most able to appreciate the benefit, risks and discomfort that may reasonably be expected from receiving psychotropic medication."[126] In so holding, the court essentially said that in nonemergency situations for a patient who had not been adjudicated incompetent, the patient herself, not the physician, knew best how to evaluate the pros and cons of taking a given medication.

6. *Rennie* and *Rogers:* The Appeals

The hospital defendants in both cases appealed the trial court's decisions. In *Rogers,* the First Circuit Court of Appeals did not dispute the fundamental holding of the lower court: that involuntarily committed patients retained, on constitutional grounds, a qualified right to refuse psychotropic medication. It did, however, reverse some aspects of the district court's decision, mostly importantly for this

121. *Id.* at 1147.
122. 478 F. Supp. 1342 (D. Mass. 1979), *modified,* 634 F.2d 650 (1st Cir. 1980), *vacated and remanded sub nom.* Mills v. Rogers, 457 U.S. 291 (1982), *on state court certification sub nom* Rogers v. Comm'r Dep't of Mental Health, 458 N.E.2d (Mass. 1983), *on remand,* 738 F.2d 1 (1st Cir. 1984).
123. *Id.* at 1360 n.9.
124. *Id.* at 1371.
125. *Id.* at 1364.
126. *Id.* at 1361.

discussion the contours of the emergency exception to this right to refuse psychotropic medication. The circuit court emphasized that in balancing the complex interests at stake in deciding whether to force medication, there must be
an "individualized estimation of the possibility and type of violence, the likely
effects of particular drugs on a particular individual, and an appraisal of alternative, less restrictive courses of action."[127] As such, the First Circuit saw the primary
decisionmaker as the physician, but put in place safeguards to ensure a qualified
doctor appropriately balanced these competing factors.

The *Rennie* decision was also appealed. The appeals court essentially affirmed
the lower court in most important aspects of its ruling. The court confirmed that
the constitutional right to liberty was not entirely extinguished by civil commitment, as had been asserted by defendants;[128] in contrast, civilly committed
patients had a qualified right to refuse medication, a right that was protected by
the due process clause of the Fourteenth Amendment to the Constitution. In so
doing, the court refused to accept the notion that involuntary administration
of medication was an inevitable aspect of a civil commitment, stating: "there is
a difference of constitutional significance between simple involuntary commitment to a mental institution and commitment with enforced administration of
anti-psychotic drugs."[129] However, utilizing the *Mathews v. Eldridge*[130] balancing
test, the court held that these due process interests could be adequately protected
through nonjudicial hearings.[131]

This decision was, in many significant respects, much like the appellate decision in Rennie.[132] Both found a qualified right to refuse medication and engaged
in a least-restrictive alternative analysis, and both required procedural due process
protections.[133] Importantly, both appellate decisions rejected the proposition asserted by defendants in the respective cases, that civil commitment equated, per
se, to incompetence to make treatment decisions;[134] in so doing, they declined to
endorse the notion that a state may rely on its *parens patriae* power to force medication absent either an emergency or a determination of incompetency.[135]

7. *Rennie* and *Rogers:* The Supreme Court

The Supreme Court granted certiorari in *Mills v. Rogers,*[136] and then remanded for
further consideration in light of an intervening Massachusetts state court case, *In*

---

127. 634 F.2 at 655–56.
128. 653 F.2d at 843.
129. *Id.* at 844.
130. 424 U.S. 319 (1976).
131. Dlugacz, *supra* note 90, at 49.
132. 2 PERLIN, *supra* note 11, at §3B-5.5c.
133. *Id.*
134. *Id.*
135. Dlugacz, *supra* note 131, at 46, *citing Rogers,* 634 F.2d at 653, *citing* cases.
136. 457 U.S.291 (1982).

re Guardianship of Roe.[137] Nonetheless, *Mills* is critical to understanding the development of this area of law for at least two reasons: (1) The Supreme Court, in *Mills,* specifically endorsed the concept that the Constitution was implicated and that some degree of due process protections attached in right to refuse litigation; and, (2) the *Mills* case is a prime example of the court's resistance to addressing the fundamental issues involved in the matter.[138]

The Supreme Court also agreed to hear but ultimately sidestepped a substantive decision in *Rennie,* remanding the case for consideration in light of the Court's contemporaneous decision in *Youngberg v. Romeo,*[139] a case involving the potential habilitation rights of a profoundly retarded, institutionalized young man with the mental capacity of an 18-month-old child.[140] Setting a low standard of scrutiny, *Youngberg* established in the federal courts a professional judgment standard against which to consider claims made against a hospital. Treatment decisions, the *Youngberg* court held, "if made by a professional, [were] presumptively valid."[141]

In retrospect, these remands for consideration, in light of both a state court decision and a Supreme Court case that paid deference to the decision-making authority of hospital staff, can be seen as harbingers of a withdrawal of the federal bench from the robust protection of rights for institutionalized individuals, and a concomitant shift of much litigation into state court forums. The seeds of this retreat can be seen in the *Rennie* remand decision, in which a deeply divided court found that, while there was still a constitutional basis for the right to refuse treatment, the least intrusive alternative analysis had not survived the high court's holding in *Youngberg.* Instead, the appropriate analysis was whether the decision to medicate was a substantial departure from accepted professional judgment.[142] Overall, it would appear fair to conclude that the lower federal courts received the message handed down by the Supreme Court: courts were not to invade the province of professionals in making specific treatment decisions or policies.

The end product, then, of this litigation was a fairly clearly delineated federal constitutional analysis on the right to refuse issue. Predicated on due process and right to privacy grounds, an institutionalized person retains, absent an emergency, a qualified right to refuse unwanted medication.

8. After *Rennie* and *Rogers:* Subsequent State Court Litigation

Despite the Supreme Court's clarity in delineating the constitutional right to refuse treatment, the establishment of a high standard for controverting a treatment

---

137. 421 N.E. 2d 40 (Mass. 1981). On the questions left unanswered by this decision to remand, *see* 2 PERLIN, *supra* note 11, § 3B-5.8, at 240–43.

138. Dlugacz, *supra* note 90, at 46.

139. 457 U.S. 307 (1982).

140. *Id.* at 309.

141. *Id.* at 323.

142. *Rennie,* 720 F.2d at 269 (quoting *Youngberg*).

decision made by a professional created great barriers to the practical enforcement of the right to refuse unwanted medication.[143] The remedy to this apparent short-coming came in the form of state court decisions. Unbound by the *Youngberg* standard, some state courts, most notably in New York and California, crafted expanded due process models for examining this issue.[144]

The most important and comprehensive of these decisions came from the New York State Court of Appeals in *Rivers v. Katz*,[145] a 1986 case expanding due process protections to include forced medication with Lithium. On strictly state constitutional grounds, the *Rivers* court held that an involuntarily committed civil patient retained a fundamental right to refuse psychotropic medications.[146] The court severed the fact of commitment from the inquiry into the patient's compe-tence to make treatment decisions.[147] Neither the state's police powers nor *parens patraie* authority was held to be inherently sufficient justification for abrogating the right to refuse treatment.[148] Consistent with other courts before it, the *Rivers* court held that this right was not unqualified and would have to give ground to a compelling state interest, generally construed as an emergency.[149] Importantly, this right was found to be sufficiently important as to require a threshold judicial finding that the person lacked decisional capacity before forcible administration of medication absent an emergency.[150] As a result of the *Rivers* decision, a New York physician wishing to administer psychotropic medication to an involuntarily hospitalized individual must be prepared to convince, by clear and convincing evidence, a Justice of the Supreme Court (or potentially a jury): (1) that the person suffers from a mental illness; (2) that as a result of that mental illness the person lacks the capacity to make a reasoned decision regarding treatment; (3) that the proposed treatment is the least restrictive alternative; and (4) that the proposed treatment is in the person's best interests.[151] Note that this right is considered so fundamental that the question of whether the proposed treatment is in the person's best interest is not addressed until lack of capacity is established. The court emphasized that this right of a competent person to make autonomous treatment decisions is so basic as to contemplate a situation where the wish to refuse medication threatens the patient's life.[152]

In 1987, in *Riese Mary's Hospital and Medical Center*,[153] a California appellate court, relying on reasoning much like that of the *Rivers* court, expanded similar protections to patients in private hospitals as those provided to public institu-

143. Dlugacz, *supra* note 90, at 51.
144. *Id.*
145. 495 N.E.2d 337 (N.Y. 1986).
146. *Id.* at 341.
147. *Id.* ad 342.
148. *Id.* at 343–44.
149. *Id.* at 343.
150. *Id.* at 343–44.
151. *Id.* at 344.
152. *Id.* at 343–44.
153. 243 Cal Rptr. 241 (Cal Ct. App. 1987) *petition for review granted*, 751 P.2d 893 (Cal. 1988), *dismissed as improvidently granted and remanded*, 774 P.2d 698 (Cal. 1989).

tional patients by the *Rivers* court. The *Riese* court cited *Rivers* for the proposition that the basic inquiry in right to refuse cases was patient competence,[154] and the determination of competence was a singularly judicial, not medical, function.[155]

This trend toward robust interpretations of the right to refuse treatment, under state constitutional theories, continued in cases such as *Anderson v. State*[156] and *People in Interest of Medina,*[157] among others. The Wisconsin Supreme Court, in *State ex. Rel. Jones v. Gerhardstein*[158] established a distinct analytical framework unrelated to the *Youngberg* standard to apply in right to refuse cases. Utilizing an equal protection analysis, the court held that forced medication, absent a finding of incompetency, was prohibited by both the federal and state constitutions.[159] In an embodiment of the split between federal and state courts on this issue, a federal court from the Western District of Wisconsin, in *Stensvad v. Reivitz,*[160] found that a state statute permitting unwanted medication was constitutional under a *Youngberg* analysis. As such, in many states it is entirely possible that an institutionalized person seeking to resist medication could be afforded significantly greater rights under interpretations of the state constitution and statutes than under the federal constitution.

9. More Recent State Court Developments

In one of the most important and far-reaching state court decisions in recent years, the Alaska Supreme Court in *Wetherhorn v. Alaska Psychiatric Institute*[161] ruled that Ms. Wetherhorn could not be involuntarily committed as "gravely disabled" unless the "level of incapacity [is] so substantial that the respondent is incapable of surviving safely in freedom."[162] In this case, Wetherhorn challenged both her order of commitment and the petition for involuntary medication. The evidence put forth in support of these petitions showed that the patient was in a manic state, homeless, had no insight and had been noncompliant with medication for 3 months.[163] The combined hearings of the two petitions took approximately 15 minutes, the testifying psychiatrist was not sworn, and no written or oral report was created by the court visitor as was required by state law.[164]

On the question of involuntary medication, the Alaska Supreme Court cited another critical recent mental disability case it had decided in 2006, *Myers v. Alaska Psychiatric Institute.*[165] There, the court held that in nonemergency situa-

---

154. *Id.* at 252.
155. *Id.* at 252–32 (quoting Rivers v. Katz, 495 N.E.2d 337,342 (N.Y. 1986)).
156. 663 P.2d 570 (Ariz. Ct. App. 1982).
157. 662 P.2d 184 (Colo. Ct. App. 1982), *aff'd,* 705 P.2d 961 (Colo. 1985).
158. 416 N.W.2d 883 (Wis. 1987).
159. *Id.*at 893.
160. 601 F. Supp. 128 (W.D. Wis. 1985).
161. 156 P.3d 371 (Alaska 2007).
162. *Id.* at 373.
163. *Id.* at 372.
164 . *Id.*
165. 138 P.3d at 240.

tions a court ordering unwanted medication must make specific findings that (1) the person is incapable of giving or withholding informed consent and has not made a previous statement that demonstrated the person to have while competently expressed a choice; (2) that the proposed treatment is in the patient's best interests, and (3) that no less intrusive alternative is available.[166]

This formulation—which, at first blush, appears to do nothing more than mirror other state court-expanded due process cases in this area such as *Rivers*[167]— breaks new ground in several key respects. It expands due process protections to the administration of Zyprexa, one of the next generation of "atypical" antipsychotic medications.[168] In so doing it declined to follow recent federal cases involving the criminal trial process that had suggested the possibility that, as new medications were developed, with supposedly lower side effect profiles, due process protections might be reduced concomitant with the—theoretically—reduced risk[169] The court relied on the Alaska constitution in providing greater privacy and due process protections to a patient wishing to resist medication than those afforded by the United State Constitution.[170] In so doing, the court endorsed judicial review of the administration of medication over objection determination, absent an emergency;[171] held that the clear and convincing standard applied to such proceedings;[172] and explicitly rejected the state's assertion that federal Supreme Court cases should form the basis of the Alaska Supreme Court's analytic framework in right-to-refuse litigation.[173] In so doing, the court refused to endorse the underlying assumption that a person is inherently dangerousness and in need of treatment simply by virtue of a civil commitment.

10. Prerequisite for Civil Commitment?

Rights granted to treatment refusers under state law tend to treat separately the need for commitment and the question of competence-to-make-treatment decisions. This bifurcated consideration of competency is, to some extent, mirrored in state commitment statutes.

166. *Weatherhorn,* 156 P. 3d at 382, citing *Meyers* ,138 P.3 at 254.

167. *See Rivers, supra* 145.

168. *Myers,* 138 P.3d at 240.

169. *See, e.g.,* United States v. Weston, 255 F. 3d 873, 886 n.7 (D.C. Cir. 2001), *cert. den.,* 5 534 U.S. 1067 (2002) ("there is a new generation of medications having better side effect profiles"); *see generally,* Michael L. Perlin, *Recent Criminal Legal Decisions: Implications for Forensic Mental Health Experts,* in FORENSIC PSYCHOLOGY: EMERGING TOPICS AND EXPANDING ROLES 333, 346–48 (Alan Goldstein ed. 2006).

170. *Myers,* 138 P. 2d at 248. On the relationship between state and federal constitutional law in mental disability law decision-making in general, *see* Michael L. Perlin, *State Constitutions and Statutes as Sources of Rights for the Mentally Disabled: The Last Frontier?* 20 LOYOLA L.A. L. REV. 1249 (1987).

171. *Myers,* 138 P. 3d at 244.

172. *Id.* at 250.

173. At 246.

For example, the Oregon civil commitment statute declares by statute that an involuntarily committed person has the presumption of competence in civil matters.[174] In contrast, the Utah civil commitment statute[175] and a model statute proposed by the American Psychiatric Association[176] both emphasize that incompetence is one of the of threshold criteria for a valid civil commitment. By making the lack of competence-to-make-treatment decision one of the hurdles for civil commitment, these formulations avoid the potentially perplexing situation in which a legally valid involuntary commitment might exist for a person who, nevertheless, is found competent to make treatment decisions, including the right to refuse treatment. Such a situation, while quite logical as a legal analysis and fully in keeping with the modern trend away from plenary findings of incompetence based upon civil commitment, can be quite challenging from a clinical management position. The situation can also cause third-party payor difficulties whereby an insurance company or managed care organization denies payment for what, in the absence of administration of ameliorative medications, is viewed as custodial care—hospitalization without active chemotherapy. It should be noted, however, that while this dilemma may be avoided by a finding of incompetence to justify the commitment, requiring this could also make it more difficult to make a prima facie case for civil commitment.

11. In Correctional Situations

In the civil commitment context, federal and state laws have, in recent history, always provided some degree of protection from unwanted medications; these protections are also provided in the correctional context, albeit in more limited form.[177]

In *Washington v. Harper*,[178] the Supreme Court examined the question of what degree of due process was required to vindicate the right of a convicted prisoner to refuse psychotropic medications. *Harper* took as its premise two basic assumptions—that a valid conviction properly extinguishes a wide variety of rights[179] and all persons, including convicted prisoners, have a "significant liberty interest" in resisting unwanted medications.[180] How to balance the two in the prison setting was the issue to be decided by the *Harper* court. While a prisoner clearly had a due process right to refuse medication, this interest had to be balanced against

---

174. Joseph Bloom, *Thirty-five Years of Working with Civil Commitment Statutes* 32 J. AM. ACAD. PSYCHIATRY & L. 430, 443 (2004), citing ORE. REV. STAT.§426.070(5)(a) (2003).

175. *Id.* at 444, citing UTAH CODE ANN. §62A-15-631 (10) (2004).

176. *Id.* at 444, citing American Psychiatric Association, *Guidelines for Legislation on the Psychiatric Hospitalization of Adults*, 140 AM. J. PSYCHIATRY 672 (1983).

177. *See infra* Chapter 3 D, discussing other situations specific to competency and correctional institutions (such as competency and disciplinary proceedings).

178. 494 U.S. 210 (1990).

179. *Id.*

180. *Id.* at 221.

the state's interest in operating lawful and safe prisons. In striking this balance, the court emphasized prison security. This led the Court to find that a state statute providing for uncounseled, administrative hearings, which were not subject to judicial review, did meet constitutional muster so long as the state's desire to medicate was "reasonably related to legitimate penological interests."[181] The court held that a security interest was sufficient to meet this standard.[182] Here, it is clear that the Court saw *Harper* as a (post-conviction) prison security case not warranting the high degree of scrutiny afforded to individuals seeking to resist the imposition of such medications during the actual criminal trial process.[183]

In contrast to the minimal protections provided required by the federal constitution as interpreted by the *Harper* court, California has established a fairly robust process for determining when a prisoner may be involuntarily medicated. The permanent injunction in *Keyhea v. Rushen*[184] established that in California, a prisoner was entitled to resist long-term unwanted medication absent a judicial finding of incompetence. The injunction outlines the process by which a prisoner undergoing mental health treatment may be given involuntary medication for a period not to exceed 72 hours; after that time, the prisoner may be certified for a further 21 days of involuntary medication on the finding that the prisoner is, "as a result of mental disorder, gravely disabled and incompetent to refuse medication for the danger to others, or danger to self."[185] However, the prisoner is entitled to contest that certification with the help of an attorney or advocate. A court-appointed hearing officer is to review the certification and if the officer does not conclude that the prisoner is either gravely disabled and incompetent or a danger to others or to self, the state may not continue to administer involuntary medication.[186]

After a total of 24 days, according to California statute, the state must bring the matter to the superior court for an order authorizing further medication over objection. At the hearing the court must find by clear and convincing evidence that the prisoner, as a result of mental disorder, is gravely disabled and incompetent to refuse medication or is a danger to self.[187] As is standard in right- to-refuse formulations, the injunction allows emergency involuntary medication if certain conditions are met.[188] In *In re Qawi*,[189] California's high court made clear that it sees a hearing under this proceeding as "'an adversarial judicial hearing and not

181. *Id.* at 223 (quoting Turner v. Safley, 482 U.S. 78, 89) (1987).
182. *Id.* at 223–24.
183. *See* 2 PERLIN, *supra* note 11, § 3B-8.3, at 327 (discussing the Supreme Court's different approaches in cases involving defendants at trial and those involving prisoners).
184. 223 Cal. Rptr. 746 (App. 1986).
185. Keyhea v. Rushen. Case No. 67432, Order Granting Plaintiffs' Motion for Clarification and Modification of Injunction and Permanent Injunction (1986), § II (A), at 6, available at http://www.documents.dgs.ca.gov/oah/forms/KEYHEA-67432.doc (*Keyhea* injunction). *See also,* Winfield v. Downing 2007 WL 656842 (E.D.Cal. 2007).
186. *Keyhea* injunction, *supra* note 101,§ II(I), (M), at 11, 13.
187. *Id.,* § III(F), at 18.
188. *Id.* at § III(J), pp. 20–21.
189. 7 Cal. Rptr.3d 780 (2004).

a perfunctory step in the process.'"[190] In this way, a prisoner in California wishing to resist psychotropic medications would have access to a considerably more robust bundle of rights under state law than under current federal constitutional formulations.

12. The Right to Refuse Treatment and Sanism

Consider the range of right-to-refuse-treatment issues that are touched on by considerations of sanism and pretextuality, and how questions of perceived competency and incompetency pervade this entire inquiry:

- The attitudes of trial judges toward patients
- The attitudes of counsel toward patients
- The implication of courts' articulating expansive remedies in right-to-refuse class action litigation, without making provision of counsel to represent patients in individualized cases
- The assignment of nonspecialized counsel and uneducated judges to represent patients in right-to-refuse cases
- The failure of appellate courts to take seriously the pro forma quality and nature of hearings in many instances
- The propensity of decision makers to equate "incompetent" with "makes bad decisions" and to assume, in the face of statutory and case law, that incompetence in decision making can be presumed from the fact of institutionalization;
- The perception of a positive relationship between implementation of the right to refuse and failed deinstitutionalization policies; and
- The perception of drugs as the only "cure" for dangerousness.[191]

The common wisdom is clear here. Drugs serve two major purposes of social control: They "cure" dangerousness, and they are the only assurance that deinstitutionalized patients can remain free in community settings.[192] Both of these assumptions are reflected in the case law that has developed in individual involuntary civil commitment cases (in which a judge's perception of the likelihood that an individual self-medicates becomes the critical variable in case dispositions);[193] they are also reflected in the public discourse that is heard in classrooms, hospital corridors, and courtrooms.

190. *Id.*, quoting Department of Corrections v. Office of Administrative Hearings, 53 Cal. App.4th at 789, 61 Cal.Rptr.2d 903 (internal citation omitted).

191. *See* Michael L. Perlin & Deborah A. Dorfman, *"Is It More Than Dodging Lions and Wastin' Time?" Adequacy of Counsel, Questions of Competence, and the Judicial Process in Individual Right to Refuse Treatment Cases,* 2 Psychology, Pub. Pol'y & L.114, 134 (1996); Michael L. Perlin, The Hidden Prejudice: Mental Disability on Trial 155 (2000).

192. *See, e.g.,* Frances Cournos, *Involuntary Medication and the Case of Joyce Brown,* 40 Hosp. & Commun. Psychiatry 736 (1989).

193. *See, e.g.,* Michael L. Perlin, *Reading the Supreme Court's Tea Leaves: Predicting Judicial Behavior in Civil and Criminal Right to Refuse Treatment Cases,* 12 Am. J. Forensic Psychiatry 37, 52–59 (1991).

Neither of these assumptions has any basis in science or in law. Yet, they continue to dominate and control the disposition of individual right-to-refuse-treatment cases.[194] It is essential that participants in these aspects of the judicial process keep these realities in mind at all times.

13. The Use of Structured Interviews

Any legal formulation of the right to refuse unwanted treatment having as a component a competency determination will frequently entail an assessment interview by a mental health professional. This section discusses some relevant factors to be considered in this effort.

In response to questions regarding an individual's competency to make treatment decisions, the examiner focuses on decision-making capacities specific to the specific treatments under consideration. This may be accomplished through interview, but data collection may be facilitated by the use of standardized instruments or structured interviews.[195]

One structured interview guide that was developed to assist clinicians in gathering relevant data from the examinee, the MacArthur Competence Assessment Tool for Treatment (MacCAT-T),[196] was created by the MacArthur Research Network for Mental Health and Law,[197] and was somewhat shorter than its predecessor research instruments, the UTD,[198] the POD,[199] and the TRAT.[200] The content of the MacCAT-T allows the examiner to focus specifically on the examinee's disorder, symptoms, and treatment options. Also distinguishing it from the prior

194. Perlin & Dorfman, *supra* note 107, at 135.

195. For a comparison of the validity and reliability of unstructured and structured interviews, *see* John Monahan, *Tarasoff at Thirty: How Developments in Science and Policy Shape the Common Law,* 75 U. Cin. L. Rev. 497 (2006).

196. Thomas Grisso & Paul Appelbaum, MacArthur Competence Assessment Tool for Treatment (MacCAT-T) (1998).

197. The MacArthur Research Network on Mental Health Law, created by the John D. and Catherine T. MacArthur Foundation with a grant to the University of Virginia in 1988, is directed by John Monahan. The network has, according to its published material, focused on developing new knowledge about the relationships between mental health and the law and applying that understanding to develop improved tools and criteria for evaluating individuals and making decisions that affect their lives. The MacArthur Research Network on Mental Health Law maintains a web site from which the foregoing description was drawn (see http://macarthur.virginia.edu/mentalhome.html).

198. For an overview of the Understanding Treatment Disclosures instrument (UTD), *see* Thomas Grisso, Evaluating Competencies 435 (2003). The UTD was developed by Thomas Grisso and Paul S. Appelbaum; *see* Thomas Grisso & Paul S. Appelbaum, Manual for Understanding Treatment Disclosures(1992).

199. For an overview of the Perceptions of Disorder (POD) instrument, *see* Grisso, *supra* note 114, at 440. The POD was developed by Paul S. Appelbaum and Thomas Grisso; *see* Paul S. Appelbaum, Manual for Perceptions of Disorder (1992).

200. For an overview of the Thinking Rationally about Treatment instrument (TRAT), *see* Grisso, *supra* note 114, at 447. *See* Thomas Grisso & Paul S. Appelbaum, Manual for Thinking Rationally about Treatment (1993).

lengthier research instruments, the MacCAT-T's clinician rating process is less standardized and more general, potentially sacrificing precision in exchange for facilitated application across settings and diagnostic conditions.[201]

The MacCAT-T focuses on the examinee's understanding of the diagnosed disorder; his or her appreciation that the diagnosis is, in fact, correct, or his or her nondelusional explication of why he or she disagrees with it; her understanding of the needed treatment and its benefits and risks; her appreciation that the treatment may provide benefit, or her nondelusional explanation for why she doubts it; her understanding of alternative treatments; the reasoning employed to make a treatment choice; and her appreciation of the consequences that might flow from or the benefits and risks that treatment may provide in her everyday life. Finally, the examinee is asked to make a treatment choice.[202]

Thus the MacCAT-T leads the examiner to make a very direct inquiry into the examinee's capacity to consider and make a reasoned judgment about relevant treatment options, standardizing the query and then providing quantification of the quality of the examinee's understanding. The resulting input to the Court from this kind of standardized but individualized approach should be testimony that assists the fact finder in making the final determination. There are a number of instruments available to assist in competency determinations in general, and in competency for treatment decisions specifically—the foregoing is illustrative of how an instrument might assist the examiner and ultimately the fact finder.

As in the area of civil commitment, so much of how a judge views the decision of whether to authorize medication over objection depends upon his or her overriding view of the nature of the proceeding. Where judges view the nature of the proceeding as fundamentally one to dispense with an obstacle—the patient has the legal right to refuse, as result of mental illness he or she does not see the need to take medication, and, therefore, the hearing is a roadblock to be circumvented to reach the desired end of the patient taking medication—there is generally little evidence to convince a judge that an order authorizing medication is not the appropriate disposition of a case. In contrast, where a court at heart sees the proceeding as having the fundamental purpose of protecting the patient's liberty interest to refuse treatment, hearings can be contentious.

Case law or statute aside, some courts will persist in viewing civil commitment as dispositive on the question of competence-to-make-treatment decisions.[203] In jurisdictions that do not include lack of competence as a commitment criterion, courts that take this distinction may seriously bifurcate the hearings, first making the hospital prove that civil commitment is justified, and only then moving

201. See Grisso, *supra* note 114, at 421, for a review of the MacCAT-T and other competency assessment tools.

202. See *generally,* Grisso, *supra* note 114; also, Thomas Grisso and Paul S. Appelbaum, *MacArthur Competence Assessment Tool for Treatment (MacCAT-T)* (1998).

203. See, e.g., Michael L. Perlin, *"And My Best Friend, My Doctor/Won't Even Say What It Is I've Got": The Role and Significance of Counsel In Right to Refuse Treatment Cases,* 42 San Diego L. Rev. 735 (2005).

on the second hearing on the question of competence-to-make treatment decisions. In such jurisdictions, a court's decision to bifurcate is a good indication that the judge understands that the legal standard for the two decisions, and to some degree the nature of the proof that must be offered, are distinct in the two instances.[204]

Those courts that choose to conduct searching inquiries into this issue will expect expert testimony on a variety of collateral matters. First, the court will likely want to know whether the patient has taken the proposed medication or a similar one before. If so, was it effective, and how is the current situation the same or different from the instant case? Did the person have any significant side effects upon past treatment? And how did the physician evaluate these data?

Although they raise evidentiary and admissibility issues,[205] review of previous records and contact with collateral sources of information tend to be the most persuasive evidence in establishing the effectiveness of previous treatment. Evidence that a patient was well stabilized on a particular medication, for example, and did not experience significant side effects, is likely to raise the comfort level of the court in ordering the same or similar medications presently. Other factors that can be important are whether the patient suffers from any medical condition or falls into any specific risk group that would place him or her at high risk for dangerousness side effects from the proposed treatment. Of course, the emergence of second-generation medications has affected litigation dispositions of this issue — at first causing judges to consider that, because of the lower visible side effect profiles of these medications, there was a reduced need to be concerned about side effect issues that animated right-to-refuse litigation in the first instance; then, as evidence began to emerge about other, serious, side effects related to the administration of these so-called atypical drugs, some courts renewed their vigilance in this regard.[206]

---

204. For example, the question of dangerousness to self or others is generally the pivotal inquiry in a retention proceeding but may be technically irrelevant to an inquiry regarding forced medication where the person's ability to understand the risks and benefits of a proposed treatment and/or whether the treatment is in the person's best interests may be the critical variables. Further, where the legal standards for the proceedings differ, a valid, involuntary civil commitment may be a predicate for consideration of a treatment over objection hearings. In such scenarios, courts declining to bifurcate the hearings will also risk blending the legal standards and proofs required much in the same way as courts continue to confuse competency to stand trial and insanity defense standards. *See, e.g.,* Michael L. Perlin, *Pretexts and Mental Disability Law: The Case of Competency,* 47 U. Miami L. Rev. 625, 642 n.78 (1993).

205. *See, e.g.,* Kirk Heilbrun et al., *Third Party Information in Forensic Assessment,* in II Forensic Psychology 69, 76 (Alan Goldstein ed. 2003), on the importance of third party information in forensic assessment, and noting that there is no evident legal bar, given its relevance as history, to the formulation of a diagnosis based, in part, on third party information.

206. The issues here are complex and the judicial interpretation of the risks involved will likely develop over time, as will the science. The process may be slowed, however, by the fact that the risks involved with second-generation drugs — such as diabetes and pancreatis — while significant and dangerous, are not visible to the layperson, as are some of the most widely known side effects of older medications such as shuffling gait or involuntary muscular movements.

A particularly vexing question regarding the judicial assessment of competence and right-to-refuse litigations in general arises in the not-uncommon situation where the patient evinces mixed motives for wishing to refuse. Such a presentation undermines a simplistic view of such proceedings. What if, for example, a patient testifies that he wishes to refuse medication for a variety of reasons, including that they make his tongue feel stiff, they produce a subjective inner feeling of great uneasiness, and, in addition, he knows that they are poison and are being proposed because the doctor is part of a CIA plot to have him killed because he "knows too much"? Does the clearly delusional aspect of this presentation negate the concern about known side effects? Should it?[207]

A related issue concerning the second-generation antipsychotics is that few of them are available in injectable form. This brings up an interesting point—what is the value or even validity of a hospital seeking an order to medicate a person over objection when the proposed treatment cannot actually be "forced"? Some are of the belief that seeking such an order is meaningless at best and improper at worst.[208] Others, though, point to the subtle influence—some say coercion—of having a judge, with all the power and authority connected with that role—"order" the person to take a certain medication, even where such medication is not available in injectable form.[209] Those subscribing to that school of thought indicate the belief that in such instances the person is much more likely to "voluntarily" take the medication, thus avoiding the potentially dangerous and certainly humiliating circumstance of having medication forcibly administered, something that can be particularly traumatizing for patients with histories of being abused.[210]

Of course, the moral authority of the judge may powerfully influence staff as well, although in some instances staff may undermine the letter if not the spirit of

---

207. *See, e.g.,* MELTON ET AL., *supra* note 33 at 349–50 (case example and discussion).

208. Two of the authors of this volume (MLP and HD) have noted this. We have discussed this with other lawyers with experience in this area, and they have reported making similar observations.

209. *Id.* On the question of voluntariness and perceived coercion in the mental health court context, *see, e.g.,* Allison D. Redlich, *Voluntary, But Knowing and Intelligent? Comprehension in Mental Health Courts,* 11 PSYCHOL., PUB. POL'Y & L. 605, 609–10 (2005).

210. *See generally* on this issue, Susan Stefan, *The Protection Racket: Rape Trauma Syndrome, Psychiatric Labeling, and Law,* 88 Nw. U. L. REV. 1271, 1274–75 (1994):

An enormous proportion of women in mental institutions have suffered from sexual abuse and violence. And when women who have been raped and sexually abused are institutionalized, the 'treatment' they receive fails to address the connection between past sexual abuse and present behavior such as anorexia, self-mutilation, severe depression, and attempts at suicide. Instead, institutional conditions and treatment replicate and exacerbate the pain of the original assaults and abuse, often leaving women patients in a condition that fulfills the prophecy of their pathology. . . . The mental health system's failure to connect sexual violence and the treatment of institutionalized women has been mirrored, rather than critiqued, by lawyers involved in civil rights cases on behalf of institutionalized persons. Although a long history of rape and sexual abuse may be relevant to forced medication, seclusion and restraint, and adequate treatment, no case dealing with these issues has ever addressed rape and sexual abuse.

a judge's order regarding medication administration. Some hospital staff do not believe that a judge should be interfering in medical decision making and resent the intrusion and loss of control, while others are comforted by the notion that an outside authority has examined the issue.[211] It is not uncommon for patients to find the exercise of an adversarial hearing beneficial in the sense that, sometimes surprisingly, seemingly for the first time, they have heard their physician explain and justify her desire to administer a particular medication.[212] This may be a result of the doctor never having taken the time to explain his rationale, it may be related to the difficulty some patients have in really focusing and appreciating the material presented, a combination of both, or other factors. In any case, the proceeding in this way can promote salutatory dialogue between doctor and patient.[213]

The issue of when and under what circumstances a person with a mental disability who is committed to a hospital can refuse medications will remain contentious. Even as the legal standards and principles become more settled within a jurisdiction, changes in science and advancements in the developments of medications will continue to influence judicial applications of those standards.

C. COMPETENCY AND OTHER INSTITUTIONAL RIGHTS

1. Introduction

Early litigation dealing with institutional rights of the mentally ill was aimed at sweeping reform in the areas of right to treatment or right to refuse treatment.[214] However, broad-based class reform and test litigation cases globally challenging all conditions within hospitals (such as the landmark case of *Wyatt v. Stickney*)[215]

---

211. *See, e.g.,* Delila M. J. Ledwith, Jones v. Gerhardstein: *The Involuntarily Committed Mental Patient's Right To Refuse Treatment with Psychotropic Drugs,* 1990 WIS. L. REV. 1367, 1393 ("a responsible psychiatric profession must accept some degree of legitimate interference from lawmakers concerned with the fate of the mentally ill. Such legal interference counters hospital staffs' understandable, though not always meritorious, self-interest in a calm and manageable patient population").

212. *See, e.g.,* Michael L. Perlin et al., *Therapeutic Jurisprudence and the Civil Rights of Institutionalized Mentally Disabled Persons: Hopeless Oxymoron or Path to Redemption?* 1 PSYCHOL., PUB. POL'Y, & L. 80, 114 (1995) (suggesting that medication hearings may have a great therapeutic usefulness in that they can permit a patient to hear and present evidence in a formal, judicial proceeding.) On a similar possibility of therapeutic value in the civil commitment hearing, see John J. Ensminger & Thomas D. Liguori, *The Therapeutic Significance of the Civil Commitment Hearing: An Unexplored Potential,* 6 J. PSYCHIATRY & L. 5 (1978), reprinted in THERAPEUTIC JURISPRUDENCE: THE LAW AS A THERAPEUTIC AGENT 245 (David B. Wexler ed., 1990).

213. *See, e.g.,* BRUCE J. WINICK, THE RIGHT TO REFUSE MENTAL HEATH TREATMENT 383–85 (1997) (on the potential therapeutic value of counseled right-to-refuse-treatment hearings). For empirical corroboration, see Julie Zito et al., *One Year under Rivers: Drug Refusal in a New York State Facility,* 12 INT'L J.L. & PSYCHIATRY 295, 357(1989).

214. *See supra* Chapter 3 B.

215. 325 F. Supp. 781 (M.D. Ala 1971), 334 F. Supp. 1341 (M.D. Ala.), 344 F. Supp. 373 (M.D. Ala.), 344 Supp 347 (M.D. Ala.), *aff'd sub nom.* Wyatt v. Aderholt, 503 F.2d 1305 (5th Cir. 1974).

were not always the appropriate vehicle through which to deal with the more granular, day-to-day issues of life of concern to people confined in institutions.[216] Subsequent litigation was necessary to address specific hospital practices and to bring these details of institutional life into a focus not achieved through more far-sweeping earlier litigation.[217]

Cases were brought seeking declarations of specific institutional rights such as free exercise of religion,[218] visitation,[219] right to publish newsletters,[220] right to free use of the mail,[221] right to use of the telephone,[222] right to exercise,[223] and right to control one's own funds,[224] to name but a few. Some of these matters, such as right to control one's own funds or to engage in sexual activity, specifically implicate the question of competency and will be discussed in more detail in the following. But, in the day-to-day life of a hospital ward, the actual effectuation of any institutional right is subject to the individual assessments of staff members regarding (if not formally) the question of competence and, implicitly, the person's ability to make autonomous decisions. As such, whether raised formally or informally, an underlying question of "competence" underpins litigation as well as day-to-day decision-making in all of these areas.

2. The Significance of *Youngberg v. Romeo*

Youngberg. v. Romeo[225] involved a profoundly retarded, institutionalized young man with the mental capacity of an 18-month-old child, and flowed from allegations of significant abuse (at the hands of institutional staff and other institutional residents).[226] The court held that an involuntarily committed person with mental retardation was entitled to "adequate food, shelter, clothing and medical care,"[227] and, further, to "minimally adequate or reasonable training to sure safety and freedom from undue restraint."[228] As previously discussed, the court also established the "professional judgment" standard for measuring liability, finding that courts were to extend great deference to the treating clinician's professional judgment, so long as the decision made did fall outside of an acceptable range of profes-

---

216. 2 Michael L. Perlin, Mental Disability Law: Civil and Criminal §§ 3C-2 to 2.1 (2d ed. 1999).

217. *Id.* at §3C-1.

218. *Id.*

219. *Id.* at §3C-3.2.

220. *Id.* at §3C-3.4.

221. *Id.* at § 3C-3.5.

222. *Id.* at §3C-3.6.

223. *Id.* at §3C-6.5.

224. Vecchione v. Wohlgemuth, 377 F. Supp. 1361 (E.D. Pa 1974), *further proceedings*, 426 F. Supp. 1297 (E.D. Pa.), *aff'd*, 558 F.2d 150 (3d cir.), *cert. denied*, 434 U.S. 943 (1977).

225. 457 U.S. 307 (1982), *see supra* Chapter 3 B.

226. *Id.* at 323.

227. *Id.* at 315.

228. *Id.* at 319.

sional practice. This ruling significantly raised the showing required by a plaintiff seeking to challenge a judgment made by a professional.[229] This standard slowed, but did not end, the development of litigation in this area.[230] Any case involving institutional rights or treatment must be read in light of the potential relevance of *Youngberg's* "professional standard" finding.

3. Money

As a matter of both case law and statutory right, it is a fairly well-established principle that mentally disabled persons in hospitals have the right to control their own funds unless they are found, through some basic due process proceeding, to be incompetent to do so.[231] *Vecchione v. Wohlgemuth,* the landmark case in this area, involved a Pennsylvania statute that had permitted the state to seize and take control of funds and property of psychiatrically hospitalized patients.[232] The statute, eventually struck down as unconstitutional by the federal district court,[233] divided patients in two groups—those found competent were then given notice and provided with a due process hearing prior to the seizure of their assets; those found to be incompetent were not provided with these basic due process protections.[234] Seized funds were then applied to cover the patients' expenses while in the hospital.[235] The *Vecchione* court found that this statute was "irrational [and] arbitrary," violating the Constitution's equal protection clause.[236] In *McAuliffe v. Carlson,* a federal district court found unconstitutional a state statute permitting the state commissioner of finance to serve as the conservator of the funds of any person confined in a state psychiatric hospital whose annual income or property was of less than $5,000 in value.[237] Importantly, the court found that the fact of

229. *See id.* at 323 note 30, the Court said: "By 'professional' decision-maker, we mean a person competent, whether by education, training or experience, to make the particular decision at issue. Long term treatment decisions normally should be made by persons with degrees in medicine or nursing, or with special training in areas such as psychology, physical therapy, or the care and training of the retarded. Of course, day-to-day decisions regarding care—including decisions that must be made without delay—necessarily will be made in instances by employees without formal training but who are subject to the supervision of qualified persons."

230. *See* 2 PERLIN, *supra* note 3, § 3A-12.3, Comment at 123 ("What is clear is that *Youngberg* is not the 'end of the road' . . . for mental disability litigation in this area").

231. In addition to *Vecchione, supra*, see also McAuliffe v. Carlson, 377 F.Supp. 896 (D.Conn. 1974), *suppl.,* 386 F.Supp. 1245 (D. Conn.) *rev'd on other grounds,* 520 F.2d 1305 (2d Cir. 1975), *cert denied,* 427 U.S. 911 (1976), and *see* so-called "patient bills of rights" statutes such as MICH. STAT. ANN. §14.800 (730) (3), (4) (1980), providing that institutionalized people may control and manage their own property and money except where denial is "essential in order to prevent the [person] from unreasonably and significantly dissipating his assets."

232. 377 F. Supp. at 1362–63.

233. *Id.*

234. 50 PA. CONS. STAT. §§4424, 2501 (1966); *see Vecchione,* 377 F. Supp. at 1369.

235. *Id.*

236. *Id.* at 1370.

237. *McAuliffe,* 377 F. Supp. at 906.

admission to a hospital did "not support even a presumption that a mental patient is incompetent."[238]

4. Voting

A growing number of states are attempting to confront the question of the degree of mental disability sufficient to render a person incompetent to vote in political elections.[239] According to recent surveys, approximately 18 states have statutes that strip people under guardianship of their right to vote, while approximately 18 states require a specific determination that a person lacks competence to vote before the right is removed.[240] Litigation in some states is beginning to provide a legal standard. A Maine case permitted persons with mental disabilities to vote if they had an understanding of the nature and effect of voting and could make a reasoned choice about voting-related issues.[241] Not surprisingly, there has been controversy concerning how to apply and assess this standard.[242] It is expected that this area will continue to be the focus of litigation in the coming years and that legal standards of competence will be at the center of these anticipated litigations.[243]

5. Intimate Interactions

The question of whether an institutionalized person with a mental disability has a right to voluntary sexual interaction is seldom raised in either the scholarly literature or case law.[244] Yet, when the issue is presented, as might be expected, it is controversial and contentious.[245] This potential right was first raised in the extensive

238. *Id.* at 904.

239. Pam Bellick, *States Face Decisions on Who is Mentally Fit to Vote,* THE NEW YORK TIMES (June 19, 2007).

240. *Id.,* quoting Jennifer Mathis, deputy legal director for the Bazelon Center for Mental Health Law.

241. Doe v. Roe, 156 F. Supp. 2d 35, 46 (D. Me. 2001) ("the State's disenfranchisement of those persons under guardianship by reason of mental illness is unconstitutional."); *see also,* Carroll v. Cobb, 354 A.2d 355 (N.J. App. Div. 1976).

242. Bellick, *supra* note 24.

243. Although the issue appears to be gaining increased attention, it is not new. *See, e.g.,* Barbara Armstrong, *The Mentally Disabled and the Right to Vote,* 27 HOSP. & COMMUN. PSYCHIATRY 577 (1976).

244. *See* 2 PERLIN, *supra* note 7, §3C-5.1; *see generally,* Michel L. Perlin, *"Limited in Sex, They Dare": Attitudes toward Issues of Patient Sexuality,* 26 AMER. J. FORENS. PSYCHIATRY 25 (2005) (Perlin, *Attitudes);* Michael L. Perlin, *Hospitalized Patients and the Right to Sexual Interaction: Beyond the Last Frontier?* 20 NYU REV. L. & SOC'L CHANGE 302 (1993–94) (Perlin, *Frontier).*

245. *See* Perlin, *Frontier, supra* note 244, at 519, quoting Rob Karwath, *Mental Center Sex Rule Studied,* CHI. TRIB., Apr. 9, 1989, at 1 (question of patient sexuality is "a public policy question as controversial as they get").

patients' rights standards articulated in the *Wyatt* case.[246] Although many states adopted most of the provisions contained in these standards without significant revision,[247] the overwhelming majority of states declined to incorporate *Wyatt's* protection of "suitable opportunities for the resident's interaction with members of the opposite sex."[248] Little subsequent litigation or legislation to protect this right has followed.[249]

What is likely the most important case examining this issue is *Foy v. Greenblott*,[250] a California case involving a suit brought on behalf of an institutionalized woman and her infant child, who was both conceived and born during the mother's hospitalization on a locked psychiatric unit. The plaintiff sought damages from the mother's attending physician on two theories: (1) that the physician did not sufficiently supervise her so that she would not have sex, or (2) that he failed to provide her with contraception and sufficient counseling on sexual matters.[251]

In declining to adopt the "improper supervision" theory, the *Foy* court found that hospitalized patients retained a right to voluntary sexual interactions including "suitable opportunities for . . . interactions with members of the opposite sex."[252] The court found that this right was based either on least-restrictive-environment theory or on reasonably nonrestrictive conditions-of-confinement theory.[253]

Thus, while rejecting the plaintiff's "improper supervision" theory of the case, the court nevertheless supported a right to reasonable sexual interaction. The court did find, however, that the failure of the medical staff to provide contraception and sexual counseling deprived the mother of her right to reproductive choice.[254]

Few legal analysts have explored the reasons for the dearth of subsequent litigation or scholarly exploration of the patient's right to sexual interaction,[255] but it seems that the overriding issue may be an unwillingness to perceive persons with mental disabilities as complete human beings with the full range of human de-

---

246. *See supra* Chapter 3 C 1.

247. *See* 2 PERLIN, *supra* note 7,§ 3 C-14.2.

248. Wyatt v. Stickney 344 F.Supp. 387, 399 (D. Ala 1972).

249. In fact, only four states—Kansas, Montana, New Jersey and Ohio—did so, and while a small number of states later added similar provisions, Kansas subsequently repealed this aspect of it statute. *See, e.g.,* Martha Lyon et al., *Patients' Bills of Rights: A Survey of State Statutes,* 6 MENT. DIS. L. REP. 194 (1982), *reprinted in* E. B. BEIS, MENTAL HEALTH AND LAW 351–53 (App. H) (1984).

250. 190 Cal. Rptr. 84 (App. 1983).

251. *Id.* at 87.

252. *Id.* at 90 n.2.

253. *Id.*

254. *Id.* at 90.

255. *But see* Perlin, *Attitudes, supra* note 31; Perlin, *Frontier, supra* note 244; Michael L. Perlin, *"Make Promises by the Hour": Sex, Drugs, the ADA, and Psychiatric Hospitalization,* 46 DEPAUL L. REV. 947 (1997); Douglas Mossman, Michael L. Perlin, & Deborah A. Dorfman, *Sex on the Wards: Conundra for Clinicians,* 25 J. AM. ACAD. PSYCHIATRY & L. 441 (1997) See also Faith B. Dickerson et al., *Sexual and Reproductive Behaviors among Persons with Mental Illness,* 55 PSYCHIAT. SERVS. 1299 (2004).

sires and wishes.[256] To the extent that the sexual impulses of persons with mental disability are acknowledged, they seem to raise fear of unbridled sexuality, thus stifling the dispassionate exploration of this important issue.

D. COMPETENCY AND CORRECTIONAL ISSUES

While it is difficult to firmly establish the prevalence of mental illness within the correctional setting, it is clear that large numbers—probably between 200,000 and 300,000 of approximately 2.1 million individuals confined on any given day in the United States—suffer from a mental disorder.[257] The presence of mentally ill persons in jails and prisons presents challenging complexities for the legal, correctional, and mental health systems throughout the country. Many of the issues raised by this conundrum are beyond the scope of this work, and some, such as the right to refuse medication and competence to stand trial, are considered in other sections.

One issue not addressed elsewhere in this volume, but clearly a rather predictable by-product of this large-scale incarceration of persons with mental disabilities, arises when one of these individuals is alleged to have violated institutional rules. Consideration of competency is implicated in that, by virtue of incapacitating mental conditions, the individual may not understand prison rules or, particularly when faced with inadequate access to quality mental health treatment, may have great difficulty in conforming behavior to the expected standards. Subsequent disciplinary hearing may not give proper consideration of mental status issues or defenses, although there are some signs that this is changing.[258] Some courts have recognized the problem; for example, in *Coleman v. Wilson*,[259] the court noted:

> Mentally ill inmates who act out are typically treated with punitive measures without regard to their mental status . . . [and] such treatment was the result of inadequate training of the custodial staff so they are frequently unable to differentiate between inmates whose conduct is the result of mental illness and inmates whose conduct is unaffected by disease. . . . There is substantial evidence in the record of seriously

256. One of us has argued that this is a manifestation of sanism. *See* Perlin, *Frontier, supra* note 244, at 537–45; MICHAEL L. PERLIN, THE HIDDEN PREJUDICE: MENTAL DISABILITY ON TRIAL 157–74 (2000). On sanism generally in the context of the issues discussed in this book, *see supra* Chapter 1 D.

257. *See, e.g.,* Jeffrey L. Metzner et al., *Treatment in Jails and Prisons,* in TREATMENT OF OFFENDERS WITH MENTAL DISORDERS 211 (Robert M. Wettstein ed., 1998); AMERICAN PSYCHIATRIC ASS'N, PSYCHIATRIC SERVICES IN JAILS AND PRISONS xix (2d ed. 2000); Jamie Fellner, *A Corrections Quandary: Mental Illness and Prison Rules,* 41 HARV. CIV. RTS.- CIV. LIBS. L. REV. 391 (2006). See generally, MICHAEL L. PERLIN & HENRY A. DLUGACZ, MENTAL HEALTH ISSUES IN JAILS AND PRISONS: CASES AND MATERIALS 2007 (in press).

258. *See generally,* HUMAN RIGHTS WATCH, ILL-EQUIPPED: U.S. PRISONS AND OFFENDERS WITH MENTAL ILLNESS (2003).

259. 912 F. Supp. 1282, 1320 (E.D. Cal. 1995) (*Coleman* is perhaps the most extensive federal class action lawsuit dealing with the treatment of people with mental illness confined in prisons).

mentally ill inmates being treated with punitive measures by the custodial staff to control the inmates' behavior without regard to the cause of the behavior, the efficacy of such measures, or the impact of those measures on the inmates' mental illnesses.[260]

There is no established right to an insanity defense in disciplinary proceedings within jails,[261] nor is competence to proceed routinely established, notwithstanding the standardization of such due process considerations in criminal proceedings outside of correctional institutions. When, as a result of a disciplinary proceeding within a correctional institution, an inmate is reassigned to segregation, there may be loss of "good-time," (or reduction in sentence for good behavior). Thus, due process considerations would arguably be implicated by these disciplinary proceedings.[262] However, under the analysis offered in *Sandin v. Conner,*[263] due process protections are only required when a punishment constitutes an atypical or significant hardship distinct from the day-to-day deprivation associated with prison life.[264]

A useful survey of the ways that states handled matters related to mental illness and inmate discipline was conducted in 2002 by Michael Krelstein, a California psychiatrist.[265] His survey found that "most, if not all, states require a determination of competency prior to proceeding with disciplinary hearings. The competency requirement is often codified into correctional administrative policy regulating the conduct of disciplinary hearings."[266] Importantly, the author found that

> [t]he determination of competency may be made with or without mental health input. The survey identified two methods among the states to deal with incompetent inmates: restoration of competency and/or provision of a staff assistant. In states in which restoration is attempted, disciplinary hearings are generally postponed and the inmate is treated . . . until competency is restored. If competency cannot be restored within a reasonable period of time (usually six months), the charge can be dropped, although rule violation is often documented in the clinical record or shadow file. In other states, determination of incompetence leads to the assignment of a staff assistant or advocate who is a prison employee, a custody officer, another inmates, or (sometimes) a law student. Inmates are usually not allowed representation by an attorney during disciplinary proceedings.[267]

260. *Id.* at 1320.
261. *See, e.g.,* Fred Cohen, The Mentally Disordered Inmate and the Law § 13-3 (2000).
262. *Cf.* Wolff v. McDonald, 418 U.S. 539 (1974). *Wolff* was a civil rights action attacking administrative practices in a Nebraska prison complex. In its decision, the Supreme Court delineated the due process requirements that would attach to a loss of "good time" or imposition of solitary confinement.
263. 515 U.S. 472 (1995).
264. *Id.* at 484.
265. Michael S. Krelstein, *The Role of Mental Health in the Inmate Disciplinary Process: A National Survey,* 30 J. Am. Acad. Psychiatry & L. 488 (2002).
266. *Id.* at 492.
267. *Id.*

As this survey illustrates, even codified procedures outlining the protections owed to inmates may be narrowly drawn, loosely enforced, and disparate across jurisdictions. While this issue of the need for competence determinations in correctional disciplinary proceedings has thus far received only modest attention, it may generate growing exploration within the larger context of the increased examination of the mentally ill in prisons in general and in disciplinary segregation in particular. How these issues are addressed has implications for the resolution of lawsuits attacking the placement of persons with disabilities in isolation as well as for other policy-driven efforts at creating community re-entry programs for incarcerated persons with mental disabilities.

4

Competency and the Civil Law

INTRODUCTION

The state has an interest in all areas of law, but the nature of its interest depends on whether the law is civil or criminal, or (as was discussed extensively earlier in this volume), whether it involves questions related to institutionalization of persons with mental disabilities. For such matters (discussed in Chapter 3 of this text), the state has a direct interest in the outcome of every case represented by state or local counsel. For criminal law matters (discussed in Chapter 2 of this text), the state has a direct interest in the outcome of every indictment or similar charge, represented by the prosecutor. For civil law matters, discussed in this chapter, the state usually has no direct interest in the outcome of any particular lawsuit, leaving litigation of the disputes to the individuals (or entities) involved.[1]

In any legal matter in which the question of competency arises, the law identifies specific elements to be considered in making a determination of competency. Often these elements are legal constructs and when mental health experts are called upon to conduct assessment of them, the legal constructs must be translated to psychologically meaningful constructions, or what have become known

---

1. Notwithstanding the generalization in the text, the state has a direct interest in many civil cases. The state may have an interest akin to the interest of a private party when the state enters into a contract with a private party. *See, e.g.,* Comm. Through Bradley v. Gerlach, 159 A.2d 915 (Pa. 1960). The state also may appear as a defendant in such a situation, but this generally requires the state to waive its sovereign immunity from lawsuits. *See, e.g.,* Ben Bolt-Palito Blanco Consolidated independent School District v. Texas Political Subdivisions Property/Casualty Joint Self-Insurance Fund, 212 S.W.3d 320 (Tex. 2006). In addition, the state, or a political subdivision of state, may bring civil actions under the doctrine of *parens patrie* for the protection of a child, an individual who lacks the legal capacity to determine his or her own best interests, and others in need of protection. *See, e.g.,* Steele v. Hamilton County Community Mental Health Board, 736 N.E.2d 10 (Ohio 2000).

as "psycho-legal constructs."[2] The principles of forensic mental health assessment[3] are then invoked to guide the assessment so that the resultant findings or opinions are both relevant and reliable.[4] While it is beyond the scope of this chapter to review the nature of such forensic assessment in detail, it is useful to review those aspects of direct relevance in the assessment of competency or prior judgment.

The forensic examiner begins with the psycholegal question clearly identified and then reviews the relevant forensic and clinical instruments available to conduct the assessment. Ethical considerations are also reviewed, with specific attention to standards and guidelines that bear on the case at hand (and in assessing the elderly and potentially cognitively impaired, those might include *What Practitioners Should Know about Working with Older Adults;*[5] *The Guidelines for the Evaluation of Dementia and Age-Related Cognitive Decline;*[6] *The Specialty Guidelines for Forensic Psychologists;*[7] *The Ethical Guidelines for the Practice of Forensic Psychiatry;*[8] *The Standard Guidelines for Forensic Psychologists;*[9] and of course, for psychologists, the overarching *Ethical Principles of Psychologists and Code of Conduct.*[10]

The forensic mental health professional should *not* adopt a different role (such as that of treatment provider)[11] in her or his relationship with the examinee but should, rather, maintain a neutral, arms-length relationship with both the examinee and retaining counsel.[12] As the discussion of civil law cases—especially in the subchapter on donative transfers—illustrates, however, courts often rely on the expert opinion of a treating professional, and in fact value that testimony more

---

2. Thomas Grisso, Evaluating Competencies: Forensic Assessments and Instruments 31–53 (2d ed. 2003).

3. *See, e.g.,* Committee on Ethical Guidelines for Forensic Psychologists (American Psychology Law Society and Division 41 of the APA 1991), *Specialty Guidelines for Forensic Psychologists,* 15 L. & Hum. Behav. 655–65 (1991); Kirk Heilbrun, Principles of Forensic Mental Health Assessment (2001).

4. As required by Federal Rules of Evidence 702 or by Daubert v. Merrell Dow Pharmaceuticals, Inc., 509 U.S. 579 (1993), in jurisdictions that have adopted the Daubert criteria or similar admissibility requirements, and as recommended by psycholegal scholars, including, for example, Grisso, *supra* note 2 and Heilbrun, *supra* note 3.

5. Norman Abeles, What Practitioners Should Know About Working with Older Adults (1998).

6. American Psychological Association, *Guidelines for the Evaluation of Dementia and Age-Related Cognitive Decline,* 53 American Psychologist 1298–1303 (1998).

7. *See supra* note 3.

8. American Academy of Psychiatry and the Law, Ethical Guidelines for the Practice of Forensic Psychiatry (1995).

9. APA, Tests and Measures (1987).

10. American Psychological Association, *Ethical Principles of Psychologists and Code of Conduct,* 57 American Psychologist 1060–1073 (2002).

11. *See, e.g.,* Stuart Greenberg et al., *Irreconcilable Conflict between Therapeutic and Forensic Roles,* 25 Professional Psychology: Research and Practice 50–57 (1997).

12. *See supra* notes 3 and 10.

highly than testimony of other experts on the basis that the treating professional had the most extensive access to the donor and thus the best foundation for an opinion about mental capacity.[13] Among the arguments against relying on a treating professional to render a forensic opinion is one well expressed by Dr. Thomas Schacht:

> Consider the potential logical dilemma of a treating physician who would opine that a patient's consent to medical treatment does NOT prove testamentary capacity. Such an opinion could be turned back on the physician and used to argue that the medical consent was not valid and that the physician committed malpractice. Put differently, the treating physician's objectivity may be questioned because the physician has an interest in maintaining that all treatment took place with proper consent.[14]

The civil law's reliance on treating professionals to serve as expert witnesses may yield to the view that an independent expert is preferable as the sophistication of lawyers and courts in the evaluation of mental health expertise continues to increase.

An extensive discussion about the psycholegal constructs and the parameters of the examination should occur with counsel so that the rights of the examinee can be properly safeguarded.[15] Following those preparatory activities, the forensic mental health evaluation should employ the most current and reliable measures, if there are objective measures available for elements of the competency in question. Data should derive from multiple sources,[16] including review of relevant records or documents, interview of both professional associates or treatment providers and personal associates (family and friends) who have useful descriptive information about the examinee at the time in question,[17] and standardized assessment tools with demonstrated psychometric strengths.

Presuming the expert is working within areas of competence, conducts the examination in comportment with standards and guidelines, keeps thorough records (including, potentially, audio or video recordings of interviews with the examinee in lifetime assessments)[18] the examination may produce information

---

13. *See, e.g.*, Drewry v. Drewry, 383 S.E.2d 12 (Va. App. 1989).

14. Personal communication between Dr. Schacht and coauthor Dr. Connell (May 27, 2007) (e-mail on file with the authors).

15. *See, e.g.*, William Foote, *Consent, Disclosure, and Waiver for the Forensic Psychological Evaluation: Rethinking the Roles of Psychologist and Lawyer,* 37 PROFESSIONAL PSYCHOLOGY: RESEARCH AND PRACTICE 437–444 (2006).

16. *See supra* notes 2 and 3.

17. *See, e.g.*, Kirk Heilbrun et al., *Third Party Information in Forensic Assessment* in COMPREHENSIVE HANDBOOK OF PSYCHOLOGY: VOL. II FORENSIC PSYCHOLOGY (Irving Weiner & Alan Goldstein eds. 69–86 (2003) (FORENSIC PSYCHOLOGY).

18. *See, e.g.*, Eric Drogin et al., *Substituted Judgment: Roles for the Forensic Psychologist,* in FORENSIC PSYCHOLOGY, *supra* note 17, at 301.

of great utility to the court in deciding questions of competency (referred to as *capacity* in most civil law matters).

The state's principal role in civil law is to express the state's public policy interests as they relate to private life. To accomplish this, the state acts through its legislature, either by enacting statutes or by refraining from legislation when the judicially developed law satisfactorily reflects the state's policy values.[19] Certain areas of civil law flow mostly from statutory law as interpreted by judges (e.g., the law of commercial transactions), and others flow mostly from judicial decisions (e.g., the law of torts).

The substantive content of civil law covers virtually every aspect of private life, from a corporation's sale of a multinational business to a couple's decision to marry. The major subdivisions of civil law affecting individuals (as opposed to business entities such as corporations) include property, contracts, torts, and domestic relations.[20] This chapter devotes one subchapter to each of these areas, with the exception of property, which is divided into two subchapters because competency considerations are different.

Tort law, covered in subchapter 4 A, involves claims of bodily injury or property damage for which one private party, the plaintiff, seeks compensation from another, the defendant.[21] The wrongful death suits against (as differentiated from the criminal prosecution of) O.J. Simpson are an example of a tort action. The purpose of tort law is to protect society against unreasonable risk of harm from accidental and unexpected injury.[22] Defamation and libel doctrines in tort law, for example, exist to dissuade the press (and others) from presenting as a fact "information" that was not adequately investigated.[23]

Like tort law, contract law covers actions between private parties for damage to an individual or the individual's property. The major difference between torts and contracts is that tort law's primary function is to vindicate social policy whereas contract law's primary function is to enforce legally binding agreements between the parties.[24] Put differently, contract law involves agreements between the par-

---

19. Norman J. Singer, 2B SUTHERLAND ON STATUTORY INTERPRETATION, §56A:10 (6th ed. 2006).

20. *See, e.g.,* E. ALLEN FARNSWORTH, AN INTRODUCTION TO THE LEGAL SYSTEM OF THE UNITED STATES (3d ed. 1996) at 121–45 (dividing private law into the categories of contracts, torts, property, domestic relations, commercial transactions, and business enterprises). *See also,* Richard C. Schragger, *Cities and Constitutional Actions: The Case of Same Sex Marriage,* 21 J.L. & POL. 47, 155 (2005) (identifying torts, contracts, property, and domestic relations as the major areas of private law that fall within the "private law exception" to the authority of localities to regulate).

21. *See, e.g.,* Palco Linings, Inc. v. Payex, Inc. 755 F. Supp. 1269 (M.D. Pa. 1990).

22. Grams v. Milk Products, Inc., 699 N.W.2d 167 (Wis. 2005); Roberts v. Williamson, 111 S.W.3d 113 (Tex. 2003); City of Louisville v. Louisville Seed Co., 433 S.W.2d 638 (Ky. 1968).

23. *See, e.g.,* Lynch v. N.J. Educ. Ass'n, 735 A.2d 1129 (N.J. 1999); Kiesau v. Bntz, 686 N.W.2d 169 (Iowa 2004).

24. *See, e.g.,* Alejandre v. Bull, 153 P.3d 864 (Wash. 2007); Francis v. Lee Enterprises, Inc., 971 P.2d 707 (Haw. 1999).

ties, and lawsuits over contracts typically assert that the defendant party either did not perform, or performed inadequately, his or her or its obligations under the agreement.[25] An example of a contract action is a movie production company's claim against an actor who agreed to appear in a movie and then failed to do so. Contract law is covered in subchapter 4 B.

Donative transfers law, a subset of property law, is discussed in subchapter 4 C. This area includes gifts made during the lifetime of the property owner as well as the distribution of an individual's property after death. The purpose of this body of law is to carry out the property owner's intentions regarding his or her property.[26] Different rules apply to different types of donative transfers, depending on the form and timing of the transfer. If the transfer occurs on the death of the property owner, then he or she definitely will be unavailable to clarify or resolve any issues about intentions for the distribution of property. The certainty of the property owner's unavailability creates a set of concerns about determining the property owner's intentions that generally do not arise when the property owner is available to clarify his or her intentions.[27] Rules designed to address those concerns apply to wills, but not to lifetime gifts.

The other subset of property law covered in this chapter is guardianship, which is the subject of subchapter 4 D. Guardianship involves determination of an individual's ability to make decisions about his or her affairs, including both property matters (e.g., paying bills, making gifts) and personal matters (e.g., where to live).[28] Although the personal matters tend to be more significant than the property matters in a large number of cases, classification of guardianship as a property law topic stems from the historic focus on property (as opposed to personal matters) in guardianship proceedings.[29] Guardianship statutes generally distinguish between personal and property matters, with some providing separate statutory schemes for personal matters and property matters.[30]

Finally, domestic relations law (also known as *family law*), covers recognition of familial relationships, such as marriage and adoption. In addition, it covers related personal and property issues, such as child custody and division of property upon divorce. A major policy running through domestic relations law is promotion of family and family stability.[31] In those areas where children or minors are involved, a policy of special concern for the protection of minors comes into play

25. Warren v. Davis, 933 P.2d 1372 (Haw. App. 1997); Loyalty Life Ins. Co. v. Fredenberg, 632 N.Y.S.2d 901 (App. Div. 1995).

26. *See, e.g.,* Pfeufer v. Cyphhers, 919 A.2d 641 (Md. 2007); Estate of Goyette, 19 Cal. Rptr.3d 760 (App. 2004).

27. *See, e.g.,* Merchants Nat. Bank v. Weinold, 138 N.E.2d 840 (Ill. App. 1956).

28. *See, e.g.,* N.Y. M.H.L. §81.01 (West 2006).

29. *See* Jennifer L. Wright, *Protecting Who from What, and Why, and How?: A Proposal for an Integrative Approach to Adult Protective Proceedings,* 12 ELDER L. J. 53, 57–58 (2004).

30. *See, e.g.,* Colo. Rev. Stat. Ann. §§15-14-102 et seq. (West 2006).

31. *See, e.g.,* Wallace v. Smyth, 786 N.E.2d 980 (Ill. 2002, *cert dismissed,* 539 U.S. 985. (2003); Estate of Martel, 32 P.3d 758 (Mont. 2001)).

as well.[32] Moreover, issues of civil rights and equal protection have been increasingly prominent in domestic relations law, introducing into domestic relations doctrine the policies underlying those constitutional law areas.[33] Domestic relations matters are discussed in subchapter 4 E.

In each of these substantive areas, legal capacity is required for acts or transactions to receive legal recognition.[34] For most activities of daily life, formal legal recognition is unnecessary. An individual can buy a cup of coffee, or even the coffee shop itself, without proving that he or she has the capacity to enter into a contract. Similarly, an individual can make gifts to family and friends, either by will or during his or her lifetime, without undergoing an assessment of mental functioning. Some family matters, like divorce and adoption, do require formal legal recognition, but even in these matters the individual participants typically do not need to establish that they satisfy the mental capacity requirements that the law imposes in order for the legal recognition to occur.[35]

To the contrary, questions of mental capacity rarely arise in civil law unless one of the participants involved in or affected by the transaction later decides that it was a bad idea.[36] If one of the participants does challenge the validity or enforceability of the transaction at a later point, a court will adjudicate the dispute and determine whether the participant whose capacity is questioned did or did not satisfy the applicable mental capacity requirement.

The mental capacity requirements in civil law reflect the state's policy interest in providing protection for those who cannot protect themselves.[37] Other policy concerns also influence civil law's mental capacity requirements because any acts or transaction affects individuals other than the one protected by the capacity requirement. The weight accorded to any particular policy concern depends on that policy's importance relative to competing policy concerns that would suggest a different legal rule. Each area of law involves different policies, requiring a particularized balancing of policies for every legal doctrine or rule.

A comparison between contract and marriage, each entered into by a person with mental disabilities, illustrates the balancing involved. In the contractual context, an important policy that competes with protection of persons with mental disabilities is the policy of fulfilling expectations by enforcing private agreements

32. *See, e.g.,* Lambert v. Lambert, 861 N.E.2d 1176 (Ind. 2007); South Carolina Dept. of Social Services v. Roe, 639 S.E.2d 165 (S.C. 2006).

33. *See, e.g.,* Lewis v. Harris, 908 A.2d 196 (N.J. 2006); Anderson v. Kings County, 138 P.3d 963 (Wash. 2006).

34. *See, e.g.,* Forman v. Brown, 944 P.2d 559 (Colo. App. 1996) (capacity to contract); Estate of Clements, 505 N.E.2d 7 (Ill. App. 1987); (capacity to make a gift); State Farm Fire & Cas. Co. v. Platt, 4 F.Supp.2d 399 (E.D. Pa 1998) (capacity to marry).

35. *See, e.g., In re* Marriage of Kutchins, 510 N.E.2d 1300 (Ill. App. 1987) (divorce).

36. *See, e.g.,* O'Rourke v. Hunter, 848 N.E.2d 342 (Mass. 2006) (presumption of capacity to execute a will); Smith v. Weir, 387 So.2d 761 (Miss. 1980) (presumption of capacity to marry); Lynn v. Magness, 62 A.2d 604 (Md. 1949) (presumption of capacity to contract).

37. *See, e.g.,* Hauer v. Union State Bank of Wautoma, 532 N.W.2d 456 (Wis. App. 1995).

upon which a market economy depends.[38] The expectations rationale would support a low standard of capacity (to minimize the number of unenforceable contracts), while the protection of persons with mental disabilities would support a higher standard of capacity (to minimize the possibility that an individual is bound to a contract he or she did not understand). In the marriage context, in contrast, the state's interest and the interest of the individual to be protected align: both support the right of the individual to marry so long as he or she understands what the marriage will mean. This unified interest supports a relatively low standard of capacity.[39]

In each context, the state balances, harmonizes, or prioritizes the relevant policy interests to arrive at the legal standard of mental capacity. The variation in policy interests from context to context makes any effort to synthesize the many different mental capacity standards in civil law a "search for a Holy Grail."[40] Each can be loosely described as requiring an understanding of the "nature and consequences" of the act or transaction undertaken, but the requirements of that standard depend entirely on what the particular act or transaction is.[41]

In each area of civil law, the states rather than the federal government have primary responsibility for developing public policy positions and the resulting legal rules.[42] Occasionally states may gravitate toward a single position, but more often there is some diversity. On heavily debated or litigated issues, states tend to follow one of a few possible approaches. On other issues, there may be a different rule in each state. The aim of this text is to present the general principles governing the law and practice of mental capacity in the covered civil law topics, and to identify the major alternative rules on divisive issues.

Each subchapter of this chapter introduces the substantive law with a description of the major policy themes and relevant legal background necessary for a fulsome understanding of the mental capacity standard or standards applicable in that area. Detailed discussion and analysis of cases follow, which illustrate the application of a particular legal capacity standard. These discussions highlight the

---

38. VA Timberline LLC v. Land Management Group, Inc., 471 F. Supp.2d 630 (E.D. Va. 2006); Reformed Church of Ascension v. Theodore Hoover & Sons, Inc., 764 A.2d 1106 (Pa. Super. 2000).

39. *See, e.g.,* Sheffield v. Andrews, 440 S.W.2d 175 (Mo. App. 1969).

40. Loren Roth et al., *Tests of Competency to Consent to Treatment,* 134 Am. J. Psychiatry, 279, 283 (1977).

41. *See, e.g.,* SunTrust Bank, Middle Georgia, N.A. v. Harper, 551 S.E.2d 419 (Ga. App. 2001).

42. This follows from the limitation on federal jurisdiction which restricts suits in federal court to those involving either diversity of citizenship or a federal question (*e.g.,* interpretation of a federal statute). 28 U.S.C.A. §§1331, 1332 (West 2006). Jurisdiction by diversity of citizenship allows many claims to be filed in court in contract and tort actions where the parties are citizens of different states and the amount at stake exceeds $75,000, 28 U.S.C.A. §1332, but the "probate exception" and the "domestic relations exception" to federal jurisdiction preclude federal courts from entertaining will contests and most domestic relations matters. *See, e.g.,* Lepard v. NBD Bank, 384 F.3d 232 (6th Cir. 2004) (probate exception); Tilley v. Anixter, Inc., 283 F. Supp.2d 729 (D. Conn. 2003) (domestic relations exception).

role of forensic psychology and psychiatry expertise in courts' evidentiary evaluations, and the qualities of expert testimony that add to or detract from its credibility. Additionally, where proactive planning is an option, the value of advance psychological or psychiatric assessments is discussed as well.

A. TORTS

1. Informed Consent

a. Historical overview[43]

Perhaps no area of the law of torts is as significant to cases involving persons with mental disability as that of the applicability of the doctrine of informed consent.[44] While the first informed-consent case was litigated over 200 years ago,[45] and the doctrine was subsequently fleshed out in the classic cases of *Salgo v. Leland Stanford Jr. University Board of Trustees*,[46] *Natanson v. Kline*,[47] and *Canterbury v. Spence*,[48] it has only been in later years[49] that the special problems involving consent of persons with *mental disabilities* have been considered in the literature[50] and the case law.[51]

---

43. This section is largely adapted from 3 MICHAEL L. PERLIN, MENTAL DISABILITY LAW: CIVIL AND CRIMINAL §§ 7A-4 to 4.2 (2d ed. 2002).

44. *See* Note, *Who's Afraid of Informed Consent? An Affirmative Approach to the Medical Malpractice Crisis,* 44 BROOKLYN L. REV. 241, 242 (1978) (citing Joseph Katz & Alexander Capron, CATASTROPHIC DISEASES: WHO DECIDES WHAT?, 82–90 (1975)):

> The doctrine of informed consent is designed not only to guarantee accordance of the patient's right to self-determination but also to promote individual autonomy, to protect the patient's status as a human being, to avoid fraud and duress in the consent to medical treatment transactions, to encourage rational decision-making, and to educate the public.

See also Loretta Kopelman, *On the Evaluative Nature of Competency and Capacity Judgments,* 13 INT'L J.L. & PSYCHIATRY 309 (1990).

45. *See* Slater v. Baker & Stapleton, 95 Eng. Rep. 860, 2 Wils. K.B. 359 (1767).

46. 317 P.2d 170 (Cal. 1957).

47. 350 P.2d 1093 (Kan. 1960), *opinion denial of motion for reh'g,* 354 P.2d 670 (Kan. 1960).

48. 464 F.2d 772 (D.C. Cir.), *cert. denied,* 409 U.S. 1064 (1972).

49. The earliest important article, however, predates *Canterbury. See* Jon Waltz & Thomas Scheuneman, *Informed Consent to Therapy,* 64 NW. U.L. REV. 628 (1970).

50. For a helpful bibliography, *see* Paul Appelbaum, *Informed Consent,* in LAW AND MENTAL HEALTH: INTERNATIONAL PERSPECTIVES 45, 79–83 (David Weistub, ed. 1986). Important articles include Loren Roth et al., *Tests of Competency to Consent to Treatment,* 134 AM. J. PSYCHIATRY 279 (1977); Alan Meisel, *The "Exceptions" to the Informed Consent Doctrine: Striking a Balance Between Competing Values in Medical Decision-Making,* 1979 WIS. L. REV. 413; Alan Meisel et al., *Toward a Model of the Legal Doctrine of Informed Consent,* 134 AM. J. PSYCHIATRY 285 (1977). *See generally* RUTH FADEN ET AL., A HISTORY AND THEORY OF INFORMED CONSENT (1986) (FADEN).

51. *See, e.g.,* Aponte v. United States, 582 F. Supp. 565 (D.P.R. 1984); Ritz v. Florida Patients' Compensation Fund, 436 So. 2d 987 (Fla. Dist. Ct. App. 1983); State Dep't of Human Servs. v. Northern, 563 S.W.2d 197 (Tenn. Ct. App. 1978); Matter of Quackenbush, 383 A.2d

The first case that ostensibly made consent to medical care a cognizable legal issue was *Slater v. Baker & Stapleton*,[52] a 1767 leg injury case. There, although the plaintiff hired the defendants to remove bandages from a partially healed leg fracture, the defendants instead—and over the plaintiff's protests—refractured the leg and placed it in an experimental apparatus so as to stretch and straighten it during healing. The plaintiff sued (basically under a breach of contract theory), and presented expert witnesses who testified that the defendants' actions were contrary to standard practice, and that such procedures should not be employed without the patient's consent.[53]

In ruling that the defendants were liable,[54] the court used reasoning "that would in subsequent centuries fall under [the doctrine of] malpractice law":[55]

> In answer to this, it appears from the evidence of the surgeons that it was improper to disunite the callous [bony material in healing] without consent: this is the usage and law of surgeons: then it was ignorance and unskillfulness in that very particular to do contrary to the rule of the profession, what no surgeon ought to have done; and indeed it is reasonable that a patient should be told what is about to be done to him, that he may take courage and put himself in such a situation as to enable him to undergo the operation.[56]

While there were several seemingly pertinent nineteenth-century American cases,[57] a series of decisions in the early twentieth century—including the frequently cited *Schloendorff v. Society of New York Hospitals*[58]—"are almost universally credited with formulating the basic features of informed consent in American law."[59] In *Schloendorff*—an unconsented-to-surgery case—Justice Cardozo formulated the "eloquent" and "classic statement of the patient's right to self-determination":[60]

---

785 (N.J. Cty. Ct. 1978). *See generally* 1 DAVID W. LOUISELL & HAROLD WILLIAMS, MEDICAL MALPRACTICE ¶8.09 at 8-119 to 8-123 n.2 (1986); 2 *id.*, ¶17A.12, at 17A-35 to 17A-43; Janice Lunde, *Informed Consent and the HIV-Positive Physician*, 39 MED. TRIAL TECH. Q. 186 (1992).

52. Slater v. Baker & Stapleton, 95 Eng. Rep. 860, 2 Wils. K.B. 359 (1767).

53. *Id.*, 2 Wils. K.B. at 360.

54. *See* FADEN, *supra* note 50, at 116, for a discussion of some of the ancillary peculiar pleading issues raised by this case.

55. *Id.* at 117.

56. *Slater*, 2 Wils. K.B. at 362.

57. FADEN, *supra* note 50, at 117–19 (discussing cases analyzed in Martin Pernick, *The Patient's Role in Medical Decisionmaking: A Social History of Informed Consent in Medical Therapy*, in 3 PRESIDENT'S COMMISSION FOR THE STUDY OF ETHICAL PROBLEMS IN MEDICINE AND BIOMEDICAL AND BEHAVIORAL RESEARCH, MAKING HEALTH CARE DECISIONS 3–14 (1982).

58. 105 N.E. 92 (N.Y. 1914).

59. FADEN, *supra* note 50, at 120.

60. FADEN, *supra* note 50, at 123. Because the narrow issue in *Schloendorff* was whether the defendant hospital was liable for torts committed by doctors using its facilities, *see* 3 PERLIN, *supra* note 43, § 7A-3.2a, no informed consent violation was found.

Every human being of adult years and sound mind has a right to determine what shall be done with his own body; and a surgeon who performs an operation without the patient's consent commits an assault for which he is liable in damages.[61]

b. Subsequent cases

Building on *Schloendorff* and its predecessors, a trilogy of subsequent cases helped craft modern consent doctrine by focusing on: (1) the explicit duty to disclose information prior to the gaining of consent; (2) the use of negligence, rather than battery, as the appropriate legal cause of action;[62] and (3) the necessity that consent be "informed."

In *Salgo v. Leland Stanford Jr. University Board of Trustees,*[63] where the plaintiff charged that the defendants failed to warn him of the risks of permanent paralysis as a result of a translumbar aortography, the court found that the defendants had a duty to disclose "any facts which are necessary to form the basis of an intelligent consent by the patient to proposed treatment."[64] It "tempered"[65] this extension of the law, however, by adding that, in discussing the element of risk, "a certain amount of discretion must be employed consistent with the full disclosure of facts necessary to an informed consent."[66]

Then, in *Natanson v. Kline,*[67] the plaintiff sued her physician for his failure to obtain informed consent to cobalt radiation therapy, from which she suffered severe radiation burns. The court, in addition to mandating a duty to disclose and explain risks to patients "in language as simple as necessary the nature of the ailment, the nature of the proposed treatment, the probability of success or of alternatives, and perhaps the risk of unfortunate results and unforeseen conditions within the body,"[68] added "strong self-determination language"[69] that flowed from *Schloendorff* and the earlier *battery* cases:

> Anglo-American law starts with the premise of thorough-going self-determination. It follows that each man is considered to be the master of his own body, and he may, if he be of sound mind, expressly prohibit the performance of life-saving surgery, or

61. *Schloendorff,* 105 N.E. at 93.

62. *See* Allan McCoid, *A Reappraisal of Liability for Unauthorized Medical Treatment,* 41 MINN. L. REV. 381 (1957).

63. 317 P.2d 170 (Cal. App. 1957).

64. *Id.,* 317 P.2d at 181. *See* FADEN, *supra* note 50, at 145 n.37, for a discussion of the roots of this phrase.

65. FADEN, *supra* note 50, at 126.

66. *Salgo,* 317 P.2d at 181. *See generally* Alan Meisel, *The Expansion of Liability for Medical Accidents: From Negligence to Strict Liability by Way of Informed Consent,* 56 NEB. L. REV. 99 (1977); Katz, *Informed Consent: A Fairy Tale? Law's Vision,* 39 U. PITT. L. REV. 150 (1977). The issue of a "therapeutic privilege" (allowing a doctor to withhold material information that would cause the patient's physical or mental condition to deteriorate) is discussed in Note, *Consent to Medical Treatment: Informed or Misinformed?* 12 WM. MITCHELL L. REV. 541, 561–63 (1986).

67. 350 P.2d 1093, 1095 (Kan. 1960).

68. *Id.,* 350 P.2d at 1106.

69. FADEN, *supra* note 50, at 130.

other medical treatment. A doctor might well believe that an operation or form of treatment is desirable or necessary but the law does not permit him to substitute his own judgment for that of the patient by any form of artifice or deception.[70]

Natanson is thus additionally important because of its holding that a patient's mere consent does not shield a defendant from negligence even where the medical performance is flawless. Liability may result if there is an injury from a known inherent risk undisclosed to the patient,[71] a new development in malpractice law.

Finally, in *Canterbury v. Spence*,[72] where a patient became paralyzed after falling from his hospital bed after undergoing a laminectomy and not having been warned that there was a 1% risk of such paralysis attendant to the operation,[73] the court addressed "all of the major aspects of informed consent law."[74] Beginning with the self-determination principles of *Schloendorff*, the court held that doctors were under an obligation to disclose all risks "material" to a patient's decision.[75] These included "the inherent and potential hazards of the proposed treatment, the alternatives to that treatment, if any, and the results likely if the patient remains untreated."[76]

Most importantly, the determination of materiality is to be made from the perspective of the patient, not the physician:

> [A risk is material if a] reasonable person, in what the physician knows or should know to be the patient's position, would be likely to attach significance to the risk or cluster of risks in deciding whether or not to forego the proposed therapy.[77]

By casting the standard in this perspective, the court thus "swam upstream against a powerful current of support for the [generally accepted professional] standard of disclosure."[78] To otherwise bind a disclosure obligation to medical usage would be "to arrogate the decision on revelation to the physician alone,"[79] a standard that the court found unacceptable, demanding instead "a standard set

---

70. *Natanson,* 350 P.2d at 1104.

71. *Id.* at 1106.

72. 464 F.2d 772 (D.C. Cir.), *cert. denied,* 409 U.S. 1064 (1972). *See also* Cobbs v. Grant, 502 P.2d 1 (Cal. 1972); Wilkinson v. Vesey, 295 A.2d 676 (R.I. 1972).

73. *Canterbury,* 464 F.2d at 776–77.

74. Appelbaum, *supra* note 50, at 48.

75. *Canterbury,* 464 F.2d at 778. On the specific issue of risks attendant to innovative therapies, *see* Waltz & Scheuneman, *supra* note 49, at 632–35.

76. *Canterbury,* 464 F.2d at 787–88.

77. *Id.* at 787. On this point, the court relied on Waltz & Scheuneman, *supra* note 49, at 640. For a slightly different formulation, *see Wilkinson,* 295 A.2d at 689 (citing Waltz & Scheuneman, *supra* note 49).

To satisfy the requirement that the plaintiff prove that the failure to disclose led to the alleged injury, he could demonstrate that a "prudent person in the patient's position," *Canterbury,* 464 F.2d at 784, would have decided not to undergo the treatment or procedure if he had known the unrevealed information.

78. FADEN, *supra* note 50, at 135.

79. *Canterbury,* 464 F.2d at 784.

by law for physicians rather than one which physicians may or may not impose upon themselves."[80]

Discussing these recent cases from the special perspective of informed consent in the prescription of drugs, Professor Tietz has thus concluded:

> Only courts can recognize the rights of individual patients and give meaning to those rights by fashioning a clear, unequivocal, and fair duty of informed consent. . . . Until courts place physicians under a duty to inform, judicial opinions will continue to perpetuate medical autonomy at the expense of individual liberty. Without judicial intervention, patients' rights of self-determination and bodily integrity, as well as the intangible dignitary interest, will continue to be little more than empty promises.[81]

Professor Meisel and his colleagues have developed a five-prong post-Canterbury[82] model of informed consent:[83] (1) voluntariness,[84] (2) provision of

---

80. *Id. See also, e.g.,* Sard v. Hardy, 379 A.2d 1014 (Md. 1977) (adopting *Canterbury, supra*).
On the collateral issue of the role of expert testimony in informed consent litigation, *see* Note, *Informed Consent Liability,* 26 DRAKE L. REV. 696, 710 (1976–77):

> The role of expert medical testimony in informed consent litigation has been an extensive one. Those jurisdictions in which the duty to disclose is premised on the materiality of the information to the patient's decision, rather than on medical custom, do not require such testimony to establish the physician's duty of care. This is the better rule. Nevertheless, even under the materiality rule, expert medical testimony is still, and should be, a relevant and necessary ingredient of informed consent litigation. Such testimony should be required to establish: (1) the existence of the proper alternatives, if any, to the medical therapy which was adopted; (2) the existence, nature and potential incidence of the collateral or inherent risks of the treatment adopted; (3) that it was medically proper, under the particular circumstances, for the physician to exercise his "therapeutic privilege," and thereby fail to disclose the potential risks of the treatment adopted; (4) that it was the undisclosed risk which materialized that was a contributing cause of the plaintiff's injury; (5) that the presence of a medical emergency was the reason for nondisclosure; (6) the probable consequences that would arise if the patient's condition went untreated; and (7) that the risk which materialized or the alternative that was not utilized was generally unknown in the medical community when the decision-making process occurred concerning the treatment adopted.

See, for a psychoanalytic perspective, Largey v. Rothman, 540 A.2d 504 (N.J. 1987) (following *Canterbury;* overruling Kaplan v. Haines, 241 A.2d 235 (N.J. 1968)); Zeichner, *The Role of Unconscious Conflict in Informed Consent,* 13 BULL. AM. ACAD. PSYCHIATRY & L. 283 (1985).

81. Tietz, *Informed Consent in the Prescription Drug Context: The Special Case,* 41 WASH. L. REV. 367, 417 (1986).

82. *See* FADEN, *supra* note 50, at 138–39, for a discussion of pertinent post-*Canterbury* cases (focusing on Truman v. Thomas, 611 P.2d 902 (Cal. 1980)).
A separate minority position developed subsequent to *Canterbury* is that of the "subjective standard," focusing exclusively on whether the particular patient in question, after knowing all of the risks, would have consented to the procedure (in which case expert testimony is unnecessary). *See* Scott v. Bradford, 606 P.2d 554 (Okla. 1979), *criticized in* Note, *supra* note 66, at 558.

83. Meisel et al., *supra* note 50, at 286. The authors divide these prongs into three main variables (provision of information, competency, and understanding), one precondition (voluntariness), and one consequence of the process (decision to consent or refuse).

84. Patients must be free from coercion, unfair persuasions, and inducements. *Id.* (citing Relf v. Weinberger, 372 F. Supp. 1196, 1202 (D.D.C. 1974)).

information,[85] (3) competency,[86] (4) understanding,[87] and (5) decision.[88] Meisel has ably summarized the competing notions:

> The vehement criticism of the doctrine of informed consent by advocates for the medical view of decisionmaking—the view that medical decisions are properly made by physicians and that the doctrine of informed consent seeks to divest them of this prerogative—results from a fundamental misunderstanding of what the doctrine requires and permits. The doctrine of informed consent allocates decisional authority within the doctor-patient relationship. In so doing, it seeks to promote patient self-determination in the realm of medical decisionmaking through the twin duties imposed upon the physician—the duty to disclose information to the patient and the duty to obtain the patient's consent before rendering treatment. Although informed consent places a heavy emphasis on patient self-determination, the exceptions that have developed for emergencies, for incompetent patients, for waiver,

85. Patients must be informed, "in simple language," of: "1) risks, discomforts and side-effects of proposed treatments, 2) the anticipated benefits of such treatments, 3) the available alternative treatments and their attendant risks, discomforts, and side-effects, and 4) the likely consequences of a failure to be treated at all." Meisel et al., *supra* note 50, at 286 (citations omitted).

The authors further suggested two general exceptions: in an emergency (where the patient is unconscious; *see Canterbury,* 464 F.2d at 788), and where disclosure "is likely to upset the patient so seriously that he or she will be unable to make a rational decision" (citing Note, *Informed Consent: The Illusion of Patient Choice,* 23 EMORY L.J. 503 (1974). Meisel et al., *supra* note 50, at 286).

86. While patients are presumed to have the capacity to understand information provided to them, if a patient is not competent, his or her decisions will not be considered valid. Meisel et al., *supra* note 50, at 287 (citing *Relf, supra*).

87. At least some authorities have suggested that doctors are obligated to take reasonable steps to ascertain whether a patient understands what has been disclosed. Meisel et al., *supra* note 8, at 287 (citing Alexander Capron, *Informed Consent in Catastrophic Disease Research and Treatment,* 123 U. PA. L. REV. 340 (1974), and Pennsylvania Department of Welfare, *Rights of Patients and Residents in Mental Health and Mental Retardation Facilities,* 5 PA. BULL. 2038 (1975)).

88. Although the authors suggest that failure to articulate a decision may, in certain circumstances, be seen as implying consent to treatment (Meisel et al., *supra* note 50, at 287, citing 139 A.L.R. 1370 (1942)), later case law calls into serious question the validity of this proposition. *See, e.g.,* Lipscomb v. Memorial Hosp., 733 F.2d 332, 335–336 (4th Cir. 1984); Hurbeson v. Parke Davis, Inc., 746 F.2d 517, 521–23 (9th Cir. 1981). *See also* Meisel, *supra* note 50, at 443–53.

Thus, a California appellate court has found that consent "implies positive action and always involves submission; mere passivity or submission does not include consent," Shea v. Board of Medical Examiners, 146 Cal. Rptr. 653, 663 (Cal. App. 1978), and at least one commentator has suggested that a patient in a mental institution may be so intimidated by the surroundings that a truly voluntary consent may be difficult to obtain. Elizabeth Symonds, *Mental Patients' Right to Refuse Drugs: Involuntary Medication as Cruel and Unusual Punishment,* 7 HASTINGS CONST. L.Q. 701, 712–13 (1980). *See generally* 2 PERLIN, *supra* note 43, § 3B-4.2 (2d ed. 1998) (discussing Kaimowitz v. Michigan Dep't of Mental Health, Civ. No. 73-19434-AW (Mich. Cir. Ct. Wayne Cty., July 10, 1973), *reprinted in* ALEXANDER D. BROOKS, LAW, PSYCHIATRY AND THE MENTAL HEALTH SYSTEM 902 (1974). *See generally* 2 PERLIN, *supra* note 43, § 3B-4.2, at notes 98–116.

and for therapeutic reasons,[89] permit this emphasis to be ameliorated in certain situations to achieve other desirable goals and to accommodate other laudable and deeply held values.[90]

c. Special problems in cases of persons with mental disabilities

Because incompetency cannot be presumed because a person is being (or has been) treated for mental illness[91] nor because of the fact that the person has been institutionalized,[92] a psychiatrist[93] is obligated to make a full and fair disclosure of risks of treatment,[94] and to obtain, in most cases, a patient's informed consent prior to the imposition of involuntary treatment.[95]

The exceptions to these doctrines arise in emergencies[96] or where a patient has been declared judicially incompetent.[97] In certain circumstances, in cases involving treatments deemed "intrusive," some sort of judicial hearing will be necessary before an incompetent patient can be treated against his or her will.[98]

89. See, e.g., Shea, *Legal Standard of Care for Psychiatrists and Psychologists*, 6 W. St. U. L. Rev. 71, 84 (1979) (listing exceptions). See Woods v. Brumlop, 337 P.2d 520, 525 (N.M. 1962).

90. Meisel, *supra* note 50, at 406. See also Roth et al., *supra* note 50, at 280, suggesting competency may be determined by examining (1) the patient's ability to evidence a choice, (2) the "reasonable" outcome of the choice, (3) whether the choice is based on "rational" reasons, (4) the patient's ability to understand the choice, and (5) the patient's actual understanding of the choice; see Barbara Atwell, *The Modern Age of Informed Consent*, 40 U. Rich. L. Rev. 591, 596 n.15 (2006) (discussing Roth's formulation).

91. See, e.g., Wilson v. Lehmann, 379 S.W.2d 478, 479 (Ky. Ct. App. 1964).

92. See, e.g., Rennie v. Klein, 462 F. Supp. 1131 (D.N.J. 1978), *supplemented*, 476 F. Supp. 1294 (D.N.J. 1979), *modified*, 653 F.2d 836 (3d Cir. 1981), *vacated and remanded*, 458 U.S. 1119 (1982), *on remand*, 720 F.2d 266 (3d Cir. 1983). See generally 2 Perlin, *supra* note 43, §§ 3B-5.1 to 3B-5.6.

93. On psychotherapy issues, see Ralph Slovenko, *Psychotherapy and Informed Consent: A Search in Judicial Regulation*, in Law and the Mental Health Professionals: Friction at the Interface 51 (W. Barton & C. Sanborn eds. 1978).

94. See Matter of K.S., 433 N.W.2d 291 (Wis. 1988) (patient adequately told of advantages and disadvantages of taking medication); Barcai v. Betwee, 50 P. 3d 946 (Hawaii 2002) (psychiatrist who did not tell patient about risk of neuroleptic malignant syndrome as possible side effect of antipsychotic medication did not properly establish therapeutic privilege exception to requirement of informed consent).

95. See, e.g., Rivers v. Katz, 504 N.Y.S.2d 74 (1986); Gundy v. Pauley, 619 S.W.2d 730, 731–32 (Ky. Ct. App. 1981). See generally supra Chapter 3.

96. The definition of "emergency" for these purposes—a "sudden, significant change in the plaintiff's condition which creates a danger to the patient himself or to others in the hospital" not greater than 72 hours in duration—is found in *Rennie*, 462 F. Supp. at 1154. See also *Rivers*, 504 N.Y.S.2d at 80.

See also, e.g., Frasier v. Department of Health & Human Resources, 500 So. 2d 858, 864 (La. Ct. App. 1986) (patient's "life-threatening" condition mooted informed consent issue).

97. See *Rennie*, 462 F. Supp. at 1144–46; *Rivers*, 504 N.Y.S.2d at 80. For a recent consideration, see David Naimark et al., *Informed Consent and Competency: Legal and Ethical Issues*, in Current Clinical Neurology: Psychiatry for Neurologists 391 (D. Jeste & J. Friedman eds.).

98. *Rivers*, 504 N.Y.S.2d at 81–82; Rogers v. Commissioner of Dep't of Mental Health, 458 N.E.2d 308, 314 (Mass. 1983). See generally 2 Perlin, *supra* note 43, § 3B-5.9. See also, e.g., In re W.S., 377 A.2d 969 (N.J. Juv. & Dom. Rel. Ct. 1977).

Here, the court exercises what has been characterized as "substituted judgment," taking into account "the decision the patient probably would have made, the patient's religious beliefs, the impact upon the patient's family, the probability of adverse effects, the consequences if treatment is refused, and the prognosis with treatment."[99] In cases involving the consent of putatively mentally disabled persons to surgery, courts have looked at the degree of the patient's disability to determine its impact on the patient's ability to meaningfully consent,[100] and have considered the appropriate party to be designated to give substituted consent when the patient is, in fact, incompetent.[101]

2. Persons with Mental Disabilities as Defendants[102]

a. Introduction

Traditionally, persons with mental disabilities were held to be responsible by an "objective standard,"[103] for both negligent[104] and intentional torts,[105] under one or more of six basic rationales:

---

99. 2 LOUISELL & WILLIAMS, *supra* note 51, ¶17A.12, at 17A-37 (discussing *In re* Boyd, 403 A.2d 744 (D.C. 1979)). *See also,* for a different formulation, Price v. Sheppard, 239 N.W.2d 905, 913 (Minn. 1976).

100. *See, e.g.,* State Dep't of Human Servs. v. Northern, 563 S.W.2d 197, 209–10 (Tenn. Ct. App. 1978) (although the patient was "lucid" and generally "of sound mind," on the subject of amputation of her frostbitten and gangrenous feet "her comprehension is blocked, blinded or dimmed to the extent that she is incapable of recognizing facts which would be obvious to a person of normal perception").

101. *See, e.g.,* Aponte v. United States, 582 F. Supp. 555, 566–69 (D.P.R. 1984) (failure to obtain presurgery consent from guardian where patient a "totally disabled schizophrenic"); Ritz v. Florida Patients' Compensation Fund, 436 So. 2d 987, 989–93 (Fla. Dist. Ct. App. 1983) (where severely mentally retarded, incompetent adult with no legal guardian in need of surgery, right to consent vested in adult's parent who had continuing legal responsibility for patient's continuing care and maintenance).

102. This section is largely adapted from 3 PERLIN, *supra* note 43, § 7B-2.

103. The development of the objective standard in general is discussed in Warren Seavey, *Negligence—Subjective or Objective?* 41 HARV. L. REV. 1 (1927).

104. *See, e.g.,* Mujica v. Turner, 582 So. 2d 24 (Fla. Dist. Ct. App.), *reh'g denied,* 592 So. 2d 681 (1991); Hudner v. Sellner, 800 F.2d 377 (4th Cir. 1986); McGuire v. Almy, 8 N.E.2d 760, 762 (Mass. 1937); William Curran, *Tort Liability of the Mentally Ill and the Mentally Deficient,* 21 OHIO ST. L.J. 52 (1960).

105. *See, e.g., In re* Meyer's Guardianship, 261 N.W. 211, 213 (Wis. 1935) (arson); Kaczer v. Marrero, 324 So. 2d 717, 718 (Fla. Dist. Ct. App. 1976) (assault and battery); Spaulding v. United States, 621 F. Supp. 1150, 1154 (D. Me. 1985) (same). Professor Ellis points out that there has been somewhat of a split in the case of intentional torts, such as defamation, which re-quire a showing of malice. *See* James W. Ellis, *Tort Responsibility of Mentally Disabled Persons,* 1981 A.B.A. RES. J. 1079, 1081 n.12 (discussing Irvine v. Gibson, 77 S.W. 1106 (Ky. 1904) (malice required)) and Ullrich v. New York Press Co., 50 N.Y.S. 788 (Sup. Ct. 1898). *Cf.* Hudner v. Sellner, 800 F.2d 377 (4th Cir. 1986) (defamation). *But see* Preferred Risk Mutual Ins. Co. v. Saboda, 489 So. 2d 768, 770–71 (Fla. Dist. Ct. App. 1986) (liability of insane person does not extend to punitive damages, nor can it be extended to any tort requiring "wanton misconduct").

For an analysis of the interplay between criminal insanity, an intentional tort, and insur-ance policy coverage, *see* Rajspic v. Nationwide Mutual Ins. Co., 718 P.2d 1167 (Idaho 1986).

1. "[W]here one of two innocent persons must suffer a loss, it should be borne by the one who occasioned it."[106]
2. Liability for negligent acts will encourage those who are responsible for persons with mental disabilities (their families or guardians) to look after them and prevent them from doing harm.[107]
3. If persons with mental disabilities are to live in liberty in society, they should pay for the damage they cause.[108]
4. Mental disability is easily feigned, and defendants might choose such an act of duplicity to avoid liability.[109]
5. It is difficult for courts to distinguish between "true" mental disability and variations in temperament, intellect, and emotional balance, and to allow all such differences to serve as excuses would erode the objective standard in all cases.[110]
6. The insanity defense and the doctrine of diminished capacity have wreaked havoc in the field of criminal law, and this chaos should not be recreated in tort law.[111]

In a careful analysis, Professor Ellis[112] has found each of these rationales wanting,[113] both as a result of: (1) their impracticality, as they presuppose a greater control over the acts of persons with mental disabilities than is exercised "by any but the most draconian of caretakers";[114] and, more importantly, (2) their "under-

---

See also Bell v. Busse, 633 F. Supp. 628 (S.D. Ohio 1986) (insanity not defense to housing discrimination suit based on federal civil rights statutes); Delahanty v. Hinckley, 799 F. Supp. 184 (D.D.C. 1992) ("insane" tortfeasors are not liable for punitive damages to the victims of their torts).

106. Ellis, *supra* note 105, at 1083 (quoting Seals v. Snow, 254 P.2d 348, 349 (Kan. 1927)).

107. Ellis, *supra* note 105, at 1083 (citing *McGuire v. Almy, supra;* G.A. SMOOT, THE LAW OF INSANITY 362–63 (1929)). According to Ellis, this is "among the most frequently cited" rationales in early cases. Ellis, *supra* note 105, at 1083 n.22.

108. Ellis, *supra* note 105, at 1083 (citing, inter alia, RESTATEMENT (SECOND) OF TORTS §283B, Comment b(3), at 17 (1965)).

109. Ellis, *supra* note 105, at 1084 (citing, inter alia, G.A. SMOOT, *supra* note 65, at 363). *See, e.g.,* Williams by Williams v. Kearbey by Kearbey, 775 P.2d 670, 672 (Kan. App. 1989) (citing RESTATEMENT on "ease" with which mental illness can be "feigned").

110. Ellis, *supra* note 105, at 1084 (citing, inter alia, RESTATEMENT (SECOND) OF TORTS, §283B, Comment b(1), at 17 (1965)). *See generally* Alexander Greer & Paul Appelbaum, *Civil Liability of Mentally Ill Persons,* 44 HOSP. & COMMUN. PSYCHIATRY 617 (1993).

111. Ellis, *supra* note 105, at 1084, (citing Jolley v. Powell, 299 So. 2d 647, 649 (Fla. Dist. Ct. App. 1974); WILLIAM L. PROSSER, HANDBOOK OF THE LAW OF TORTS 1001 (4th ed. 1971).

112. Other commentators agree. *See generally* sources cited in Note, *Tort Liability of the Mentally Ill in Negligence Actions,* 93 YALE L.J. 153 n.3 (1983), especially David Seidelson, *Reasonable Expectations and Subjective Standards in Negligence Law: The Minor, the Mentally Impaired, and the Mentally Incompetent,* 50 GEO. WASH. L. REV. 17, 38 (1981) (characterizing tort standard as "almost facially unfathomable").

113. *See generally* Ellis, *supra* note 105, at 1084–90.

114. *Id.* at 1084.

See also, White v. Muniz, 999 P. 2d 814 (Colo. 2000) (person with mental disability suffering from Alzheimer's may be liable for intentional torts, but fact-finder must first conclude that actor intended the harmful consequences of his act); Berberian v. Lynn, 809 A. 2s 865 (N.J. App. Div. 2002) (nursing home resident with dementia did not have mental capacity to appreciate and control violent behavior in pushing nurse down stairs).

lying attitude,"[115] reflecting, "at best, a grudging acceptance of the fact that persons with mental disabilities do, in fact, live in the world."[116] Since "conventional wisdom" was that the disabled constituted a "grave threat to society," it should not be surprising, he concluded, that "such an atmosphere would foster a rule that refused to absolve such persons from compensating victims for the damage they caused."[117]

On the question of the "fear of faking,"[118] Ellis saw two subissues: (1) whether current scientific knowledge had advanced sufficiently to allow for more accurate diagnosis and thus the detection of false claims,[119] and (2) whether a subjective rule would be unmanageable because of the "subtle variations of intelligence, temperament, and emotional balance which are common to all people and thus to all tort defendants."[120] Neither of these, he concluded, is ultimately persuasive.[121]

At least one well-known case[122] has attempted to reach an intermediate position between the two standards. In *Breunig v. American Family Insurance Co.,*[123] a mentally ill person believed that God had taken the steering wheel of her car, and was directing the car's movement.[124] When she saw a truck coming, she stepped on the gas so as to become airborne like Batman.[125] When the car came to rest,

115. *Id.* at 1085.

116. *Id.*, commenting on RESTATEMENT (SECOND) OF TORTS, §238B, Comment b(3), at 17 (1965) ("Mental defectives, if they are to live in the world, should pay for the damage they do").

117. Ellis, *supra* note 105, at 1086.

118. This is an issue that continues to plague the legal system in a variety of fact settings. *See supra* Chapter 2 H (competence to be executed).

119. While Ellis concludes that, even with these advances, "for a substantial number [of persons with mental disabilities], expert opinion is unlikely to be unanimous" (Ellis, *supra* note 105, at 1087), he also points out that, given the combination of stigma—far more significant here than in a criminal context where, presumably, feigned insanity might, in the worst case scenario, save a defendant from the death penalty; *see* Michael L. Perlin, *The Supreme Court, the Mentally Disabled Criminal Defendant, Psychiatric Testimony in Death Penalty Cases, and the Power of Symbolism: Dulling the Ake in Barefoot's Achilles Heel,* 3 N.Y.L. SCH. HUM. RTS. ANN. 91, 96 (1985); Michael L. Perlin, *The Supreme Court, The Mentally Disabled Criminal Defendant, and Symbolic Values: Random Decisions, Hidden Rationales, or "Doctrinal Abyss"?* 29 ARIZ. L. REV. 1, 49–62, 76–78 (1987)—and the fact that many tort defendants are substantially insured, "it seems unlikely that false claims by tort defendants would present an insurmountable problem if a subjective standard were thought otherwise desirable." Ellis, *supra* note 105, at 1087.

120. Ellis, *supra* note 105, at 1087. Ellis notes, however, that other instances of such subjectivity—*e.g.*, cases involving children and physically disabled persons, *see* RESTATEMENT (SECOND) OF TORTS at §§283A & 283C (1965)—are commonplace in negligence law, and, conversely, a subjective standard is common in other *non*tort areas of the law as well (*e.g.*, guardianship, commitment, and testamentary capacity). Ellis, *supra* note 105, at 1088–89.

121. Ellis concludes, though, that proponents of a subjective standard will still have to show that rejection of such a standard works an "extraordinary injustice" on mentally disabled defendants. Ellis, *supra* note 105, at 1088.

122. *See* Ellis, *supra* note 105, at 1101–02; Irwin Perr, *Liability of the Mentally Ill and Their Insurers in Negligence and Other Civil Actions,* 142 AM. J. PSYCHIATRY 1414, 1415 (1985).

123. 173 N.W.2d 619 (Wis. 1970).

124. *Id.*, 173 N.W.2d at 622.

125. *Id.*

she was unable to speak, and was subsequently hospitalized for acute paranoid schizophrenia.[126]

In response to the insurance company's argument that she could not have been negligent because she had no prior knowledge or warning that she would suffer the delusion that caused her to lose control of her car,[127] the court reasoned that, for mental disability to exculpate the driver for such a negligent act, the actor must not have been forewarned that she was prone to such mental illness as would affect her capacity to drive.[128] Analogizing to conditions such as heart disease, the court concluded that when the actor has no warning of the condition's likelihood—either, presumably, from prior occurrence[129] or medical indication of susceptibility—the actor will be absolved from civil liability for a resulting accident on the theory that it was unavoidable.[130] Since there was evidence in the case before the court that the driver had preexisting knowledge of both her condition and the likelihood of hallucinations (she had been delusional previously), the court upheld a jury's finding of liability.[131]

This decision has been mildly criticized by both lawyers, finding its attempts to distinguish between cases involving "sudden" and less sudden mental disability "unpersuasive,"[132] and psychiatrists, questioning the assumption that a previously delusional or hallucinating individual would reasonably have the concomitant insight to subsequently avoid driving a car.[133] However, Professor Ellis has concluded that, while the decision is a "less than satisfactory half-measure," it is based on a policy that, "if applied even-handedly, would result in a subjective standard for the vast majority of mentally handicapped defendants."[134]

---

126. *Id.*

127. *Id.* at 623.

128. *Id.* at 624.

129. Persons with epilepsy, for example, have been held liable for accidents in cases where they were aware of their epileptic condition, but nonetheless had operated motor vehicles without having taken their prescribed medication. *See, e.g.,* Derdiarian v. Felix Contracting Corp., 434 N.Y.S.2d 308 (1980). *Cf.* Hammontree v. Jenner, 97 Cal. Rptr. 739 (Cal. App. 1971) (defendant who had become unconscious during epileptic seizure while driving after having taken his medication not absolutely liable for injuries).

For a linkage between these cases and the "duty to protect" cases (*see* 3 PERLIN, *supra* note 43, §§ 7C-2 to 7C-2.4h), *see* Myers v. Quesenberry, 193 Cal. Rptr. 733 (1983) (sustaining cause of action against doctors for negligently failing to warn patient against driving in uncontrolled diabetic condition complicated by a missed abortion).

130. *Breunig,* 173 N.W.2d at 624.

131. *Id.* at 625.

132. Ellis, *supra* note 105, at 1101.

133. Perr, *supra* note 122, at 1415.

134. Ellis, *supra* note 105, at 1102. For a different sort of fact pattern, *see* Johnson v. Insurance Co. of America, 350 S.E.2d 616 (Va. 1986) (insurance policy coverage of mentally ill individual who shot friend precluded by intentional injury exclusion clause). *See also* Stuyvesant Assocs. v. Doe, 534 A.2d 448 (N.J. Law Div. 1987) (mentally disabled tenant subject to a summary repossession/eviction action where property damage caused during psychotic episode brought on by tenant's failure to maintain treatment regimen).

For a scholarly investigation of the full range of problems presented, *see* Catherine Salton,

Subsequent courts have again begun to grapple with these issues.[135] A recent Florida decision carved out an exception for cases in which a defendant with a mental disability has been institutionalized and, because of mental disability, injures one of her caretakers.[136] While the court acknowledged the standard rationales for holding such defendants responsible for their tortious acts,[137] it found that such imposition of responsibility would serve no purpose in cases involving defendants "with no control over [their] actions and [are] thus innocent of any wrongdoing in the most basic sense of that term,"[138] especially where the defendant is institutionally confined and the injured party is employed to care for or control him.[139] And another case has held that the assumption of risk doctrine prevented recovery from the estate of an incompetent person in a case in which the patient struck and injured a nurse's aide in a convalescent hospital.[140]

b. A new standard?

Professor Ellis clearly and forcefully states the argument for the adoption of a new standard in cases[141] involving mentally disabled defendants:

The objective standard of care for mentally disabled defendants was an outgrowth of the ideology of confinement—an ideology that society has since abandoned. The

---

Mental Insurance and Liability Insurance Exclusionary Clauses: The Effect of Insanity upon Intent, 78 CALIF. L. REV. 1028 (1990).

135. *See, e.g.,* Bashi v. Wodarz, 53 Cal. Rptr. 2d 635 (Cal. App. 1996) (sudden and unanticipated onset of mental illness not defense to action based upon negligent operation of motor vehicle).

136. Anicet v. Gant, 580 So. 2d 273 (Fla. Dist. Ct. App.), *review denied,* 591 So. 2d 181 (1991); *see also Mujica, supra.* For a recent case from another jurisdiction, *see* Gould v. American Family Mut. Ins. Co., 543 N.W.2d 282 (Wis. 1996) (person institutionalized with mental disability who lacked capacity to control or appreciate behavior could not be found negligent for injuries caused to caretaker). *See also* Colman v. Notre Dame Convalescent Home, 968 F. Supp. 809 (D. Conn. 1997) (nursing home resident with senile dementia could be held liable for battery).

Scholars have begun to consider the parallel question of liability implications in the cases of individuals with sleep disorders. *See* Daniel Shuman, *Civil Liability Issues Arising out of Sleep Deprivation and Sleep Disorders,* in FORENSIC ASPECTS OF SLEEP 189 (C. Shapiro & A. McCall Smith eds., 1997).

137. *Anicet,* 580 So. 2d at 275, quoting Jolley v. Powell, 299 So. 2d 647, 647 (Fla. Dist. Ct. App. 1974), *cert. denied,* 309 So. 2d 7 (Fla. 1975) (citing rationales discussed *supra* text accompanying notes 64–65).

138. *Anicet,* 580 F.2d at 276.

139. *Id.* at 277, relying on Van Vooren v. Cook, 75 N.Y.S.2d 362, 367 (A.D. 1947) (Taylor, P.J., dissenting). *Compare Colman, supra* (institutionalized patient not liable for injuries to paid caregiver resulting from patient's negligence).

Subsequently, another Florida court has distinguished *Anicet* where there was no evidence that the mentally disabled defendant was "violently insane" or "lacked the capacity to control his violent behavior." Cowen v. Thornton, 621 So. 2d 684, 687–88 (Fla. App.), *reh'g denied* (1993), *review denied,* 634 So. 2d 629 (Fla. 1994).

140. Herrle v. Estate of Marshall, 53 Cal. Rptr. 2d 713 (Cal. App. 1996), *review deniew* (1996).

141. On the special issues affecting defendants with mental disabilities and cases involving either employers or insurance companies, *see* Perr, *supra* note 122, at 1415–18.

rule has remained in force because very little litigation involving such defendants has reached the appellate courts and because no alternative of stunning superiority has presented itself. Adoption of a subjective standard would not right a vast number of grave injustices, nor would it dramatically ease the burdens of the courts. It would probably have no effect on the overall number of accidents in society, nor would it significantly shift the burden of their cost. But on balance, it may be seen as a modest step toward equitable treatment of the mentally handicapped before the law.[142]

In contrast, one student commentator has taken a revisionist position, in a provocative article arguing that, given current mental health policy, treatment, and research, an objective standard[143] is still appropriate, albeit for different reasons than had traditionally been articulated.[144] An objective tort liability standard, she suggests, meets the present requirements and aims of community treatment by minimizing the burden on the community, helping foster community acceptance of persons with mental illness, and encouraging such persons to become self-sufficient and responsible community members.[145]

Since deinstitutionalization—which increases the number of individuals with mental disabilities in the community—will, according to the author, likely result in more torts committed by such individuals, holding persons with mental disabilities to an objective tort standard of liability may make such individuals behave more "conscientiously,"[146] even if they are unable to satisfy judgment because of indigency and/or lack of insurance.[147] In addition, if persons with mental disabilities were allowed to escape tort liability, "there is a risk that the public might become outraged by the perceived injustice of denying compensation to innocent victims."[148] The author concludes:

> The aim of community treatment is to integrate discharged mental patients into the community as responsible and independent functioning members. Attainment of this goal requires that the mentally ill be treated as ordinary citizens. Hence, they should be held to the same standards of tort liability which apply to the rest of society. . . . [T]he use of a subjective standard in primary negligence cases, rather than being a humanitarian reform, would actually run counter to current mental health policies and would work to the decided disadvantage of the mentally ill. Similarly,

142. Ellis, *supra* note 105, at 1108–09. At least one case has explicitly rejected Ellis' thesis on the grounds that it purportedly failed to reach the question of "fairness to the victim of the wrongful conduct." Goff v. Taylor, 708 S.W.2d 113, 115 (Ky. Ct. App. 1986).

143. For an earlier view that the objective standard is appropriate because mental illness is a "myth," *see* George Alexander Thomas & Szasz, *Mental Illness as an Excuse for Civil Wrongs*, 43 NOTRE DAME LAW. 24 (1967).

144. Note, *supra* note 112, at 160–70.

145. Note, *supra* note 112, at 163–64.

146. *Id.* at 166. There is a deterrent, "admonitory objective" of tort law that transcends the fact of monetary judgments: the individual's knowledge that he may be faced by a lawsuit if he behaves in a certain way is expected to motivate the individual to act with additional care. *Id.* at n.112.

147. *Id.* at 167.

148. *Id.*

the current use of the subjective standard in determining contributory negligence is inappropriate and should be replaced by the objective standard.[149]

Although this is a well-thought-out and, on the surface, appealing argument, on closer analysis it appears somewhat meretricious. While couched in humanitarian rhetoric and broadly supportive of modern deinstitutionalization policies, the argument is, in the end, little more than a restatement of the third of the traditional arguments in support of an objective standard: If persons with mental disabilities are going to live with the rest of society, they must pay for the damage they cause.

The author's conceded fear of community outrage—"it takes only a few well-publicized cases absolving the mentally ill from tort liability to start a public outcry"[150]—implies that such outrage is a legitimate tool in shaping judicial and/or legislative policy in cases involving persons with mental disabilities.[151] If public pressure, which results from jury verdicts finding no cause of action in tort cases,[152] succeeds in both reversing deinstitutionalization policies[153] and "substantially circumscrib[ing]" the opportunities for the disabled to obtain licenses, employment, or housing,[154] the doctrinal threads upon which such policies and opportunities have been premised will be exposed as so slender that, at the least, total rethinking of such policies would be warranted.

B. CONTRACTS

1. Introduction

Contracts—voluntary agreements to purchase, sell, or exchange property or services, are the bedrock of a free market system.[155] Contract law covers a broad

---

149. *Id.* at 170.

150. Note, *supra* note 112, at 165.

151. *Cf.* City of Cleburne v. Cleburne Living Center, 473 U.S. 432, 448 (1985) (quoting Palmore v. Sidotti, 466 U.S. 429, 433 (1984) ("Private biases may be outside the reach of the law, but the law cannot, directly or indirectly, give them effect")). On the Supreme Court's more recent consideration of the issue of stigma and bias in cases of persons with mental illness, *see* 3 PERLIN, *supra* note 1, § 5A-2.4b, discussing Olmstead v. L.C., 527 U.S. 581 (1999).

152. This is a doubtful proposition at best. Public furor in tort cases involving individuals with mental disabilities will probably be limited to cases in which such persons are third parties, and the defendants are mental health professionals, public safety officials, or governmental entities (*see* 3 PERLIN, *supra* note 1, §§ 7C-2 to 7C-8), in these latter cases, the issue of an objective/subjective standard is practically irrelevant. For a consideration of such a case in an international context, *see* Michael L. Perlin, *Faden "You Got No Secrets to Conceal": Considering the Application of the Tarasoff Doctrine Abroad*, 75 U. CIN. L. REV. 611 (2006), discussing the case of Osman v. United Kingdom, 29 Eur. Ct. H.R. 245, 277 (1998).

153. On the question of whether deinstitutionalization can be legitimately seen as a "policy," *see* 3 PERLIN, *supra* note 43, § 4B-2.

154. *See* Note, *supra* note 112, at 165.

155. *See, e.g.,* Len Cao, *Reflections on Market Reform in Post-War Post-Embargo Vietnam*, 22 WHITTIER L. REV. 1029, 1054–1056 (2001); Sandra J. Levin, Comment, *Examining Restraints*

range of transactions, from mergers and acquisitions involving corporations and other entities to the sale of vegetables at farmers' markets. The essence of a contract is a voluntary exchange of value (referred to as *consideration*)[156] between the parties. The presence of consideration distinguishes a contract from a gift or other donative transfer, in which one party gives another party something of value but receives nothing of value (or nothing recognized by law as consideration) in return.[157] The voluntariness of the exchange distinguishes contract law from tort law, where the law imposes legal duties and consequent liability without the need for agreement between the parties.

To induce contractual exchanges, the law protects the expectations of the parties by enforcing contracts.[158] Not all contracts, however, are enforceable. Illegal contracts, such as a contract to violate a criminal statute or to commit a tort, are unenforceable,[159] as are contracts that violate a fundamental public policy of the state, such as a contract to preventing a litigant from selecting a particular lawyer to represent his or her interests.[160] Generally, the conflicts between the policy of enforcing contracts and other important public policies have been balanced by courts or legislatures and embodied in statutes or judicial doctrines that guide or dictate the outcome of disputes involving those conflicting policies.[161]

---

on Freedom to Contract as an Approach to Purchaser Dissatisfaction in the Computer Industry, 74 CAL. L. REV. 2101, 2115–2116 (1985).

156. *See, e.g.*, Wise v. City of Chelan, 135 P.3d 951 (Wash App. 2006) (contract to perform services in exchange for salary).

157. *See, e.g.*, McRay v. Citrin, 706 N.Y.S.2d 27 (App. Div. 2000) ("love and affection" did not constitute consideration sufficient to support a promise to pay yearly sum of money). In the case of a contract that has already been performed, however, "love and affection" generally will support enforcement of the contract. Lancaster v. Boyd, 927 So.2d 756 (Miss. App. 2005), *reh'g den. reh'g en banc den.*, 2006 Miss. App. LEXIS 346, 348.

158. *See, e.g., In re* Sauder, 156 P.3d 1204 (Kan. 2007); Wellington Power Corp. v. CAN Corp., 614 S.E.2d 680 (W. Va. 2005).

159. *See, e.g.*, Anabus Export Ltd. v. Alper Industries, Inc., 603 F. Supp. 1275 (S.D.N.Y. 1985) (contract to sell and deliver stickers featuring portrait of Michael Jackson made without securing the celebrity's consent held unenforceable); Blue Dolphin Investment Ltd. v. Kane, 687 P.2d 533 (Colo. App. 1984) (evidence of alleged oral agreement to tortiously interfere with contract held inadmissible under the parole evidence rule, because contract to commit a tort violates public policy, and thus court refused to apply exceptions otherwise available under parole evidence rule).

160. *See, e.g.*, Jarvis v. Jarvis, 758 P.2d 244 (Kan. App. 1988) (contract preventing wife from retaining a particular lawyer to represent her in post-divorce proceedings void as against public policy). *See also*, RESTATEMENT (SECOND) OF CONTRACTS §192 (1981) (classifying contracts to commit or induce commission of tort as unenforceable on grounds of public policy rather than as illegal contracts).

161. One such example is the parole evidence rule, which excludes evidence of an oral agreement that conflicts with an integrated written agreement. RICHARD A. LORD, WILLISTON ON CONTRACTS §33:23 (4th ed. 2003) hereinafter "WILLISTON ON CONTRACTS". This rule generally advances the goal of fulfilling parties' expectations, but fundamental fairness requires an exception when the oral evidence is offered to show that the written contract is illegal, fraudulent, or otherwise void or voidable. *See id. See also*, RESTATEMENT (SECOND) OF CONTRACTS, *supra* note 160.

A principal policy that counterbalances protection of expectations through enforcement of contracts is assuring that contractual agreements are truly voluntary on the part of both parties.[162] In contracts, as in every other area of law, the state has a strong interest in protecting those who are incapable, or deemed incapable, of protecting their own interests.[163] Contract law balances this policy of protection and the policy of fulfilling the expectations created by a contract with the doctrine of contractual capacity.[164]

The policy of protection that underlies the requirement of capacity to contract also buttresses other doctrines that limit enforcement of contracts. "Agreements" induced by fraud, duress, or undue influence, or agreements that are so unfair as to be unconscionable, are unenforceable because they are deemed to be involuntary. In the application of these doctrines, mental weakness short of incapacity may play a role in determining whether the facts satisfy the elements of the particular doctrine involved.[165]

Conversely, the policy of enforcing expectations limits the protection that the capacity doctrine otherwise would provide in particular contexts. The additional policies that affect the basic policy balance articulated in the doctrine of contractual capacity may appear in the form of express doctrine or alternatively as discussion of policies relevant to a particular case.

Each state has primary authority to adopt and implement doctrine and policy in the realm of contracts, resulting in variations from jurisdiction to jurisdiction. For many types of contracts federal law preempts (trumps) some aspects of otherwise applicable law,[166] and in a few areas federal law preempts an area of contract law entirely.[167] When federal law does not preempt state law, the states may adopt strikingly similar statutory schemes for particular types of contracts, which are often modeled on a uniform code or statute specifically designed to bring about this result. The Uniform Commercial Code, for example, adopted (with some variations) in every state, governs sales of goods (as opposed to services), pledges

162. *See, e.g.*, New Welton Homes v. Eckman, 830 N.E.2d 32 (Ind. 2005), *reh'g den.*, 2005 Ind. LEXIS 2004; Wilkie v. Auto-Owners Ins. Co., 664 N.W.2d 776 (Mich. 2003); Manufacturer's Trust Co. v. Podvin, 89 A.2d 672 (N.J. 1952).

163. *See generally*, Alexander Meiklejohn, *Contractual and Donative Capacity*, 39 CASE W. L. REV. 307, 320–23 (1989); Milton D. Green, *Public Policies Underlying the Law of Mental Incompetency*, 38 MICH. L. REV. 1189, 1207–08 (1940).

164. Otelere v. Teachers' Retirement Board of the City of New York, 250 N.E.2d 460, 567-468 (Jasen, J., dissenting).

165. *See infra* Chapter 4 B.

166. *See, e.g.*, Title Max of Birmingham v. Edwards, 2007 WL 1454456 (Ala. Sup.) (Federal Arbitration Act preempts some aspects of state law); Guice v. Charles Schwab & Co., 674 N.E.2d 282 (N.Y. 1996), *cert den.* 520 U.S. 1118 (1997) (Securities and Exchange Commission requiring disclosure to retail customers of securities firms' use of wholesalers preempted state law).

167. *See, e.g.*, Wall v. CSX Transportation, Inc., 471 F.3d 410, 423 n.11 (2nd Cir. 2006) (identifying the Labor Management Relations Act, the Employee Retirement Income Security Act, and the National Bank Act as the only statutes completely preempting contract claims).

of a security interest in support of performance of a contractual obligation (e.g., a finance company's right to repossess a car if the purchaser defaults on the car loan) and other transactions.[168]

On the other hand, real estate contracts, property agreements between a couple, and many other transactions vary much more from state to state. The rules applicable to specific types of contracts incorporate policy interests that are not implicated in other types of contracts. The policies underlying these rules modify, in one way or another, the basic policy of fulfilling expectations by enforcing contracts, and in some cases may influence the policy of protection inherent in the requirement of contractual capacity. In these areas, as well as all of the others covered elsewhere in Chapter 4, the prevailing standards as well as notable exceptions are covered.

This chapter presents contractual capacity, its related doctrines, and the use of forensic mental health expertise to facilitate proof of legal capacity or incapacity to contract.[169] The first section describes the standard of contractual capacity, which applies to the entire range of transactions that fall within the realm of contracts, the effect of timing of contractual incapacity in relation to the execution and performance of the contract, the effect of contractual incapacity on the transaction, and the interplay between the capacity doctrine and other doctrines that involve mental weakness short of contractual incapacity. Additionally, the first section illustrates the application of how courts apply the contractual capacity standard in the context of different types of contracts. Cases were selected to illustrate the role that policy plays and its effects on the evidence mental health expertise can provide. The final section illustrates application of the role of mental health expertise in proving "mental weakness" that, together with other grounds, plays a role in judicial determinations.

2. Capacity to Contract

a. In general

Traditionally, the legal standard of contractual capacity was purely cognitive.[170] The cognitive standard requires the individual to understand the nature of the act of entering into the contract and to appreciate the consequences of the contract.[171] Diminished (or limited) intelligence or other mental weakness does not

---

168. *See generally,* U.C.C. §2-105 (1977). *See, e.g.,* Sonja A. Soehuel, *What Constitutes a Transaction, Contract for Sale or a Sale within the Scope of UCC Article 2,* 4 A.L.R.4th 85 (1991).

169. This Chapter covers only contracts of individuals who are not adjudicated incompetents or under guardianship. After an adjudication of incompetency, contracts executed by the incapacitated person are void automatically if the incapacitated person did not retain authority to execute the contract in question pursuant to the guardianship determination. Guardianship is covered *infra* in Chapter 4 D.

170. WILLISTON ON CONTRACTS, *supra* note 161 at §10.8.

171. RESTATEMENT (SECOND) OF CONTRACTS, *supra* note 161 at §15(1). *See also, In re* Marriage of Davis, 89 P.3d 1206 (Ore. App. 2004), *rev. den* 99 P.3d 290 (2004).

itself establish incapacity to contract;[172] instead, the individual seeking to avoid the contract must establish that the cognitive impairment resulted in the individual having no reasonable perception of the nature or terms of the contract.[173]

The traditional standard for contractual capacity disregards the devastating impact that mental conditions may wreak upon an individual's volition to control his or her conduct in relation to the contract, even though he or she understands the contract's content and effect. In a recent Oregon case, for example, the court rejected a claim of contractual incapacity despite diagnoses of depression, post-traumatic stress disorder, and battered women's syndrome, in part because the diagnosed conditions did not impair the wife's cognitive abilities.[174]

In most jurisdictions, the standard for contractual capacity includes both the traditional cognitive standard and also an alternative standard, referred to as the *affective test,* the *modern test,* or the *volitional test.*[175] Under the affective test, an individual lacks contractual capacity even though he or she understands the nature and consequences of the transaction, if by reason of the mental impairment he or she cannot act reasonably in relation to the transaction. The affective standard may justify a determination of contractual incapacity, however, only if the other party to the contract has reason to know of the other party's impairment.[176]

In one of the first decisions to apply the affective test, the New York Court of Appeals held that a surviving spouse was entitled to set aside a retirement plan benefit election executed by his deceased spouse approximately 2 months before she died.[177] The court clearly indicated that the deceased spouse had no intellectual impairment that would amount to incapacity under the traditional cognitive standard. On the other hand, the deceased spouse had been placed on disability leave due to mental illness. Her treating psychiatrist testified that she had suffered from a medically diagnosed psychosis, as well as volitional and affective impediments in personality that left her unable to control her conduct or make a rational decision.[178] By applying the affective test, the court was able to set aside the deceased spouse's election, allowing her survivors to receive the retirement funds the deceased spouse had worked for decades to earn.

---

172. *See, e.g.,* Mason v. Acceptance Loan Co., Inc. 850 So.2d 289 (Ala. 2002), *reh'g den.* 2002 Ala. LEXIS 391 (purchasers of credit life and disability insurance had contractual capacity despite evidence that many of the purchasers' IQs fell into the "mildly retarded" range; many of the purchasers were illiterate; the purchasers had very limited education (and some had received special education); and many of the purchasers could not understand legal or business terminology). *See generally,* WILLISTON ON CONTRACTS, *supra* note 161, at §10.10.

173. *See, e.g.,* Myers v. US, 943 F. Supp. 815 (1996) (W.D. Mich 1996), *rev'd on other grounds,* 1997 US LEXIS 9378 (6th Cir. 1998) (applying the traditional cognitive test of contractual capacity, court determined that drug defendant's wife had the capacity to enter a plea agreement; emotional distress was not relevant to contractual capacity).

174. *In re* Marriage of Davis, 89 P.3d 1206 (Or. App. 2004).

175. RESTATEMENT (SECOND) OF CONTRACTS, *supra* note 160, at §15(1)(b).

176. *Id.* This reflects the importance of the policy of effectuating expectations. Why cognitive disorders and affective disorders should be subject to different standards is not clear.

177. Ortelere v. Teachers' Retirement Board, 250 N.E.2d 460 (1990).

178. *Id.* at 463.

The affective standard recognizes that the cognitive test had been formulated when the field of psychiatry was far less developed; the range of recognized mental impairments has broadened considerably since then.[179]

Despite this enhanced understanding of mental disabilities, several courts have rejected depression as a basis for negating contractual capacity, reasoning that inclusion of depression would interfere excessively with the policy of fulfilling expectations of the parties.[180] In the words of one court:

'If mere depression, serious or otherwise, can be considered a valid reason to avoid a contract . . . then the courts will be confronted with a plethora of claims by litigants declaring that they were too depressed or unhappy to know what they were doing and should, thus, be relieved, from the effects of their conduct.' Treating depression as a basis for avoiding a contract would undermine 'the fundamental integrity and reliability of contracts.'[181]

Consistent with the traditional standard's cognitive focus, addiction and intoxication fell outside the scope of the contractual capacity concept.[182] A parallel rule developed in most jurisdictions, however, to cover this situation: If substance abuse deprives the individual of the ability to understand the nature and effect of the transaction at the time he or she enters into it, the contract is unenforceable by the impaired party.[183]

i. Timing of incapacity: Lucid intervals and ratification   Generally, contract capacity doctrine holds that the incapacity must exist at the time of the transaction in order to excuse performance by the impaired party. For the many types of mental impairments that may fluctuate in severity or periodically remit, contractual capacity may be present one day but absent the next. To account for these fluctuations, and avoid disappointing expectations of the unimpaired party to the transaction, courts developed the "lucid interval doctrine."[184] Under this doctrine an individual whose impairment has receded at the time of the transaction has contractual capacity so long as he or she understands the nature and consequences of the transaction (or satisfies the alternative (modern) test of contractual capacity, if applicable).[185] The lucid interval doctrine still prevails in a number of

179. *Id.* at 464–67.
180. *See, e.g.,* Wurst. Blue River Bank of McCool Junction, 454 N.W.2d 665, 668–670 (Neb. 1990).
181. Willgerodt v. Majority Peoples' Fund for the 21st Century, Inc. v. Hohri, 953 F. Supp. 557, 560 (S.D.N.Y. 1997) (quoting Blatt v. Manhattan Medical Group, PC, 519 N.Y.S. 2d 973, 975 App. Div. 1989), *aff'd* 159 F.3d 1347 (2nd Cir. 1998).
182. *See* Seminara v. Grisman, 44 A.2d 492, 494 (N.J. Ch. 1945) ("Under ancient common law, intoxication, if voluntary and not fraudulently procured, merited neither relief nor extenuation in a contractual transaction,") *citing* Beverly's Case (1603), 4 Coke 124, 76 Eng. Reprint 1119, and Johnson v. Madlicott (1734), 3 P.Wms. 130.
183. *See, e.g.,* Williams v. Matthews, 379 So.2d 1245 (Ala. 1980); Olsen v. Hawkins, 408 P.2d 462 (Idaho 1965); Poole v. Hudson, 83 A.2d 703 (Del. Super. 1957).
184. WILLISTON ON CONTRACTS, *supra* note 161, at §10.8.
185. *Id.*

jurisdictions,[186] although some states have rejected it in order to provide greater protection for impaired individuals.[187]

The converse of a contract executed during a lucid interval is a transaction entered into when a party lacks contractual capacity but later acquires (or re-acquires) it. In this situation, the contract will be enforceable if the previously incapacitated party, or a party who has the authority to bind the incapacitated party,[188] affirms or ratifies the contract. Ratification, whether explicit or implicit, includes three elements: (1) an unauthorized act performed by an individual for and on behalf of another and not on account of the actor himself; (2) knowledge of all material facts by the person to be charged with the unauthorized act; and (3) acceptance of the benefits of and unauthorized act by the person charged with the act.[189] In other words, an individual who lacked contractual capacity to enter into the contract but later gained contractual capacity will be held to the contract if he or she began fulfilling the terms of the contract or accepting benefits due from the unimpaired party to the contract.[190]

ii. Consequences of contractual incapacity

Generally, contracts entered into by a party who lacks contractual capacity are either void or voidable.[191] A void contract is a nullity, unenforceable in any way by any party. A voidable contract,

---

186. *See, e.g.*, Bank IV v. Capital Fed'l Sav. & Loan Ass'n, 828 P.2d 355 (Kan. 1992); Williams v. Wilson, 335 So.2d 110 (Miss. 1976); Uribe v. Olson, 601 P.2d 818 (Or. App. 1979) (even where there are substantial indications of mental incapacity it is possible for an individual to have a "lucid interval" during which he or she possesses the requisite capacity to contract); Briggs v. Briggs, 325 P.2d 219 (Cal. App. 1958).

187. *See, e.g.*, Jackson v. Van Dresler, 219 S.W. 2d 896 (Tenn. 1949), *superseded by statute on another issue as stated in* Edward v. Edwards, 1995 Tenn.App. LEXIS 56; Farnum v. Silvano, 540 N.E.2d 202 (Mass. App. 1989) (contractual capacity presupposes something more than transient surge of lucidity). The ambivalence about the lucid interval doctrine in contract law contrasts sharply with its universal acceptance in the law of donative transfers. *See infra* Chapter 4.C. This reflects the greater interest in enforcing donative transfers, particularly wills as compared to contracts. *See id.*

188. An attorney-in-fact (one who holds a power of attorney on behalf of another) has the power to bind the agent who gave the power of attorney to the extent of the powers conferred. A power of attorney becomes ineffective, however, upon the death or disability of the agent, unless the power of attorney provides otherwise (a "durable" power of attorney). Hedgepeth v. Home Sav. & Loan Ass'n, 361 S.E.2d 888 (N.C. App. 1987) (enforcing transaction by an attorney-in-fact, based on equitable considerations, despite the mental incapacity of the principal). A guardian may execute or ratify a transaction of an incapacitated person as well. *See, e.g.*, Banker's Trust. Co. of Albany, N.A. v. Martin, 381 N.Y.S.2d 1001 (App. Div. 1976) (bank, as conservator [guardian of an incapacitated person's property] ratified contract).

189. *See, e.g.*, Wilcox Mfg. Group, Inc. v. Marketing Services of Indiana, Inc., 832 N.E.2d 559 (Ind. App. 2005).

190. *Id.*

191. *See, e.g.*, Matter of Rothko, 372 N.E.2d 257 (1977); *see also,* WILLISTON ON CONTRACTS, *supra* note 161, at §1:2. Guardianship operates prospectively, limiting the right of the incapacitated person (IP) to make decisions and engage in legal acts that the IP would have held in the absence of the guardianship. Consequently, contracts made by an IP who is subject to guardianship that covers property matters generally are void. *Id.*

on the other hand, may be set aside on behalf of the party who lacked capacity so long as there are not countervailing considerations (such as a ratification). The phrase *void contract* is an oxymoron because "contract" presupposes some degree of enforceability, whereas an ostensible agreement between two parties that is void is not a contract and cannot be enforced at all.[192]

Although many courts refer to contracts of individuals who lack contractual capacity as void or invalid, most jurisdictions treat such contracts as voidable.[193] For incapacity based on intoxication or addiction, the contract is never void; at most it is voidable.[194] The voluntary nature of intoxication, as compared to mental illness, has been offered as a justification for this rule.[195]

A condition to allowing rescission of a voidable contract is the ability to restore the parties to their precontract positions. In addition, the competent party must not have known of the other party's incapacity, the competent party must not have taken advantage of the incompetent party, and the contract must have been performed in whole or in part.[196] Under these circumstances, fairness demands enforcement of the contract.[197]

iii. Relationship of contractual capacity to other doctrines that support setting aside contract

An impairment that falls short of establishing contractual incapacity may nevertheless be relevant to excusing performance of the contract by the impaired party under other contract doctrines.[198] These doctrines include, among others, fraud, undue influence, duress, and unconscionability. Each of them addresses whether there is a true agreement between the parties, and incorporates the notion that the voluntariness or validity of an agreement to contract capacity may be affected by mental weakness, age, physical condition, effects of drug or alcohol abuse, the relationship between the contracting parties, the adequacy of consideration, and other factors.[199] The interrelationship of these doctrines and the capacity doctrine is discussed in Chapter 4 B (3).

---

192. *See Annubus Expert*, 603 F. Supp. at 1276–77.

193. WILLISTON ON CONTRACTS, *supra* note 161, at §1:2. *Accord, LeBovici, supra;* Thorton v. Carpenter, 476 S.E.2d 92 (Ga. App. 1996); Apfelbat v. Nat'l Bank Wyandotte-Taylor, 404 N.W.2d 725 (Mich. App. 1987) (all holding that mental incapacity renders contract voidable rather than void). *But see,* Lau v. Behr Heat Transfer System, 150 F. Supp.2d 1017 (D.S.D. 2001) (holding that mental incapacity may result in a void contract or alternatively a voidable contract, depending on the severity of the incapacity.)

194. WILLISTON ON CONTRACTS, *supra* note 161, at §10.11.

195. *Id.* This reasoning stems from the period before social science research began to question the voluntariness of substance abuse.

196. WILLISTON ON CONTRACTS, *supra* note 161, at §10.6 (accords with the determination of assent based on actions and words rather than "acute assent.")

197. RESTATEMENT (SECOND) OF CONTRACTS, *supra* note 160, agrees with the majority rule. It states that if the contract is fair and the other party is without knowledge of any infirmity, any power of avoidance that might otherwise exist is terminated if the K has been performed in whole or in part or the circumstances have otherwise so changed that avoidance would be unjust. WILLISTON ON CONTRACTS, *supra* note 161, at §10.6.

198. ARTHUR L. CORBIN et al., CORBIN ON CONTRACTS §27.15 (2006).

199. Green, *supra* note 163.

b. The role of mental health expertise—Illustrative contexts

The standard of contractual capacity (whatever that standard may be in a particular jurisdiction) remains constant across the wide range of subject matter that contracts cover. Yet different types of contracts may call forth considerations that emphasize the policy of protecting mentally impaired individuals while others may invoke the policy of protecting expectations of the other party. The subject matter of the contract as well as the context of a particular transaction also may influence the availability of evidence, the analysis of that evidence, and perceptions about fairness and equity that implicitly or explicitly affect the determination of contractual capacity. A firm understanding of the principles and policies governing common types of contracts facilitates an understanding of how mental health expertise can contribute most fruitfully to determinations of contractual capacity.

i. Real estate   Transactions in real property follow different rules from those governing transactions in personal property.[200] The two sets of rules overlap, but they differ in important respects for historic, policy, and practical reasons. From an historical perspective, real property was far more important than personal property in feudal times, when the law of real estate transfers developed, and many of the rules developed have been retained despite the absence of any policy justification for those rules in modern society.[201] From a policy perspective, each particular parcel of real estate has been considered unique, a view much more supportable in the context of a tract of land than a "cookie cutter" condominium apartment.[202]

---

200. The distinction between real and personal property grew out of the feudal system in England, where land was much more important than money or other forms of property. RICHARD R. POWELL, ET AL., POWELL ON REAL PROPERTY §5.04 (2007). Today, there are no political or procedural strictures that would require the creation of a real-personal property dichotomy. *Id.* Nevertheless, the dichotomy is alive and well. *See, e.g.*, MINN. STAT. ANN. §272.03 (b) (West 2006) (defining real property for purposes of taxation as "building or structure . . . together with all improvements or fixtures attached to the building or structure which are integrated with and a permanent benefit to the building or structure and which cannot be removed without substantial damage to itself or the building or structure"). Estate of Wartels, 357 So.2d 708 (Fla. 1978) (holding that cooperative apartment is not a "homestead for purposes of inheritance other than the homestead exemptions"; determination depended on real versus personal property distinction because the applicable statute, though it did not define the term "homestead," clearly contemplated real estate as property qualifying for the exemption).

201. A classic example is the common law prohibition against severing a joint tenancy by transferring the jointly held property to one joint tenant. In order to effectuate the severance and consequently destroy the rights of survivorship in the property, the transferring party would have to convey the jointly held property to a third person ("strawman") as a predicate to transferring the property into the sole name of the transferring joint tenant. *See, e.g.*, Knickerbocker v. Cannon, 912 P.2d 969 (Utah 1996) (discussing prevalence of the common law strawman requirement and the increasing number of states that have rejected it).

202. *See* Somer v. Kreidel, 378 A.2d 767 (N.J. 1977) (employing the uniqueness rationale to explain why imposing on landlords a duty to mitigate damages when tenants breach their leases would not require the landlord to market the breaching tenant's property first: each apartment is unique, so the tenant may prefer one apartment in the building to another).

As a practical matter, real estate transactions require more extensive formalities than do typical purchases and sales of personal property. Whereas transactions in personal property generally do not require a written agreement, real estate contracts generally do require a written agreement, or at least evidence of a written agreement.[203] The formality of the writing underscores the seriousness of the transaction, and also gives the parties time to re-think the transaction while the contract is being prepared.[204] In addition, there is typically a time period between the signing of the real estate contract and the actual transfer of the property, which occurs upon transfer of the deed, after any conditions in the contract have been satisfied and other issues resolved.[205] Although contractual capacity is not an explicit contingency in a typical real estate contract, if the issue arises before the deed is delivered, the parties often may find their way to a solution, obviating the need for a lawsuit.

When a lawsuit alleging contractual incapacity does arise, it involves mental health experts less often than one might expect, and less often than many other civil matters, such as wills, guardianships, and domestic relations disputes. The reason for this is not clear. One possibility is that the claim of contractual incapacity is specious or simply weak. If, for example, there is no evidence of incapacity other than testimony from the party alleging incapacity, the nature of the problem is not well articulated, and the problems causing the incapacity are not reported until that party attempts to rescind the contract, the claim may not merit retention of a mental health expert.[206]

Another possible explanation is an attitude of indifference about the potential value that mental health expertise may provide.[207] In a recent decision that held that the grantor lacked the mental capacity to deed property to his daughter-in-law, for example, the court said "the requisite proof regarding mental capacity is within

---

203. The writing requirement for the sale of land originated in England's Statute of Frauds. Several other transactions in personal property were covered by that statute as well, including, for example, agreements in consideration of marriage, agreements that could not be performed within 1 year from the original contract date, and trusts. STATUTE OF FRAUDS 1677, 29 Car. 2, c.3. WILLISTON ON CONTRACTS, *supra* note 161, at §21:3. Although the transactions within the Statute of Frauds vary among jurisdictions, land contracts continue to be the most important, or at least one of the most important, transactions within the statute of frauds.

204. *See generally, In re* Maycock, 33 P.3d 1114 (Wyo. 2001) (discussing policies underlying the statute of frauds). Similar policies underlie the Statute of Wills, discussed in Chapter 4 C 3, *infra*.

205. *See, e.g.,* Michael Braunstein, *Structural Change and Inter-Professional Competitive Advantage: an Example Drawn from Residential Real Estate Closings,* 62 Mo. L. REV. 242, 265–67 (1997) (describing the actions required between contract signing and contract closing).

206. *See, e.g.,* Masoner v. Bates County Nat'l Bank, 781 S.W.2d 235 (Mo. App. 1989).

207. *See generally,* Douglas Mossman and Marshall D. Kapp, *"Courtroom Whores"? or Why Do Attorneys Call Us?: Findings from a Survey on Attorneys' Use of Mental Health Experts,* 26 J. AM. ACAD. PSYCHIATRY & L. 27 (1998); *Richard E. Redding et al., What Judges and Lawyers Think about the Testimony of Mental Health Experts: A Survey of the Courts and Bar,* 19 BEHAV. SCI. & L. 583, 584 (2001) (recognizing that not all expert testimony is equally valid or probative and discussing appropriateness of different types of expert mental health testimony).

the common knowledge and experience of laypersons and therefore, medical testimony is not required."[208] In that case, the court concluded that the evidence was sufficiently clear to obviate the need for expert testimony. As contract law evolves and the doctrine of contract capacity is applied with increasing attention to shares of cognitive or mental impairment, however, there may be greater appreciation for the potential contribution of mental health testimony. Further stimulating this shift may be heightened receptivity as courts addressing contracts and other civil law matters become increasingly familiar with principles of forensic psychology and psychiatry.

Litigating contractual capacity without the assistance of a mental health expert is risky, particularly if the other side offers expert testimony in support of his or her position. In cases involving contractual capacity, appellate decisions (which comprise the vast majority of reported state cases) typically apply a holistic approach to reviewing evidence that led to the trial court's decision rather than specifying any particular item of evidence as determinative. In a departure from that approach, a Florida appellate court reversed the trial court's determination that the grantor had the capacity to enter into a real estate contract, stating:

> The trial court should accept unrebutted expert testimony on highly technical matters, unless it is palpably illogical and unreasonable as to be unworthy of belief or otherwise open to doubt from some reasonable point of view. However when facts sought to be proved by expert testimony are within the ordinary experience of the fact finder or disputed by lay testimony, the conclusion to be drawn for the expert testimony will be left to the finder of fact.[209]

In that case, both sides had experts testifying on the purchaser's capacity to contract. The purchaser's expert, his treating psychiatrist,[210] stated that his patient was a paranoid schizophrenic for more than 30 years, and that this condition affected the patient-purchaser's ability to understand a basic real estate transaction.[211] The seller's expert, a psychologist, also testified that the purchaser, though he was capable of understanding the financial aspects of the real estate transaction, was not competent to negotiate a sale or purchase that involved extended payments over time (as this real estate contract did).

In the most typical case, each side in the litigation has an expert who testifies in a manner supportive to the client's position. In these cases, much depends on the quality of the expert testimony, which includes not only the expert's knowledge of forensic psychology or psychiatry principles, but also familiarity with the facts of the case that bear on the application of those principles. The case of *Slorby v. Johnson*[212] vividly illustrates how the quality of expert testimony affects its value.

---

208. Decker v. Decker, 192 S.W.3d 648 (Tex. App. 2006).

209. Long v. Moore, 626 So.2d 1387 (Fla. App. 1993).

210. The psychiatrist began treating the purchaser after the contract had been executed. *Id.* at 1388.

211. *Id.*

212. 530 N.W. 307 (N.D. 1995).

In that case, the seller sought to rescind the sale of his farm based on incapacity to contract. In support of his position, the seller offered the testimony of his personal physician, who had no specialized training in psychiatry or psychology but did have considerable experience treating the elderly. The physician testified candidly that his principal concern was the seller's physical condition, but also said that the seller was "obviously quite senile when I first saw him."[213] Elaborating, the physician testified that he had to rely on others to obtain a medical history of the seller because the seller was incapable of providing one.

The purchaser's expert, a clinical psychologist, testified that the seller did have capacity to understand the real estate transaction.[214] The weakness in this testimony lay in the psychologist's unfamiliarity with facts relevant to the seller, the transaction, and the litigation. The court specifically noted that the psychologist never met, evaluated, or interviewed the seller personally; that the psychologist did not know of the purchaser's attempts to get the seller's attention during the seller's deposition; and that the psychologist was unaware that the seller and purchaser spent 8 hours together the day before the deposition.[215] In this case, the clinical psychologist may have had a stronger background in assessing mental capacity, but the inadequacies in the factual foundation for his opinion undermined its persuasiveness.

ii. Goods and services   Reported cases involving capacity to contract for goods and services are far less plentiful than one might expect. One important reason for this is the doctrine of necessaries, which generally require individuals who lack the requisite mental capacity to contract to pay restitution for certain goods and services.[216] This doctrine recognizes that the importance of facilitating access to items such as food, clothing, and medical care, and the corresponding equity in compensating the provider for the goods or services rendered.[217] The incapacitated person may not have had to purchase the necessary items from the particular seller involved, or under the particular terms of the parties' contract, but he or she would have been compelled to secure the necessary items or services from someone. The doctrine of necessaries does not compel enforcement of the contract according to its terms, but rather requires the incapacitated party to pay or make restitution.[218]

The doctrine of necessaries presupposes incapacity, making the issue of mental competency to contract relevant generally only when there is a question whether the subject of the contract qualifies as a "necessary" so that restitution (as opposed

213. *Id.* at 311.
214. *Id.* at 312.
215. *Id.*
216. A substantially similar rule applies to necessaries acquired by a minor, but details of the rule as well as its consequences differ. *See, e.g.,* Hauer v. Union State Bank, 532 N.W.2d 456 (Wis. App. 1995) (relief from liability for depreciation or use of property applicable to disaffirming infant is not applicable to an incapacitated adult who contracts for necessaries).
217. E. ALLEN FARNSWORTH, FARNSWORTH ON CONTRACTS §4.8 (4th ed. 2004).
218. *See, e.g., In re* Hays, 98 N.W.2d 430 (Wis. 1959); Breaux v. Allied Bank of Texas, 699 S.W.2d 599 (Tex. App. 1995).

to no remedy at all) would be available, or when the contract price is substantially higher than the amount that would be required to be repaid as restitution.[219] In the case of *Landmark Medical Center v. Gauther*, for example, the court noted that a surviving spouse's alleged contractual incapacity would have no effect on her obligation to pay hospital bills of herself and her deceased spouse where all parties agreed the hospital charges were reasonable.[220]

A more significant issue, in theory, is whether the competent party knew of the other party's contractual incapacity and acted unfairly, because that may relieve the obligation to provide restitution.[221] In practice, however, there is a paucity of recent cases on that issue as well. To the extent those cases arise, mental health expertise would seem to be of little relevance because the issue is what the other contracting party perceived (or should have perceived) about the incapacitated party as opposed to the incapacitated party's actual situation.[222]

In the realm of goods, as opposed to services, there is an additional doctrine that weighs against claims of contractual incapacity. The state's version of the UCC, which governs such transfers, disallows rescission of voidable contracts[223] where the property transferred by an individual lacking contractual capacity comes into the hands of a "good faith purchaser for value."[224] This protection of the competent party reflects not only protection of expectations but the fairness of such transactions. Where the transaction is tainted by fraud, undue influence, inadequacy of purchase price, or knowledge of the incapacitated party's condition, the competent party will not qualify as a good-faith purchaser entitled to this special protection.[225]

Attempts to rescind contracts for personal or professional services based solely on a party's contractual incapacity are brought infrequently and won even less frequently. One relatively recent case involved a medical college's suit for reimbursement by a graduate who, at the time of application and admission, signed a contract to practice medicine in the state of Ohio for 5 years.[226] After graduating, completing his internship and residency, and practicing medicine in Ohio for

---

219. *See id.*

220. *See, e.g.*, Landmark Medical Center v. Gauthier, 635 A.2d 1145, 1148–49 (R.I. 1994).

221. *See* Farnsworth, *supra* note 217, at §4.8, *citing* Tubbs v. Hilliard, 89 P.2d 535 (Colo. 1939).

222. *But see*, Nalty v. Nalty, 64 So.2d 216 (La. 1953) (allowing expert testimony on the issue whether an individual was "notoriously insane" so that the competent party could not have been deceived as to the other party's incapacity).

223. *See* WILLISTON ON CONTRACTS, *supra* note 161 (noting that the vast majority of states treat contracts by individuals lacking contractual capacity as voidable rather than void).

224. A similar rule applies in some jurisdictions to cases outside the scope of the UCC, such as real estate transactions. *See, e.g.*, WILLISTON ON CONTRACTS, *supra* note 161, at §10.4 and cases cited therein (noting a split of authority as to whether a contractual incapacity justifies rescission of the contract when the other party is a bona fide purchaser for value). *See also* U.C.C. § 2-403(1).

225. *See infra* Chapter 4.B.3, for a discussion of doctrines other than contractual capacity that mix mental weakness and fairness.

226. Ohio Board of Trustees v. Smith, 724 N.E.2d 1155 (Ohio App. 1999).

1 year, the doctor left Ohio for a position at Stanford University. Rejecting the doctor's claims that he lacked contractual capacity due to his inability to hire a lawyer or understand the legalities of the contract himself, the court easily granted summary judgment for the medical college.[227]

In another case alleging contractual incapacity, a widow sought to rescind a contract with a law firm she had hired to prosecute a claim for the wrongful death of her husband.[228] The widow's proof of incapacity consisted of her testimony that she was "in shock" on the day she learned of her husband's death, and also 3 days later when she entered into a contingency fee arrangement with the law firm.[229] The widow also testified, however, that on the date she entered into the contract she did understand that she was employing lawyers to file suit for her husband's death, and that she was agreeing to pay the lawyers one third of any sum recovered. Based on that testimony, the court held that, as a matter of law, the widow failed to establish contractual incapacity.[230]

Neither of these cases involved expert testimony or other medical evidence, making it difficult for courts to justify the conclusion that the party alleging incapacity in fact fell short of the legal standard. That type of evidence is "important" and "potent,"[231] suggesting that those who have a bona fide claim of contractual incapacity in a services case ought to consider arranging for a forensic evaluation.

iii. Settlement agreements between unrelated parties   Legal folklore has it that the mark of a fair settlement is one in which all parties are a bit disappointed. Perhaps it is this judicial attitude, "buyer's remorse" on the part of one or more of the parties, the efficiency of closing a litigation file, or a combination of these factors that makes settlement agreements one of the most difficult types of contracts to set aside on the basis of mental incapacity. The same standard of contractual capacity that applies to other contracts applies to settlement agreements as well, but application of the standard appears to be more rigorous for settlement agreements. This strict application extends to all evidence of incapacity, including expert testimony.

A rather extreme example is *In re Rains*,[232] a case involving a settlement of a creditor's claim in bankruptcy in which the debtor drove himself to a hospital emergency room following the execution of the settlement agreement. There he was diagnosed with a ruptured cerebral aneurysm, sub-archoid hemorrhage, and stroke. Mr. Rains had surgery the next day and was in the intensive care unit for approximately 1 month until released from the hospital.

---

227. *Id.*
228. Mandell & Wright v. Thomas, 441 S.W.2d 841 (Tex. 1969).
229. *Id.* at 845.
230. *Id.*
231. Simmons First Nat'l Bank v. Luzader, 438 S.W.2d 25 (Ark. 1969) (holding that evidence, which consisted entirely of lay testimony, fell short of proving contractual incapacity despite the apparent weakness of the individual, who had since died).
232. 428 F.3d 893 (9th Cir. 2005).

Afterward, Rains claimed to have no recollection of the events preceding his hospitalization. In support of Rains' claim of contractual incapacity, the neurologist who treated him for his aneurysm stated that Mr. Rains would have lacked the mental capacity to engage in business on the date of the mediation agreement and subsequent hospital admission, and that the incapacity would have existed for a number of days before and after that date.[233] The clinical psychologist who provided follow-up care for Mr. Rains concurred, stating that Mr. Rains would not have had his normal mental capacity and would have been incapable of conducting business affairs with competence.[234]

Rains' adversaries, the creditor and the trustee in bankruptcy, offered no expert testimony about Rains' condition. Instead, they submitted their own declarations describing their impressions of Rains as an active participant in the settlement discussions. On this evidence, the Ninth Circuit upheld the bankruptcy court's determination that Rains possessed the capacity to enter into the settlement.[235]

In a similarly reasoned case, the Supreme Court of Utah held that an individual who suffered a severe brain contusion causing permanent mental impairment possessed the mental capacity necessary to execute a settlement of his personal injury claims.[236] In so holding, the court reversed the trial court's directed verdict, holding that no reasonable jury could have found by "clear, unequivocal and convincing evidence" (the standard applicable in Utah) that Mr. Jiminez, the impaired party, was incompetent to contract on either of the two dates he signed the releases that settled his personal injury claim.[237]

The determination that Mr. Jiminez had contractual capacity conflicted with the opinion of three doctors, all of whom testified on behalf of Jiminez: the neurosurgeon who attended Mr. Jiminez while he was hospitalized (the doctor in the "best" position of the three experts to judge Jiminez' capacity, according to the court), the deposition testimony of Dr. J. L. Rosenbloom (specialty unspecified), who saw Jiminez approximately 7 months after the accident, and a third doctor, Garland H. Pace (specialty unspecified), who examined Jiminez 2 years after the accident. Dr. Rosenbloom diagnosed Jiminez' condition as posttraumatic personality or constitution and expressed an opinion that Jiminez "would always show some residual symptoms of the trauma in the nature of decreased emotional control, decreased capacity for working and probable impairment of concentration."[238]

All three experts expressed the opinion that Jiminez suffered permanent brain injury and that he was "not normal" on the dates he signed the releases, although the trial court precluded them from offering their opinion on the ultimate ques-

233. *Id.* at 898.
234. *Id.*
235. *Id.* at 907.
236. Jimenez v. O'Brien, 213 P.2d 337 (Utah 1949).
237. *Id.* at 88.
238. *Id.* at 343.

tion of contractual capacity.[239] The Utah Supreme Court praised that preclusion, stating that if the doctors had known of the substance of the conversations about settlement between Jiminez and the insurance company employee, there was "a good probability that their opinions as to Jiminez' mental competency would have been modified."[240] While the court did express a positive view of expert testimony, it found this testimony fell short because it was made in the context of medical examinations, as opposed to observation of the transaction as it occurred (or perhaps similar transactions near in time to the transaction at issue).[241] An alternative view of the evidence (expert testimony, lay testimony, and other evidence), set out in a vigorous dissent, would have upheld the determination of contractual incapacity.[242]

This case is an example of how the foundation and presentation of expert testimony may dictate the outcome of a case. Here, the experts limited the foundation of their testimony to their experience with Mr. Jiminez rather than exploring collateral data that would support their diagnoses. Moreover, they did not explicitly specify how inability to concentrate would have affected Mr. Jiminez' ability to understand the nature and consequences of the settlement agreement. The expert testimony would have been stronger if it had included those facts.

Even in cases involving a policy concern on behalf of the impaired party beyond the usual protection, courts have a tendency to enforce the settlement agreement. In *Cornell v. Delco Electronics Corporation*,[243] for example, Mr. Cornell asserted age and disability discrimination claims against his employer. With the assistance of a magistrate judge, the parties reached a settlement and signed it in the judge's presence.[244] Cornell sought to rescind the settlement agreement based on incapacity to contract on the day the settlement agreement was signed. Cornell had been diagnosed 3 years earlier with attention deficit disorder (ADD) as well as obsessive-compulsive disorder (OCD). He had been receiving medical treatments for these disorders since he was diagnosed, and took Ritalin, Dexedrine, and Prozac to help control manifestations of his illness.[245] Cornell also testified that when he did not take his medicine, he had difficulty focusing and "shuts down."

---

239. *Id.* at 343. Precluding experts from testifying about the ultimate legal issue in the case, in this context an opinion on whether a party had or lacked capacity to contract, is consistent with the traditional view that "ultimate issue" opinions usurp the role of the jury. KENNETH M. MOGILL, EXAMINATION OF WITNESSES §6:43 (2d ed. 2006). The modern trend takes the opposite view, allowing such testimony so long as there is an adequate foundation and the testimony is otherwise admissible. *Id.* Jurisdictions split on this issue, some following the tradition approach and others adopting the modern rule. *Compare* Doster v. Bates, 568 S.E.2d 736 (Ga. 2002) (adhering to traditional approach) *with* Pyasky v. Oyama, 641 N.E.2d 552 (Ill. App. 1994) (applying the modern rule applies). In federal civil cases, the modern rule applies. F.R.E.704(a).

240. *Jiminez* 213 P. 2d at 343.

241. *Id.*

242. *Id.* at 344–52 (Wade, J., dissenting).

243. 13 F. Supp. 2d 1116 (S.D. Ind. 2000).

244. *Id.* at 1117.

245. *Id.* at 1119.

Cornell was unable to take his afternoon dose of Dexedrine and Prozac because he did not anticipate that the settlement conference, which began late and kept him away from home for more than 9 hours, would go beyond the 1-hour period that the first settlement conference consumed.[246] Without the aid of an expert, Cornell described the effect that the missed dosages had on his ability to "bring everything into perspective" and wrote late that day that he "felt like he really shouldn't have signed it; but under the conditions that he was in at the time, that was what happened."[247]

Evaluating Cornell's claim of contractual incapacity, the Indiana Federal District Court stated:

> The contract approach does not give sufficient weight to federal interests in ensuring that the goals of anti-discrimination statutes are not undermined by agreements made between parties with unequal bargaining power. (citation omitted) Therefore, when a party to a settlement agreement purports to waive or release federally-based claims, courts will examine the totality of the circumstances in which the parties made the agreement to ensure that any waiver of civil rights was knowing and voluntary. (citation omitted)[248]

After considering Cornell's evidence in light of the special protection afforded to a waiver of civil rights, the court had no difficulty concluding that Cornell possessed the requisite capacity to enter into the settlement.[249]

iv. Settlement of divorce and spousal separation claims   Settlement of claims involving divorce and spousal separation merits consideration separate from settlement agreements between unrelated parties for two reasons.[250] First, the passions that grow out of the intimacy of marriage[251] may engender severe emotional reactions that generally would not occur in the context of other types of settlement agreements. The second reason spousal separation requires special consideration is the flip side of the first: The highly charged emotional context of marriage termination often creates vexatious litigation and makes settlement

---

246. *Id.*

247. *Id.*

248. *Id.* at 1120 (the court goes on to enumerate the following nonexclusive list factors: (1) the employee's education and business experience; (2) the employee's input in negotiating the terms of the settlement; (3) the clarity of the agreement; (4) the amount of time the employee had for deliberation before signing the release; (5) whether the employee actually read the release and considered its terms before signing it; (6) whether the employee was represented by counsel or consulted with an attorney; (7) whether the consideration being given in exchange for the waiver exceeded the benefits to which the employee was already entitled by contract law; and (8) whether the employee's release was induced by improper conduct on the defendant's part).

249. *Id.* at 1122.

250. In this chapter, we discuss one type of agreement that fits conceptually better here than in other sections: separation or dissolution agreements between spouses. Other agreements involving spouses are discussed in Chapter 4 E, *infra*.

251. The same is true of domestic partnerships and civil unions, whether they receive formal legal recognition or not. These alternatives to marriage are discussed *infra* in Chapter 4 E.

of the litigation more difficult than settlement of other types of claims. The combination of these two factors means that courts have an especially strong interest in settling marriage termination cases, even as one (or both) of the parties may be so emotionally affected as to impair his or her ability to understand or to act rationally with respect to the end of the relationship.

Balancing these two considerations may justify modification or elaboration of the legal standard for contractual capacity, incorporating the particularized mental health issues that marriage termination presents.[252] Presently, however, claims of incapacity in an action to set aside a settlement of divorce or spousal separation are subject to the same stringent standards that apply to settlements in other types of litigation.[253] The greatest difficulty with the present standard is that it almost never recognizes the debilitating effect that depression can have on contractual capacity. This is problematic in the context of claims other than those involving spouses,[254] but it is particularly problematic in the context of separation and divorce because this situation commonly brings on or exacerbates depression.[255] As one court has stated, "if agreements between husbands and wives could be set aside on the ground that one of the parties was severely depressed when he or she signed the agreement, separation agreements and other agreements executed by persons involved in dissolution or divorce proceedings would tumble like pins in a bowling alley."[256]

In one case, for example, the wife, Mrs. Drewry, had been receiving psychological counseling for unhappiness caused by her marriage for almost a year before she signed the agreement to divorce.[257] Her condition worsened and she was hospitalized for depression for approximately 1 month. At the hospital she came under the care of a psychiatrist, Dr. Luedke, who released her for a trip to Florida, apparently as part of her treatment. When she returned to Virginia she was again hospitalized, this time for a week due to a psychological breakdown.[258]

---

252. *See generally,* Connie J. A. Beck, et al., *Defining a Threshold for Client Competence to Participate in Divorce Mediation,* 12 Psychol. Pub. Pol'y & L. 1, 25 (2006) (proposing the following legal standard for divorce mediation):

> A person is incompetent to participate in mediation if he or she cannot meet the demands of a specific mediation situation because of functional impairments that severely limit a rational and factual understanding of the situation:
> 1. An ability to consider options, appreciate the impact of decisions, and make decisions consistent with his or her own priorities; or
> 2. An ability to conform his or her behavior to the ground rules of mediation.

253. *See supra* Chapter 4.B.2.b.iv.

254. For a case expressing skepticism about depression's relevance to contractual capacity in the context of a loan agreement, *see, e.g.,* Wurst. v. Blue River Bank of McCool Junction, 454 N.W.2d 665 (Neb. 1990).

255. *See, e.g.,* Juliani v. Juliani, 531 N.Y.S.2d 322 (App. Div. 1988); Drewry v. Drewry, 383 S.E.2d 12 (Va. App. 1989).

256. Flint v. Flint, 1990 WL 8465 (Ohio App. 1990), quoting DiPietro v. DiPietro, 10 Ohio App. 44, 49 (1983).

257. Drewry v. Drewry, 383 S.E.2d 12 (Va. App. 1989).

258. *Id.* at 13–14.

Dr. Luedke saw Mrs. Drewry the day before she signed the separation agreement and testified by deposition that she suffered from severe depression, and that she was "totally incompetent due to her illness to reason through any important legal document" when she signed the agreement.[259] Mrs. Drewry's clinical psychologist, who treated her prior to referring her to Dr. Luedke, agreed with Dr. Luedke's view. After expressing the view that treating doctors' and psychiatrists' opinions should be accorded "great weight" as compared to an expert witness who appears solely as a consultant in the litigation, the court rejected the treating doctors' opinions, stating that the trial court had found that they were based, in part, on fabricated and exaggerated information provided by Mrs. Drewry.[260]

Depression over divorce or separation also may lead the depressed individual to act in a way that creates legal liability if he or she has the mental capacity. For example, if the depressed individual physically harms another who is involved with the depressed individual's ex-spouse or separated spouse, the harmed individual may have a claim in tort law.[261] Where a homeowner's insurance policy covers claims for personal injury, a contract claim may arise, as occurred in *St. Paul Property and Liability Ins. Co. v. Eymann*.[262] The question of mental capacity arises if, as in *Eymann*, the insurance policy coverage excludes intentional acts that cause injury.

In *Eymann*, Cindy Cusumano (then Cindy Eymann) established a separate residence during her separation from "Sonny" Eymann. After Cindy filed for divorce from Sonny, she began a relationship with Stan Cusumano (whom she later married), an employee of the Eymanns (who then jointly owned a photography shop).[263] Sonny discovered this when he came to Cindy's apartment unannounced. Several days later Sonny again went to Cindy's apartment unannounced, and Stan again was there. When Cindy saw through the window that it was Sonny at the door, she did not open it. Sonny broke the door open with his shoulder, shouted at Cindy, and intentionally hit Stan on the head.[264] After Stan fell to the floor, Sonny apologized, hugged Stan, fell to the floor himself, and then began crying. He then got up, called Cindy a whore, hit her, and left the apartment.[265]

Evidence of incapacity included testimony of a psychologist who examined Stan the following day. The psychologist diagnosed Stan as suffering from "acute major depression," and testified that the depression together with the incident

259. *Id.*
260. *Id.* at 15–16. The reported appellate decision does not identify the statements found to be fabricated or exaggerated.
261. *See supra* Chapter 4 A.
262. 802 P.2d 1043 (Ariz. App. 1990), *superseded by statute on other grounds as stated in* K.B. v. State Farm Fire & Cas. Co., 941 P.2d 1288 (Ariz. App. 1997).
263. *Id.* at 1045.
264. *Id.*
265. *Id.*

significantly compromised Stan's judgment and reasoning, leaving him "not fully in control of his actions."[266] In addition, Stan testified he had never been in the same frame of mind or experienced the same emotions before or since the incident in question. Cindy testified that she had never seen Stan like that before or since.[267]

In Arizona (where the incident occurred), the test applied to determine whether an individual lacks the mental incapacity to commit a "voluntary" act to which the insurance exclusion would apply is whether the insured was suffering from a derangement of his intellect, which deprived him of the capacity to govern his conduct in accordance with reason, and while in that condition acted on an irrational impulse."[268] Noting that this standard was not limited to intellectual impairment, psychosis, or any other particular diagnostic category, the court nevertheless held that Sonny had the requisite capacity, so that the insurance exclusion applied.[269]

Together, these cases illustrate the extraordinary difficulty of establishing contractual incapacity based on depression, particularly in the context of settlements and related spousal matters. However, the cases do not preclude the possibility of proving contractual incapacity resulting from depression. Instead, they highlight the importance of explaining the connection between the depression's effects and the applicable contractual capacity standard.

3. The Role of Other Contract Doctrines Involving Mental Weakness

When an individual's mental capacity is impaired to some degree, but nevertheless satisfies the standard for contractual capacity, proof of the impairment (referred to in the case law as "mental weakness," to signify that it falls short of contractual incapacity) may contribute to invalidation of a contract under one or more other contract law doctrines. These other doctrines, which developed in different ways and at different times, are all concerned with the overall fairness of the transaction.[270] As illustrated in the following discussion, when one party to a contract suffers from a mental weakness, that may be a central factor in determining the validity of the contract.

a. Undue influence

Undue influence, a close cousin to the doctrine of contractual capacity, justifies setting aside a contract when a contracting party has contractual capacity to understand the nature and effect of the transaction, but is impelled by artifice, force,

266. *Id.* at 1051.
267. *Id.* at 1046.
268. *Id.* at 1050.
269. *Id.*
270. Green, *supra* note 163.

or fear to do what he or she does not want to do and what he or she would not have done but for such influence.[271] It is difficult to articulate a general rule that can be predictably applied distinguishing ordinary or appropriate influence from undue influence that justifies setting aside a contract (or other transaction). Factors tending to show undue influence include: (a) discussion of the transaction at an unusual or inappropriate time, (b) consummation of the transaction in an unusual place, (c) insistent demand that the business be finished at once, (d) extreme emphasis on untoward consequences of delay, (e) use of multiple persuaders by the dominant side against a single servient party, and (f) absence of third party advisers to the servient party.[272]

The close connection between capacity and undue influence often leads to assertion of both claims in an attempt to set aside a contract, particularly when the parties involved are related or otherwise close.[273] Limited mental capacity together with undue influence may merit cancellation of a contract even though the contract would be upheld absent evidence of fraud or undue influence.[274] In *Wood v. Wood,* another case seeking to vacate a decree of dissolution of a marriage, the plaintiff, Carol Wood, coupled her claim of mental incapacity with a claim of undue influence.[275]

Carol's mental health problems began approximately a year before she and her husband of 20 years, David, entered into the dissolution decree.[276] Her symptoms included difficulty sleeping, hair loss, mood swings, despondency, feelings of helplessness and hopelessness, and a loss of interest in activities she had previously enjoyed. She had also contemplated suicide. These problems affected her performance at work as well as her relationship with her only child, and they continued throughout the period of separation and dissolution.

Several months after the onset of Carol's mental health problems, Carol's friend took her to the hospital, where she was diagnosed with major depression and admitted for treatment of depression and suicidal ideation. This was precipitated by a fight between Carol and David the evening before, when David observed Carol with a man David believed was having an affair with Carol, based on a phone call from an anonymous coworker of Carol's. After 3 days she was released and David

---

271. Kelly v. Perault, 48 P. 45 (Idaho 1897); Howell v. Landry, 386 S.E.2d 610 (N.C. App. 1989). *See also,* RESTATEMENT (2ND) OF CONTRACTS, *supra* note 160, at §177 (defining undue influence as "unfair persuasion of a party who is under the domination of the person exercising the persuasion or who by virtue of the relation between them is justified in assuming that the person will not act in a manner inconsistent with his welfare").

272. Odorizzi v. Bloomfield School District, 546 Cal. Rptr. 533 (App. 1966) (undue influence existed where schoolteacher, who had been arrested on charges—later dismissed—of homosexual activity, was persuaded by school officials to resign his position after 40 hours without sleep). *See also,* Howell v. Landry, 386 S.E.2d 610 (N.C. App. 1989).

273. Libelt v. Liebelt, 801 P.2d 52 (Idaho App. 1990). *See also, infra,* Chapter 4.C.3.

274. Collins v. Isaacs, 21 S.W.2d 484 (Ky. 1929).

275. 1999 WL 4300710 (Ohio App. 1999).

276. *Id.* at 2.

drove her home. Carol was referred to a mental health service, and she continued with treatment but saw no improvement in her condition.

Two months later, David presented Carol with a separation agreement prepared by his lawyer, which already included hand-written changes to the agreement. The substance of the agreement provided that Carol would receive 20 percent of the assets from their 9-year marriage, and no spousal support. David also discouraged Carol from retaining an attorney. Carol later asserted that when the parties went to David's attorney's office to sign the final documents to dissolve the marriage, she did not see the financial disclosure of marital assets, and in fact some major assets (e.g., retirement accounts, airplane) were not listed or not valued.

Approximately 2 weeks after signing the separation agreement, Carol met with a psychiatrist, Dr. Scarnati, who performed a psychiatric evaluation. The psychiatrist diagnosed Carol with "major depression recurrent" and "marital problems." He indicated that the depression had worsened due to, among other things, the disintegration of her marriage. He also believed that physical and sexual abuse Carol suffered as a child contributed to her depression. Although Carol had doubts about terminating the marriage during the month between the execution of the dissolution documents and the hearing on the final dissolution, which she discussed with David, she did not discuss those doubts with a lawyer. At the final hearing, she affirmed that she wanted to go through with the dissolution. She later testified that she was in a daze on that date, and she felt she had to go through with the dissolution in order to reconcile with David.

The following month, Carol was evaluated by Dr. Guanzon, a psychiatrist who had taken over Dr. Scarnati's patients. Dr. Guanzon diagnosed Carl with "major depressive episode recurrent with no psychotic features" and "profoundly depressed," but a change in medication eventually improved Carol's condition.

At trial, Dr. Scarnati testified that Carol's ability to make decisions was impaired by her depression; that her insight, judgment, and memory were poor; that she had problems concentrating; and that "there was no way Carol could have understood her rights or what she would be getting from the dissolution." Dr. Guanzon, who gave deposition testimony, agreed.[277]

To counteract the testimony of Carol's experts, David offered the testimony of a psychiatrist and a forensic psychiatrist. David's two experts agreed that neither of Carol's experts had adequate information from which to draw any conclusion about Carol's competency.

After considering this evidence the trial court held for Carol on the basis of mental incapacity and undue influence. On appeal, the court chose to affirm the trial court's decision on the grounds of undue influence, obviating the need to consider whether the evidence justified setting aside the dissolution on the ground of mental incapacity.[278]

---

277. *Id.* at 6.
278. *Id.* at 11.

b. Duress

Duress, the legal antecedent of the equitable doctrine of undue influence, invalidates transactions of individuals deprived of the free will to choose whether to enter into the transaction.[279] Duress is determined based on consideration of all surrounding circumstances such as age, mental capacity, relation of the parties, and any other relevant factors.[280] In other words, the determination of duress depends not only on the actions of the alleged wrongdoer but also their effect on the other party. Consequently, actions that would fall short of duress with respect to an individual of ordinary strength and vigor may well constitute duress with respect to a weaker individual.

In *Tallmadge v. Robinson*,[281] for example, one daughter (Luetta) threatened to testify in a will contest that her estranged deceased father committed acts of incest with her. Luetta agreed to drop her objections to probate if her half sister, Jane, who also was a daughter of the decedent, gave Luetta $10,000. After 2 days of discussion with Luetta's brother (Jane's half brother), Jane agreed to pay the requested amount to Luetta. Luetta dropped the will contest but Jane did not pay, and Luetta brought suit.[282] In the suit, Luetta's threatened allegations were found to be untrue, and the threats, expressed through Luetta's brother, tormented and distressed Jane. Stating that the threat of personal and family disgrace may be grave enough to deprive an individual of the mental capacity to execute a valid contract, the Ohio Supreme Court held that Luetta's actions constituted duress, and Jane therefore had no obligation to make the promised payment to her.[283]

In a more recent case, the surviving spouse of a decedent attempted to set aside her separation agreement with the decedent on the grounds of duress.[284] In support of her position, the surviving spouse offered the expert testimony of a psychologist who opined "to a reasonable degree of psychological certainty" that the surviving spouse was convinced she had no choice but to sign the agreement or risk physical abuse from her husband.[285] She could not contest the agreement after it was signed, she said, because she was fearful of her husband until he died.

The psychologist performed a clinical evaluation of the surviving spouse, subjected the surviving spouse to psychological testing, and reviewed the separation

279. *See, e.g.,* Clark v. Riverview Fire Protection Dist., 354 F.3d 752, 759 (8th Cir. 2004) (the "central question with duress is whether, considering all surrounding circumstances, one party to the transaction was prevented from exercising his free will by the threats or conduct of another").

280. *See, e.g.,* Maenno v. Mutual Ben. Health & Acc. Ass'n 187 N.Y.S.2d 709 (N.Y. Sup. 1959); McCandish v. Linker, 231 S.W.2d 162 (Mo. 1950).

281. 109 N.E.2d 496 (Ohio 1952).

282. *Id.*

283. *Id.* at 501. Luella's withdrawal of her objections to the will had no effect on the determination that Jane had no obligation to pay Luella, because withdrawing objections did not necessarily have financial value. *Id.*

284. Goodwin v. Webb, 568 S.E.2d 311 (N.C. App. 2002), *rev'd* 577 S.E.2d 621 (2003).

285. *Id.* at 313.

agreement as well as other relevant documents.[286] The psychologist's affidavit affirmed, among other things, that: (a) the surviving spouse did not have the mental or emotional capacity to understand or appreciate the content of the separation agreement, (b) the surviving spouse's history and clinical testing were all consistent with a woman who had been abused and battered, mentally and physically, for her entire life, and (c) the surviving spouse's verbal IQ was in the low 70s, and her ability to understand written materials accordingly low. According to the psychologist, it was extremely unlikely that the surviving spouse understood, and the psychologist believed the surviving spouse did not understand, the separation agreement.[287]

The appellate court determined that the agreement was executed under duress, but remanded to the trial court to hear evidence on the question whether the facts established the surviving spouse had ratified the agreement.[288] The defendant offered no expert testimony about the surviving spouse's condition, but there was evidence that the surviving spouse had engaged in other business dealings that suggested that she had acquired or regained capacity. The surviving spouse appealed to the Supreme Court of North Carolina, which dealt the final blow to her claim, holding that the other business dealings and acceptance of benefits under the separation agreement constituted ratification as a matter of law.[289] Although the surviving spouse lost the appeal, the psychologist presented the argument for ongoing contractual incapacity well.

c. Fraud

In general, fraud requires proof of: (a) a material misrepresentation of presently existing or past fact, (b) the maker's intent that the other party rely on it, and (c) detrimental reliance by the other party.[290] Where the party alleging fraud suffers from mental illness or weakness, his or her mental condition may ease the showing necessary to establish fraud.[291] In considering a claim of fraud, a court will consider mental weakness of an allegedly impaired party. This may have the effect of lowering the threshold showing required to prove fraud.

Jason v. Drane, for example, involved a contract to repair damages to a house caused by fire, which Mr. Drane signed within 1 hour of the fire, despite many uncertainties about the necessary repairs. On the day of the fire (in December), the temperature in Chicago was zero degrees. The fire cut off the electricity and

---

286. *Id.* at 314.
287. *Id.*
288. *Id.* For a discussion of ratification see *supra* notes 189–190.
289. 577 S.E.2d 621 (2003).
290. *See, e.g.,* American Title Ins. Co. v. Lawson, 827 A.2d 230 (N.J. 2003); *See also,* McClain v. Shenandoah Life Ins. Co., 32 S.E.2d 592 (N.C. 1945) ("Fraud is a representation of fact materially affecting the value of the contract which is peculiarly within the knowledge of the person making it and with respect to which the other person in the exercise of proper vigilance has not an equal opportunity of ascertaining the truth.").
291. *See, e.g.,* Jason v. Drane, 237 N.E.2d 862 (Ill. App. 1968).

the firefighters had to knock out the building's windows, leaving Mr. Drane in a precarious position.

About a month before the fire Mr. Drane had been diagnosed with chronic paranoid schizophrenia, with much reoccupation (*sic*) and physical symptomotology.[292] Mr. Drane had physical illness as well. The case was referred to a Master for hearing on the issue of fraud, but ultimately held that the contract should be set aside based upon contractual incapacity. The appellate court affirmed the decision,[293] holding that the connection between mental weakness and fraud justified the consideration of Mr. Drane's mental capacity. Although the basis of the decision was contractual incapacity, the Master's findings as well as the appellate court's review did not explicitly reject the fraud claim and in fact discussed the inverse relationship between evidence of fraud and evidence of mental weakness: the greater the mental weakness, the lower the threshold for providing fraud.[294]

d. Unconscionability

Unconscionability, like undue influence, is a doctrine that is both difficult to encapsulate into a general rule lending itself to predictable application but yet sufficiently explicit to fulfill law's commitment to fundamental fairness. The common law doctrine of unconscionability has remained the same for nearly 3 centuries, stemming from a 1750 English case that defined an unconscionable contract as one that "no man in his senses and not under delusion could make on the one hand, and no honest and fair man would accept on the other. . ."[295] The Second Restatement of Contracts modifies the standard for unconscionability by specifying a substantive component—inadequacy of consideration—and a procedural element, namely whether the parties were in unequal bargaining positions at the time they entered into the contract.[296] The Restatement identifies the following factors as relevant to the determination of procedural aspect of unconscionability: belief by the stronger party that there is no reasonable probability that the weaker party will fully perform the contract; knowledge of the stronger party that the weaker party will be unable to receive substantial benefits from the contract; knowledge of the stronger party that the weaker party is unable reasonably to protect his interests by reason of physical or mental infirmities, ignorance, illiteracy, or inability to understand the language of the agreement, or similar factors.[297]

In *Lang v. Derr*, for example, plaintiff sought a declaratory judgment on her contract to sell her $60,000 interest in her deceased father's estate for $100 on

---

292. *Id.*
293. *Id.*
294. *Id.* at 864.
295. Hume v. United States, 132 U.S. 406 (1889), *quoting* Earl of Chesterfield v. Janssen, 28 E.R. 82 (1750).
296. Lang v. Derr, 569 S.E.2d 778, 781 (W. Va. 2002), *citing* RESTATEMENT OF CONTRACTS 2d §208, cmt. a.
297. RESTATEMENT OF CONTRACTS 2d §208, cmt. d.

the grounds of unconscionability.[298] The court held that the grossly inadequate price established the substantive inadequacy of consideration, and that plaintiff's grief over the death of her only surviving parent together with the close relationship she had enjoyed with defendants, sufficed to establish the procedural aspects of unequal bargaining power necessary to an unconscionability claim. Consequently, plaintiff prevailed.[299] Although this case did not involve any expert testimony, it illustrates how mental health expertise may be helpful in proving a claim of unconscionability.

4. Summary

Presently, contract law cases generally avoid using derogatory or discriminatory terminology,[300] describing functional limitations that bear directly on the capacities necessary for a showing of capacity to contract.[301] Additionally, contract law is beginning to distinguish different types of cognitive impairments, recognizing that a person may be mentally incompetent for purposes of some legal transactions and yet be competent for others.[302] The objective of this section is to describe how mental health expertise presently contributes to determinations of capacity (or incapacity) in contractual disputes, as well as to heighten awareness of the additional contributions that mental health expertise has to offer.

C. WILLS, TRUSTS, AND OTHER DONATIVE TRANSFERS

1. Introduction

This subchapter describes wills, trusts, and other forms of donative transfers with specific attention to potential challenges that might be raised in future litigation. The capacity standard by which the donor may be measured upon such contest will be explored, examining similarities and differences among state statutes and relevant case law holdings. Finally, the role of mental health expertise in the assessment of those capacities will be explored.

The law of donative transfers covers all types of gifts from one property owner to another. The multibillion-dollar gift from Warren Buffet to the Bill and Melinda Gates Foundation falls in this domain, as do bequests of property having

---

298. *Lang,* 569 S.E.2d at 781.

299. *Id.*

300. WILLISTON ON CONTRACTS, *supra* note 161, at §10.1. Many of the older cases speak of lunacy or lunatics, and judicial decisions, even relatively modern ones, often use the terms *insanity* or *insane persons.* The Restatement (Second), adopting a more modern approach, classifies these persons as suffering from mental illness or defect. The Williston text occasionally still uses the terms insanity and insane persons, although it primarily uses such terms as *mentally incompetent, mentally infirm,* and *mentally ill,* or those suffering a *mental defect.*

301. *Id.*

302. *Id.*

only sentimental value in a will. Outright gifts given during the donor's lifetime, gifts in trust that last throughout or beyond the donor's lifetime, property transferred from the donor to the donor and another jointly, and proceeds of life insurance policies, individual retirement accounts, pay-on-death bank accounts, and other similar arrangements also come within the scope of donative transfers.

The level of mental capacity required to make a donative transfer of property traditionally (though not universally)[303] depends on the form and timing of the transfer: Transfers by will require less capacity than gifts made during the donor's life. The higher standard for lifetime transfers implements the policy interest in maintaining the donor's ability to provide for his or her own needs and obligations.[304] The death of the donor obviates this consideration, resulting in a lower-capacity standard for wills. "Will substitutes," which take the form of a lifetime transfer but result in a property transfer upon the donor's death, may be governed by the lower wills standard or the higher standard applicable to contracts,[305] depending on the jurisdiction.[306]

Disputes over donative capacity—whether the transfer occurs during life or after death—share two important similarities that affect the evidence of a donor's capacity and the court's perception of it. First, donative transfer disputes usually begin after the donor's death, when he or she is unavailable for examination and unable to explain the reasons for making a gift or choosing particular beneficiaries. Second, members of the donor's family are virtually always on at least one side of the dispute, and frequently on both sides, which brings to the litigation the history of intrafamilial dynamics.

The reason for the timing of donative transfers litigation is different for wills than for other forms of transfer. Wills take effect only upon the death of the donor (referred to as the "testator" with respect to his or her will) and so no legal proceeding is possible before then.[307] For other donative transfers, the legal impediment to immediate challenge is that a plaintiff must have a stake in the outcome of the dispute ("standing" to sue).[308] The only person who has standing to challenge a donative transfer is the one who would receive the property if the transfer is set aside. During the donor's life, this would be the donor or a person who has authority over the property owner's transactions, such as a court-appointed guardian, attorney in fact, or other legal representative.[309]

303. *See infra* notes 431–33, and accompanying text.

304. RESTATEMENT (THIRD) OF PROP.: DONATIVE TRANSFERS §8.1, cmt. b (1999).

305. *See supra* Chapter 4.B (Contracts).

306. *See infra* notes 396–398, and accompanying text.

307. In three jurisdictions "pre-mortem probate" is available, but apparently has never been used. *See infra* notes 359–361 for an explanation of pre-mortem probate.

308. *See, e.g.,* Goff v. Weeks, 517 N.W. 2d 387, 391 (Neb. 1994) (former beneficiary of life insurance policy had standing to sue present beneficiary of life insurance policy because former beneficiary would have received life insurance proceeds if lawsuit had been successful).

309. A disappointed family member could petition the appropriate court for appointment as guardian of the donor. Few family members choose this course because it offers no assurance that they ultimately will receive any of the property. Even if the court does appoint a guardian

After the donor's death, those who may be entitled to receive the deceased donor's estate (or property that passes upon the donor's death outside the probate system)[310] may challenge the donor's lifetime transfers, either directly or through the estate's personal representative. This group always includes the decedent's intestate heirs, who are the decedent's closest relatives as identified by the state's intestacy statute.[311] In the absence of a valid will, the intestate heirs are automatically entitled to the estate, and they divide it as the intestacy statute provides.[312] If the decedent did leave a will, the intestate heirs have standing to challenge it, and their interest in the estate continues for the duration of the will contest. If the will is admitted to probate (recognized as valid), a disinherited surviving spouse will still have an interest in the estate by virtue of the "elective share" statute, which confers on the spouse the right to claim a share of the testator's estate.[313]

The legal restrictions on who can sue when have an adverse impact on the court's ability to assess donative capacity, regardless of the particularities of the applicable capacity standard. Deferring the litigation until after the donor's death precludes the possibility of direct expert examination of the donor on behalf of those challenging the transfer. Expert examination of capacity during the donor's life is possible, but its value is uncertain because there are no widely known or accepted standards for, or checks on, the conditions of such an examination. Consequently, few donors include capacity testing as part of their estate planning.

Without the probative evidence that expert examination under controlled conditions could provide, the litigants cobble together bits and pieces of less probative evidence to paint competing portraits of the decedent-donor's capacity at the time the document was executed. In some cases, the relative accuracy of one or

---

and the lifetime gift is set aside, the donor might have the capacity to make a transfer upon death. The guardianship will not resolve that question. *See, e.g.,* Estate of Gallavan, 89 P. 3d 521 (Colo. App. 2004) (will executed after conservator had been appointed for testator was valid).

310. *See infra* Chapter 4.C.5 (Will Substitutes).

311. *See, e.g.,* UNIF. PROB. CODE §2-102 et seq. All jurisdictions employ an objective definition rather than a qualitative conception of family to identify intestate heirs. This objective approach precludes claims of family status that otherwise would be possible. *Compare,* Matter of Cooper, 592 N.Y.S. 2d 797 (App. Div. 1993) (decedent's unmarried partner denied status as "surviving spouse") *with* Braschi v. Stahl Assoc. Co., 543 N.E. 2d 49, 54 (decedent's unmarried partner qualified as family member entitled to rent-controlled apartment). *See also, In re* Estate of Hall, 707 N.E.2d 201, 204 (Ill. App. 1st Dist. 1998) (same as *Cooper*).

312. *See, e.g.,* UNIF. PROB. CODE §2-102 (surviving spouse is entitled to 100 percent of the decedent's estate if (i) no parent or descendant of the decedent survives the decedent, or (ii) all of the decedent's surviving descendants are also descendants of the surviving spouse and no other descendant of the surviving spouse survives the decedent); N.Y. E.P.T.L. 4-1.1 (McKinney 1998) (estate of decedent survived by spouse and descendants is allocated first to the surviving spouse to the extent of $50,000, and above that the estate is allocated one-half to the spouse and one-half to the descendants by representation).

313. *See, e.g.,* UNIF. PROB. CODE §2-201 et seq. (providing for the surviving spouse to receive a specified fraction of the total assets of the couple, depending on the length of the marriage); N.Y. E.P.T.L. 5-1.1-A (providing for the surviving spouse to receive 1/3 of the "augmented estate," which includes the probate estate plus specified testamentary substitutes).

the other portrait is clear. In many others, however, the outcome depends on subjective perceptions about the character of parties on each side of the dispute.[314]

A vivid example of this is the will contest over the estate of Seward Johnson, "the largest, costliest, ugliest, most spectacular and most conspicuous will contest in American history."[315] Mr. Johnson died an octogenarian, survived by his third wife and six adult children from his earlier marriages. Mr. Johnson's will, signed approximately 1 month before he died, devised the bulk of the estate to his wife and virtually disinherited all six children.

Mr. Johnson had spent significant time on his estate planning over the years, but his lawyers never arranged for a psychological assessment of his capacity in connection with the execution of his wills. His lawyers did secure an affidavit affirming Mr. Johnson's testamentary capacity from a cardiologist who attended to Mr. Johnson on the day of the will execution and signed the affidavit that same day. The basis of the cardiologist's opinion, however, was casual conversation. The experts testifying on behalf of the children, including a doctor specializing in geriatric medicine, a neurologist, and a geriatric psychiatrist, effectively discredited the cardiologist's testimony despite the fact that they had not known, much less examined, Mr. Johnson.

As media reports and interviews with the jurors later showed, the opinions of the case depended largely on character assessments of the children as compared to Mrs. Johnson. Mrs. Johnson ("Basia"), less than half the age of Mr. Johnson, was a Polish immigrant who met her future husband while working as a housekeeper for him and his second wife. The children eschewed financially productive endeavors, preferring pursuit of hobbies like horse breeding, art collecting, and movie production. The gold-digger versus the disinherited children, or the devoted wife versus the dilettantes? The ultimate outcome of the will contest was anyone's guess. At the eleventh hour, after the jury had begun to deliberate but before they had returned a verdict, the parties settled. The children received approximately $6 million and a charity founded by Mr. Johnson received $1 million, leaving Mrs. Johnson with the balance, estimated at $350 million.

To forensic psychologists and lawyers who practice in areas other than trusts and estates, the evidence offered regarding testamentary capacity in the Johnson case may seem amazingly unsophisticated. But it is also typical. Certainly, forensic psychologists have much to offer that will contests and other donative transfer disputes often do not reflect.

The aim of this subchapter is to describe how mental health expertise can contribute to proof of capacity (or incapacity) in will contests and other donative transfer disputes. The subchapter is divided into four categories of donative trans-

---

314. Pamela Champine, *Expertise and Instinct in the Assessment of Testamentary Capacity,* 51 VILL. L. REV. 25 (2006) (testamentary capacity); *cf.,* Melanie Leslie, *The Myth of Testamentary Freedom,* 38 ARIZ. L. REV. 235 (1996) (undue influence).

315. DAVID MARGOLICK, UNDUE INFLUENCE: THE EPIC BATTLE FOR THE JOHNSON & JOHNSON FORTUNE (1993).

fers: wills, lifetime outright gifts, irrevocable trusts, and will substitutes. Each section of this subchapter begins with a description of the nature of the transfer and its essential legal characteristics. A statement of the capacity standard applicable to that type of transfer follows, with case analysis to illustrate how courts apply the standard. Each subsection concludes with discussion and analysis of the opportunities and pitfalls presented by the use of mental health expertise.

2. Wills

A will is the traditional method of transferring property upon death for individuals who wish to select their beneficiaries rather than to accept the default scheme of intestacy. Wills are written documents, executed with formalities specified by statute. The statutory formalities vary in their specifics from state to state, but most require the will to be in writing, signed by the testator, and witnessed.[316] In addition, every jurisdiction requires the testator to have the mental capacity to execute a will.[317] Finally, the will must not be the product of insane delusion, undue influence, or fraud.[318] Only if all of these requirements are met will the will be valid.

The will validity requirements are concerned with the authenticity of the will as opposed to the testator's choice of beneficiaries. This reflects the policy of effectuating the intent of the testator in two ways: by confirming that the will is the will of the testator as opposed to some other person, and by assuring the testator's freedom to select beneficiaries of his or her choosing (testamentary autonomy).[319] The validity requirements for wills advance both aspects of this policy by denying probate to instruments that do not appear to embody the testator's intent.

Some of the validity requirements advance this objective directly while others are more indirect. The statutory formalities indirectly advance the objective of effectuating the testator's intent by limiting the opportunity for fraud or mistake. The doctrines of testamentary capacity and undue influence, on the other hand, directly address whether the will represents the testator's intent.

a. The testamentary capacity standard

The testamentary capacity standard, articulated in different ways from jurisdiction to jurisdiction, generally requires the testator to know the nature and extent of his or her property, the natural objects of his or her bounty, and the nature of the testamentary act.[320] This task-specific standard allows for defects in capacity so

---

316. WILLIAM J. BOWE ET AL., PAGE ON WILLS §19.4 (Anderson Pub. Co. 2003) *hereinafter* PAGE ON WILLS; *See, e.g.,* N.Y. E.P.T.L. 3-2.1 (McKinney 1998); UNIF. PROB. CODE § 2-502.

317. PAGE ON WILLS, *supra* note 316, at §§ 12.1 et seq.

318. *Id. at* §§ 14.1 et seq., 15.1 et seq.

319. *See supra* note 304.

320. CAL. PROB. CODE §6100.5 (West Supp. 2007); *In re* Estate of Dokken, 604 N.W. 2d 487 (S.D. 2000).

long as the testator is able to reach decisions about the disposition of his or her estate.[321] A cognitively impaired individual who functions at the level of a 10- or 12-year-old child may nevertheless have testamentary capacity.[322] Diseases like Alzheimer's and other forms of dementia do not automatically deprive an individual of testamentary capacity,[323] nor does serious mental illness.[324] Moreover, an individual who lacks testamentary capacity much of the time nevertheless may execute a valid will during a "lucid interval."[325]

Many courts have described the testamentary capacity standard as low relative to standards of capacity for other legal acts, such as entering into contracts or engaging in ordinary business transactions.[326] This ranking of capacity standards overlooks their substantive differences as well as the role of contextual factors in defining the capacity requirement applicable to a particular case.[327] Nevertheless, the generalization accurately captures the policy choice of erring on the side honoring wills executed by testators lacking capacity rather than invalidating wills of testators who possess the requisite capacity.

The testamentary capacity standard explicitly embraces the policy of testamentary freedom by focusing on the testator's cognitive ability to make estate planning decisions rather than the outcome of the decision-making process.[328] The emphasis on testamentary autonomy tends to obscure another policy in the law of wills: protection of the testator's family. The testamentary capacity standard's reference to the "natural objects of the testator's bounty," the standing of intestate heirs to challenge a will, and the right of a surviving spouse to claim a share of the estate regardless of the provisions of the will, evidence an abiding concern for the testator's family.[329]

While the family generally has no entitlement to inherit from the testator, neither should they be disinherited unintentionally by a testator who did not understand the substance of his or her will. To this extent, family protection and the policy of testamentary autonomy align: In cases where the testator clearly lacks capacity, an act the testator did not understand (execution of the will) could not

---

321. Estate of Khazeneh, 2006 WL 3872843 (Sur. N.Y. Nov. 28, 2006); *In re* Conservatorship of Groves, 109 S.W.3d 317, 333–35 (Tenn. Ct. App. 2003).

322. Leventhal v. Baumgartner, 61 S.E.2d 810 (Ga. 1950); *In re* Teel's Estate, 483 P. 2d 603, 605 (Ariz. App. 1971).

323. *See, e.g.,* Wilson v. Lane, 614 S.E.2d 88 (Ga. 2005); Estate of Buchanan, 665 N.Y.S.2d 980 (App. Div. 1st Dept. 1997).

324. Estate of Romero, 126 P.3d 228 (Colo. App. 2005), *cert den.* 2006 W.L. 349702 (Colo. 2006). (schizophrenia); *In re* Estate of Ellis, 616 N.W. 59, 65–66 (Neb. Ct. App. 2000) (schizotypal personality).

325. *See, e.g.,* Maxwell v. Dawkins, 2006 WL 3692427 (Ala. 2006).

326. *In re* Estate of Farr, 49 P. 3d 415 (Kan. 2002); Hess v. Arbogast, 376 S.E. 2d 333 (W. Va. 1988); Hilbert v. Benson, 917 P. 2d 1152, 1156 (Wyo. 1996).

327. THOMAS B. ATKINSON, THE LAW OF WILLS 240 (2d ed. 1953).

328. RESTATEMENT (THIRD) OF PROP.: DONATIVE TRANSFERS §8.1 cmt. b (1999). This is exactly the same as the test for competency to waive counsel. *See supra* Chapter 3.C.

329. Estate of Herbert, 979 P. 2d 39, 50 (Haw. 1999); *see also,* Norris v. Bristow, 219 S.W. 2d 367, 370 (Mo. 1949) (defining natural objects of the testator's bounty).

have been autonomous. Beyond this, the policies conflict, because family protection policy generally favors denying probate while testator protection favors admission of the will to probate.

The testamentary capacity standard in some jurisdictions emphasizes the interest in family protection by adding to the basic elements a requirement of "rational judgment" to make a will.[330] In other jurisdictions, courts consider the testator's relationship with family members as part of the overall evidentiary picture of the testator's capacity.[331] The weaker the evidence of capacity, the more pivotal becomes the evidence of the testator's relationships.

In *Estate of Romero,* for example, the testator's children challenged the will, which devised the entire estate to the testator's sister.[332] The testator suffered from schizophrenia and had a V.A. guardianship to handle his financial affairs. Neither the mental illness nor the guardianship raised a presumption of incapacity, but each constituted evidence relevant to testamentary capacity.[333] The testator's sister offered no evidence of testamentary capacity beyond the testimony of the will's drafter and the attesting witnesses. The court affirmed probate of the will, relying expressly on the drafter's testimony about the testator's wish to provide for his sister, who had cared for him, rather than his children, whom he rarely saw.[334]

Although *Romero* held against the testator's intestate distributees,[335] the subjective assessment of relationships is the same analysis that courts use to implement the family protection policy. The sister's claim on the testator's estate was more in the nature of reciprocity or fairness than family protection. Decades ago, family protection and fairness were fairly synonymous because family structure and familial obligations were largely homogenous. In contemporary society, with its ever more diverse family structures, fairness better captures the objective of "family protection" that capacity doctrine reflects.

i. Insane delusion   In rare cases, an individual of otherwise unquestioned mental competence may suffer from an *insane delusion*. An insane delusion is a belief that has absolutely no foundation in fact; even slight evidence that provides a basis for the belief negates the conclusion that it constitutes an insane

---

330. *See, e.g.,* Norwest Bank v. Minnesota North, N.A. v. Beckler, 663 N.W.2d 571 (Minn. App. 2003) (listing the reasonableness of the proposed disposition as the first of four factors to be considered in evaluating testamentary capacity, followed by the testator's conduct before and after the will execution, any prior adjudication of the testator's capacity, and finally, expert testimony regarding the testator's physical and mental condition).

331. *See, e.g.,* Estate of Hastings, 347 N.W.2d 347 (S.D. 1984); Fletcher v. DeLoach, 360 So.2d 316 (Ala. 1978); Pardue v. Pardue, 227 S.W.2d 403 (Ky. 1950); Adams v. Adams, 101 P.3d 344 (Ok. App. 2004); Schwartz v. Lamberson, 407 So.2d 358 (Fla. App. 1981).

332. Estate of Romero, 126 P.3d 228 (Colo. App. 2005).

333. *See, e.g.,* Estate of Hastings, 347 N.W.2d at 350–51 (neither appointment of a guardian nor diagnosis of organic brain syndrome precluded testamentary capacity, but both constituted evidence supporting determination of testamentary incapacity).

334. Estate of Romero, 126 P.3d at 231–32.

335. *See supra* note 9.

delusion.[336] An insane delusion that materially affects a testator's will deprives the testator of capacity, even if he or she would otherwise satisfy the testamentary capacity standard.[337]

This stringent standard generally prevents family members or other objectants to a will from claiming that the testator's reasons for disinheriting them were the product of an insane delusion. In *Estate of Kottke,* for example, the testator's stepdaughter claimed that the testator revoked the will and executed a new one disinheriting her based on the delusion that she had stolen the will and jewelry of her mother (the testator's first wife) after her death.[338] The court rejected the stepdaughter's characterization of this belief as an insane delusion because the fact that the will and jewelry were missing supported the testator's belief, even if he was mistaken.

In another case, a testator disinherited children whom he seriously abused while they lived together and largely ignored after the children moved away with their mother.[339] One of the testator's sons argued that his father suffered from an insane delusion because he had no reason to hate or fear the children. The court rejected the argument because another son had threatened the testator, creating a basis in fact for the testator's fear. After lamenting the testator's poor treatment of his children, the court held that it did not deprive the testator of capacity to make a will.[340]

Expert testimony may facilitate proof of an insane delusion,[341] as happened in *Miami Rescue Mission, Inc. v. Roberts.*[342] In that case, the testator executed a will on the day before she died, benefiting various charities. In so doing, she revoked an earlier will that left her estate to her long-time caregiver and friend. The reason for the change, the caregiver argued, was the testator's insane delusion that the caregiver had abandoned her, stolen from her, and left her dog to die. The doctors supported this position with their own testimony about the testator's deteriorating mental condition, the effects of the drugs they gave her, and their notes of the testator's distress about being abandoned by the caregiver. This, together with evidence that the caregiver visited the testator every day, established an insane

---

336. *See, e.g.,* Matter of Kottke, 6 P. 3d 243 (Alas. 2000); Dougherty v. Rubenstein, 914 A.2d 184 (Md. App. 2007); Russell v. Russell. 197 S.W.3d 265 (Tenn. App. 2005).

337. *See, e.g.,* McCabe v. Hanley, 886 So.2d 1053, 1055 (Fla. App. 2004) (insane delusion must affect provisions of the will in order to invalidate it).

338. *Matter of Kottke,* 6 P. 3d at 246–47.

339. Estate of Schnell, 683 N.W.2d 415 (S.D. 2004).

340. *Id.*

341. The phrase *insane delusion* rarely appears anymore in insanity defense law, and when it does, it is usually limited to what are called "deific decree cases." *See, e.g.,* Grant Morris et al., *"God Told Me to Kill": Religion or Delusion,* 38 San Diego L. Rev. 973 2001. An insane delusion may raise the defense of insanity "only to the extent that the delusional facts would have justified or excused the criminal offense if those facts had been true rather than delusional." Miller v. State, 940 S.W.2d 810, 812 (Tex. App. 1997, *pet. ref'd*).

342. 943 So.2d 274 (Fla. App. 3d Dist. 2006).

delusion that invalidated the will benefiting the charities, leaving the caregiver free to probate the earlier will.[343]

ii. The interrelationship of testamentary capacity and undue influence

Undue influence is closely connected to testamentary capacity because both involve the testator's mental state. Undue influence differs from capacity in that undue influence invalidates a will executed by a testator under such coercion that the testator carried out the wishes of another person instead of the testator's own wishes because he or she was unable to refuse or too weak to resist.[344] Theoretically, an allegation of undue influence is relevant only if the testator had capacity to execute the will, because an incapacitated testator has no will that undue influence could overcome.[345] As a practical matter, however, objectants to a will often join the two claims where the testator's capacity is marginal. Usually courts consider the two claims separately, but occasionally the claims are considered in tandem.[346]

The elements usually present in an undue influence case include a will that makes an "unnatural" disposition, a testator who was susceptible to undue influence, and a wrongdoer who had the opportunity to exercise undue influence and acted on that opportunity.[347] The conduct of the alleged wrongdoer is important, but the real issue, and the one forensic mental health assessment would address, is the effect of that conduct on the testator.[348] The weaker the testator's mind, the lower the threshold for undue influence.[349] A weakened mind in this context typically involves persistent confusion, forgetfulness, and disorientation.[350]

The same evidentiary problems that plague testamentary capacity determinations apply equally to the "mental weakness" element of undue influence, and the ultimate question of whether a wrongdoer subverted the testator's will. To help fill that void, courts analyze the relationship between the testator and the alleged wrongdoer. *Confidential relationship* describes an individual's dominance over the testator that arises either through trust or from mental or physical weakness.[351] Will drafters, physicians, and attorneys-in-fact (those who hold a power of attorney enabling them to act on behalf of another), by virtue of their position, have a confidential relationship with the testator because they owe the testator

---

343. *Id.*

344. *See, e.g.,* Smith v. Liney, 631 S. E. 2d 648 (Ga. 2006); Estate of Ryan, 824 N.Y.S. 2d 20 (App. Div. 1st Dept. 2006).

345. Estate of Aageson, 702 P. 2d 338 (Mont. 1985).

346. *Id.; In re* Rogers' Estate, 47 N.W.2d 818 (Iowa 1951).

347. O'Rourke v. Hunter, 848 N.E.2d 382 (Mass. 2006).

348. Estate of Slusarenko, 147 P. 3d 920 (Or. App. 2006).

349. *See, e.g., In re* Blake's Will, 120 A.2d 745 (N.J. 1956).

350. Owens v. Mazzei, 847 A.2d 700 (Pa. Super. 2004).

351. Mullins v. Ratcliff, 515 So.2d 1183, 1191–92 (Miss. 1987).

legal duties that justify the testator's trust.[352] Family members, friends, caregivers, and others may owe the testator a moral or personal duty that results in a "confidential relationship" with the testator.[353] Where a confidential relationship exists, the proponent of the will bears a heightened responsibility to explain the circumstances of the testator's dispositive choices.[354]

In the end, undue influence analysis amounts to a highly subjective inquiry into the testator's motives in making the will. The doctrine's real contribution to the law of wills is to "allow courts to invalidate wills which contain plans of distribution that the court finds shocking or objectionable. It permits a very low standard of testamentary capacity while simultaneously providing a means to nullify suspect wills of marginally capacitated testators."[355]

a. When an expert testifies on both testamentary capacity and undue influence

An expert who renders an opinion in a case involving allegations of both incapacity and undue influence should clearly separate his or her analysis of testamentary capacity undue influence. The same factors bear on testamentary capacity and the mental weakness element of undue influence. Separating the analysis, however, underscores the expert's understanding that a lower threshold applies to mental weakness than to testamentary incapacity. Moreover, it segregates from the testamentary capacity analysis any aspects of the testator's mental abilities or disabilities that bear on susceptibility to persuasion or undue influence.

b. The role of mental health expertise

The coupling of undue influence and incapacity claims emphasizes the familial context of donative transfers relative to more direct evidence of cognition. While context is critical in the legal analysis of evidence as well as the psychological assessment of mental capacity, context ought not to overshadow probative evidence of cognition. In a groundbreaking study, Dean Milton Green argued that this is exactly what has occurred in cases involving wills: Expert testimony mattered least and the content of the will mattered most in testamentary capacity determinations.[356] When the study was published in 1942, expert testimony arguably deserved this dismal ranking. Forensic psychology had not yet emerged

---

352. *E.g.,* Bailey v. Edmundson, 630 S.E.2d 396 (Ga. 2006).

353. *In re* Estate of Duebendorfer, 721 N.W. 2d 438 (S.D. 2006) (power of attorney); Matter of Henderson, 605 N.E.2d 332 (N.Y. 1992); Matter of Satterlee, 119 N.Y.S. 2d 309 (App. Div. 1953).

354. *In re* Neenan, 827 N.Y.S. 2d 164 (App. Div. 2006); Fla. Stat. Ann. §703.107(2).

355. Lawrence A. Frolik, *The Strange Interplay of Testamentary Capacity and the Doctrine of Undue Influence: Are We Protecting Older Testators or Overriding Individual Preferences,* 24 INT'L J. L. & PSYCHIATRY 253, 266 (2001).

356. Milton D. Green, *Proof of Mental Incompetency and the Unexpressed Major Premise,* 53 YALE L. J. 271, 278–79 (1944).

as a recognized discipline,[357] and forensic assessment instruments scientifically designed to elicit relevant information about a specific legal capacity had not yet been developed.[358]

Today, forensic psychology's potential to improve the quality of testamentary capacity law remains largely unrealized. The major problem with integrating forensic psychology into testamentary capacity determinations is that they occur after the death of the testator. The obvious remedy would be to change probate procedures so that they authorize assessment of capacity during the testator's life that will be binding on all parties in any subsequent will contest. Law reformers recognized this almost a century ago, and they began to design alternative procedural structures for "living probate."[359] None of the alternatives attracted general support, however, because none effectively balanced family protection and testator autonomy. Allowing the family to challenge a will in "living probate" protected their interests but compromised the testator's by forcing disclosure of the will content and imposing the costs of litigation during the testator's lifetime. Excluding the family from living probate would be viable only if the family protection policy could be implemented in an alternative way.[360] In the late 1970s and early 1980s, when the last serious discussion of living probate occurred, no such alternative was available.[361] Consequently, the "obvious" solution to evidentiary shortcomings in testamentary capacity determinations has not found its way into probate procedures.

a. Estate planning   In cases where the testator or the testator's lawyer anticipates a will contest, it may be advisable to arrange for an expert to examine the testator in order to document testamentary capacity contemporaneously with the will execution. The preliminary question is whether the lawyer has any doubt about the testator's capacity to execute the will. If the lawyer does have doubts,

357. Ronald Roesch, Stephen D. Hart, and James R. P. Ogloff, eds., Psychology and Law: The State of the Discipline 122–23 (1999).

358. Thomas Grisso, Evaluating Competencies: Forensic Assessments and Instruments, *supra* note 2, at 31–53.

359. The first living probate statute in the United States was enacted by Michigan in 1883, but it was declared unconstitutional a few years later because, among other things, it allowed the testator to circumvent the inchoate rights of the surviving spouse and child in the estate. Lloyd v. Wayne Circuit Judge, 23 N.W. 28, 29 (Mich. 1885); *see also,* Howard Fink, *Ante-Mortem Probate Revisited: Can an Idea Have Life After Death?,* 37 Ohio St. L.J. 264, 268–83 (1976); Harold S. Hulbert, *Probate Psychiatry, A Neuro-Psychiatric Examination of Testator from the Psychiatric Viewpoint,* 25 U. Ill. L. Rev. 288, 288–89 (1930); Samuel J. Stephens, Probate Psychiatry: Examination of Testamentary Capacity by a Psychiatrist as a Subscribing Witness, 25 U. Ill. L. Rev. 276, 279–80 (1930).

360. Mary Louise Fellows, *The Case Against Living Probate,* 78 Mich. L. Rev. 1066, 1095–09 (1980).

361. Gregory S. Alexander & Albert M. Pearson, *Alternative Models of Ante-Mortem Probate and Procedural Due Process Limitations on Successions,* 78 Mich. L. Rev. 89 (1979); John H. Langbein, *Living Probate: The Conservatorship Model,* 77 Mich L. Rev. 63, 66 (1978).

persuasive but nonbinding ethical guidance suggests that the lawyer ought to resolve those doubts by consulting with an expert.[362] Even when no will contest is anticipated, the lawyer arguably has a duty to prevent the client from harming his or her own best interests by preparing a will that the client does not understand. On the other hand, some lawyers believe that their personal doubts about a client's testamentary capacity do not justify consultation with an expert, even when a contest is anticipated.[363]

Where the lawyer has no doubt that the client possesses testamentary capacity, a high-quality expert examination presents little risk and great reward. A study of cases reported between 2000 and 2005 found that five of the cases involved a lifetime assessment of testamentary capacity conducted by a knowledgeable expert, contemporaneously or very close in time to the will execution.[364] In each of the five cases the judicial determination of testamentary capacity followed the expert's opinion.[365] From those and other cases, the attributes of an optimal examination appear to include: (a) a knowledgeable expert, (b) who examines the testator (c) contemporaneously with the will execution (d) in order to ascertain testamentary capacity.

A *knowledgeable* expert ought to have a background or experience in assessing mental capacity, a substantial factual basis upon which to base opinions about the capacity of the testator, and knowledge of the legal standard for testamentary capacity.[366] In each of the five cases in the study covering 2000–2005, the expert had either a mental health background or long-term familiarity with the testator, but none had both. Of the three cases involving experts who did not have an extended relationship with the testator, two involved social workers (one medical, one clinical) and the other involved a psychologist.[367] A background in forensic psychology would be ideal for most situations, but so long as the examining expert understands the legal standard, elicits the relevant facts, applies a recognized test or methodology to analyze the relevant facts, and connects those facts to his or her conclusion about testamentary capacity, the expert contributes valuable evidence.

The timing of the examination is also critical. An expert examination that is significantly before (or significantly after) the will execution leaves open the possibility that the testator's capabilities changed in the intervening period. The

---

362. Am. Coll. of Trust & Estate Counsel (ACTEC) Commentaries on the Model Rules of Prof'l Conduct 218 (ACTEC Found. 3d ed. 1999).

363. *Compare* Drope v. Missouri, 420 U.S. 162 (1975) (if defense counsel has bona fide doubt as to his client's incompetence to stand trial he must raise issue to the court).

364. Champine, *supra* note 314, at 36–37.

365. Baun v. Kramlich, 667 N.W.2d 672 (S.D. 2003); Singleman v. Singleman, 548 S.E. 2d 343 (Ga. 2001); *In re* Estate of Garrett, 100 S.W. 3d 72 (Ark. App. 2003); *In re* Schott Estate, 2001 WL 34069931 (Ct. Com. Pl. 2001); Estate of Jensen v. Quayle, 2003 WL 1889983 (Cal. Ct. App. 2003).

366. *See, e.g., In re* Powers' Estate, 134 N.W. 2d 148 (Mich. 1965).

367. *Baun, supra* (medical social worker); *Singleman, supra* (licensed clinical social worker); *Garrett, supra* (treating physician); *Schott, supra* (family practitioner); *Jenssen, supra* (psychologist).

shorter the interval between the forensic examination and the will execution, the less likely it is that the testator's capabilities will differ for the two events.[368] Even in situations where the testator's capacity is not fluctuating, it is important to limit the objectant's opportunity to argue that the testator's capacity changed.

An examination conducted for the express purpose of ascertaining testamentary capacity is preferable over physician notes for the period in question because the examiner's attention is focused on different aspects of mental capacity. Examination by the physician might address competency to make medical decisions, for example, which would potentially rely on different information than that required to assess competency to execute a will.[369] No specific questions or tests are mandated for the expert's examination. So long as the expert understands the requirements for testamentary capacity, the translation of those requirements into appropriate questions is left to the discretion of the expert. However, the attorney should review with the expert the kinds of information that might be sought by the expert, its relevance to the requirements for testamentary competency, methods by which the expert intends to collect the information and to maintain records of the process, and any anticipated obstacles to completing a comprehensive assessment. Limits of confidentiality must be understood (though they are often waived in will contests), and consequent consideration must be given to areas of potential concern so that the testator's privacy is not unduly violated.

b. Estate litigation   In the vast majority of will contests, the testator did not undergo a prophylactic assessment of testamentary capacity contemporaneously with the will execution. In these cases, the value of expert testimony turns on many factors, including the expert's qualifications in the relevant field of expertise, the thoroughness of information available to the expert regarding the testator, the expert's ability to relate his or her expertise to the testator's situation, and the expert's experience or effectiveness in dealing with cross-examination techniques designed to undermine the value of his or her testimony.

Knowledge of the testator is a most important factor in courts' evaluation of expert testimony, because an expert opinion can be no stronger than the foundation on which it rests.[370] This principle accounts for the weight accorded to testimony based on examination of or interaction with the testator for an extended period.[371] It also accounts for the derogation of expert testimony resting

368. Maxwell v. Dawkins, 2006 WL 3692427 (Ala. 2006).
369. *See* McGough v. McGough, 2005 WL 2293555 (Ark. App. 2005).
370. *See, e.g., In re* De Maio's Estate, 70 A.2d 339 (Pa. 1950).
371. *See, e.g.,* Arac v. Jacobs, 289 N.E.2d 839 (Mass. 1972) (testimony of attending physician at the time of the will's execution that the testator was "perfectly rational and normal," supported by the opinions of the attesting witnesses, was sufficient to establish that the testator had capacity to execute the will); Estate of Bennight, 503 P.2d 203 (Okla. 1972) (trial court's judgment that the testator possessed capacity to execute the will was clearly against the weight of evidence, which included the testimony of testator's long-time physician); Estate of Abram, 213 A.2d 638 (Pa. 1965) (will drafted by attorney and proved by attesting witnesses requires compelling evidence to prove incapacity, especially if attending physician corroborates the will

on review of the testator's medical records alone, and the practice of granting summary judgment[372] to the proponents of a will where the sole evidence offered by objectants is expert testimony based solely on review of the testator's medical records.[373]

One methodology that may be useful when the expert never met the testator is the so-called *psychological autopsy,* or retrospective analysis of the testator's relevant functional abilities at the time the document was executed.[374] The sources of information beyond the testator's medical records—such as interviews with family, friends, physicians, care providers, and those involved with the preparation or execution of the will—lend weight and credibility to the expert's conclusions.[375] The reliability of the psychological autopsy technique has been challenged in the handful of will contest cases involving this type of testimony, but those challenges generally fail.

In one relatively recent case, the South Dakota Supreme Court affirmed probate of a will based on the opinion of a forensic psychiatrist who evaluated, in accordance with forensic psychiatry principles, the testator's medical records and interviewed individuals who knew the testator.[376] In so holding, the court explic-

---

proponents); Succession of Lafferanderie, 84 So.2d 442 (La. 1955) (rejecting testimony of notary and attesting witnesses in favor of attending physicians' testimony).

372. Summary judgment is a procedure that authorizes the court to render a judgment without conducting a trial. The purpose of a trial is to resolve questions of fact, and so the grant of summary judgment is appropriate when there is no disputed issue of material fact for a trial to resolve. *See, e.g.,* Boone v. Nelson, 264 N.W.2d 881 (N.D. 1978). Generally, the rules of civil procedure of each jurisdiction authorize the use of summary judgment, but that procedure is not necessarily available for every type of suit. *See, e.g.,* O'Rourke v. Hunter, 848 N.E.2d 382 (Mass. 2006) (explaining statutory change, effective in 2000, that permitted use of summary judgment in probate contests); Estate of Davis, 132 P.3d 609 (Okla. App. 2006) (interpreting Oklahoma's probate procedures to preclude use of summary judgment).

373. Estate of Dupree, 20 Phila. Co. Rptr. 349, 1990 WL 902402 (Pa. Orph.), *aff'd,*8 594 A.2d 787 (Pa. Super. 1991); Estate of Swain, 509 N.Y.S.2d 643 (App. Div. 1986) (holding that psychiatrist's opinion that the testator lacked testamentary capacity was entitled to no weight where the psychiatrist did not know the testator and did not consult with those who treated the testator; psychiatrist's review of records, the sole basis of his testimony, did not include the month during which the will was executed; treating physician's testimony was credited). Estate of Friedman, 809 N.Y.S.2d 667 (App. Div. 2006).

374. *See* K. Hawton et al., *The Psychological Autopsy Approach to Studying Suicide: A Review of Methodological Issues,* 50 JOURNAL OF AFFECTIVE DISORDERS 269–76 (1998); N. Polythress et al., *APA's Expert Panel in the Congressional Review of the USS Iowa Incident,* 48 AMERICAN PSYCHOLOGIST 8–5 (1993); J. BESKOW ET AL., *Psychological Autopsies: Methods and Ethics,* 20 SUICIDE AND LIFE THREATENING BEHAVIOR, 307–23 (1990).

375. Estate of Dankbar, 430 N.W.2d 124 (Iowa 1988) (forensic psychiatrist's testimony, based on interviews with family, friends, and physicians, as well as review of medical and family records accumulated from the testator's adolescence to her death at age 56, generated a jury question on each essential element of testamentary capacity). *But see,* Matter of Skulina, 468 N.W.2d 322 (Mich. App. 1991) (refusing to admit testimony of psychologist about the decedent's personality traits based on review of deposition transcripts, whether characterized as "psychological profile" or "psychological autopsy," holding that the testimony offered jurors nothing more than they could glean if they had reviewed the transcripts themselves).

376. Estate of Dokken, 604 N.W.2d 487 (S.D. 2000).

itly approved the lower court's reliance on this testimony in the face of contrary reports of field examiners from the Veteran's Administration who periodically checked in on the testator.[377]

In a Louisiana case, the objectant appealed the lower court's judgment probating the will, asserting that, among other things, the testimony of the proponent's forensic psychiatrist lacked the requisite reliability for expert testimony based on scientific principles.[378] Applying the relevant state standard, which essentially adopted the Daubert[379] criteria applicable in federal cases, the court held that the proponents use of a methodology "essentially the same as the psychological autopsy" satisfied the reliability requirement for expert testimony. The court went on to affirm probate of the will, despite the testimony of the objectant's own forensic psychiatrist, who had applied the psychological autopsy technique and, based on that, concluded the testator lacked capacity to execute a will.[380] In approving admission of the proponent's expert's testimony, the court rightly emphasized the substance and thoroughness of the database relied upon by the experts rather than the particular psychological methodology or technique used to develop that database.

An exemplary presentation of the application of forensic mental health principles to reach a determination about testamentary capacity is set forth in the Texas case of *Estate of Robinson*.[381] In that case, a forensic psychiatrist exhaustively reviewed the testator's medical records and explained how elements of medical history ranging from reported tiredness to diagnosis of atherosclerotic heart disease to CT scans showing progression of brain atrophy led to his conclusion that the testator suffered a progression of pathological disease process that caused her to lose brain cells.[382] The appellate court not only affirmed the admissibility of that testimony,[383] it held that this testimony was itself legally sufficient evidence

---

377. *Id.*

378. Succession of Pardue, 915 So. 2d 415 (La. App. 2005).

379. Daubert v. Merrell Pharmaceuticals, Inc. 509 U.S. 579 (1993) held that FRE 702, which governs the admissibility of novel scientific evidence in federal cases, superseded the standard previously applied to determine admissibility of such evidence. Under the Daubert standard, the role of the federal district courts is to play a "gate-keeping" role in determining admissibility of new scientific evidence. In addition to considering the level of general acceptance of such evidence within the community, which the superseded standard relied on exclusively, Daubert requires courts to consider whether the method can and has been tested, whether it has been subjected to peer review and publication, the known or potential error rate, and whether the method has gained general acceptance within the relevant scientific community. *Id.* For a summary of the states that have adopted the Daubert standard, and cases decided under that standard, see Alice B. Lustre, *Post-Daubert Standards for Admissibility of Scientific and Other Expert Evidence in State Courts,* 90 A.L.R.5th 453 (2001).

380. *Id.*

381. Estate of Robinson, 140 S.W. 3d 782 (Tex. App. 2004).

382. *Id.*

383. Texas' standard for determining scientific reliability is substantially similar to the *Daubert* standard used in federal courts. For testimony that is not readily susceptible to analysis under the *Daubert* test, Texas uses the analytic gap test, which rejects expert testimony when there is too great an analytic gap between the data and the opinion in order for the opinion to be

of testamentary incapacity.[384] Mental health testimony, then, tightly linked to the question before the court, can be dispositive.

3. Lifetime Outright Gifts

Outright gifts immediately and irrevocably transfer ownership of property from the donor to a donee. To make a valid gift, the donor must deliver the property to the donee with the intent of transferring ownership immediately and irrevocably.[385] The element of donative intent, which implicitly requires mental capacity, distinguishes this type of transfer from a loan or temporary transfer of custody of property.[386]

Lifetime outright gifts may consist of the entire interest in property or a fractional interest in property held in some form of co-ownership: tenancy in common,[387] joint tenancy with right of survivorship (JWROS),[388] or tenancy by the entirety.[389] A change in the title of property from individual name into the

---

reliable. The six factors in *Robinson* are: (1) the extent to which the theory has been tested, (2) the extent to which the technique relies on the expert's subjective interpretation, (3) whether the theory has been subject to peer review and/or publication, (4) the technique's potential rate of error, (5) whether the underlying theory or technique has been generally accepted as valid by the relevant scientific community, and (6) the nonjudicial uses that have been made of the theory or technique (*E.I. du Pont de Nemours & Co. v. Robinson*, 923 S.W.2d 549, 557 [Tex.1995]).

384. The reliance on the forensic psychiatrist's testimony in *Robinson* is a sharp contrast to an earlier (pre-*Daubert*) Texas court's refusal to admit expert testimony based on the psychological autopsy technique in dispute between will beneficiaries. In the earlier case, one beneficiary sought to disqualify the other beneficiary, who had killed the testator and later himself, from receiving his share of the estate. The personal representative of the estate of the deceased beneficiary offered the testimony of an expert in order to prove that the deceased beneficiary did not have the intent required for forfeiture of his interest in the estate. The court rejected this testimony, holding that the psychological autopsy technique used by the expert was not sufficiently accepted to satisfy the then-applicable standard for reliability of expert testimony applying scientific techniques. Notably, the expert testified that he was unaware of any other case in which the psychological autopsy was used in "this" way. Thompson v. Mayes, 707 S.W.2d 951 (Tex. App. 1986).

385. Ruffel v. Ruffel, 900 A.2d 1178 (R.I. 2006); Keyon v. Abel, 36 P. 3d 1161 (Wyo. 2001).

386. *See. e.g.*, Park Station Ltd. Partnership LLP v. Bosse, 835 A.2d 646 (Md. 2003) (sale v. gift); Burkle v. Burkle, 46 Cal. Rptr. 3d 562 (App. 2006) (gift v. loan).

387. *See, e.g.,* Taylor v. Canterbury, 92 P.3d 961 (Colo. 2004); Richmond v. Hall, 460 S.E.2d 103 (Va. 1996).

388. A joint tenancy with right of survivorship is classically characterized by the existence of four unities: time, title, interest, and possession. Estate of Quick, 905 A.2d 471 (Pa. 2006). The "four unities" require the joint tenants to receive their interest in the property at the same time, and under the same instrument, each with the right to possess the whole of the property subject to the rights of other joint tenant(s).

389. Tenancy by the entirety, a form of co-ownership recognized in a diminishing number of jurisdictions, classically is characterized by five unities: the four unities of joint tenancy plus the unity of marriage. *See, e.g.,* Finley v. Thomas, 699 A.2d 1163 (D.C. 1997); Sawada v. Endo, 561 P.2d 1291 (Haw. 1977); N.Y. E.P.T.L. 6-1.2 (McKinney 2002).

name of the original property owner and another is presumptively a gift from the original property owner to the other joint tenant, although the contributing joint tenant may defeat the presumption by proving he or she did not intend to make a gift to the other joint tenant.[390] Generally, the size of the fractional interest(s) transferred to each new co-owner is equal to the interest retained by the donor (i.e., 1 divided by the total number of co-owners).[391] The gift to other joint tenants is irrevocable, just as a gift of the entire interest in property would be.[392]

The JWROS is popular because property held in that form becomes the property of the surviving joint tenant(s) upon the death of one, without the need for probate or any other legal proceeding.[393] This feature of JWROS may motivate use of this form of ownership, but a gift still occurs upon the transfer of property into joint name.[394]

a. Standard of capacity

The mental capacity required to make a gift requires the donor to understand the nature and effect of the gift.[395] Most jurisdictions do not specify particular elements that the donor must understand, but courts and other authorities traditionally have interpreted this standard as higher than the testamentary capacity standard.[396] The policy protecting the donor from his or her own improvidence supports the traditional approach, as does judicial suspicion about an individual's intent to transfer property while he or she may yet need it, as compared to dispositions under a will.[397] In some jurisdictions, however, the testamentary capacity standard governs not only wills but also lifetime gifts.[398] This precludes the possibility of conflicting capacity determinations for gifts and wills executed the same day.

---

390. *See, e.g.,* Long v. Long, 697 A.2d 1317 (Me. 1997); Treschek v. Moreville Nat'l Bank, 604 N.E.2d 1081 (Ill. App. 1992); Becker v. McDonald, 488 N.E.2d 729 (Ind. App. 1986), *on rehearing* 499 N.E.2d 210 (Ind. App. 1986).

391. *See, e.g.,* Ga. Stat. App. 44-6-120 (Michie 1991) (tenants in common may have unequal interests in property, but in the absence of contrary evidence, equal interests are presumed).

392. *See, e.g.,* Kleeman v. Sheridan, 256 P. 2d 553 (Ariz. 1953). *Compare,* KAN. REV. STAT. ANN. 59-3501 (authorizing a nonprobate transfer-on-death deed, which vests no interest in the beneficiary until the death of the donor).

393. Trust of Rosenberg, 727 N.W.2d 430 (Neb. 2007) (joint tenancy property, other than accounts governed by statute, vests in the surviving joint tenant(s) upon the death of the other joint tenant); Estate of Roloff, 143 P.3d 406 (Kan. App. 2006) (survivorship is the "distinctive characteristic and grand incident" of an estate in joint tenancy).

394. *See supra* note 385.

395. *See, e.g.,* Wyman v. Dunne, 359 P.2d 1010 (Idaho 1961); *In re* Estate of La Douceir, 2006 WL 3719701 (Minn. App.); Whalen v. Harvey, 653 N.Y.S.2d 159 (App. Div. 3d Dept. 1997); Matter of Estate of Clements, 505 N.E.2d 7 (Ill. App. 5th Dist. 1987).

396. *See supra* note 326.

397. Horner v. Horner, 719 A. 2d 1101, 1104–05 (Pa. Super. 1998).

398. Brown v. Ainsworth, 943 So.2d 757 (Miss. App. 2006); Hilco Property Services, Inc. v. U.S., 929 F. Supp. 526 (D. N.H. 1996); Rose v. Dunn, 679 S.W. 2d 180 (Ark. 1984); Nagle v. Wakefield's Adm'r, 263 S.W.2d 127 (Ky. 263). *See also,* Landmark Trust (USA), Inc. v. Goodhue, 782 A.2d 1219 (Vt. 2001)(raising but not answering the question whether Vermont's gift standard is equivalent to or substantively different from the testamentary capacity standard).

A subcategory of outright gifts, gifts *causa mortis,* allows a donor in imminent danger of death to make a gift conditional upon death. If the donor survives the contemplated danger (however long it may last), he or she may demand return of the property because the contemplated condition did not materialize.[399] The revocability of a gift *causa mortis* substantially reduces the concern about improvident gifts jeopardizing the donor's financial security,[400] which suggests that the testamentary capacity standard ought to apply. At least one court has reached this conclusion.[401]

b. The role of mental health expertise

The role that mental health expertise plays in disputes over outright gifts depends largely on who seeks to set aside the gift. Where intestate heirs (or others with standing) bring the suit, the role of mental health expertise is essentially equivalent to its role in will contests. On the other hand, suits brought by the donor or by the donor's guardian are more likely to involve circumstances or evidence that shift the role of the mental health expert in gift litigation.

For example, a donor who sues to set aside a gift on the grounds of incapacity asserts that, though he or she now has capacity to bring suit, he or she lacked capacity at the time of the gift. In this situation, the donor may have simply changed his or her mind about the gift. In such a case expert testimony cannot help the donor, and should not be needed by the donee.

In *Hill v. Brooks,* for example, a father of five daughters changed the title of a tract of land from the father individually to a JWROS deed naming him and one of the daughters as joint tenants.[402] The next day, Mr. Brooks married his second wife. Several years later, Mr. Brooks brought suit to rescind the deed, alleging among other things, that he had lacked the capacity to make a gift.[403] Finding the testimony of the donor to be inconsistent and receiving no expert testimony from either side of litigants, the court easily upheld the deed.[404]

In contrast to a suit by the donor, a suit brought by the guardian on behalf of the donor usually involves a bona fide question of capacity because the need for a guardian suggests incapacity of some sort.[405] The question for the mental health expert in the gift litigation is whether the donor's capacity fell short of the legal standard applicable to gifts when the gift was made. The evidence of capacity relied upon in the guardianship proceeding may provide a useful starting point for the mental health expert's development of background information relevant to his or her own examination of the donor's capacity to make a gift.

---

399. Estate of Pina v. Flaglore, 443 N.W.2d 627 (S.D. 1989); Kesterseon v. Cronan, 806 P.2d 134 (Or. App. 1991) (holding purported gift *causa mortis* to be invalid testamentary disposition).
400. Bergman v. Greenwise Sav. Bank, 74 N.Y.S.2d 638 (N.Y. City Court 1947).
401. Estate of Vardalos, 320 N.E.2d 568 (Il. App. 1974).
402. 482 S.E.2d 816 (Va. 1997).
403. *Id.*
404. *Id.*
405. *See, e.g.,* NY MHL 81.02 (defining standard for appointment of a guardian).

Although examination of the donor is important, it does not ensure that the expert testimony will carry significant weight, as illustrated by *Landmark Trust (USA) v. Goodhue*.[406] In that case, the donor, Mr. Holbrook, deeded his apple farm to Landmark Trust, a landmark preservation organization. Mr. Holbrook had acquired one half of the apple farm by inheritance from his mother, and he later acquired his sister's one-half interest in the farm by transferring to her his one-half interest in the family home, which he also had inherited from his mother. The value of the house exceeded the value of the apple farm, but the transaction advanced Mr. Holbrook's goals by giving him the power to arrange for preservation of the farm.[407] Mr. Holbrook achieved his goal when he transferred the apple farm to Landmark Trust on June 23, 1995.

Mr. Holbrook's cognitive capabilities declined precipitously beginning in the fall of 1995. He began to have difficulty understanding financial matters generally and the transaction with Landmark specifically, he lost interest in the day-to-day operation of the apple farm in the midst of harvest season, and he did not recognize his lawyer in a chance meeting on the street. A guardian was appointed for Mr. Holbrook in 1996. In light of Mr. Holbrook's decline, Landmark Trust brought suit for a declaratory judgment that the gift of the apple farm was valid.

Two neurologists testified on behalf of the guardian, both of whom had administered the MMSE [408] and other tests of cognition to Holbrook.[409] Ultimately, both testified that Mr. Holbrook had lacked the capacity to make the gift to Landmark. Earlier, however, one of these two experts testified that he could not offer an opinion on capacity and the other testified that Holbrook did have capacity to give the apple farm to Landmark.[410] The equivocation of the experts devalued their testimony, leading the court to validate the gifts based on lay testimony of individuals who interacted with Mr. Holbrook at or near the time of the gift.[411]

In cases involving a claim of undue influence, as opposed to incapacity, the testimony of an expert may be useful to prove (or disprove) that the donor suffered from a mental weakness that made the donor susceptible to undue influence.[412] Where the dispute involves no claim of incapacity and rests heavily on unfairness as opposed to mental weakness, the value of expert testimony may be negligible.[413] Similarly, where the expert offers an opinion without an accurate understanding of the underlying facts or an explanation of how the expert's

406. 782 A.2d 1219 (Vt. 2001).

407. *Id.*

408. The *MMSE* is the *Mini-Mental State Examination,* developed by Folstein, Folstein, and McHugh. Marshal F. Folstein et al., *"Mini-Mental State": A Practical Method for Grading the Cognitive State of Patients for the Clinician,* 12 J. PSYCHIATRIC RESEARCH 189–98 (1975).

409. *Id.*

410. *Id.*

411. *Id.*

412. For a description of undue influence doctrine, *see supra* Section C.3.b.ii.

413. Estate of Tipp, 933 P.2d 182 (Mont. 1997) (allegation of undue influence in execution of JWROS deed and will brought by one sister against another sister who served as testator's caregiver).

foundation connects to the elements of undue influence, the testimony may be inadmissible altogether, or if admitted, may carry little weight.[414] Although the foundation of an expert's opinion is important in every case, the risk that an expert may offer an unfounded opinion is greater in undue influence cases than it is in capacity cases because the role of fairness in the undue influence doctrine may make it difficult for the expert to segregate his or her views about the fairness of the gift from the specialized contribution he or she is qualified to make about the cognitive, personality, or other aspects of the donor's mental state.

On the other hand, expert testimony in an undue influence case may be quite valuable if the expert effectively connects psychological principles to one or more of the elements of undue influence. In *Mattingly v. Mattingly,* for example, the guardian of a ward, who was her husband, sought to set aside deeds of land given to the ward's brother.[415] The parties stipulated that "Buddy," the donor-brother, possessed the mental capacity to make the transfers; the primary issue was whether the donee-brother, Aubry, brought about the transfer by exercising undue influence.[416]

The transaction may have been considered natural in the sense that the donee-brother and his wife managed the family excavation business to which the deeds related. On the other hand, the ward had recently married and apparently was not in a position to make such a significant transfer to a collateral relative. To buttress her case, the guardian introduced testimony of a forensic psychiatrist who diagnosed Buddy with dependent personality disorder, a condition characterized by difficulty in decision-making and excessive deference to the wishes of others.[417] The overlap between the symptoms of dependent personality disorder and the concept of undue influence gave this testimony potentially powerful probative value. On the wife-guardian's appeal of the judgment upholding the transfer, the appellate court remanded the case to the trial court, explicitly noting that the trial court had discretion to admit (or reject) this testimony, and determine its probative value.[418]

4. Irrevocable Trusts

A trust is an alternative to an outright gift, either during the donor's life or under a will. A trust is a relationship created by a donor between two sets of parties: the trustee or trustees, who hold the legal title of the transferred property, and the beneficiary or beneficiaries, who hold the equitable or beneficial title in the transferred property.[419] The purpose of a trust is to divide legal and beneficial

414. *See, e.g.,* Will of Smoak, 334 S.E.2d 806 (S.C. 1985) (expert opinion had no probative value on undue influence where physician knew nothing about the circumstances and gave no basis for his conclusion).
415. 607 A.2d 575 (Md. App. 1992).
416. *Id.*
417. *Id.*
418. *Id.*
419. Mark L. Ascher, 1 Scott & Ascher on Trusts §2.3 (2006).

ownership of property so that one person (the trustee) manages the property and others (the beneficiaries) enjoy the benefits of it.[420] Basic provisions for any trust include the duration of the trust relationship, the rights of beneficiaries to receive distribution of trust property, and the responsibilities of the trustee. Examples of reasons to create a trust include: beneficiaries who are incapable of managing the property themselves; accumulating property over an extended period of time for the benefit of future generations of the family; controlling beneficiaries after death by stating in the trust who receives how much, when, and under what circumstances; minimizing estate taxes; and avoiding probate.

Trusts ought to be, and usually are, memorialized in writing, although oral trusts are recognized in some jurisdictions.[421] The document that creates a trust established during the donor's life is either a declaration of trust, which is used when the donor is the sole trustee, or a trust agreement, which is used when there is a trustee other than the donor. A deed of trust also may be used for lifetime transactions. Trusts that take effect upon the donor's death, referred to as *testamentary trusts,* are not separate documents but rather a set of provisions in the donor's will.

a. Capacity standard

Generally, the applicable standard for irrevocable trusts established during the donor's life (rather than under a will) is the same as the standard applicable to outright lifetime transfers.[422] Variously described as the standard applicable to gifts, the standard applicable to deeds, or the standard applicable to contracts, the standard of capacity requires the donor to understand the nature and consequences of the transaction. Legal challenges to irrevocable trusts are relatively rare, in part because irrevocable trusts are appropriate only when an outright gift cannot accomplish the donor's objectives. If complexities of the estate plan do justify an irrevocable trust, it will be designed and drafted by an estate-planning lawyer, either alone or in collaboration with other estate-planning professionals. These professionals will form an opinion about the donor's capacity before the trust is executed, and will not participate in an estate plan or a donor who they believe lacks the requisite capacity. Most typically, the lawyers and other professionals will make their judgment without any formal assessment of capacity by a mental health professional.

When challenges do arise, the extensive planning process required for an irrevocable trust creates a record that often suffices for the court to uphold the trust.

420. *See id.*

421. *See, e.g.,* Estate of Fournier, 902 A.2d 852 (Me. 2006) (upholding oral trust); UNIF. TRUST CODE §407, 7C U.L.A. 233 (West Supp. 2005).

422. Queen v. Blecher, 888 So.2d 472 (Ala. 2003) (rejecting application of testamentary capacity standard to irrevocable trust, and defining legal capacity standard as requiring donor to understand and comprehend the nature of the act); *In re* Noland, 956 S.W 2d 173 (Ark. 1997) (applying testamentary capacity standard to irrevocable trust because testamentary standard applies to all donative transfers); Hilbert v. Benson, 917 P.2d 1152 (contract standard applied). Harrison v. Grobe, 790 F. Supp. 443 (S.D.N.Y. 1992) (contract standard applied).

In *Rudolf Nureyev Dance Foundation v. Noureeva-Francois*, for example, the famous ballet dancer established and funded a foundation shortly before his death.[423] After his death, his sister and niece objected to the transfer on the grounds of incapacity and undue influence allegedly exercised by the lawyer who drafted the instruments of transfer. Applying the standard applicable to contracts, the court had no trouble concluding that Nureyev had the requisite capacity to establish the foundation and that undue influence did not interfere in the expression of his donative intent.[424]

Heavy reliance on the opinion of the drafter of the trust is not ideal because the drafter, in essence, is defending the judgment of capacity to execute the trust that he or she originally made. Yet this is consistent with the heavy reliance on the drafter's testimony in will contests as well as the significant weight attached to the testimony of the witnesses to a will, who affirm at the time of witnessing that the testator appeared to possess the requisite capacity to make a will.

b. The role of mental health expertise

Where the donor or the donor's advisers anticipate a challenge to the trust, psychological or psychiatric confirmation of capacity may be invaluable. This proved true for a most unlikely candidate, Hon. Donald Stuart Russell, a judge of the United States Court of Appeals for the Fourth Circuit and former governor of South Carolina, United States senator from South Carolina and president of the University of South Carolina.[425] Acrimony between his children and some of his grandchildren led him to anticipate a challenge to his estate plan, which included an irrevocable trust as well as a revocable trust and a will.

In an effort to minimize the probability of a potential challenge to the estate-planning documents, Judge Russell arranged for a psychiatric examination to confirm his capacity to execute the estate-planning documents.[426] After his death, the anticipated contest occurred, but the children alleged only undue influence and not incapacity as the basis for their contest. It is likely that the psychiatric examination influenced the children's decision to forgo a claim of incapacity.

To support their claim of undue influence, the children presented testimony of medical doctors who testified that Judge Russell could have been subject to undue influence, and lay witnesses who described instances of confusion, physical deterioration, and other facts bearing on undue influence. The Supreme Court of South Carolina affirmed the grant of summary judgment upholding the validity of all of Judge Roberts' estate-planning instruments.[427]

Particularly significant is the court's conclusion that the testimony of the medical doctors on behalf of the objectants did not raise a question of fact justifying

423. 7 F. Supp. 2d 402 (S.D.N.Y. 1998).
424. *Id.* Accord, Harrison v. Grobe, 790 F. Supp. 443 (S.D.N.Y. 1992).
425. Russell v. Wachovia Bank, N.A., 578 S.E.2d 329 (S.C. 2003).
426. Russell v. Wachovia Bank, N.A., 633 S.E.2d 722 (S.C. 2006).
427. *Russell*, 578 S.E.2d at 334–36.

a trial because it did not relate to the circumstances surrounding the execution of the estate-planning instruments.[428] While this testimony could have had some value in assessing mental capacity if that had been challenged, the court said, evidence of undue influence must be based on the donor's particular circumstances.[429] This statement strongly suggests that if the children had chosen to object to the will and trusts on the basis of incapacity, a trial might have been required. Thus, the lifetime assessment of legal capacity may have spared the Roberts estate from the risk and expense of an undue influence trial, as well as from litigation over mental capacity.

5. Will Substitutes

As the name implies, a *will substitute* is an instrument that replaces one or more dispositions in a will. Unlike wills, will substitutes take effect according to their own terms without the need for probate. Examples of will substitutes include life insurance, individual retirement accounts (IRAs), pay-on-death (POD) bank accounts that allow the depositor to designate a beneficiary to receive the account on death, "Totten Trust" accounts, substantively equivalent to POD accounts, transfer-on-death (TOD) securities accounts, and revocable trusts. Property held in joint tenancy with right of survivorship is also a will substitute in the sense that surviving joint tenants succeed to a deceased joint tenant's interest without the intervention of probate.[430]

a. Standard of capacity
The standard of capacity required to execute a testamentary substitute is less settled than capacity standards for other donative transfers. Traditionally, the capacity standard depended on the type of instrument used to transfer the property: the testamentary capacity standard applied to wills, and the contract standard applied to transfer by other instruments.[431] The increasing use of will substitutes to dispose of all, or a large portion of, an estate underscores the formalistic nature of determining the applicable capacity standard based on the form of the instrument.[432] A more modern approach is to apply the testamentary capacity standard to revocable arrangements, because their consequences are much closer to the consequences of a will than to an irrevocable transfer during the donor's

428. *Id.* The court refers to the will in discussing the probative value of the medical doctors, but the point apparently applies to the trusts as well, since all of them were subject to the undue influence claim and all of the instruments were upheld.

429. *Id.*

430. *See supra* note 310.

431. *See supra* note 304.

432. *See* Eunice L. Ross et al., Will Contests §9:1 (2d ed. 2006) (increasing importance of will substitutes); 14A McKinney's Forms: Estates and Surrogate Practice §3:146 (McKinney 1999) (increasing use of revocable trust as will substitute in New York); Lawrence M. Friedman, et al., *The Inheritance Process in San Bernardino County, California, 1964: A Research Note,* 43 Hous. L. Rev. 1445, 1472 (discussing trends in California).

lifetime.[433] The extent of debate about the appropriate capacity standard for will substitutes depends largely on the particular will substitute under consideration.

i. Revocable trusts   The revocable trust is the most comprehensive and arguably most important will substitute, because it is functionally identical to a will. It is widely agreed that the functional equivalence of wills and trusts makes the testamentary capacity standard appropriate despite the higher capacity standard applicable to other trusts.[434] A revocable trust has all of the essential traits of a trust,[435] but it has an additional feature that allows the donor (or other individual designated in the trust instrument) to terminate the trust and take back the property. Revocable trusts avoid probate with respect to assets held in the trust at the donor's death, because legal title to those assets is in the name of the trustee rather than the donor's individual name. At the donor's death, the trust property becomes distributable to the beneficiaries named in the trust document, who are the same beneficiaries that would have been named in a will if the donor had chosen that form of transfer. The revocable trust affords the donor the same flexibility that a will does, because the revocability feature of the trust allows the donor to change the beneficiaries of the trust and to access the trust assets for himself or herself at will.

One virtue of a revocable trust as compared to a will is that the revocable trust needs no affirmative validation similar to probate. The trustee need not give formal notice to intestate heirs nor must he or she place the trust in the public record as would be required for a will. This may make it marginally more difficult for intestate heirs or other interested parties to learn about the decedent's estate plan, and in the case of remote relatives, the decedent's death.

If intestate heirs or others do challenge a revocable trust, the litigation will involve the same problems of proof that plague wills because, like wills, litigation over a revocable trust cannot occur until after the donor's death. This is not an extension of wills law but rather application of the general principal of standing, which requires a litigant to have an interest in the outcome of a suit.[436]

ii. Assets passing by beneficiary designation   Creation of an asset that passes by beneficiary designation requires a contract between the owner and the financial institution that will pay the designated beneficiary upon the owner's death. The parties to the contract must have contractual capacity, which is generally consid-

---

433. *See supra* note 304.

434. Lah v. Rogers, 707 N.E.2d 1208 (Ohio App. 1998); UNIF. TRUST CODE § 601.

435. *See supra* notes 419–21, and accompanying text.

436. *See, e.g.,* McKinnon v. R.I. Hosp. Trust Nat. Bank, 713 A.2d 245 (R.I. 1998); Linthicum v. Rudi, 148 P.3d 746 (Nev. 2006); UNIF. TRUST CODE §603. After the death or incapacity of the donor, the beneficiaries may be entitled to challenge the trust's predeath transactions, depending on whether the donor explicitly or implicitly approved of those transactions while having the legal capacity required to so approve. *See* Siegel v. Novak, 920 So.2d 89 (Fla. App. 2006) (applying New York law).

ered to be higher than testamentary capacity.[437] In a dispute between the owner of the account and the financial institution, the contractual standard of capacity unquestionably would apply. In a dispute over the beneficiary designation, on the other hand, the testamentary capacity standard arguably ought to apply, because it is effective only upon the death of the owner.

Which standard applies depends on the jurisdiction as well as the particular type of will substitute. For POD accounts, both the contract standard and the testamentary standard have been applied.[438] For life insurance and annuity contracts, on the other hand, some jurisdictions apply the testamentary standard[439] while others require contractual capacity to change a beneficiary designation.[440]

It can be difficult to reconcile capacity standards for different assets passing by beneficiary designation even within a particular jurisdiction. In Georgia, for example, the Court of Appeals has held that a 15-year-old owner of annuity contracts received in settlement of a personal injury claim had capacity to designate beneficiaries, analogizing the nature of the transaction to a testamentary disposition.[441] Five years later, the same court applied the contractual capacity standard to a change in the beneficiary designation of an IRA account.[442] The IRA case did not discuss the earlier annuity case, leaving open the question whether the unique circumstances of the annuity case justified use of the testamentary capacity standard, or alternatively, that the testamentary capacity standard applies to all annuities. In all jurisdictions, determination of the capacity standard applicable to assets passing by beneficiary requires careful consideration.

iii. Joint tenancy accounts   Unlike joint tenancy interests in other types of property,[443] a bank account held in joint tenancy (JWROS) is owned by the joint tenants in proportion to their respective contributions.[444] Revocability would justify use of the testamentary capacity standard for creation of a joint tenancy in a

---

437. *See supra* note 304.

438. Compare Giurbino v. Giurbino, 626 N.E.2d 1017 (Ohio App. 1993) (contract standard applied); *with* Union Nat. Bank of Wichita v. Mayberry, 533 P.2d 1303 (Kan. 1975) (testamentary standard applied); Rogers v. Frayer, 1995 WL 408196 (Ohio App. 11 Dist. 1995) (same).

439. Bergen v. Travelers Ins. Co. of Illinois, 776 P.2d 659 (Utah App. 1989); Fulbroad v. Ofate, 463 A.2d 1155 (Pa. Super. 1983).

440. *See, e.g., In re* Estate of Marquis, 822 A. 2d 1153 (Me. 2003); Rawlings v. John Hancock Mut. Life Ins. Co., 78 S.W. 3d 291 (Tenn. Ct. App. 2001).

441. Bacon v. Smith, 474 S.E.2d 728 (Ga. App. 1996).

442. Sun Trust Bank, Mill Ga. N.A. v. Harper, 551 S.E. 2d 419 (Ga. App. 2001).

443. As discussed in connection with lifetime gifts, a joint tenancy generally vests each co-owner with an equal undivided interest in the property, resulting in a gift from one joint tenant to the other(s) (in an amount equal to the interests of the others) if one joint tenant contributes all of the property held in joint tenancy. Estate of Quick, 905 A. 2d 471 (Pa. 2006). The different rule for joint bank accounts exists by virtue of statute. *See* UNIF. PROB. CODE §6-211.

444. *See, e.g.,* Caldwell v. Walraven, 490 S.E.2d 384 (Ga. 1997); Hogan v. Hogan, 855 S.W.2d 905 (Ark. 1993); *contra* N.Y. BANKING LAW §675 (creation of joint bank account constitutes irrevocable gift to noncontributing joint tenant).

deposit, which some jurisdictions have adopted.[445] Others apply the contractual capacity standard because that is the form of the transaction.[446] In New York, which treats creation of a joint account by one joint tenant as a completed gift of a proportionate amount of the account value to the other joint tenant, the lifetime transfer standard arguably ought to be applicable, but it is not.[447] As with assets passing by beneficiary designation, determination of the applicable capacity standard requires careful consideration of the law of the jurisdiction.

b. Mental health expertise

One of the virtues of will substitutes is their simplicity. Not only do they avoid probate, most (with the notable exception of the revocable trust) can be created without the involvement of a lawyer. Without the involvement of a lawyer, the chances that the donor will arrange for a preemptive assessment of capacity to execute the will substitute are remote. Challenges to these arrangements usually occur after the donor's death, when examination of the donor is no longer possible, so the considerations applicable to use of mental health experts in will contests apply equally in this context.

6. Summary

The law of donative transfers includes several different capacity standards. Which standard applies depends on the jurisdiction involved, as well as the form and the substance of the transfer. Whichever standard applies, the core question always is whether the donor understood the essence of the transaction and its consequences.

The typical circumstances of litigation over donative transfers, specifically the unavailability of the donor for examination at the time of trial and the moral or equitable claims of family members to the donor's property, complicate the court's assessment of the donor's capacity. Mental health expertise has the power to add much-needed objectivity to judicial analyses of capacity in donative transfer disputes. Recent cases have established the persuasiveness of opinion testimony by an expert familiar with the applicable capacity standard, which is based on the application of well-established psychological principles or methodologies to the facts of the case.

Expert examination of the donor to assess capacity to make a donative transfer is relatively rare, but the persuasiveness of such testimony in recent cases may encourage this practice in cases where the donor anticipates litigation. In the many cases where there was no contemporaneous expert assessment of capacity to make a donative transfer, an opinion based on a psychological autopsy may carry significant weight. So long as the expert develops a foundation from whatever

445. *In re* Estate of Felt, 647 N.W. 2d 373 (Wis. App. 2002).
446. Knight v. Lancaster, 988 S.W.2d 172 (Tenn. App. 1988); *In re* Estate of Nordorf, 364 N.W. 2d 877 (Minn. App. 1985).
447. Estate of Coon, 539 N.Y.S.2d 534 (App. Div. 1989).

sources are available, applies accepted principles of forensic psychology to draw conclusions, and connects those conclusions to the legal standard of capacity, the opinion should be well received.

D. GUARDIANSHIP

1. Introduction

Guardianship overlaps considerably with commitment proceedings, discussed in Chapter 3 A. Both aim to protect alleged incapacitated persons (AIP) from harm, and historically focused on that benevolent goal to the detriment of an AIP's right to due process and other civil rights.[448] There are many differences between guardianship and commitment proceedings as well. Guardianship proceedings may but usually do not involve the state as a party. A family member or other individual interested in the well-being of an AIP petitions for appointment of a guardian in order to transfer control of decision-making authority from the AIP to the guardian.[449] The imposition of a guardianship does not result in confinement of the AIP to a mental institution, although it may authorize the guardian to determine where an incapacitated person (IP) should live, what, when, and how medical care should be provided, and a host of other personal matters. Guardianship may also extend to control of the AIP's property.

These and other differences between guardianship and commitment proceedings flow from the different interests at stake in the two proceedings. Guardianship is concerned exclusively with the AIP, while civil commitment involves the state's interest in protecting not only the AIP but others as well.

Another important difference between commitment proceedings and guardianship that flows from guardianship's exclusive focus on the AIP is that the availability of an individual with the means, foresight, and mental capacity to enter into a private arrangement for asset management or personal decision-making may obviate the need for guardianship. A health care proxy and a living will (if a living will is desired) foreclose, as bases for seeking guardianship, many health care matters, sparing the AIP the potential trauma and expense that often accompany an application for guardianship.[450] Similarly, a durable power of at-

---

448. *See* Jennifer L. Wright, *Protecting Who from What and Why, and How: A Proposal for an Integrative Approach to Adult Protective Proceedings,* 12 ELDER L.J. 53, 57–66 (2004). *See also,* J. Howard Ziemann, *Incompetency and Commitment Proceedings,* 8 AM. JUR. TRIALS 483 (2007).

449. *See* Wright, *supra* note 448, at 72.

450. Statutory living wills are available in most jurisdictions, as are health care proxies. *See, e.g.,* ARIZ. STAT. ANN. §§36-3221, 36-3261 (West 2003) (health care power of attorney and living will, respectively); FLA. STAT. ANN. §§765.203, 765.303 (West 2005) (statutory form for appointment of health care proxy and living will, respectively); OKLA. STAT. 63, § 3101.4 (statutory form for advance directive including living will and health care proxy). Not all jurisdictions recognizing living wills by statute, *see, e.g.,* MICH. COMP. LAWS ANN. §§ 700.5501–700.5502 (Lexis-Nexis 2005) (authorizing designation of "Patient Advocate for Health Care"), although the U.S. Supreme Court has recognized a constitutional right to refuse medical treatment by executing a living will. Cruzan v. Missouri Dept of Health, 497 U.S. 261 (1990).

torney and revocable trust are two common methods of providing for property management of an individual who is later alleged to be incompetent to enter into contracts, pay bills, make gifts, or engage in any other financial transaction. With these or similar arrangements in place, there often will be no need for a guardian.[451] Since these arrangements occur as a result of foreplanning, it is the most vulnerable members of society who are most frequently left to be the subjects of guardianship proceedings.

At best, the guardianship will provide the personal care and property management that the individual alone cannot handle. At worst, guardianship will deprive the individual of decision-making authority that he or she has the capacity to handle, and create the opportunity for personal or financial abuse.

In general, guardianship involves judicial appointment of one person (the guardian) to act on behalf of another person (AIP or ward) who lacks legal capacity due to infancy or mental disability. Guardianship law for these two types of legal incapacity overlaps substantially,[452] but there are important differences as well. The most important of these differences is how the need for guardianship is determined.[453] The sole criterion for guardianship of an infant is whether the infant has reached the age of majority in the relevant jurisdiction. Appointment of a guardian for an adult, on the other hand, requires a determination of mental abilities and disabilities under the legal standard established in the particular jurisdiction.[454] Most importantly, adult guardianships deny IPs the right to make decisions and engage in legal acts that the IP would have had in the absence of the guardianship.

This subchapter addresses adult guardianships, with a focus on the role that mental health experts play in determining whether the AIP meets the legal standard for guardianship. Following this introduction (section 1), section 2 describes

---

451. *See, e.g., In re* Nellie, 831 N.Y.S.2d 473 (App. Div. 2007) (appointment of guardian reversed where power of attorney covered needs of the AIP); *In re* Teeter, 537 N.W.2d 808 (Iowa App. 1995), *rev. den.,* Jones v. Dane Cty, 540 N.W.2d 200 (1995) (irrevocable trust obviated need for guardian); *In re* Magro, 655 A.2d 341 (Me. 1995) (revocable trust obviated need for conservator); *but see,* Rice v. Floyd, 768 S.W.2d 57 (Ky. 1989) (durable power of attorney does not obviate need for guardian).

452. In some states, the same statutory scheme governs infants and mentally impaired individuals. *See infra* note 15. Others have separate statutes for adults and minors. *See, e.g.,* CAL. PROB. CODE §§1500, 1800.3 (West 2002) (conservatorship statute applies to adults and guardian statute applies to minors). Low IQ and developmental disability are often treated under separate statutory schemes as well. *See, e.g.,* N.Y. S.C.P.A. §§ 1750-A, 1750-B (McKinney Supp. 2007).

453. Guardianship over an AIP and guardianship over an infant also differ in that parents have the status of "natural guardian" over their infants, obviating the need for guardianship except where a parent cannot serve this role (due to death or their own incapacity or otherwise) or where the infant receives assets (because natural guardians do not, by virtue of that status alone, control infants' property). In addition, mentally impaired adults often have property that requires management, and they also may have children or other relatives who are keenly interested in the preservation of that property for future inheritance.

454. If the guardianship is consensual, the jurisdiction may relax the requirements considerably, such as in Wyoming, where the sole criterion for a voluntary guardianship is the best interest of the AIP. Guardianship of McNeel, 109 P.3d 510 (Wyo. 2005).

the statutory law that governs guardianship, highlighting the different types of competency standards that jurisdictions use. The third section addresses the role of mental health expertise in guardianship proceedings, focusing on important rights in the personal realm. The fourth section covers additional considerations arising in property guardianships and discussion of how lawyers have begun to use mental health expertise in guardianship proceedings to advance their clients' interests in future will contests.

2. A Statutory Overview

The guiding principle underlying guardianship is *parens patrie,* the state's interest in assuring care for those who cannot care for themselves.[455] Courts have no inherent authority to restrict an individual's civil rights, even when the motivation is paternalistic concern for the AIP's well-being. The state first must exercise the *parens patrie* power by enacting a statute to authorize guardianship and to specify the conditions under which guardianship may be imposed.[456] Every state has adopted a statutory scheme for guardianship of adults who require assistance in meeting their personal needs, handling their finances, or both.

Historically, the standard of competency for guardianship was an "all or nothing" test.[457] For AIPs who had the capability to handle some matters but not others, appointment of a guardian would unnecessarily terminate civil rights of the impaired individual. The guardianship system offered no alternative short of complete ("plenary") guardianship for an individual who could handle most matters but needed help managing others.

The unnecessary deprivation of civil rights that occurred whenever an IP required the assistance of a guardian for some but not all matters passed unnoticed, even as the U.S. Supreme Court addressed these same civil rights issues in the context of criminal matters, civil commitment, and other areas.[458] In the 1980s, a confluence of events drew national attention to the shortcomings of the procedural processes applicable to appointment of a guardian as well as the treatment of incompetent persons (IPs) after appointment of a guardian.[459]

---

455. Translated literally, *parens patriae* means "parent of the country." English common law recognized this doctrine in the fourteenth century, and also under the statute *De Prerogative Regis.* Sallyanne Payton, *The Concept of the Person in the* Parens Patriae *Jurisdiction over Previously Competent Persons,* 17 J. MED. & PHIL. 605, 625–26 (1992).

456. *See, e.g.,* Guardianship of Heden, 528 N.W.2d 567 (Iowa 1995). *See also,* Jennifer L. Wright, *supra* note 448; Jan Ellen Rein, *Preserving Dignity and Self-Determination in the Face of Competing Interests and Grim Alternatives: A Proposal for Statutory Refocus and Reform,* 6 GEO. WASH. L. REV. 1818, 1886 (1992).

457. Charles P. Sabatino, *Refining Our Legal Fictions* 1, 3–28; *Statutory Definitions of Incapacity: The Need for a Medical Basis* 40, 40–57, in OLDER ADULTS' DECISION-MAKING AND THE LAW (Michael K. Smyer et al. eds. 1996).

458. *See supra* chapters 2 and 3.

459. *Id. See also,* Charles P. Sabatino et al., *Competency: Reforming Our Legal Fictions,* 6 J. OF MENTAL HEALTH & AGING 119 (2000).

In response to the public outcry that followed, most states reconsidered and revised their guardianship statutes.[460] Some states follow one of the available model statutes, the Uniform Guardianship and Protective Proceedings Act of 1982 (UGPPA 1982),[461] the Uniform Guardianship and Protective Proceedings Act of 1997 (UGPPA 1997) that revised the UGPPA 1982,[462] or the ABA's model for reform.[463] Other states designed their own guardianship statutes to remedy the substantive and procedural shortcomings that had been identified by the exposés and studies on the topic.[464] Despite these variations, most states have addressed several core issues, including the definition of competence that establishes who is subject to guardianship, the procedures that govern the determination whether an AIP requires a guardian, the availability of "limited guardianship" that allows the court to tailor the authority of the guardian and delimits the corresponding deprivation of the IP's rights, and post-appointment procedures for protecting the IP's interests.[465] All of these changes are directed to the basic goal of preserving the autonomy of AIPs to the extent possible while providing necessary support for matters beyond the IP's competency.[466]

a. Terminology

The varieties of adult guardianship (as opposed to guardianship of infants), together with the differences in the substance of guardianship law from jurisdiction to jurisdiction, have resulted in a multiplicity of terms for specific types of guardians: guardian of the person, guardian of the property, conservator, committee, and others. "Conservator," for example, often refers to guardianship of property only, with no powers over personal matters—but some jurisdictions use this term to govern a different type of guardianship,[467] while others have replaced that term with "guardian of the property" or simply "guardian." This text uses the term "guardian" to cover all types of adult guardianships except when use of a jurisdiction-specific term facilitates clarity.

---

460. ABA Comm. on L. & Aging & Am. Psychological Assn., *Assessment of Older Adults with Diminished Capacity: A Handbook for Lawyers* 131–32 (2005).

461. Unif. Guardianship and Protective Proceedings Act of 1982 §1-101 et seq., 8A U.L.A. 439 (West 2003) [hereinafter "UGPPA 1982"].

462. Unif. Guardianship and Protective Proceedings Act of 1997 § 1-101 et seq., 8A U.L.A. 312 (West 2003) [hereinafter "UGPPA 1997"].

463. ABA Comm'n on the Mentally Disabled, *Legal Issues in State Mental Healthcare: Proposals for Change—Model Guardianship Statute*, 2 Mental Disability L. Rep. 444 (1978).

464. N.Y. M.H.L. §81.01 et seq. (2006). It should be noted that there is a Uniform Veterans Guardianship Act, adopted in about half of the states, which governs proceedings involving certain veterans. These statutes, last revised during World War II, apply in conjunction with the state's general guardianship statutes. Unif. Veterans Guardianship Act § 1 et seq., 8C U.L.A. 287 (2001).

465. A. Kimberly Dayton et al., Advising the Elderly Client §34:1 et seq. (Westlaw 2007).

466. *See, e.g.,* N,Y, M.H.L., at §81.01.

467. *See, e.g.,* Cal. Prob. Code, at §1800.3 (defining conservatorship as covering adults and married minors as to personal as well as property matters).

One new term brought into common use through guardianship reform is "limited guardianship." Limited guardianships allow the court to tailor the guardian's authority to the needs of the incapacitated person, allowing the IP to retain decision-making authority over matters within his or her capabilities.[468] The pre-reform recognition of conservators or guardians of the property is an example of limited guardianship. The statutory reform expands on that example by allowing the court to tailor a guardian's authority to the IP's needs. This approach is designed to maximize the autonomy of the IP while simultaneously providing the assistance that the IP requires for particular matters. The creation of limited guardianship is a critical aspect of reform measures.

b. Definitions of competency

The centerpiece of any guardianship statute is the definition of competency that triggers imposition of guardianship. One of the principal aims of guardianship reform was to replace the all or nothing definition of capacity with a more focused test in order to maximize the autonomy of AIPs with partially diminished capacity. The major alternative definitions developed include a status-oriented approach, a purely behavioral (functional) approach, and a cognitive approach.[469]

The status-oriented approach to defining competence relies on criteria that have some degree of objectivity, such as a diagnosed mental disability. The status-oriented approach requires the finding of a disabling condition such as a "mental illness" or "mental disability" that impairs the AIP's ability to adequately man-

468. *See, e.g.*, N.Y. M.H.L., at §81.01, which provides:

The legislature hereby finds that the needs of persons with incapacities are as diverse and complex as they are unique to the individual. The current system of conservatorship and committee does not provide the necessary flexibility to meet these needs. Conservatorship which traditionally compromises a person's rights only with respect to property frequently is insufficient to provide necessary relief. On the other hand, a committee, with its judicial finding of incompetence and the accompanying stigma and loss of civil rights, traditionally involves a deprivation that is often excessive and unnecessary. Moreover, certain persons require some form of assistance in meeting their personal and property management needs but do not require either of these drastic remedies. The legislature finds that it is desirable for and beneficial to persons with incapacities to make available to them the least restrictive form of intervention which assists them in meeting their needs but, at the same time, permits them to exercise the independence and self-determination of which they are capable. The legislature declares that it is the purpose of this act to promote the public welfare by establishing a guardianship system which is appropriate to satisfy either personal or property management needs of an incapacitated person in a manner tailored to the individual needs of that person, which takes into account the personal wishes, preferences, and desires of the person, and which affords the person the greatest amount of independence and self-determination and participation in all the decisions affecting such person's life.

See also, UGPPA 1997, at 302–04 (Prefatory Note).

469. *See, e.g.*, Mary Radford, *Is the Use of Medication Appropriate in Adult Guardianship Cases?* 31 Stetson L. Rev. 611, 627–32 (2002); Eleanor M. Crosby et al., *Adult Guardianship in Georgia: Are the Rights of Proposed Wards Being Protected? Can We Tell?* 16 Quinnipiac Prob. L.J. 249, 271–74 (2003).

age his or her personal affairs.[470] The original version of the UGGPA exemplifies the status-oriented approach to defining competency. Under that statute, an IP is "any person who is impaired by reason of mental illness, mental deficiency, physical illness or disability, chronic use of drugs, chronic intoxication, or other cause (except minority) to the extent lacking sufficient understanding or capacity to make or communicate responsible decisions."[471]

The purely functional approach considers the AIP's ability to perform functions required for his or her daily living, including financial transactions, without a prerequisite identifiable mental disability. Florida's guardianship statute exemplifies this approach by defining the incapacitated person as an individual "who has been judicially determined to lack the capacity to manage at least some of the property or to meet at least some of the essential health and safety requirements of the person."[472]

Both the status-oriented approach and the purely functional approach to defining competency have been criticized on the grounds that they allow for overly subjective and arbitrary judicial determinations. The arbitrariness of the status-oriented approach lies in its over-reliance on diagnostic labels and corresponding inadequate consideration of the actual limiting effects of the diagnosed illness or disability on the activities of the AIP.[473] Conversely, the problem with the purely functional approach is its failure to distinguish behavior caused by a mental illness, disability, or other condition as opposed to mere eccentricity, for which guardianship would be an unwarranted imposition on the autonomy of the AIP.[474]

In an effort to rectify these problems, the UGPPA of 1997 adopted the cognitive functioning test to accomplish the consideration of requisite mental illness or other mental disability embodied in the status-oriented approach. The cognitive functioning approach to competence defines an IP as "an individual who, for reasons other than being a minor, is unable to receive and evaluate information

---

470. ABA Comm. on L. & Aging & Am. Psychological Assn., Assessment of Older Adults with Diminished Capacity: A Handbook for Lawyers 7 (2005).

471. UGGPA 1982, at §1-201(7).

472. Fl. Stat. Ann. §744.102(12). For a description of this standard as compared to other approaches to determining competency in guardianship proceedings, see Jan Ellen Rein, *Clients with Destructive and Socially Harmful Choices—What's an Attorney to Do?: Within and Beyond the Competency Construct*, 62 Fordham L. Rev. 1101, 1118–30 (1996).

473. Am. Bar Ass'n Comm'n on the Mentally Disabled & Comm'n on Legal Problems of the Elderly, Guardianship: An Agenda for Reform (1989); Stephen Anderer, *Determining Competency in Guardianship Proceedings* (1990). *But see,* Alison Barnes, *The Liberty and Property of Elders: Guardianship and Will Contests as the Same Claim* 11 Elder L. J. 32 (2003) (arguing that the status-oriented approach was adequate as stated, but failed when courts did not examine the nature of the behavior that arguably justified guardianship). *See also,* Robert P. Roca, *Determining Decisional Capacity: A Medical Perspective*, 62 Fordham L. Rev. 1177, 1188 (1994) (commenting that diagnosis is "critical anchor and validator in competency judgments"); Paul R. Tremblay, *On Persuasion and Paternalism: Lawyer Decisionmaking for the Questionably Competent Client*, 3 Utah L. Rev. 515, 536, 538 (1987) (same).

474. *See, e.g.,* Mary Radford, *supra* note 473 at 627–32; Alison Barnes, *supra* note 473, at 32–34.

or make or communicate decisions to such an extent that the individual lacks the ability to meet essential requirements for health, safety or self-care, even with appropriate technological assistance."[475]

States do not necessarily adopt any of these three models verbatim. Some state statutes have combined aspects of the basic alternatives; other states have followed one of the alternative definitions of competence but modified it in some way; yet other states have adopted their own unique statutes. Additionally, several states retain the distinction between guardianship over personal matters and guardianship over property matters in their statutory definitions and procedures. Consequently, an understanding of the jurisdiction's scheme for guardianship is important to ensure that the case is developed around the applicable statutory definition of competency.

c. Procedural protections for the AIP

A major focus of guardianship reform was improving the due process protection of AIPs.[476] Basic elements of due process, such as notice, an opportunity to be heard, and a right to assistance of counsel were defective or altogether absent in many cases.[477] The major elements of reform are briefly described in the following.

i. Notice to AIP   Notice to the AIP was often inadequate; some jurisdictions may not have required it, others may have easily dispensed with it, and yet others may have fulfilled notice requirements by serving on the AIP a document he or she could not read or understand, or the notice may have allowed insufficient time to retain a lawyer or otherwise plan to defend a guardianship proceeding. Guardianship reforms rectify this by requiring notice to the AIP that is understandable as well as timely, so that an AIP can prepare appropriately.[478]

ii. Representation of AIP   In criminal cases, the accused has a right to counsel.[479] AIPs in guardianship proceedings, by contrast, were historically not af-

---

475. UGGPA 1997, at §102(5).

476. *See, e.g.,* Nancy M. Coleman et al., *Report on the Work of the ABA Commission on Law and Aging,* 31 Hum. Rts. 13 (2004).

477. *Id.*

478. *Compare,* UGPPA 1997, at §113 (notice must be given at least 14 days in advance, and its contents must be set forth in plain language; additional notice requirements apply for guardians of the person and also for guardians of property ("conservators" in the UGPPA nomenclature) and *id.* at §§ 309, 404 (notice to AIP of application for guardianship of the person requires personal service on AIP, together with a description of the nature, purpose and consequences of an appointment as well as a statement that the AIP must be physically present at the guardianship hearing unless excused by the court, and a statement of the AIP's rights at that hearing; notice of petition for conservatorship substantially similar); *with* N.Y. M.H.L., at §81.07, (requires notice by personal service at least 14 days but no more than 28 days in advance, and specifying content of notice must include "a clear and readable statement of the [AIP's] rights. . . ").

479. *See supra* Chapter 2 A; *see also,* Gideon v. Wainright, 372 U.S. (1963) (indigent defendant's right to counsel); Strickland v. Washington, 466 U.S. 668 (1984) (Constitutional right to counsel guarantees at least minimally effective assistance of counsel).

forded this right. The earlier view of legal counsel as dispensable in guardianship proceedings stems from the paternalistic view of guardianship as a nonadversarial process in which all parties pursue the best interests of the AIP.[480] That view, however benevolent and well-intentioned, has no place in the initial determination of whether an AIP ought to be deprived of civil rights.[481] Today, a majority of jurisdictions confer a right to counsel in guardianship proceedings.[482] Those that do not provide for counsel automatically typically provide for appointment of counsel upon the AIP's request, or in the court's discretion.[483] The right to counsel, however, does not necessarily mean a right to an advocate; rather, it may mean that there will be a guardian *ad litem* or other representative who is entitled to represent his or her view of the AIP's best interests when they are inconsistent with the AIP's view.[484]

iii Court-appointed visitor or evaluator   Another protection incorporated into many states' guardianship reforms is the creation of the role of "visitor" or "evaluator."[485] This is a neutral role rather than an advocacy role, designed to elicit relevant facts from the AIP and others. Its purpose is to facilitate the development of the factual record so the court has the best, most complete information possible in making guardianship determinations.[486] The role of visitor or evaluator, in some jurisdictions, is integral to satisfying basic due process requirements.[487]

In general, only an individual with some expertise or experience may be appointed as a visitor or evaluator, but the requirements for this role vary widely. In Florida, for example, the statute requires the court to appoint an examining committee consisting of three members, one of whom must be a psychiatrist or other physician.[488] Each of the remaining members must be either a psychologist, gerontologist, another psychiatrist or other physician, a registered nurse, nurse practitioner, licensed social worker, a person with an advanced degree in gerontology from an accredited institution of higher education, or other person who by knowledge, skill, experience, training, or education may, in the court's discretion, advise the court in the form of an expert opinion. In addition, each member of the examining committee must have been prepared for the role by completing a program of guardianship study.[489]

---

480. *See supra* notes 448, 22.
481. *Compare*, UGPPA 1997, at 302–04.
482. DAYTON ET AL., *supra* note 465, at §34.21.
483. *Id.*
484. *See, e.g.*, N.C. GEN. STAT. §35A-1107 (Lexis-Nexis 2005) (providing for representation of AIP by a guardian ad litem (GAL) who may recommend an approach different than that desired by the AIP).
485. *See, e.g.*, N.Y. M.H.L. §81.09.
486. *Id.*
487. Guardianship of Therese B., 671 N.W.2d 377 (Wis. App. 2003), *rev. den.* 671 N.W.2d 852 (2003).
488. FLA. STAT. ANN., at §744.331(3).
489. *Id.* at § 744.331(2(d).

In contrast, one need not be a psychologist, psychiatrist, or physician in order to serve in the role of court evaluator in New York.[490] Like Florida, however, New York requires candidates for the role of court evaluator to complete a prescribed course of study in guardianship law.[491]

iv. Hearing   Before the reform of guardianship law, it was not uncommon for a court to issue a guardianship order without conducting a hearing. As a result of reform, a hearing is required in many jurisdictions to enhance the court's ability to ascertain the relevant facts and protect the AIP's due process rights.[492] Where there is any evidence that appointment of a guardian may be appropriate, it is reversible error for the judge to dismiss the case without conducting a hearing.[493] Conversely, some jurisdictions preclude appointment of a guardian for an AIP who initially contests guardianship but later consents to appointment of a guardian.[494] The effect of requiring a new, voluntary petition for guardianship is to prevent avoidance of the required hearing by convincing the AIP to consent to an undesired guardianship.

d. The role of mental health expertise

The statutory integration of mental health expertise into the determination of an IP or AIP's competency (or competencies) is a critical aspect of guardianship reform. By incorporating the place of mental disability (relative to other facts) in the legal standard for competency, modern statutes facilitate appropriate, effective use of mental health expertise. The explicit articulation of policy objectives, most preserving autonomy of an AIP to the extent possible without jeopardizing the AIP's well-being, guides mental health experts in the relevance of different aspects of their assessment of an AIP.[495] This, in turn, increases the probability that an expert will offer testimony that is not only relevant but also understandable to courts. In cases where this occurs, the evidence offered by the expert will be more likely to reduce the influence of heuristics or sanist assumptions imbedded in the popular understanding of mental disabilities.[496]

i. Simultaneous service as expert witness on behalf of a party and court-appointed evaluator   A mental health expert may serve as a witness on behalf of a party to the guardianship proceeding or as an evaluator or other neutral expert on behalf of the court. Presumably, however, an expert should not serve

---

490. N.Y. M.H.L., at § 81.09.

491. *Id.* at § 81.40.

492. *See supra* note 476.

493. *See, e.g., In re* Eggleston, 757 NYS2d 24 (NY 2003).

494. Matter of Conservatorship of Leonard, 563 N.W.2d 193 (Iowa 1997).

495. *See supra* note 466.

496. *See* Michael L. Perlin, *"Half-Wracked Prejudice Leaped Forth": Sanism, Pretextuality and Why and How Mental Disability Law Developed as It Did,* 10 J. CONTEMP. LEGAL ISSUES 3, 5 (1999).

both roles in the same case.[497] In either role, the mental health professional's evaluation of an individual ought to be the same,[498] but the advocacy role of the lawyer representing the IP (or AIP) should highlight favorable aspects of the professional's testimony and downplay unfavorable aspects. The element of advocacy, appropriate and indeed required for representation of an individual, interferes with the neutrality that a court evaluator is appointed to provide.[499] At the very least, the duality of roles creates an appearance of impropriety that ought to be avoided.[500]

This issue arose in South Carolina, where the trial court designated as neutral experts the same two professionals previously identified as witnesses for the AIP.[501] Not surprisingly, the professionals testified that the AIP was competent to handle her $60 million estate. The AIP appealed to the South Carolina Supreme Court, which granted certiorari, but has not yet decided the case. In other jurisdictions, duality of roles is specifically prohibited.[502]

---

497. *Cf.,* MODEL RULES OF PROFESSIONAL CONDUCT R. 1.7 (2003) (rule preventing lawyer's representation of clients with conflicting interests), *reprinted in* 2 GEOFFREY C. HAZARD, JR. & W. WILLIAM HODES, THE LAW OF LAWYERING app. A, A-19 (3d ed. 2001). Regarding the principle of "one case, one role," see, e.g., KIRK HEILBRUN PRINCIPLES OF FORENSIC MENTAL HEALTH ASSESSMENT, *supra* note 3, at 73–82 (discussing the importance of determining the role to be played in a forensic case, and arguing (at 73) that "it is undesirable to blend the roles of court-appointed, defense/prosecution/plaintiff's expert, or consultant in a single case."). *See generally,* Stuart A. Greenberg & Daniel W. Shuman, *The Expert Witness, the Adversary System and the Voice of Reason: Reconciling Impartiality and Advocacy,* 34 PROF' PSYCHOL: RES. & PRAC. 219 (2003).

498. Regardless of who retained them, forensic psychologists are bound by professional guidelines to retain neutrality and objectivity. Committee on Ethical Guidelines for Forensic Psychologists, *Specialty Guidelines for Forensic Psychologists,* 16 LAW & HUM. BEHAV. 655, 658 (1991) (Guideline VII Public Communications, (B) "Forensic psychologists realize that their public role as 'expert to the court' or as 'expert representing the profession' confers upon them a special responsibility for fairness and accuracy."

499. R. 1.3, cmt. 12 (establishing a duty of diligence and providing that the "lawyer must . . . act with zeal in advocacy on client's behalf ").

500. R. 1.10 (establishing duty to avoid the appearance of impropriety). *Cf.,* Greenberg & Shuman, *supra* note 497, at 221, further discusses the role of the retained expert, who, by maintaining a posture of impartiality and practicing squarely within the bounds of professional guidelines and ethical standards, can provide the strongest possible advocacy for the retaining party, stating:

> Expert witnesses face evidentiary demands imposed by courts, ethical demands imposed by professional licensing agencies, liability demands imposed by disgruntled litigants, and economic demands imposed by the attorneys who employ them. How should experts respond to these demands, which seem to ask them to play both neutral and partisan roles? Our proposal, impartiality as the best advocacy, does not ask experts to choose between these roles but offers guidance on how to fulfill both roles simultaneously. The crucial assumption that guides this proposal is that an expert's credibility is an essential component of being an effective advocate and that credibility derives from the expert's impartiality. An expert's absence of impartiality is fatal not only for its impact on neutrality but also for its impact on advocacy.

501. *In re* Campbell, 625 S.E.2d 233 (S.C. App. 2006).
502. *See supra* note 500.

ii. As evaluator   The neutral role of court-appointed evaluator is a more natural fit for most mental health experts not specifically trained in forensics than is the role of expert witness. While the evaluator participates in the adversarial process that due process requires, the evaluator himself or herself is not advocate but rather more in the nature of a special assistant to the court. A mental health expert who is appointed to this role should be mindful of the significant differences from jurisdiction to jurisdiction (and from court to court) in what is expected of the evaluator. In Florida, for example, where a mental health expert is required to serve on the neutral committee that aids the court in guardianship proceedings, the investigation, report, or other aspects of the evaluators' work may require more specific information than that required of a court evaluator in New York. The court evaluation process in New York is accomplished by an individual rather than a committee of neutral experts, and this individual's background need not include the same level of mental health expertise.[503] By following the statutory requirements as well as the specific practices that a particular court prefers, the evaluator maximizes the effectiveness of his or her input.

iii. As expert witness   The role of expert witness in a guardianship proceeding differs from the role of expert witness in other areas of civil law, particularly torts, contracts, and donative transfers, because the competency determination is in the present rather than retrospective: The AIP is available for direct observation by the court when the court is being asked to make a determination in response to the AIP's plea to avoid imposition of an unwanted guardianship. Not only the court but also, if statute allows, the neutral evaluator will have the opportunity to observe the AIP and the surrounding circumstances. The court's opportunity for observation of the AIP heightens the scrutiny of the expert's testimony because the testimony must not only be clear, cogent, and accurate in the abstract, it must explain or reconcile any differences between the court's observations and the expert witness' observations or opinions. Conversely, the evaluator may enjoy the added advantage, in explaining assessment results, of having examples of the described cognitive facilities or limitations at hand for the court's observation.

In cases where the evaluator has no mental health expertise, it is important to identify the background of the evaluator and determine the experience, data collection strategies, and other factors that form the basis of the evaluator's opinion. The availability of this data will assist the retained rebuttal expert to review the evaluator's findings and identify deficits, oversights, or misinterpretations.[504] Conversely, a retained expert witness in this situation may lend support for the conclusions drawn by an evaluator who has done a good job of collecting and integrating the data. In any event, it is critical that the expert witness obtain as much information as possible about the AIP, his or her circumstances, and other relevant information.

---

503. *See supra* notes 490, 493.
504. *See, e.g.*, Schaefer v. Schaefer, 52 P.3d 1125 (Or. App. 2002).

e. The effect of guardianship reform

Empirical studies of the effect of guardianship reforms show that they have had little impact in terms of replacing plenary guardianships with less intrusive limited guardianships, enforcing due process protections for AIPs, or accomplishing other aspects of reform.[505] As one commentator noted, what is now needed is not another set of statutory revisions but rather stringent enforcement of the requirements that exist.[506] One way to advance this objective is to analyze how courts use mental health expertise in their determinations of an AIP's or IP's competencies as a means of identifying the approaches or techniques of mental health experts that are most (and least) helpful to courts in adjudicating guardianship proceedings.

In this endeavor, it bears noting that most guardianship cases are unreported, and thus the reported cases (upon which legal analysis heavily relies) may not be representative of guardianship cases as a whole.[507] Nevertheless, review of reported cases remains the best source of information available for detailed analysis of the use of mental health expertise in contemporary guardianship cases.

3. The Role of Mental Health Expertise—Personal Matters

After a guardian has been appointed, conflicts between the guardian and the IP are usually resolved by determining whether the authority to decide the matter is vested in the guardian, retained by the IP, or a matter reserved for the court's judgment. In the case of a plenary guardianship, the IP loses virtually all rights, potentially including (depending upon the jurisdiction), the right to vote, the right to select health care providers, and the right to refuse medical treatment (absent a valid advance directive).

a . Living arrangements

One of the most important rights an IP may lose is the ability to choose where to live. In many cases, that issue triggers the guardianship proceeding. The AIP seeks to remain at home, or at least avoid a nursing home, while relatives or others concerned with the care of the AIP assert that a nursing home or other institutional arrangement is necessary in order to provide adequate care. In this type of conflict, as in all guardianship cases, the motivation or self-interest of the party petitioning for guardianship ought to be considered. This examination of motivation helps to minimize the possibility that transfer of judgment would infringe on

505. See Crosby, *supra* note 469, at 279–83; Wright, *supra* note 448, at 82–83.

506. Lawrence A. Frolik , *Statutory Definitions of Incapacity: The Need for a Medical Basis* 40, 40–57, in Older Adults' Decision-Making and the Law (Michael K. Smyer et al. eds. 1996).

507. In most jurisdictions, opinions of trial-level state courts are not officially reported. Even in a jurisdiction where trial-level state court opinions are published, only selected decisions will be published. Moreover, a case can be concluded without any written decision, such as when settlement occurs or the court issues an order or decree that contains the information required for disposition of the case.

an AIP's autonomy simply for the sake of the petitioner's convenience or for any objective other than the AIP's best interests. Where there is no expert testimony at all, or expert testimony only on behalf of the petitioner, the danger of an overly restrictive (or entirely unnecessary) guardianship is significant.

In *Matter of Richman,* for example, a hospital sought appointment of a guardian for an individual who had been an inpatient for several months because the hospital, an acute care facility, could not find an appropriate living arrangement for her.[508] The AIP, Harriet Richman, did not require hospitalization for medical reasons. She did, however, suffer from morbid obesity, a condition that required her to use an oversized wheelchair that could not pass through a standard doorway. Hospital staff located appropriate nursing homes that could accommodate her wheelchair, but when the nursing home personnel came to meet her, she would agree to go to the nursing home only if certain unspecified "unrealistic" conditions were met.[509] Ms. Richman also made life difficult for the hospital staff, the court found, by refusing physical therapy and other care, most notably when the care came at an inconvenient or unexpected time.

Another item of evidence suggesting functional limitation was Ms. Richman's accumulation of a year's worth of unnegotiated checks at the time of her hospitalization, with no arrangements for them to be deposited. The only evidence presented on behalf of Ms. Richman (who was represented by counsel) was a signed lease for an apartment obviating the hospital's concern about housing a patient who did not require acute medical care.[510]

In concluding that Ms. Richman required a guardian to handle specified personal and property matters,[511] the court accepted, and appears to have relied heavily, on the testimony of a licensed psychiatrist (who apparently was called by the hospital as a witness) who diagnosed Ms. Richman with a thinking disorder of "borderline personality."[512] The court went on to describe the psychiatrist's testimony:

---

508. 625 N.Y.S.2d 443 (N.Y. Sup. 1995), *aff'd* 639 N.Y.S.2d 39 (App. Div. 1996), *app. den.*, 646 N.Y.S.2d 985 (1995).

509. *Id.* at 406.

510. *Id.*

511. *Id.* at 446–47.

512. *DMV IV* describes borderline personality disorder as:

A pervasive pattern of instability of interpersonal relationships, self-image and affect, and marked impulsivity beginning by early adulthood and present in a variety of contexts, as indicated by five of more of the following:

1. Frantic efforts to avoid real or imagined abandonment
2. Pattern of unstable and intense interpersonal relationships characterized by alternating extremes of idealization and devaluation
3. Identity disturbance markedly and persistently unstable self-image or sense of self
4. Impulsivity in at least two areas that are potentially self-damaging (e.g., spending, sex, substance abuse, reckless driving, binge eating)
5. Recurrent suicidal behavior, gestures, or threats or self-mutilating behavior
6. Affective instability due to a marked reactivity mood (e.g., intense episodic dyspho-

> Although Richman appears competent in terms of her verbal ability, at the same time she is relatively without insight and self-destructive. Although Richman's behavior looks like it is self-confounding, so-called passive-aggressive and infantile behavior, it is in actuality a thinking disorder. This type of behavior is often seen in people who are morbidly obese. . . .[513]

The court's determination appears to focus on Ms. Richman's belligerence as the primary basis for determining that she required a guardian. In the words of the court, Ms. Richman needed a guardian "not because of her functional limitations, but because she would not accept any help from aides to take care of her personal needs and property management."[514] Reconciling the quoted language with the court's holding (appointment of a guardian) seems to require the conclusion that choices deemed inappropriate by the court (e.g., refusing care) may substitute for the statutory requirement of functional limitations as a prerequisite to imposition of a guardianship.

The testimony of the psychiatrist attaches a diagnostic label to the AIP's behavior, but there is no indication in the decision that anyone probed the diagnosis, or addressed the likelihood of Ms. Richman overcoming the functional limitations that the court found to exist. More fundamentally, there is no discussion of why the signed lease did not satisfy the petitioner-hospital's interest in finding an appropriate placement for Ms. Richman, obviating the need to continue with the proceeding at all. While the court's ultimate conclusion could be appropriate, the decision does not disclose legal reasoning or critical analysis of the psychiatric testimony that would explicate the court's reasoning.

b. Health and bodily integrity

Loss of decisional authority over health care matters, such as the right to select treatment providers, may be traumatic, particularly if the guardian replaces a known and trusted care provider with a stranger. Life-and-death decisions, such as whether to terminate life support, may be in the guardian's control as well. If the ward executed any advance directive, such as a health care proxy or organ donation consent, when he or she had the requisite capacity, the advance directive should control.[515] Even where an advance directive was executed before there was any doubt about the IP's competence, however, judicial intervention still may be necessary to ensure that the hospital, doctor, or other care provider follows the

---

ria, irritability, or anxiety usually lasting a few hours and only rarely more than a few days)

7. Chronic feelings of emptiness
8. Inappropriate intense anger or difficulty controlling anger (e.g., frequent displays of temper, constant anger, recurrent physical fights)
9. Transient, stress-related paranoid ideation or severe dissociative symptoms

513. 625 N.Y.S.2d at 445–46.
514. *Id.* at 447. *See also,* Matter of Ryan, 2004 WL 2891933 (Ohio App. 2004).
515. *See supra* note 451.

IP's wishes as expressed in the advance directive.[516] In the absence of either a valid advance directive, a statute explicitly addressing the issue, or a specific provision in the guardianship order, a guardian must obtain authorization before authorizing removal of life support or other similar life-or-death decisions.

i. Organ donation   Decisions involving organ donation fall outside the usual medical authority that a guardian would have.[517] Cases in which a guardian seeks to subject the IP to a medical procedure that offers a life-saving opportunity for a family member or other individual who is close to the IP through biology, consanguinity, or otherwise, presents the question of how to determine the IP's best interests. An exclusive focus on the physical condition of the IP virtually mandates a prohibition on organ donation or other procedures that offer physical benefits to another individual with no corresponding physical benefit (and often actual physical risk) to the IP.

This traditional view is reflected in some guardianship statutes that prohibit a guardian or court from consenting to such procedures, as well as in case law.[518] The reasoning underlying this approach is that the interplay of personal values that bear on organ donation decisions makes this an issue that ought to be outside the scope of matters any surrogate, including the court, can presume to decide for an IP.[519] It also prevents courts from acting on the temptation to weigh the benefit to the recipient of the organ donation (or other procedure) against the risk to the IP rather than focusing exclusively on the IP's best interests.

The traditional analysis comports with the instinct to protect IPs, but this protection may not necessarily be consistent with the IP's best interests. In *Strunk v. Strunk*, a Kentucky case dating back to 1969, the court authorized the guardian to consent to the donation of one of the kidneys of the IP, who had a mental age of six. The proposed recipient of the kidney was the IP's sibling, who needed a kidney to survive and had no other viable prospects. The other members of the family, including a brother, had been eliminated as candidates; the brother who refused to donate his kidney asserted that the risks involved would jeopardize his family's financial and emotional security. The court permitted the donation, reasoning that losing a kidney would serve the IP's best interests by lengthening the time the kidney recipient would have to visit the IP.[520]

If the issue at hand is beyond the scope of the court's authority to adjudicate,

---

516. *See, e.g.,* Matter of Gordy, 658 A.2d 613 (Del. Ch. 1994).

517. *See, e.g.,* Ky. Rev. Stat. Ann. 387.660(4) (Lexis 1999) (court consent required, except in emergency, for guardian to authorize organ donation by ward).

518. *See* Guardianship of Pescinski, 226 N.W.2d 18 (Wis. 1975).

519. *Cf.,* Guardianship of Eberhardy, 307 N.W.2d 881 (Wis. 1981) (holding court had authority over all guardianship matters, including authority to permit sterilization, but declined to authorize procedure without legislative guidance on the important policy questions involved). Subsequently, Wisconsin addressed this matter by statute, as did a number of other jurisdictions. Wis. Stat. Ann. §54.25 (West 2003 & Supp. 2006). *See also,* Alas. Stat. Ann. §13.26.150 (Lexis-Nexis 2006); Cal. Prob. Code Ann., at §§1958, 1959.

520. 445 S.W.2d 145 (1969).

the IP is deprived of choice because the default rule—no organ donation—applies automatically. In the context of divorce involving an IP,[521] courts have recognized that automatic application of a default rule is not necessarily the most appropriate outcome or the outcome most protective of an IP. In the context of organ donation and other similar medical procedures, however, the opportunities for abuse are higher, providing greater justification for an absolute prohibition. On the other hand, it is not unreasonable to provide a legal procedure for consenting to organ donation (or similar medical procedure). Donation to a family member is a choice that many individuals make, and that ought to be considered in such cases, particularly where there is evidence of an IP's prior actions in accordance with (or against) the proposed action.[522] It is equally clear, however, that protection of the IP must be the primary concern.[523]

In jurisdictions where it is possible to seek consent for organ donation, medical expertise about the expected physical consequences for the IP will be of utmost importance. Mental health experts may play an important role as well, however, in assessing the IP's ability to make this particular decision, notwithstanding the inability to make other personal decisions. Mental health expertise could also be useful to assist the court in determining the likelihood that the IP, though incompetent to make the decision, would have the capacity to enjoy (or conversely to experience negative feelings about) any aspect of the organ donation.

ii. Forced medication　The issue of forced medication has received much attention in the area of criminal law, resulting in the imposition of restraints on the state's power in this area.[524] In the area of guardianship this issue has received much less attention, and there is correspondingly less specificity in the requirements necessary to justify forced medication in this context. A comparison of two recent Massachusetts cases addressing this issue illustrates the value that mental health expertise has in this area, and also underscores the qualities that are important in the presentation of mental health expertise in any civil case.

In the first case, *Guardianship of Jackson,* the AIP son of petitioners was diagnosed with paranoid schizophrenia by two psychiatrists.[525] Both psychiatrists testified that Jackson, the AIP, was incompetent by virtue of his mental illness to make decisions regarding his medication. One of the psychiatrists had examined Jackson in connection with the temporary guardianship that had been imposed

---

521. *See infra* Chapter 4.E.3.

522. Guardianship statutes typically do not address the authority of the IP's guardian to consent to organ donation on behalf of the IP. Reported decisions on this issue are sparse as well. A law review article dating back 30 years noted a trend in unreported cases to authorize guardians to consent to organ donation. *See* Annot., Lisa K. Gregory, *Propriety of Surgically Invading Incompetent or Minor for Benefit of Third Party,* 4 A.L.R. 5th 1000, 1008 (1992), *citing* Robertson, *Organ Donations by Incompetents and the Substituted Judgment Doctrine,* 76 COLUM. L. REV. 48 (1976).

523. *Id.*

524. *See supra* Chapter 2.B.

525. 814 N.E.2d 393 (Mass. App. 2004).

in February, 2002; the other psychiatrist last examined Jackson approximately 1 month before the trial (on the matter of whether a permanent guardian ought to be appointed).[526] A third psychiatrist, Dr. Goderez, who was called as a witness by the AIP, examined only the most recent hospitalization records of the AIP, did not speak with other physicians who had treated or examined the AIP, did not determine that the AIP was not mentally ill, and did not offer a definitive diagnosis of the AIP. In addition, Dr. Goderez' examination occurred approximately 4 months before trial, during a period in which the AIP's condition had significantly improved.

Although the parents-petitioners hoped to undermine Dr. Goderez' testimony, their effort failed, resulting in a determination that the AIP was competent to make his own medical decisions. One possible reason that the parents' strategy failed to undermine Dr. Goderez' testimony is that the AIP's condition at the time of Dr. Goderez' examination did not change during the 4 months between the doctor's testimony and the trial. Another reason may be that Dr. Goderez did not overstate his findings or reach definitive conclusions based on the incomplete information that he had. The modesty of his testimony deflected the petitioners' opportunity to challenge Dr. Goderez' objectivity, or his conclusions. At most, petitioners could argue that Dr. Goderez' testimony alone would not support a determination of legal competency (hardly a valuable concession, given the presumption of capacity). Most importantly, perhaps, is the failure of the petitioners' experts to explain how the AIP's condition (diagnosed by them as paranoid schizophrenia) interfered with the AIP's ability to make decisions about medication. The nexus between this diagnosis and decision-making capacity may seem obvious to psychiatrists, but without a clear explanation of the relationship between paranoid schizophrenia and the legal standard for competency in guardianship proceedings, the conclusion reached by the petitioners' two psychiatrists may appear to have been based on a medical standard for competence rather than a legal one.

Guardianship of Arlene, decided 2 years later, offers an interesting contrast.[527] In that case, the trial court heard expert testimony, uncontradicted, that Arlene, the AIP, suffered from schizoaffective disorder, a major mental illness that impaired her thought process and ability to recognize reality. The court did not discuss the expert testimony in detail but instead applied a "substituted judgment" standard under which the court must ascertain what the AIP in the case (as opposed to some fictionalized, objective AIP) would choose if he or she were competent.[528] Arlene's denial that she was ill, her statement that she would take her medication if she were ill, the uncontroverted diagnosis of schizoaffective disorder,[529] and the

---

526. *Id.* at 396.

527. 857 N.E.2d 46 , 2006 WL 3349572 (Mass. App. 2006) (table only).

528. *Id.,* 2006 WL 3349572 at *1.

529. Schizoaffective disorder is similar to schizophrenia in that it is characterized by some combination of delusions, hallucinations, disorganized speech, grossly disorganized or catatonic behavior, negative symptoms (affective flattening, alogia, or avolition), none of which

risk of developing catatonia[530] formed the basis of the court's determination that Arlene, if competent, would take the medication.[531] If the factual foundation of the decision is accurate, then the conclusion logically follows. The real question is the factual accuracy of the determination that Arlene's mental illness caused her to reject her medication. A mental health expert, whether a neutral expert appointed by the court or a retained expert called as a witness by Arlene, could have probed not only the testifying expert's diagnosis but also the basis for that expert's conclusion about the causal link between the mental illness and the refusal to take the medication.

As the case law under modern guardianship continues to develop, disparities between AIPs who have the benefit of mental health expertise through either an advocate or a neutral party and AIPs who do not may become more apparent. In the interim, AIPs without the benefit of mental health expertise may suffer from the deprivation.

4. Additional Considerations—Property Matters

In theory, expert assessment of an AIP should be similar, whether the proposed guardianship involves personal matters, property matters, or both.[532] In reality, finances influence not only the AIP's need for assistance but also the motivation of those seeking to impose guardianship and the resources available for litigating the guardianship proceeding. Moreover, if guardianship is established, the funds of the IP will be available for gratuitous transfers at the death of the IP, and also, in many jurisdictions, during the IP's lifetime. The guardian may also seek to set aside transactions the IP entered into before the guardian was appointed. Furthermore, the powers vested in guardians present the opportunity for conflicts of interest and outright abuse; for example, using guardianship funds for the benefit of the guardian or any individual other than the IP.

a. Conflicts of interest
In too many cases, a family member or other individual close to the AIP may seek guardianship to protect or preserve the assets of the AIP for future inheritance. This interest alone falls short of establishing the need for a property guardian. In the words of one court ". . . [O]ne may not have his or her property taken away

---

are attributable to medical condition, medication, or substance abuse, whereas schizophrenia may be a lifelong condition. Also, schizoaffective disorder involves major manic, depressive, or mixed episodes concurrent with the active phase symptoms whereas schizophrenia does not. *DSM IV* §295.40.

530. *DSM IV* describes manifestations of catatonia to include motoric immobility, excessive motor activity that is apparently purposeless and not influenced by external stimuli, extreme negativism or mutism, peculiarities of voluntary movement, and echolalia or echopraxia. §293.89(A).

531. *Arlene*, 2006 WL 3449572 at *2.

532. Of course, the functional abilities required for guardian of the person as compared to guardian of the property may differ significantly.

and placed in the hands of a conservator merely because potential heirs believe there will be more left for them if the owner of the property is not free to deal with the property as he or she chooses."[533]

When a petitioner's self-interest coexists with a sincere concern for the AIP, the pursuit of self-interest may inflict harm on the AIP. In *Guardianship of Kelly,* for example, the AIP was an elderly man whose ability to care for himself had declined with age.[534] While his wife was living, she cared for him. After her death, an adult daughter moved in with the AIP to care for his needs. In the course of probate proceedings for the AIP's deceased wife, the AIP's five children learned that the couple's estate plan provided for their home to pass to one grandchild, with the remainder of the estate passing equally to the five children. This created a conflict among the children, resulting in competing petitions for guardianship. In adjudicating the petition, the court held that the AIP did require a guardian, and further held that the intersibling conflicts required an independent guardian for the AIP.[535] Thus, the children's financial expectancies in their father's estate led them to destroy the familial care arrangement and replace it with a guardianship.

Conflict of interest also prompted litigation in the case of an IP who had inherited from her husband, Edward Pflueger, a $17 million estate that included a world-renowned porcelain collection.[536] In that case, a guardian was appointed for Mrs. Pflueger after Mr. Pflueger's death. The guardian, Mrs. Pflueger's sister, asserted that Mrs. Pflueger was the owner of one-half of some of the porcelain, notwithstanding that the porcelain was titled in Mr. Pflueger's name, or alternatively that Mr. Pflueger had given some of the porcelain to Mrs. Pflueger during his lifetime. Additionally, the guardian asserted that Mrs. Pflueger ought to exercise her statutory right of election against Mr. Pflueger's estate so that she would receive one third of the estate property outright rather than the benefits provided by Mr. Pflueger's will.[537] Under the will, the bulk of Mr. Pflueger's estate would be held in trust for Mrs. Pflueger's benefit during her lifetime, and upon her death the Boston Museum of Fine Arts would receive the porcelain collection while Mrs. Pflueger's closest relatives (her siblings and their descendants) would receive the other assets of the trust.[538]

For Mrs. Pflueger personally, neither the right of election nor the joint property claim would provide any benefit.[539] As lifetime beneficiary of the trust, she would enjoy the porcelain (which she referred to as her "children"), as well as the financial support from the trust. Exercising the right of election would give Mrs. Pflueger one third of the assets of Mr. Pflueger's estate, but Mrs. Pflueger

---

533. Estate of Wagner, 367 N.W.2d 736, 738 (Neb. 1985). *See also,* Guardianship and Conservatorship of Teeter, 547 N.W.2d 808 (Iowa App. 1995).
534. Guardianship of Kelly, 901 P.2d 665 (Ariz. App. 1996).
535. *Id.*
536. Estate of Pflueger, 693 N.Y.S.2d 419 (Sur. 1999).
537. *See supra* Chapter 4.C.2, note 313.
538. Pflueger, 639 N.Y.S.2d at 296.
539. *Id.* at 425.

would have to give up all provisions for her under the will. Moreover, the Boston Museum would receive two thirds of the porcelain (the portion of the porcelain not subject to the right of election) immediately rather than at the death of Mrs. Pflueger.

In an effort to protect Mrs. Pflueger's best interests, the court appointed a special guardian to represent Mrs. Pflueger in this litigation.[540] The special guardian succeeded in reaching a settlement with all parties, under which Mrs. Pflueger's relatives exchanged their legal claims for a distribution of $1.2 million to Mrs. Pflueger's trust, an annual payment of $100,000 to Mrs. Pflueger (with a guaranteed minimum of $400,000), and distribution of porcelain valued at $500,000, all to be funded by the Boston Museum. In addition, counsel to the executor and trustee of Mr. Pflueger's estate agreed to reduce legal fees by $150,000. Concluding the settlement met the applicable New York statutory substituted judgment standard[541] and also accorded with Mrs. Pflueger's previously expressed wishes, the court approved the settlement.[542]

b. Gifts of property

Gifts of property from the estate of an IP to another beneficiary offer no direct financial benefit to the IP, and in fact harm the IP's financial interest to the extent that they reduce the assets available for the IP. Gifts from an IP's estate parallel in the property context the issue of organ donation by the IP in the personal context.[543] In neither case does the IP receive direct benefit, but an expanded concept of "benefit" may justify what a narrow conception of "benefit" would prohibit.

In contrast to the restrictive approach courts have taken to organ donation, several courts have approved gratuitous transfers of an IP's property, applying either a standard established by statute or the common-law doctrine of "substituted judgment."[544] Some statutes establish a specific standard for gifts from a guardianship estate, while states without specific statutory guidance follow common-law principles in determining whether to authorize a gift of the IP's property. In New York, for example, the guardianship statute authorizes gifts from an IP's estate under the following conditions:

1. The [IP] lacks the requisite mental capacity to perform the act or acts for which approval has been sought and is not likely to regain such capacity within a reasonable period of time or, if the incapacitated person has the requisite capacity, that he or she consents to the proposed disposition;

---

540. The court appointed a special guardian to represent Mrs. Pflueger in the litigation of the claims due to the general guardian's status as a presumptive remainderman of the trust, and beneficiary of a purported will executed after Mr. Pflueger's death.

541. *See infra* note 545.

542. *Id.*

543. *See supra* notes 517–523 and accompanying text.

544. *See generally,* Annot., *Power of Court or Guardian to Make Noncharitable Gifts or Allowances Out of Funds of Incompetent Ward,* 24 A.L.R.3d 863 (1969 & Supp.). Not all jurisdictions have adopted the doctrine of substituted judgment. *See, e.g.,* Guardianship of Stanley B., 540 N.W.2d 11 (Wis. App. 1995).

2. A competent, reasonable individual in the position of the [IP] would be likely to perform the act or acts under the same circumstances; and

3. The [IP] has not manifested an intention inconsistent with the performance of the act or acts of which approval has been sought at some earlier time when he or she had the requisite capacity or, if such intention was manifested, the particular person would be likely to have changed such intention under the circumstances existing at the time of the filing of the petition.[545]

The most common bases for seeking court approval of a gift from an IP's estate include the desire to provide support for a dependent family member, to save estate taxes, or to impoverish the IP so that the IP qualifies for Medicaid. Approval of gifts that will minimize estate taxes upon the IP's death is not particularly intuitive, but neither is it antithetical to the IP's interests. Central to this conclusion, however, is the determination that the funds remaining after the gift will be more than adequate to provide for whatever the IP's future needs may be.

If there is any real risk that the gift may jeopardize the ability to meet the IP's needs, the gift ought to be disapproved, as the Montana Supreme Court did in Estate of West.[546] In that case, a limited guardian sought to terminate a conservatorship and replace it with a trust arrangement in order to accomplish multiple purposes, one of which was to increase the IP's flexibility to make gifts to his mother, who was his guardian. In addition, the IP (but not the guardian) sought to terminate the limited guardianship on the grounds that he had recovered sufficiently from the physical and mental injuries he incurred in an accident. The IP's physician reported that a less restrictive method of providing for the IP's needs would be appropriate, and the lower court relied on that opinion to limit but not terminate the guardianship and to keep the conservatorship in place.[547] In this case, the shortfall in expertise came not from the mental health expert, but from financial professionals who did not support their allegation that a trust would save taxes. More importantly, no one had analyzed the prospective needs of the IP, who still required significant care.[548] Without such evidence, the court properly refused to approve the termination of the conservatorship, a conclusion the Montana Supreme Court affirmed.

Even less intuitive than gifts to save taxes are gifts to impoverish the IP so that the IP qualifies for Medicaid. The interest of the IP arguably is served because it preserves assets for the IP's heirs rather than allowing health care expenses to deplete the IP's assets. The New Jersey Supreme Court accepted this rationale in a case involving a son-guardian's application to sell his mother's house and divide the proceeds between himself and his brother, less the amount needed to cover health care expenses for the statutory period of Medicaid disqualification following any gratuitous transfer(s).[549] Adopting a series of factors, developed by the

---

545. N.Y. M.H.L. 81.21(e).
546. 887 P.2d 222 (Mont. 1994).
547. *Id.* at 225.
548. *Id.* at 229.
549. *In re* Keri, 853 A.2d 909 (N.J. 2004).

lower courts in New Jersey that parallel the statutory test applied in New York, the court approved of the transfer.[550]

Another type of Medicaid transfer that courts have approved is creation of a trust known as a "payback," "spend down," or "supplemental needs" trust.[551] Federal legislation[552] permits the creation of such trusts without jeopardizing Medicaid eligibility, and several states, either by case law or statute, have authorized adoption of such trusts as well. Under the terms of a supplemental needs trust, a parent, grandparent, legal guardian of an IP, or a court may establish a trust without jeopardizing Medicaid eligibility if the trust provides that amounts remaining in the trust upon the death of the IP are distributable to the state in an amount equal to the total medical assistance paid on behalf of the IP by Medicaid.[553]

Even a jurisdiction that has rejected the common-law doctrine of substituted judgment may approve an application to establish a supplemental needs trust with guardianship funds. In *Guardianship of Scott,* for example, a mother-guardian sought to establish a supplemental needs trust for her son, the IP.[554] Distinguishing tax savings from Medicaid planning, the court stated that transfer to a payback trust (supplemental needs trust) advances the goal of preserving resources available to the IP that gifts, for tax purposes or otherwise, do not.[555] Accordingly, the court held that transfer to a payback trust was permissible and remanded the case to the trial court for a factual determination as to whether such a trust was appropriate in this case.[556]

c. The link between mental health expertise in guardianship proceedings and will contests

As noted in the discussion of wills, contemporaneous expert assessment of testamentary capacity is rarely available.[557] States have offered no workable opportunity to definitely determine testamentary capacity during an individual's life-

---

550. *Id.* at 914. In New Jersey, the criteria include: (1) the mental and physical condition of the incompetent are such that the possibility of her restoration to competency is virtually nonexistent, (2) the assets of the estate of the incompetent remaining after the consummation of the proposed gifts are such that, in light of her life expectancy and her present condition of health, they are more than adequate to meet all of her needs in the style and comfort in which she now is (and since the onset of her incompetency has been) maintained, giving due consideration to all normal contingencies, (3) the donees constitute the natural objects of the bounty of the incompetent by any standard. . . , (4) the transfer will benefit and advantage the estate of the incompetent by a reduction of death taxes, and (5) there is no substantial evidence that the incompetent, as a reasonably prudent person, would, if competent, not make the gifts proposed in order to effectuate a saving of death taxes. For criterion (2), the court considered the continuation of care in a facility rather funds in the guardianship account. For criterion (4), the court considered the savings in medical expenses rather than tax savings. *Id.*

551. *See, e.g.,* Estate of Kane, 40 Cal. Rptr. 3d 378 (App. 2006).

552. THE OMNIBUS BUDGET RECONCILIATION ACT OF 1993, *codified at* 42 U.S.CA. 1396p(d)(4)(A) (West 2003 & Supp. 2007).

553. *Id.*

554. 659 N.W.2d 438 (Wis. App. 2003).

555. *Id.* at 444.

556. *Id.* at 445.

557. *See supra* section 4.C.3.

time. In the absence of an explicit opportunity to accomplish such assessment for testamentary capacity, lawyers have begun to use guardianship as a vehicle for a lifetime assessment of testamentary capacity. A guardianship proceeding gives the petitioner (as well as the respondents) the opportunity to present expert opinion about the AIP's capacity. While the capacity determination in a guardianship proceeding is not aimed at testamentary capacity, lawyers have used the guardianship proceeding to preserve evidence that bears on the determination of testamentary capacity.[558] Lawyers also have used the threat of this maneuver as leverage for settlement of claims of competing heirs and beneficiaries of the AIP's (or IP's) estate. Although property guardians historically could not and typically cannot execute (or revoke) a will on behalf of an IP, the same effect can be achieved through use of testamentary substitutes that can be executed, revised, or revoked by a property guardian authorized to do so.[559]

This type of legal maneuvering is clearly inconsistent with the historic prohibition against executing a will on behalf of an IP. Yet efforts to prohibit such maneuvering by statute have met with the same difficulty that arose in earlier debates over living probate: The conflicting policy interests at stake have precluded any clear path to the desired result. In the guardianship context, the principal obstacle to precluding this type of maneuvering is the interest in affording the estate of an IP the same opportunities to engage in estate planning that competent individuals enjoy. A rule specifically barring use of evidence developed in a guardianship proceeding for the purpose of proving (or disproving) testamentary capacity in a later will contest would reduce the efficacy of this approach, but not by much. So long as the guardian has the power to deal with will substitutes, the substantive effect of changing the IP's will can be achieved. More ominously, the threat of a guardianship proceeding can force an AIP, who may be perfectly competent, to choose between incurring significant litigation expenses to avoid guardianship and entering into a "settlement" of the guardianship proceeding that includes estate-planning changes the AIP does not desire.

Statutory recognition of lifetime assessment of testamentary capacity determinations is a superior alternative. Not only does it directly address the real objective of the party seeking the verification of testamentary capacity (or incapacity), it also reduces the possibility that guardianship proceedings will be used to threaten rather than to benefit AIPs and IPs.

To further limit the opportunity to use the threat of property guardianship to force an AIP into adopting undesired estate planning changes he or she does not desire, limitations on the circumstances under which a property guardian may change an IP's estate plan through testamentary substitutes would be necessary. The likelihood of adopting such limitations is remote, however, because of the longstanding precedent allowing gifts of IPs' property and the natural extension of that to testamentary substitutes included as part of the estate plan.

558. *See, e.g.*, Matter of Joseph S., 808 N.Y.S.2d 426 (App. Div. 2006) (reversing trial court's *sua sponte* invalidation of any will executed after a certain date).
559. *See, e.g.*, N.Y. M.H.L., at §81.21.

5. Summary

Statutory schemes for guardianship vary infinitely in their detail, precluding any sweeping generalizations or conclusions about the law governing appointment of guardians in general, or use of mental health expertise in the determination of competency in particular. The reforms adopted by most jurisdictions in recent years reflect an increased concern for protection of AIPs from invasions of their autonomy that are not necessary for the AIP's protection. Mental health expertise plays a central role in these reforms, maximizing the opportunity for appropriate use of such expertise in guardianship proceedings.

Specifically, neutral and objective assessment can provide the court with rich and reliable data that is relevant to the elements of guardianship establishment. The assessment may include both standardized measures of cognitive capacity and a wide-ranging assessment of the contextual issues at play, including the decision-making propensities of the IP or AIP, the nature of relationships among the parties, and the vulnerability for exploitations. A court-appointed expert would enjoy the ideal posture for neutrality, but a retained expert should be held to the same standard of giving equal consideration to all reasonable hypotheses, actively seeking data to support or refute each, and offering for the court's consideration the data that support each possible view of the need for guardianship.

E. DOMESTIC RELATIONS

1. Introduction

The family is an important social structure that the law seeks to encourage.[560] *Domestic Relations Law* defines and regulates the foundational relationships of family: the union of two individuals in marriage or domestic partnership, and (or) the relationship of parent and child. This includes the creation and termination of familial relationships as well as property rights that arise from familial status, such as the right to equitable distribution upon divorce, the right to a statutory elective share of a deceased spouse's estate and, in jurisdictions that have adopted community property, the applicable principles governing that form of ownership.

Historically, federal law has recognized domestic relations as an area uniquely suited to state (as opposed to federal) authority, because the range of reasonable policy choices vary widely.[561] Contemporarily, some of the most heated policy de-

---

560. *In re* Anderson's Estate, 194 P.2d 621 (Mont. 1948); Simpson v. Neely, 221 S.W.2d 303 (Tex. App. 1949).

561. 28 U.S.C.A.§ 1332 (West 2006). *Compare* Kahn v. Kahn, 21 F.3d 859 (8th Cir. 1994) (under domestic relations exception to diversity jurisdiction, the District Court lacked subject matter jurisdiction over former wife's claim against former husband for breach of fiduciary duty conversion, constructive fraud, and fraud because these claims were inextricably intertwined with property settlement to divorce proceedings); *with* Forton v. McOsker, 407 F.3d 501 (1st Cir. 2005) (spurned paramour's action alleging promissory estoppel and intentional infliction

bates concern domestic relations matters, such as whether to recognize same-sex marriage, how to balance rights of children and parents in termination of parental rights, and what criteria should define a prospective parent's eligibility to adopt. In this area of civil law, more than any other discussed in this chapter, issues of constitutional significance have arisen and continue to arise.

In this subchapter, we discuss selected topics that illustrate a variety of approaches, in legal principle as well as public policy, to the determination of mental capacity in domestic relations law. Following this introduction (section 1), we begin with the topic of marriage (section 2), describing the legal standard of capacity required to enter this relationship, the application of this standard in a variety of contexts, and the utility of mental health expertise in proving (or disproving) capacity to marry. Domestic partnership and civil unions are discussed in a separate section (3). This section is brief, in part because the domestic partnerships and civil unions are relatively new and in part because the statutes recognizing these relationships are designed to follow the rules of marriage other than the rule restricting marriage to opposite-sex couples. The final subsection in the discussion of familial partners is divorce (section 4). This section discusses not only capacity to divorce but also mental disability as grounds for or defense to a divorce, with case illustrations highlighting the role of mental expertise in the adjudication of such claims.

This subchapter then turns to the legal relationship of parents and children, beginning with termination of parental rights (section 5), focusing on the legal bases of parental rights terminations involving, directly or indirectly, mental disability of the parent as well as the role of mental health expertise in the application of these legal standards. The final subsection of domestic relations (section 6) addresses adoption. This subsection considers the legal standards applicable to all parties involved in the prospective adoptive relation, including prospective adoptive parent and child, and the parent(s) relinquishing the child. The role of mental health expertise also is discussed, including illustrative cases as well as a discussion of best practices.

2. Marriage

Marriage is a fundamental right guaranteed by the Fourteenth Amendment to the U.S. Constitution.[562] This constitutional protection restricts the flexibility states otherwise would have in regulating marriage, but it does not preclude regulation of marriage.[563] The state may impose reasonable requirements if they pose no significant

---

of emotional distress in connection with husband's alleged promise to divorce wife and support paramour was not within domestic relations exception to federal jurisdiction).

562. Loving v. Virginia, 388 U.S. 1 (1967).

563. *See, e.g.,* Anderson v. King County, 138 P.3d 963 (Wash. 2006) (rejecting Constitutional challenge to state's Defense of Marriage Act ("DOMA") precluding same sex marriage). *See also,* Baehr v. Lewin, 852 P.2 44 (Haw. 1993) (ban on same sex marriage violated state constitution), *superseded by state Constitutional Law Amendment as stated in* Lewis v. Harris, 875 A.2d 259 (N.J. Super. 2005).

interference with the marital relationship.[564] Substantial interference with the decision to marry, on the other hand, is permissible only if important state interests are at stake and the regulation is closely tailored to effectuate the state's interests.[565]

Consistent with constitutional guarantees, the statutory requirements for marriage are minimal.[566] For common-law marriage, which is still recognized in a handful of jurisdictions, the presumption of validity does not apply. The requirements for common-law marriage are not stringent, but proof of common-law marriage may be difficult.[567]

Every marriage (whether common-law or ceremonial) requires capacity on the part of both individuals to enter into the relationship.[568] This stems from the conception of marriage as a contract as well as a social status.[569]

a. Mental capacity to marry

As in other areas of civil law, individuals are presumed to possess the capacity in the absence of a determination to the contrary.[570] Moreover, a presumption of validity applies to ceremonial (formal) marriages, reflecting the state's interest in promoting and protecting marriage and family.[571]

The best accepted standard for mental capacity to marry is whether the individual understands the nature of the marriage contract and the duties and responsibilities it creates.[572] The language of this standard parallels the capacity standard

---

564. *See, e.g.,* Turner v. Safley, 482 U.S. 78 (1978) (held valid an inmate marriage regulation that prohibited inmates from marrying other inmates or civilians unless prison superintendent determined that there were compelling reasons that were not reasonably related to any penological objective).

565. *Id.*

566. *See, e.g.,* MICH. COMP. LAWS ANN. §551.103 (Lexis-Nexis 2007); TEX. FAM. CODE ANN. §2.001 (West 2006).

567. *In re* Marriage of Martin, 681 N.W.2d 612 (Iowa 2004) (proof of common-law marriage rests with the party asserting the claim; elements of common-law marriage include (i) present intent and agreement to marry, (ii) continuous cohabitation, and (iii) declaration that parties are husband and wife); DeMelo v. Zompa, 844 A.2d 174 (R.I. 2004) (affirming lower court's determination that common-law marriage had not been proved; insufficient evidence that parties seriously intended to enter into husband-wife relationship); Bahruth v. Jacobus, 2007 WL 104175 (Kan. App. 2007) (reversing trial court's determination that common-law marriage under Kansas law had been established; elements of common-law marriage include: (1) capacity of the parties to marry, (2) a present marriage agreement between the parties, and (3) a holding out of each other as husband and wife to the public).

568. *See, e.g.,* Mahan v. Mahan, 88 So.2d 545 (Fla. 1956).

569. Edmunds v. Edwards, 287 N.W.2d 420 (Neb. 1980).

570. Accounts Management Inc., v. Litchfield, 576 N.W.2d 233 (S.D. 1998) (marriage statute should be construed to favor validation even when full compliance with formalities may be defective); De la Montanya v. De la Montanya, 281 P. 825 (Or. 1939) (presumptive validity of marriage). *But see,* Gamez v. Industrial Comm'n, 559 P.2d 1094 (Ariz. App. 1976) (marriage that fails to comply with statutory requirements is invalid).

571. Greathouse v. Vogsburg, 169 N.E.2d 97 (Il. 1960); Eygabrood v. Gruis, 79 N.W.2d 215 (Iowa 1946); Brown v. State, 6 6 S.E.2d 745 (Ga. App. 1951).

572. *See, e.g.,* Estate of Hendrickson, 805 P.2d 20 (Kan. 1991); Johnson v. Johnson, 104 N.W.2d 8 (N.D. 1960); Cook v. Cook, 243 S.W.2d 900 (Ky. App. 1951).

for ordinary contracts, but the meaning is quite different due to the vast differences in the responsibilities and consequences of marriage as contrasted with ordinary business transactions.[573] As one court described it:

> [Marriage] in many cases, depends more on sentiments of mutual esteem, attachment, and affection, which the weakest may feel as well as the strongest intellects, than on the exercise of a clear, unclouded reason, or sound judgment, of intelligent discernment and discrimination, and in which it differs in a very important respect from all other contracts.[574]

Few cases specify what an individual must understand about the "nature of marriage" or the attendant "duties and responsibilities" in order to satisfy the marriage capacity standard. A contractual perspective would suggest that the material provisions of the marriage contract would define the understanding required for capacity to marry. Cases eschew such a formalistic approach, instead emphasizing the fact-specific nature of the capacity determination.

The formalistic approach was explicitly rejected in the case of *Ivery v. Ivery,* involving a daughter's challenge to the marriage of her deceased father. The jury found that the father lacked capacity to marry, and the father's wife appealed. The Supreme Court of North Carolina reversed and ordered a new trial on the grounds that the jury instructions given by the trial court incorrectly suggested that marriage capacity required the ability to understand the applicable intestacy statute as well as the revocatory effect of marriage on wills predating the marriage.[575] In other words, capacity to marry does not necessarily require an appreciation of the panoply of property rights of a surviving spouse.

As in the case of other capacity doctrines in the civil law, capacity to marry need exist only at the time of marriage.[576] Proof of a mental disability that ordinarily compromises the capacity to marry will not invalidate a marriage entered into

573. *See, e.g.,* MINN. STAT. ANN. §517.01 (West 2006) (establishing contractual capacity as applicable to marriage).

574. *Johnson,* 104 N.W.2d at 14. *See also,* Edmunds v. Edwards, 287 N.W.2d 420, 425 (Neb. 1980), *quoting University of Michigan v. McGuckin,* 64 Neb. 300, 89 N.W. 778 (1902). (". . . marriage is not a contract resembling in any but the slightest degree, except as to the element of consent, any other contract with which the courts have to deal, is apparent upon a moment's reflection. * * * What persons establish by entering into matrimony, is not a contractual relation, but a social status; and the only essential features of the transactions are that the participants are of legal capacity to assume that status, and freely consent so to do").

575. 129 S.E.2d 457 (N.C. 1963).

576. Briggs v. Briggs, 325 P.2d 219 Cal. App. 1958); Mahan v. Mahan, 88 So.2d 545 (Fla. 1956); De Medio v. De Medio, 257 A.2d 290 (Pa. Super. 1969). Several years after the DeMedio decision, the Pennsylvania Supreme Court rejected DeMedio's conclusion that Pennsylvania's divorce statute prohibits a party from raising equitable defenses to an annulment. Diamond v. Diamond, 461 A.2d 1227 (Pa. 1983). The effect (though not necessarily the purpose) of recognizing the availability of equitable defenses to annulment is to support the policy of preserving marriage.

during a "lucid interval."[577] This is another means by which courts can enforce the policy of preserving marriage.[578]

b. Context and standing

Claims of incapacity to marry arise in three basic contexts: (1) one spouse seeks annulment after a period of living with the other spouse as husband and wife; (2) a guardian or family member seeks annulment during the lifetime of the spouses; and (3) a guardian or family member seeks annulment after the death of one of the spouses. Not all of these claims are viable in all jurisdictions. Restrictions on who has standing to sue, the time in which the annulment suit must be brought, and the form of the suit vary by jurisdiction, depending on statutes governing marriage, guardianship, and civil procedure as well as common-law principles of standing, collateral attack of judgments, and other doctrines.

i. Spouse seeks annulment   In general, one spouse may seek annulment of a marriage to the other spouse based on incapacity. In a few jurisdictions, however, only the spouse alleged to lack capacity may assert the claim; a competent spouse who wants to dissolve the marriage must pursue divorce.[579]

Historically, annulment did not justify judicial rearrangement of the parties' property rights because alimony, property division, and community property all flowed from marriage. Annulment of the marriage would void it from inception, leaving no basis upon which to order spousal support, alimony, or division of property.[580] Early cases reflect the advantage that annulment offered to a proper-

---

577. *Id.*

578. Lott v. Toomey, 477 So.2d 316 (Ala. 1985) (once established, common-law marriage is presumed valid and party attacking marriage has burden of proof); Estate of Wagner, 893 P.2d 211 (Idaho 1995) (same); Guzman v. Alvarez, 205 S.W.3d 375 (Tenn. 2006) (ceremonial marriage presumed valid).

579. ALAS. STAT. ANN. §§ 25.05.031, 13.26.150(e)(8) (Lexis-Nexis 2006) (cannot prohibit marriage or divorce of a ward; only mentally impaired spouse may seek annulment on grounds of incapacity); N.Y. DOM. REL. §140 (McKinney 1999) (competent spouse cannot seek annulment of marriage to a mentally retarded spouse; competent spouse cannot seek annulment of marriage to mentally ill spouse after mentally ill spouse's death); 42 OKLA. STAT. ANN. §128 (West 2001); WASH. REV. CODE ANN. § 26.04.130 (West 2005) (marriage voidable only at the election of the party under disability); Florida specifically denies the guardian the power to determine whether a ward marries, instead requiring court approval. FL. STAT. ANN. § 744.3215(2)(a) (West Supp. 2007).

580. Some jurisdictions adhere to the common law rule. *See, e.g,* Williams v. Williams, 97 P.3d 1124 (Nev. 2004), *reh'g den.*, 2004 Nev. Lexis 115 (2004); Shoustari v. Zamari, 574 S.E.2d 314 (Va. App. 2002), *reconsideration den.* (Nov., 2004), *reconsideration en banc den.* (Dec. 2004). Several jurisdictions, however, have deviated from the common-law rule in order to provide relief for the spouse requiring permanent maintenance (alimony) or property division. *See, e.g.,* White v. White, 323 S.E.2d 521 (S.C. 1984); Callaway v. Callaway, 739 So.2d 1134 (Ala. App. 1999); Falk v. Falk, 462 N.W.2d 547 (Wis. App. 1999); Ramieri v. Ramieri, 539 N.Y.S.2d 382 (1989), *appeal dismissed,* Ranieri v. Ranieri, 545 N.Y.S.2d 106 (1989).

tied spouse, as compared to divorce, where alimony and property division were routine.

In *Forbis v. Forbis,* for example, Mrs. Forbis petitioned the court for separate maintenance after Mr. Forbis refused to permit her to return to her marital home following a stay in an insane asylum.[581] Mr. Forbis responded to the claim by seeking annulment on the grounds of Mrs. Forbis' incapacity to marry. After observing that the presumption of validity of a marriage is "one of the strongest known to the law," the court affirmed the lower court's judgment awarding separate maintenance to Mrs. Forbis and denying Mr. Forbis' claim for annulment.[582]

Before the advent of no fault divorce, annulment offered potential for relief for a spouse who had no grounds for divorce but did have grounds for arguing incapacity. In some cases, a decade or more elapsed between the marriage and the application for annulment.[583] In these cases, the spouse alleged to lack capacity to marry typically suffered from a chronic mental illness or other disability that predated the marriage. Courts usually refused to annul such marriages, invoking the lucid interval doctrine to refute the contention that chronic mental illness could itself establish incapacity to marry.[584]

The availability of no fault divorce eliminates the motivation to use one spouse's mental illness as a means of annulling the marriage where no grounds for divorce exist. The property motive for preferring annulment to divorce also has largely disappeared because many jurisdictions, recognizing the potential for unfairness, expanded courts' authority to order alimony or property division upon annulment. This development has decreased the incentive for a spouse to seek annulment rather than divorce.[585]

ii. Guardian or family member seeks annulment during spouse's life-time

In order for a guardian to maintain an action for annulment on behalf of the ward, the guardian must have that particular authority, either by statute or by court order. Several jurisdictions have enacted statutes that specifically authorize guardians to petition for annulment on behalf of their wards.[586] In most other

581. 274 S.W.2d 800 (Mo. App. 1955).

582. *Id.* at 807–08.

583. DeMedio v. DeMedio, 257 A.2d 290 (Pa. Super. 1969); Cook v. Cook, 243 S.W.2d 900 (Ky. App. 1951).

584. *Id. See also,* Larson v. Larson, 192 N.E.2d 594 (Ill. App. 1963); Forbis v. Forbis, 274 S.W.2d 800 (Mo. App. 1955).

585. *See, e.g.,* Callaghan v. Leonard, 387 A.2d 390, 391–2 (N.J. Super. 1978), *quoting* Final Report to the Governor and Legislature of the Divorce Commission (liberal divorce laws or no-fault divorce rules tend to reduce the actions for annulment because annulment sometimes involved embarrassing grounds such as impotency or incapacity); (N.Y. Dom. Rel. §140, Commentaries C 140:1 ("reasonable explanation" for the drop in annulments is that it is easier to plead and obtain divorce)).

586. *See, e.g.,* Haw. Stat. §580-26-3 (1993); 42 Ok. Stat. Ann. §128; S.D. Stat. Ann. §25-3-2 (Lexis 1999); Tex. Fam. Stat. Ann. §6.108(a) (Vernon/West 2006); Wyo. Stat. Ann. § 20-2-101(d) (Lexis-Nexis 2005).

jurisdictions, courts have concluded that the guardian's general authority includes the power to seek annulment on behalf of the ward.[587]

In a few cases, courts have based their decisions about a guardian's authority over a ward's marriage on their guardianship statute's provision governing the effect of guardianship on contracts.[588] Under this analysis, marriage, like any other contract executed after authority over the subject matter of the contract has been transferred from ward to guardian, is void. Without a specific reference to marriage in the guardianship statute, "contracts" could be interpreted more narrowly, applying only to ordinary business contracts. The difference between the capacity required for ordinary contracts and the capacity required for marriage would seem to justify the more restrictive interpretation of the statutory consequences of guardianship. Another factor weighing in favor of the narrower statutory interpretation, consistent with the ward's protection, is the policy favoring the least restrictive limitations on a ward's autonomy.[589]

Courts have not missed these points; instead they have focused on protection of the ward. This approach is understandable in the context of *Knight v. Radmoski,* a case that involved the marriage of an institutionalized, severely brain damaged young man to his treating psychologist.[590] The psychologist sought, but did not receive, the approval of her fiancé's father for the marriage. The father, who had previously been appointed conservator of his son's estate, sought appointment as guardian of the person of his son. On the same day the guardianship was approved, the son married the psychologist, and the two left the Maine institution to live in Colorado. Noting the severe harm that the marriage and the move had caused the ward, the court held that a guardian's approval was a necessary prerequisite to marriage and that marriage without consent is voidable. On this theory the guardian had standing to seek annulment, which the court granted.[591]

iii. Guardian or family member seeks annulment after death of a spouse   After the death of either party to a marriage, annulment may be unavailable. Traditional legal theory allows suits after the death of a spouse if the marriage was void, but not if it was merely voidable.[592] At common-law, mental

---

587. *See, e.g.,* Marriage of Drews, 503 N.E.2d 339 (Ill. 1986), *cert den. and appeal dismissed,* 483 U.S. 1001 (1987); Nave v. Nave, 173 S.W.3d 766 (Tenn. App. 2005), *appeal den.,* 2005 Tenn. Lexis 904; Krukowsky v. Krukowsky, 49 Pa. D&C 651 (1970). *See generally,* Annot., David E. Rigney, *Power of Incompetent Spouse's Guardian or Representative to Sue for Granting or Vacation of Divorce or Annulment of Marriage, or to Make Compromise or Settlement in Such Suit,* 32 A.L.R. 5th 673 (1995).

588. Knight v. Radmoski, 414 A.2d 1211 (Me. 1980); Matter of Johnson, 658 N.Y.S.2d 780 (N.Y. Sup. 1997).

589. *See supra* Chapter 4 D.2.

590. Knight, 414 A.2d at 1212–14.

591. *Id.* at 1216.

592. *In re* Santolino, 895 A.2d 506 (N.J. Super 2005) (discussing history of void versus voidable distinction as applied to marriage annulment after the death of a spouse, and concluding that the prevailing rule continues to provide that a void marriage may be annulled after the death of one of the parties absent a statutory to the contrary).

incapacity resulted in a void marriage as did bigamy, incest, and other fundamental violations of public policy.[593] Less serious defects in a marriage, such as fraud, resulted in the marriage being merely voidable.[594]

Today, several jurisdictions classify a marriage involving a spouse who lacked capacity to marry as voidable rather than void. Following the common-law distinction between void and voidable transactions, classification of a transaction as voidable causes the action to abate after the death of either of the spouses.[595] Some states specify by statute when and whether an annulment action abates.[596] Where statutes do not specifically address the right to pursue annulment after the death of a party, a court may interpret other provisions of the statute governing annulments to prohibit such an action.[597]

c. Mental health expertise

In the context in which disputes over capacity to marry arise, there is generally no planning opportunity to secure an advance judicial determination or expert opinion on capacity. The personal nature of the decision to marry, as compared to the more objective nature of business and property decisions, may make it even more difficult to establish the probative value of expert opinion. On the other hand, the value of expert testimony may be significant, particularly if the alleged incapacitated person is under the care of a mental health professional at the time the marriage occurs, or a mental health professional examined the individual close in time to the marriage.

3. Civil Unions and Domestic Partnerships

Historically, same-sex couples had no right to marry. Efforts to change the law to permit same-sex marriage laid important groundwork for the cause, but at

---

593. *See generally,* WILLISTON ON CONTRACTS, *supra* note 161 at § 1:2.

594. *Id.*

595. *See, e.g.,* Davidson v. Davidson, 151 N.W.2d 53 (Wis. 1967) (for voidable marriage, action abates upon death of a party); Nunley v. Nunley, 210 A.2d 12 (D.C. App. 1965) (same).

596. CAL. FAM. CODE §2111 (c); 13 DEL CODE ANN. §1506(b) (Michie 1975) (after death action permissible only if brought by either putative spouse or the legal representative of the alleged incapacitated party not more than 90 days after the petitioner learned of the incapacity); 750 ILL. COMP. STAT. ANN. §5/302(b)(1) (West's Smith-Hurd 1999) (same as Delaware); MONT. STAT. ANN. §40-1-402(2) (West 2005) (action must be brought within 1 year of petitioner's knowledge of impaired party's condition); N.Y. DOM. REL. L. §140(c) (after-death action permissible on the basis of mental illness if brought by an interested relative but not if brought by next friend); OHIO REV. CODE § 3105.32 (c) (Page 2003) (action for annulment abates upon death of either party); S.D. CONS. L. 25-3-2; TEX. FAM. STAT. § 6.201 (after-death proceeding for idiot permissible during either party's lifetime; for lunatics (all those of unsound mind except idiots). *See also,* Estate of Fuller, COLO. REV. STAT. ANN. § 14-10-111(2)(a) 862 P.2d 1037 (Colo. App. 1993) (holding that marriage could not be annulled after death of one of allegedly incapacitated spouse because marriage was voidable rather than void).

597. Hooten v. Jensen, 94 Ark. App. 130 (2006) (interpreting annulment statute to preclude post mortem challenge).

the same time triggered a powerful backlash. Today, only one state, Massachusetts, permits same-sex couples to marry.[598] A few more jurisdictions mediated the political conflict by creating a parallel status available to same-sex couples, the domestic partnership or civil union.[599]

Generally, civil union and domestic partnership statutes do not specify the mental capacity required for entering into or terminating the relationship, but all mandate equality or equivalence with marriage.[600] This general statutory provision, as well as equal protection guarantees of the U.S. Constitution, supports the proposition that the same standard of capacity should apply to domestic partnership, civil union, and marriage. Reported case law has not confirmed this proposition, however, due to the short time in which domestic partnerships and civil unions have been available.[601]

4. Divorce

To terminate a marriage, domestic partnership, or civil union requires either death of one of the parties or divorce. As previously noted, annulment does not terminate the relationship but rather voids its legal recognition on the grounds that the parties did not qualify for legal recognition of the relationship in the first place.[602] A spouse's mental disability affects the ability to divorce in several ways, some of which may be particularly detrimental to that spouse.

a. Capacity to divorce

The capacity standard applicable to divorce parallels the capacity standard for marriage. The standard for capacity to divorce is whether the spouse has "sufficient mental capacity to understand fully the meaning and effect of the petition and whether the spouse is able to determine in his or her own interest that he or she desires a final separation."[603] The consequences of incapacity differ depending on whether the incapacitated spouse is seeking divorce or defending against it.

If the defendant-spouse lacks capacity to divorce, he or she will be represented by a guardian, if guardianship was previously established; if not, a guardian *ad litem* will represent the defendant-spouse in the divorce proceeding.[604] Thus, a

---

598. Goodridge v. Dept. of Public Health, 798 N.E.2d 941 (Mass. 2003) (declaring unavailability of marriage to same-sex couples as violative of the state constitution). *See generally,* Robin Miller & Jason Minimow, Annot., 1 A.L.R. FED.2d 1 (2005).

599. CAL. FAM. CODE §297.5; CONN. GEN. STAT. §46b-38aa (Supp. 2007); NEW HAMP. STAT. §457-A:1 et seq.; N.J. STAT. ANN. §37:1-1 et seq. (West. Supp. 2007); VT. STAT. ANN. § 1201 et seq. (Lexis-Nexis Supp. 2006). Other states have statutory schemes that afford same-sex couples some, but not all, of the incidents of marriage. *See, e.g.,* HAW. STAT.§ 572C et seq. (reciprocal beneficiaries).

600. *Id.*

601. *Cf.,* C.Y. v. H.C., Index No. 10265806 (N.Y. Sup. 2007).

602. *See supra* note 580.

603. Marriage of Kutchings, 482 N.E.2d 1005 (Ill. App. 1985).

604. *See, e.g.,* HAW. STAT. §580-6; MASS. GEN. LAWS ANN. 208, § 15 (West 1998).

defendant-spouse's incapacity cannot thwart the ability of the competent spouse to secure a divorce.

A plaintiff-spouse with questionable competency, on the other hand, is not necessarily entitled, either on his or her own or through a guardian, to bring a divorce action. The right of a mentally disabled spouse to seek divorce depends primarily on the relevant jurisdiction's statutory law governing authority of guardians and requirements for divorce, as interpreted by the courts of that jurisdiction. Some states now address this specific issue by statute, expressly authorizing guardians to file for divorce on behalf of their wards, either with judicial preauthorization[605] or without it.[606]

In states without a specific statute, the authority of the guardian to bring a divorce action on behalf of the ward depends on the interpretation of more general statutes governing guardianship, divorce, or both. Many guardianship statutes confer broad general authority on the guardian, defining the guardian's powers by reference to the authority of infants' guardians, by enumeration of several nonexclusive powers, or both.[607] Several courts have considered this issue, with varying results.

In the early cases, a substantial majority of courts narrowly interpreted the guardian's authority, holding that divorce was outside the scope of actions that could be taken on behalf of a ward.[608] While principles of statutory construction influenced these cases to some degree, the principal rationale for denying the guardian authority to file for divorce on behalf of the ward was that divorce, like marriage, is so personal that only the individual involved can choose whether to pursue it.[609] This interpretation protected the ward against the possibility of an unwanted divorce, but simultaneously created the possibility that the ward would be trapped in an unwanted marriage unless and until the competent spouse sought to terminate it.[610] Subsequently, several changes in the social and legal environment occurred that undermined the rationale of the traditional rule.

First, the traditional rule prohibiting guardians from seeking divorce came about when law and society, as a means of encouraging marriage, stigmatized divorce. Law's approach on this matter changed with the advent of no-fault divorce permitting spouses to divorce without proving fault on the part of either party.[611]

---

605. *See, e.g.,* Colo. Rev. Stat. Ann. §15-14-315.5; (Lexis-Nexis 2006); Fla. Stat. Ann. §744. 3215(e); Mo. Stat. Ann. §475.091 (West 1992).

606. *See* Mass. R. Dom. Rel. P., Rule 17(b).

607. *See supra* Chapter 4.D.

608. *See, e.g., In re* Marriage of Drews, 503 N.E.2d 339, 340 (Ill. 1987), *cert den.* 482 U.S. 1001 (1987) (citing several older cases adopting the traditional interpretation); Murray v. Murray, 426 S.E.2d 781, 783–84 (S.C. 1993) (same). *See also,* Annot., *Power of Incompetent Spouse's Guardian or Representative to Sue for Granting or Vacation of Divorce or Annulment of Marriage, or to Make Compromise or Settlement in Such Suit,* 32 A.L.R.5th 673 (1995).

609. 426 S.E.2d at 784.

610. *Id.*

611. For a review and critique of no-fault divorce, see generally, Lynn D. Wardle, *Divorce Reform at the Turn of the Millenium: Certainties and Possibilities,* 33 Fam. L. Q. 783 (1999).

Just as the state's interest in marriage no longer justified denial of divorce to spouses who could not establish fault, the state's interest in marriage did not justify a conclusive presumption that a ward would want to preserve rather than dissolve his or her marriage.[612]

Second, major changes in views about guardianship reflect a shift away from the paternalistic view of guardianship and toward maximum preservation of the ward's autonomy.[613] In tandem with these changes, courts began to grant guardians authority over many highly personal decisions that the ward lacked capacity to make, recognizing that a prohibition against a surrogate decision-making effectively decided the matter, foreclosing any possibility of considering the ward's values. On this reasoning, courts have authorized guardians to decline medical treatment, to authorize abortion, to seek sterilization, and to pursue other medical procedures for their wards. As compared to those matters, it is difficult to say, as the traditional rule does, that the decision to divorce is too personal to be made by a guardian.

For these reasons, most of the recent cases that have considered the issue do not absolutely prohibit commencement of a divorce action by a guardian.[614] These cases usually do not give guardians carte blanche authority to determine whether to sue on behalf of their wards for divorce. In some jurisdictions, the guardian may file for divorce only if the ward has capacity to decide whether to divorce;[615] in others, an expression of desire to divorce before incapacity arose will suffice;[616] in yet others, a guardian may pursue the divorce if it is in the "best interests" of the ward even though the ward did not and cannot express an opinion on the divorce.[617] These checks on the guardian's authority are an attempt to maximize the probability of advancing the ward's desires, rather than simply change from an absolute rule prohibiting the right to divorce to an absolute rule allowing it. Thus, the modern interpretation affords equal protection to competent and incapacitated spouses in divorce proceedings.[618]

b. Mental disability as grounds for, or defense to, divorce

In an effort to reduce the disharmony that accompanies divorce, most states have adopted some form of no-fault divorce.[619] In addition to these newer no-fault provisions, most states retain the traditional grounds for divorce, including adul-

---

612. *See, e.g.,* Nelson v. Nelson, 878 P.2d 335, 340 (N.M. App. 1994).

613. *See supra* Chapter 4 D.

614. *See, e.g.,* Wahlenmaier v. Wahlenmaier, 762 S.W.2d 575 (Tex. 1988); Nelson v. Nelson, 878 P.2d 335 (N.M. App. 1994); Ruvalcaba v. Ruvalcaba, 850 P.2d 674 (Ariz. App. 1993); Murray v. Murray, 426 S.E.2d 781 (S.C. 1993); Syno v. Syno, 594 A.2d 307 (Pa. Super. 1991), *appeal den.* 600 A.2d 1259 (1991); Northrop v. Northrop, 1996 W.L. 861489 (Del. Fam. Ct.).

615. *See, e.g.,* Murray, 426 S.E.2d at 341–42; Syno, 594 A.2d at 311–12.

616. *See, e.g.,* Ruvalcaba, 850 P.2d at 682–83.

617. *See, e.g.,* Nelson, 878 P.2d at 335; *In re* Marriage of Gannon, 702 P.2d 465 (Wash. 1985).

618. *See, e.g.,* Stubbs v. Ortega, 977 S.W.2d 718, 722 (Tex. App. 1998), *pet'n reh'g den., and motion for reh'g on pet. for review overruled* (1998).

619. *See supra* note 52.

tery, cruelty, and the like.[620] The fault provisions may be invoked when no-fault divorce is unavailable, as for example, when the jurisdiction requires both spouses to agree to no-fault divorce.[621]

If the competent spouse brings an action for divorce alleging fault on the part of the mentally disabled spouse, the mental disability may serve as a defense to the action. In order for the defense to prevail, the disability must have prevented the defendant spouse from appreciating the nature of his or her actions at the time they occurred.[622] In *Cosgrove v. Cosgrove,* for example, the Massachusetts Supreme Court upheld divorce based on cruel and inhuman treatment based on the wife's cutting the husband with a razor and other acts.[623] The court held, although she had been diagnosed with schizophrenia and institutionalized for mental illness, the wife's insanity defense failed because she did not prove inability to understand the nature or consequences of her acts, or that her mental illness caused those acts.

Mental disability also may serve as grounds for divorce in some jurisdictions. The specific requirements for this ground of divorce vary from jurisdiction to jurisdiction.[624] Alabama, for example, requires the defendant spouse to have been confined to a mental hospital for 5 consecutive years, and to be "hopelessly and incurably insane."[625] In the absence of a specific statute, mental disability is not itself grounds for divorce.

c. Mental health expertise

Unlike marriage, mental health expertise may be helpful to prove grounds for, or a defense of, a divorce action. In this situation, the mental state at the time of divorce is relevant, and so a contemporaneous expert evaluation is possible. Of course, in the case of a statute like Alabama's,[626] proof of the grounds for divorce must be established by a prior adjudication, obviating any need for a contemporaneous expert assessment.

5. Termination of Parental Rights

Parents have a fundamental right to custody and control over their children, which affords them significant autonomy in decisions affecting family life.[627] When parental autonomy would interfere with a compelling state interest, how-

---

620. *See, e.g.,* Ebbert v. Ebbert, 459 A.2d 282 (N.H. 1983) (original 13 grounds for divorce based on fault were not repealed when no-fault divorce based on irreconcilable differences was enacted); N.Y. Dom. Rel. §170 (grounds for divorce); Miss. Code Ann. § 93-5-1 (same); 750 Ill. Comp. Stat. Ann. § 5/401 (same).

621. *See, e.g.,* Alexander v. Alexander, 493 So.2d 978 (Miss. 1986).

622. *See, e.g.,* Mikkelsen v. Mikkelsen, 174 N.W.2d 241 (Minn. 1970).

623. 217 N.E.2d 754 (Mass. 1966).

624. *See, e.g.,* Ark. Stat. Ann. § 9-12-301 (Lexis-Nexis Supp. 2005).

625. Ala. Code Ann. § 30-21-1(a)(8) (Michie 1989).

626. *Id.*

627. Santosky v. Kramer, 455 U.S. 745 (1982) (clear and convincing evidence required in order to terminate parental rights).

ever, parental autonomy must yield.[628] This principle underlies mandatory education, restrictions on child labor, the minimum-age requirement for drinking alcohol, and many other laws specifying parameters for conduct of, or relating to, children. A state department of social services (or other similar administrative agency) may intervene in a parent's relationship with his or her child where abuse, neglect, or other shortcomings in the child's care put the child at risk of harm.[629] If the interventions fail to bring the parent's parenting skills to an adequate level within a reasonable period of time, the intervention of last resort is termination of parental rights.[630]

In general, termination of parental rights requires the state, or more precisely the state social services agency charged with protecting children's interests in receiving appropriate parental care, to prove that: (a) the parent's acts or circumstances fall within one of the statutory bases for terminating parental rights, and (b) termination of the parent-child relationship is in the child's best interest.[631]

Each state has its own procedures leading up to a termination proceeding, and for the termination proceeding itself. The U.S. Supreme Court has held that there is a qualified right to counsel in parental rights termination proceedings,[632] and in compliance with this mandate several states authorize or require appointment of counsel for indigent parents.[633] Similarly, several statutes provide for counsel or a guardian *ad litem* to represent the child involved in the termination proceeding.[634] Statutes generally do not mandate appointment of a psychologist or other individual with a mental health background to evaluate the defending parent, but the agency seeking to terminate parental rights often does retain an expert when mental illness or deficiency is an aspect of the case to be proved.[635]

a. Mental disability sufficient to terminate parental rights

The statutory bases for terminating parental rights include several different behavior-based grounds (e.g., criminal conviction, abuse), and mental deficiency that impairs parenting ability. Some jurisdictions use only behavior as a basis for

---

628. See id.

629. Federal law mandates that the state must make reasonable efforts to prevent placement of a child in foster care and termination of parental rights. 42 U.S.C.A. §§620–28, 670–79(a).

630. See generally, Sherry S. Zimmerman, Parents' Mental Illness or Mental Deficiency as Ground for Termination of Parental Rights—Constitutional Issues, 110 A.L.R. 5th 579 at §2a (2003).

631. See, e.g., In re Cornica J. 814 N.E.2d 618 (Ill. App. 2004), appeal den. 824 N.E.2d 284 (2004).

632. Lassiter v. Dept. of Social Services of Durham County, 452 U.S. 18 (1981), reh'g den., 453 U.S. 927 (1981).

633. See, e.g., ALA. CODE §12-15-63(b) (Michie 1995); D.C. CODE ANN. §16-234(b)(1); OHIO REV. STAT. ANN. §2151.35.2.

634. See Zimmerman, supra note 630, at §2.

635. See generally, THOMAS JACOBS, 1 CHILDREN AND THE LAW: RIGHTS AND OBLIGATIONS §3:21 (expert evidence often essential to termination proceedings) (West 2006).

termination of parental rights,[636] while others include mental deficiency, where the deficiency impairs parenting ability such that it creates a risk of harm to the child, as a separate basis for terminating parental rights.[637] In some cases, mental disability insulates the disabled individual from the possibility of losing his or her children, even though the disability may prevent a parent from satisfying duties owed to the child.[638]

i. Mental disability—Interferes with parenting abilities Mental disability, in and of itself, does not justify termination of parental rights.[639] If, however, the

636. *See, e.g.,* MINN. STAT. ANN. §260C.301(1)(b) (grounds for termination of parental rights include: (1) abandonment, (2) substantial, continuous or repeated refusal or neglect of parental duties, if the parent is physically and financially able, and either reasonable efforts of the social services agency have failed to correct the conditions that led to the petitioner or reasonable efforts would be futile, (3) failure to comply with a court order to contribute to the support of the child or financially aid in the child's birth continuously without good cause (inapplicable to a non-custodial parent who has not been ordered to or cannot financially contribute to the support of the child or aid in the child's birth), (4) palpable unfitness to be a parent because of a consistent pattern of specific conduct before the child or of specific conditions directly relating to the parent and child relationship either of which are of a duration or nature that renders the parent unable, for the reasonably foreseeable future, to care appropriately for the ongoing physical, mental, or emotional needs of the child, (5) following the child's placement out of the home, reasonable efforts, under the direction of the court, have failed to correct the conditions leading to the child's placement, (6) the child encountered egregious harm while in the parent's care which is of a nature, duration, or chronicity that indicates a lack of regard for the child's well-being, such that a reasonable person would believe it contrary to the best interest of the child or of any child to be in the parent's care, (7) that in the case of a child born to a mother who was not married to the child's father when the child was conceived nor when the child was born the person is not entitled to notice of an adoption hearing under applicable statute and the person has not registered with the fathers' adoption registry under applicable statute, (8) that the child is neglected and in foster care, or (9) that the parent has been convicted of a crime listed in applicable statute.

637. *See, e.g.,* MO. STAT. ANN. §211.447 (West 2004), which includes in the list of bases for termination of parental rights:

    a. A mental condition which is shown by competent evidence either to be permanent or such that there is no reasonable likelihood that the condition can be reversed and which renders the parent unable to knowingly provide the child the necessary care, custody, and control; and

    b. Chemical dependency which prevents the parent from consistently providing the necessary care, custody, and control of the child and which cannot be treated so as to enable the parent to consistently provide such care, custody, and control.

638. As discussed, *infra* at note 649, mental disability as a defense to termination of parental rights is grounded in interpretation of the applicable state statutory grounds for termination as requiring specific intent. One who lacks the requisite capacity may lack the required specific intent to terminate parental rights on the grounds asserted. In a small number of jurisdictions, the Americans with Disabilities Act (ADA) has been used as a defense to parental termination proceedings. In most jurisdictions, however, courts have held that the ADA is inapplicable to termination proceedings. Sherry S. Zimmerman, *Parents' Mental Illness or Mental Deficiency as Ground for Termination of Parental Rights,* 119 A.L.R. 5th 351 (2004).

639. *See, e.g.,* Matter of Lillian, 837 N.E.2d 269 (Mass. 2005); Matter of JPA, 928 So.2d 736 (La. App. 2006).

mental illness interferes with the ability to parent in a way that puts the child at substantial risk or serious harm, the state's interest in protection of the child justifies termination of parental rights. In several cases, parents have challenged the validity of these statutes, arguing that they violate the constitutional guarantee of equal protection because they discriminate against individuals who have a mental disability without an adequate basis for doing do.[640] Courts have roundly rejected the contention that this statutory framework violates equal protection,[641] and at least one court has also held that this type of statute satisfies the constitutional requirements of substantive due process as well.[642]

ii. Mental disability—Impact on other bases for termination   As an alternative to proving mental disability that endangers the child's well-being, the state may rely on one of the behavioral bases for terminating parental rights. These vary from jurisdiction to jurisdiction, but common bases include abandonment, neglect, unfitness, inability to remedy conditions that led to the child's removal from the parent's custody initially, inability to parent, and criminal conviction.[643] In *Matter of J.W.,* for example, the Alaska Supreme Court upheld on termination of a biological father's parental rights based on his inability to provide for his children's most basic needs, where alcoholism contributed to his parenting deficiencies.[644] Rejecting the father's claim that the lower court terminated his parental rights on account of his mental illness, the court stated that chronic intoxication was a form of conduct even if the condition that underlay it is classified as a mental illness.[645]

b. Mental health expertise

Testimony of a mental health expert is not required in all cases,[646] but it is likely to play a crucial role in most cases involving a parent whose mental disability forms the basis for the termination proceeding.[647] In cases where parental rights are terminated on other grounds, but mental disability contributes to the proof of those

640. See, e.g., Bartell v. Lohiser, 215 F.3d 550 (6th Cir. 2000) (applying "rational basis" standard of review); *In re* Eugene W., 105 Cal. Rptr. 736 (Cal. App. 1972) (same).
641. See Id.
642. *In re* R.C., 745 N.E.2d 1233 (Ill. 2001) (applying "strict scrutiny" standard of review to substantive due process claim).
643. See *supra* note 80. See also, Sherry S. Zimmerman, *Parents' Mental Illness or Mental Deficiency as Ground for Termination of Parental Rights—General Considerations,* 113 A.L.R. 5th 349, at §§11–15 (2003).
644. Matter of J. W., 921 P.2d 604 (Alaska 1996).
645. *Id.*
646. *In re* Dependency of C.T., 798 P.2d 1170 (Wash. App. 1990), *rev den. sub nom. State Dept. of Soc.* Services v. Osborne Tanner, 807 P.2d 883 (Wasj 1991), *rev. den. sub nom In re Dependency of Tanner,* 807 P.2d 884 (Wash. 1991); *In re* J.B., 428 So.2d 84 (Ala. App. 1983).
647. See *generally,* Karl A. Menninger II, *Defense in Proceeding for Termination of Parental Rights on Ground of Mental Disability,* 46 Am. Jr. Proof of Facts 3d 231 (West 2007). See also, Sherry S. Zimmerman, Annot., *Parents' Mental Illness or Mental Deficiency as a Ground for Termination of Parental Rights—Evidentiary Issues,* 122 A.L.R. 5th 385 (2004).

grounds, expert testimony can be equally helpful. In a recent Louisiana case, for example, the court dispensed with the mother's consent to adoption based on her failure to pay child support for at least 6 months without just cause.[648] In that case, the failure to pay child support was attributable to the biological mother's inability to maintain employment. That, in turn, was attributable to the mother's refusal to seek a treatment plan for her diagnosed conditions of ADD and bipolar disorder, or even acknowledge her mental illnesses. If the inability to pay child support was beyond the mother's control, the court stated, there would be justification for the failure of support and parental rights could not be terminated. In this case, however, the court concluded that the failure to acknowledge her illness and seek treatment was within the mother's control and thus could not excuse the failure to pay child support. Consequently, the biological mother's parental rights were terminated.

In the Louisiana case, the mental health expertise benefited the agency seeking termination of parental rights. If, however, the biological mother's mental disabilities had been believed to interfere with her ability to acknowledge her illnesses or seek treatment, persuasive expert testimony to that effect would have changed the result in the case. Similarly, if the basis for terminating parental rights requires specific intent to engage in the conduct justifying termination of parental rights, a mental disability that precludes formation of the requisite intent may be a defense to the termination proceeding. In Connecticut, for example, abandonment as a basis for termination of parental rights requires specific intent. Consequently, a Connecticut court refused to terminate the parental rights of a schizophrenic mother who lacked the mental capacity to formulate a reasonable degree of interest, concern, or responsibility toward the child.[649]

6. Adoption

Adoption is the mechanism used to create a legally recognized parent-child relationship between two individuals who have not otherwise acquired that relationship.[650] Unlike marriage, there is no fundamental right to create an adoptive relationship.[651] The right to adopt is conferred by each state through statute,[652] setting forth the substantive standards and procedural rules for adoption. The rules reflect the jurisdiction's balancing of the public policies involved, most notably the best interests of the child, protection of the natural parents in the adoption process, and protection of the stability of the adoptive family after it is established.[653]

648. *In re* DDD, 2007 WL 1300698 (La. App. 2007).
649. *In re* Gene M., 1992 W.L. 91787 (Conn. Super. 1992).
650. *See, e.g., In re* Fleming, 21 P.3d 281 (Wash. 2001) (quoting statutory definition of "parent" for purposes of adoption as excluding "any person whose parent child relationship has been terminated by the act of a court of competent jurisdiction").
651. *See supra* note 562.
652. *See, e.g., In re* Jeramie N. 688 A.2d 825 (R.I. 1997).
653. *See, e.g.,* Adoption by P.S. 716 A.2d 1171 (N.J. Super 1998).

Generally, adoption terminates the biological parent-child relationship (or previous adoptive parent-child relationship) that has not been terminated earlier by death of a parent, a legal proceeding based on statute,[654] or the natural parent's voluntary consent. This principle eliminates the conflicts that would arise if the child maintained the familial relationship with two sets of families.[655] A prospective adoptive parent may locate a prospective adoptive child privately or by using a public or private adoption agency. Once the prospective parents locate a child that is available for adoption, the legal proceeding to adopt may begin.

a. Capacity of parties to adoption
i. Capacity of parent to relinquish child   In situations where parental rights have not been and are not expected to be terminated, the prospective adoptive parent must secure the biological parent's (or parents') consent in order to proceed with the adoption.[656] Statutes in several jurisdictions provide that a minor parent may consent to adoption.[657] Most states include procedural safeguards to minimize the possibility of an uninformed consent, such as requiring consent to be signed or confirmed before a judge, written certification that the individual accepting the biological parent's consent explained the consequences of consent, or providing counsel for the biological parent.[658]

The procedural requirements for consenting to relinquishment of a child make

---

654. *See supra* Ch. 4 E. 5.

655. Inheritance rights are a principal concern in adoption. In limited situations, an adoption may occur without terminating parental rights of the natural parents. For example, many jurisdictions allow a stepparent to adopt the child of his or her spouse without terminating the custodial spouse's parental rights. *See, e.g.,* Hall v. Vallandingham, 540 A.2d 1162 (Md. App. 1988) (interpreting inheritance statute to permit inheritance through no more than two parents). Some jurisdictions allow the other natural parent (i.e., the parent who is not the spouse of the adopting stepparent) to retain parental rights as well. The later type of statute results in three parents for the child: the two natural parents and the adopting stepparent. *See, e.g.,* UNIF. PROB. CODE § 2-114.

656. Identifying the natural father may be problematic or impossible if he is not involved with the child or the natural mother, and he has not signed a document of parentage or obtained a judgment declaring his parental status. States deal with this problem in a variety of ways. The Uniform Adoption Act, for example, distinguished between fathers who have manifested "parenting behavior" by: (i) marrying the mother before the child's birth or within 300 days after termination of the marriage, (ii) entered into a purported marriage that ultimately was or could be declared invalid if the child was born during the attempted marriage or within 300 days after the attempted marriage was terminated, or (iii) obtaining a judicial determination that he is the child's father or signing a document that has the effect of establishing his paternity AND either (A) visiting or communicating with the child and supporting the child financially, to the extent of his ability or (B) marrying the biological mother after the child's birth but before the child's placement for adoption, or attempted to marry the biological mother in apparent compliance with the law even if the marriage is or could be declared invalid, or (iv) receiving the child into his home and openly holding out the child as his own. UNIF. ADOPTION ACT §2-401.

657. *See, e.g.* Mass. Ch. 210 § 2 (West 1998 & Supp. 2007).

658. UNIF. ADOPTION ACT OF 1994 §2-406, 9 U.L.A. 57 (West 1999).

it difficult for a biological parent to revoke consent on the grounds of incapacity.[659] Adoption statutes generally do not provide for appointment of a mental health expert to assess a biological parent's capacity, leaving open the possibility that a "consent" to relinquish parental rights is not at all voluntary. In the adoption context, unlike most other areas of civil law, cases generally do not dwell on the doctrinal definition of capacity to adopt beyond the general principle that legal capacity for a particular act requires understanding the nature and effect of the act.[660] As discussed in more detail in section b, following, the results of recent cases seem to suggest that the threshold capacity to consent to relinquish parental rights is quite low.[661]

A regretful parent also may assert that the consent was obtained by mistake, fraud, or undue influence. In these cases, general contract principles apply. Thus, unilateral mistake by the biological parent will not invalidate an otherwise valid consent, but fraud or undue influence may. Paralleling other areas of civil law, adoption cases involving claims of fraud are difficult to prove,[662] and claims of undue influence are highly unpredictable.[663]

---

659. *See, e.g.,* Arkansas Dept. of Human Services v. Couch, 832 S.W.2d 265 (Ark. App. 1992) (consent of biological mother held valid where court appointed an attorney, who had been appointed based on court's concerns about mother's incapacity, concluded that mother understood consent; court also questioned biological mother before it concluded that she possessed the requisite capacity); *In re* Adoption of J.A.B., 997 P.2d 98 (Kan. App. 2000) (acknowledgment before court or officer authorized by law to take acknowledgments constitutes prima facie proof that the consent is valid; biological mother's status as ward of the court due to her drug addiction and temporary suspension of her parental control as a result of drug abuse fell short of proving incapacity); *In re* R.I.C., 800 S.W.2d 655 (Tex. App. 1990), *writ. den.* (1991) (consent of biological mother who suffered from schizophrenia at times held valid because mother's counsel did not bring any concern about capacity to the attention of the trial court, and court had no duty to inquire); *In re* J.N., 95 P.3d 414 (Wash. App. 2004), *rev. den. sub nom. Nightengale v. Conrad,* 114 P.3d 1198 (Wash. 2005). (consent held voluntary where GAL appointed for 15-year-old biological mother reviewed consent document "line by line" with her; failure to provide her with copy of consent document, which stated she had 48 hours to revoke her consent, held inconsequential); adoption of Hernandez, 607 P.2d 879 (Wash. App. 1980) (consent held voluntary where agency and biological mother jointly petitioned for an order relinquishing custody of infant, judged questioned biological mother "extensively" regarding the nature and effect of her decision, consent was executed before the court, and biological mother admitted she understood the nature and effect of the consent).

660. *See* Hernandez, 607 P.2d at 883 (applying statutory definition of mental incompetency, which exists when the individual "does not possess sufficient mind or reason to enable him to comprehend the nature, terms, and effect of the particular transaction in which he is engaged").

661. *Accord,* Webb v. Webb, 677 So.2d 630 (La. App. 1996), *cert. den.* 682 So.2d 774 (1996) (analogizing capacity to adopt an adult to testamentary capacity).

662. *Compare, In re* J.N., 95 P.3d at 419–21 (no fraud); *with* Matter of Adoption of P.E.P., 407 S.E.2d 505 (N.C. 1991) (fraud).

663. *See supra* Chapters 4 B 3(a) & 4 C 3(a) (ii). *See also,* Marich v. Knox Cty. Dept. Of Human Services, 543 N.E.2d 776 (Ohio 1989), *reh'g den.,* 545 N.E.2d 909 (Ohio 1989) (majority and dissenting opinions on whether consent to relinquish child was invalidated by undue influence).

ii. Capacity of prospective parent to adopt   The significant attention to the capacity of a parent to relinquish a child is essential to protect the relinquishing parent's rights. The capacity of the prospective adoptive parent also is equally important, but for a different reason. In order to advance the best interests of the child, the prospective adoptive parent must have the functional ability to satisfy the child's needs. In recent years, public policy issues at the forefront of qualifications to adopt have included whether unmarried partners, same-sex or opposite sex, may adopt,[664] the importance to be attached to racially and culturally matching children and prospective adoptive parents,[665] and whether adoption of one adult by another violates public policy where the two adults do not have a parent-child relationship.[666]

Statutory criteria governing who may adopt generally do not address mental disability.[667] Instead, the prospective adoptive parent's mental stability, along with virtually every other aspect of his or her life, is considered during a home study.[668] The home study criteria for a particular agency, whether public or private, may (and presumably do) exclude any discriminatory factors. It is difficult to know, however, whether this might include diagnoses of mental illness, because most statutes do not specify the criteria for the home study.[669]

---

664. *See, e.g.,* FLA. STAT. ANN. §63.042 (prohibiting gay adoption). *See also,* Scott D. Ryan et al., *Florida's Gay Adoption Ban: What Do Floridians Think?* 15 U. FLA. J. L. & PUB. POL'Y 261 (2004); Jehnna I. Hanan, *The Best Interest of the Child: Eliminating Discrimination in the Screening of Adoptive Parents,* 27 GOLDEN GATE UNIV. L. REV. 167 (1997).

665. *See, e.g.,* Margaret F. Brinig, *Moving toward a First-Best World: Minnesota's Position on Multiethnic Adoptions,* 28 WM. MITCHELL L. REV. 553 (2001).

666. *See, e.g.,* In the Matter of BB and SB for the Adoption of LB, 920 A.2d 155 (N.J. Super. Law Div. 2006) (refusing to waive statutory requirement that prospective adoptee be at least 10 years younger than prospective adoptive parent(s), based on the absence of a parent-child relationship). *Accord, In re* Adoption of Robert Paul P., 471 N.E.2d 424 (N.Y. 1984) (precluding one homosexual partner from adopting the other based on the absence of a parent-child relationship). *Contra, In re* Adoption of James Swanson, 623 A.2d 1095 (Del. 1993) (approving adoption of one homosexual partner by the other).

667. *See, e.g.,* UNIF. ADOPTION ACT § 1-102.

668. Whether the adoption is arranged through a public agency, a private agency, or privately without the involvement of an agency, a home study of the adoptive parents provides information about the qualities of the prospective adoptive parents to fulfill their role as parents. JACOBS, *supra* note 76, at §4:12.

669. The Uniform Adoption Act is an exception in this regard. It requires two evaluations: one before a child is placed with a prospective adoptive parent, and one during the course of the adoption proceedings. The preplacement evaluation requires the following information about the prospective adoptive parent:

1. Age and date of birth, nationality, racial or ethnic background, and any religious affiliation.
2. Marital status and family history, including the age and location of any child of the individual and the identity of and relationship to anyone else living in the individual's household.
3. Physical and mental health, and any history of abuse of alcohol or drugs.
4. Educational and employment history and any special skills.

Moreover, there is an opportunity for discrimination in the application of the criteria to a prospective parent. Discrimination based on mental disability is entangled with sanist myths and heuristics to such a degree that those conducting or reviewing a home study may not recognize discriminatory aspects of the home study evaluation.[670]

The Americans with Disabilities Act specifically prohibits discrimination, by private or public adoption agencies, based on a mental or physical disability.[671] A mental or physical illness or other disability may compromise an individual's parenting ability so that adoption by that individual would be inappropriate. On the other hand, a mental (or physical) disability ought not to preclude adoption if it does not interfere with parenting ability. Reported cases involving allegations

---

5. Property and income, including outstanding financial obligations as indicated in a current credit report or financial statement furnished by the individual.
6. Any previous request for an evaluation or involvement in an adoptive placement and the outcome of the evaluation or placement.
7. Whether the individual has been charged with having committed domestic violence or a violation of the State's child protection statute, and the disposition of the charges, or whether the individual is subject to a court order restricting the individual's right to custody or visitation with a child.
8. Whether the individual has been convicted of a crime other than a minor traffic violation; and
9. Any other fact or circumstance that may be relevant in determining whether the individual is suited to be an adoptive parent, including the quality of the environment in the individual's home and the functioning of other children in the individual's household.

UNIF. ADOPT. ACT §2-203.

After the adoption petition is filed, another evaluation is required. This evaluation must contain:

1. An account of any change in the petitioner's marital status or family history, physical or mental health, home environment, property, income or financial obligations since the filing of the preplacement evaluation.
2. All reasonably available information concerning the physical, mental, and emotional condition of the minor adoptee that is not included in any report on the minor's health, genetic and social history filed in the proceeding for adoption.
3. Copies of any court order, judgment, decree, or pending legal proceeding affecting the minor adoptee, the petitioner, or any child of the petitioner.
4. A list of the expenses, fees, or other charges incurred, paid or to be paid, and anything of value exchanged or to be exchanged, in connection with the adoption.
5. Any behavior or characteristics of the petitioner that raise a specific concern regarding significant physical or psychological risk of harm to the prospective adoptive child; and
6. A finding by the evaluator concerning the suitability of the petitioner and the petitioner's home for the minor adoptee and a recommendation concerning the granting of the petition for adoption.

Id. at §3-602.
670. *See generally,* Michael L. Perlin, *On Sanism,* 46 SMU L. REV. 373 (1992).
671. 42 U.S.C.A. §12101 et seq.

of ADA violations by adoption agencies are rare, leaving little guidance for those who counsel a prospective adoptive parent who has a mental disability.[672]

No widely published empirical studies establish the effect of a mental illness or disability on a prospective parent's likelihood of successfully adopting. Internet sites dedicated to the adoption process suggest, as those who advocate on behalf of those with mental disabilities probably surmise, that the nondiscrimination contemplated by the ADA is more theoretical than real.[673] Empirical studies of prospective adoptive parents who have a mental illness or other mental disability would facilitate study of the extent to which such discrimination exists, and the scope of the problem. It may be that few cases arise because individuals who have a mental impairment pursue adoption less frequently that do those without such an impairment, possibly because of fear of automatic (illegal) disqualification based on the existence of a past or present disability. If initial skepticism does not deter prospective parents, the home study or other aspects of the adoption process requiring discussion of the prospective parent's mental condition may. Investigation of these questions would help to understand the existence and extent of discrimination in this area of law.

iii. Consent by prospective adoptee　The other party to the adoptive relationship, the child to be adopted, if the child has attained the age specified by statute, also has a right to consent or object to the adoption under most statutes.[674] Under some statutes, the required consent may be waived at the discretion of the court.[675]

b. Mental health expertise

Mental health expertise has a role in virtually every aspect of adoption, including voluntary and involuntary relinquishment of a biological parent's rights as well as the acquisition of parental rights by prospective adoptive parents. Termination of parental rights often involves expert assessment by an employee or appointee

672. One case that did arise is Adams v. Monroe County Dept. of Social Services, 21 F. Supp.2d 235 (S.D.N.Y. 1998). That case involved a blind woman who claimed the agency violated the ADA by refusing to place a child with her, either for foster care or adoption. The court dismissed the case, holding that the agency's concerns related to the ability to care for specific children as opposed to a blanket rejection based on the plaintiff's blindness. *See also,* 3 MICHAEL L. PERLIN, MENTAL DISABILITY LAW: CIVIL AND CRIMINAL § 5A-2.4, at 201 (2d ed. 2002) (citing cases that discuss the ADA in domestic relations contexts).

673. *See, e.g.,* www.bipolar.about.com/od/adoption (describing the effect of author's bipolar disorder on her quest to adopt); www.2girlsandawebsite.com (lists mental illness along with unstable job history, prior marriages, and other factors as concerns for adoptive parents); www .flhomestudies.com (including history of mental illness or chemical dependency among factors that probably will preclude adoption).

674. *See, e.g.,* UNIF. ADOPTION ACT, at § 2-401 (age 12).

675. *See, e.g.,* Matter of Frederick S., 678 N.Y.S.2d 448 (Fam. Ct. 1998) (consent of 14-year-old prospective adoptee waived because court determined that adoption was in his best interest).

of the agency pursuing the termination. The adversarial nature of the litigation, however, makes it desirable for a second expert, either a neutral expert appointed by the court or an expert retained on behalf of the parent defending the termination, to probe the opinion of the first expert and offer either endorsement or critique of the agency's expert opinion.

In the context of consent to relinquish a child, mental health expertise would decrease reliance on procedural measures intended to ensure understanding of the consent that fall on deaf ears when a biological parent is in distress. A 15-year-old girl in foster care sought to revoke her consent to relinquish her child based on her postpartum depression.[676] The court rejected this argument, because the 15-year-old mother did not present expert testimony to prove her mental condition on the date she signed the relinquishment document. Moreover, the court held "emotional stress alone does not vitiate an otherwise voluntary decision to relinquish parental rights."[677]

Mental health expertise also might have raised a red flag in the case of Maria, a single mother who vacillated on the question whether she ought to relinquish her child, resulting in the child moving back and forth between Maria and foster care.[678] Six days after the hearing on Maria's petition (brought jointly with an agency) to relinquish the child, Maria attempted suicide. After spending 4 days in a psychiatric ward, she contacted an attorney in an effort (ultimately unsuccessful) to regain her parental rights.[679]

Mental health expertise also could be helpful to a prospective adoptive parent who has a mental disability, particularly during the home study aspect of the application process. An expert assessment of how the prospective parent's disability affects his or her parenting abilities could allay a caseworker's concerns, educate the caseworker about the fallacies underlying any sanist myth that the caseworker treats as fact, or at the very least alert the caseworker to the illegality of discrimination based on mental disability. The examination should be focused specifically on the impact, if any, of the disability on parenting ability,[680] the effectiveness of treatment in controlling symptoms, and the individual's history of compliance with treatment. Additionally, the examination might reasonably include explora-

---

676. *In re* J.N. 95 P.3d 414 (Wash. App. 2004).

677. *Id.* at 419.

678. Adoption of Hernandez, 607 P.2d 879 (Wash. App. 1980).

679. *Id.* at 881.

680. *See generally,* THOMAS GRISSO, EVALUATING COMPETENCIES, *supra* note 2, at 25 (2d ed. 2003) (indicating the most fundamental objective of a forensic assessment for legal competency is to obtain information about the person's functional abilities—"what the person understands, knows, believes, or can do that is directly related to the competence construct"). *See also, id. at* 250 ("current legal precedent require[es] consideration of functional consequence of mental disabilities, rather than presuming incapacity on the basis of mental disability alone. Thus, forensic assessments that describe only diagnoses, personality characteristics, or general intellectual capacities of parents and fail to assess the caretaker's childrearing abilities are of little value.").

tion of the prospective parent's parenting plan, availability of family or community supports, and other protective factors that might be expected to minimize any anticipated impact of the mental disability on parenting capacity.

In a case involving an adult adoption, the question of capacity to adopt may arise after the adoption has been completed. This occurred in *Webb v. Webb*,[681] where Mrs. Webb adopted the son of her deceased husband (Mrs. Webb's stepson), apparently without the knowledge of Mrs. Webb's siblings or other presumptive heirs. After Mrs. Webb's death they learned of the adoption and challenged it on the ground that Mrs. Webb lacked capacity to execute the adoption petition.[682] The validity of adoption was at issue because that would affect the distribution of Mrs. Webb's estate under a will that everyone agreed was valid.

To support their case, family members of Mrs. Webb stated that she had a long history of mental illness. Furthermore, she had been admitted to a medical center, on the day before the adoption decree was issued, and diagnosed with psychosis and cerebral arteriosclerosis.[683] Applying a standard similar to the standard for testamentary capacity, the court noted the strong presumption in favor of capacity. The court's summary of the evidence mentioned medical records and the expert testimony of the psychiatrist, who had examined Mrs. Webb in connection with Mrs. Webb's admission to the medical center and one other time.[684] The psychiatrist, who had been retained by the heirs who were challenging the adoption, testified that Mrs. Webb exhibited symptoms compatible with a psychotic disorder and opined that her mental condition most likely had been the same that morning. He also testified that she had difficulty understanding her own business affairs, but acknowledged that she might have known about her assets and probably knew who were her relatives and the important persons in her life. The psychiatrist's testimony that Mrs. Webb "possibly" understood the relationship she created by the adoption was "significant" in the eyes of the court.[685] In addition, the judge who presided over the adoption expressed the view that Mrs. Webb had the capacity to adopt, as did one of Mrs. Webb's brothers.[686] Based on all of the evidence in the record, the court concluded that Mrs. Webb possessed the requisite capacity to enter into the adoption.

Although they lost the case, the heirs challenging the adoption could not have hoped to secure any stronger expert opinion evidence than the psychiatrist actually provided. A more conclusive opinion (e.g., Mrs. Webb could not possibly have understood the relationship that the adoption had created) offered by any expert, much less someone who had limited contact with the individual in question, would strike many as arrogant. The existence of conflicting evidence, especially the testimony of the judge who presided over the adoption, would only add

681. 677 So.2d 630 (La. App. 1996).
682. *Id.*
683. *Id.* at 632.
684. *Id.* at 634.
685. *Id.*
686. *Id.*

to the tendency to devalue an unequivocal conclusion by an expert in this situation. It is certainly possible that Mrs. Webb lacked capacity, as the lower court had concluded. The appellate court's emphasis on the presumption of capacity, however, led the appellate court to the opposite conclusion.

7. Summary

The legal status of individuals as married, partnered (pursuant to a domestic partnership or civil union), or single, as well as the legal status of parent and child, affect virtually every area of civil law in one way or another. Legal recognition of family status establishes who qualifies as an intestate heir for purposes of inheriting a decedent's estate and challenging a will. Similarly, familial status is a factor in establishing priority to serve as a guardian for an incapacitated relative. Contracts and other property claims may be directly influenced by familial status, such as the availability of tenancy by the entirety to only married couples or their equivalent, or indirectly by the confidential nature of the spousal relationship, and in some cases, the parent-child relationship. In each aspect of an intrafamily action that involves a family member whose mental capacity is impaired, mental health expertise will be relevant, and in some cases, pivotal. The legal standard for capacity depends on the particular claim involved, but in all civil cases, it is the individual's understanding of the nature and consequences of the act or transaction in question that frames the parameters for each legal test of mental capacity.

5

Principles and Their Wider Implications

A. COMMONALITIES

We have attempted in this volume to cover a wide range of substantive areas of the law that inevitably involve inquiries into a party's competency (no matter how that phrase is defined). Superficially, it would appear that the question of a contract's validity has little in common with the question of whether a mentally disabled death row inmate may be put to death or whether an institutionalized individual can engage voluntarily in sexual relations. Yet, in each instance (and in all of the other topics covered in this volume), the individual's *competence* (to enter into a contractual relationship; to understand the meaning of the ensuing execution; to comprehend the meaning of sexual intercourse) is often at the center of the legal dispute. As the footnotes to this volume make abundantly clear, these and others are questions that recur time and time again, whether the topic is criminal law, institutional law, or private civil law.

The legal system has, for centuries, treated competence as an inquiry that is appropriately before the courts, *and* has recognized that expert witnesses can offer their opinions on matters that are not typically within the knowledge base of laypersons.[1] But the fact that this is a "given" in the law does not mean that it is a topic free from confusion and uncertainty.[2] We hope this volume has demonstrated to the reader that there are commonalities in these inquiries into competence, no matter what the underlying subject matter:

---

1. *See, e.g.,* Ross A. Oliver, *Testimonial Hearsay as the Basis for Expert Opinion: The Intersection of the Confrontation Clause and Federal Rule of Evidence 703 After Crawford v. Washington,* 55 Hastings L.J. 1539, 1548–49 (2004) ("The expert witness could testify only if necessary to provide information that was beyond the ken of the average juror. . .").

2. *See* Jack B. Weinstein, *Rule 702 of the Federal Rules of Evidence Is Sound; It Should Not Be Amended,* 138 F.R.D. 631, 632 (1991) ("Expert evidence can be both powerful and quite misleading because of the difficulty in evaluating it. Because of this risk, the judge in weighing possible prejudice against probative force under [the Federal Rules of Evidence] of the present rules exercises more control over experts than over lay witnesses.")

• Expert testimony is a precondition to a judicial decision in virtually every area of the law in which competency is an issue. (certainly, every area that involves liberty issues). Although for some civil matters, there is no mandate for expert testimony, as a practical matter it has become increasingly necessary.

• The Supreme Court's language in *Drope v. Missouri*—that the question of competency "is often a difficult one in which a wide range of manifestations and subtle nuances are implicated"[3]—is too often ignored by judges.

• Mental health professionals who participate in the judicial process as testifying witnesses *must* be familiar with the controlling legal standards *and* the reasoning processes used by courts in coming to decisions. By reviewing the historical development of the particular competency requirement at question, the testifying expert will develop an appreciation of how the assessment is to be used by the fact finder and of particular areas of sensitivity in the case law.[4]

• Mental health participants and attorneys working in this area must also recognize how the use of expert testimony varies depending on the subject matter of the controversy. The historical development of a particular competency requirement, the frequency with which cases raise that issue, the existence (or nonexistence) of a legal mandate to obtain a mental health evaluation of an individual, and many other aspects of forensic mental health participation inevitably depend upon the specific subject involved.

• Evaluations that are done as part of treatment planning or even for forensic purposes are often done in an unstructured and forensically inadequate fashion, in contrast to the structured evaluations endorsed by the leading thinkers in the behavioral science community.

• Competency is not a unitary concept: It varies depending upon the context, the person, and the task that is the subject of evaluation. A person can be competent for one purpose and incompetent for another.[5] For an expert to offer information that is both relevant and reliable, the expert must have specialized knowledge in assessing the particular competency at question. Expertise in assessing one kind of competency does not necessarily translate to expertise in assessing another. The competency to execute a will requires specific manifestations of understanding far different from competency to waive one's *Miranda* rights, for example. Forensically useful expertise rests on knowing where to look for the requisite functional capacities or manifestations and how to assess their presence

---

3. 420 U.S. 162, 180 (1975).

4. The Supreme Court's most recent decision on a competency question—Panetti vs. Quarterman, 127 S. Ct. 2842 (2007); *see supra* Chapter 2H 2 (a)—is an excellent example to keep in mind.

5. *See* Godinez v. Moran, 509 U.S. 389, 413 (1993) (Blackmun, J., dissenting):

But the majority cannot isolate the term "competent" and apply it in a vacuum, divorced from its specific context. A person who is "competent" to play basketball is not thereby "competent" to play the violin. The majority's monolithic approach to competency is true to neither life nor the law. Competency for one purpose does not necessarily translate to competency for another purpose.

or absence. Forensic mental health instruments have been developed to assist in the assessment of some competencies but would be useless for the assessment of others. Similarly, different measures of response style and impression management are employed depending on the competency in question. Finally, the expert must know how to present the results of the assessment to the court in a way that is direct, clear, and understandable. The expert has an affirmative obligation to link opinions to the underlying data in a way that can be tracked by laypersons, and to refrain from stepping beyond that data in formulating opinions.

• Competency is also not a static concept; it changes over time, depending on the situation and the psychological and medical condition of the person before the court[6] as well as on such contextual variables as drug interactions. Clinical expertise must be combined with forensic sophistication to fully develop the facets of an individual's competency that are relevant for the time period of interest to the law.

• There is a significant disconnect between the sort of evaluations generally done in contested cases (unstructured interviews) and the sort of evaluations generally endorsed by the leading thinkers in the behavioral science community (structured interviews).

• Competency is often, in its practical application, "in the eye of the beholder."[7] A ruling on competency may hinge on some misapprehension of the legal elements.[8] Also, decisionmakers consistently believe that individuals are competent when they agree with the decisionmaker's perspective on a critical issue and incompetent when they do not.[9]

---

6. Although this has been acknowledged by the Supreme Court in the context of competency to stand trial in *Drope*, 420 U.S. at 178–79 (*see generally*, Justine A. Dunlap, *What's Competence Got to Do with It: The Right Not to be Acquitted by Reason of Insanity*, 50 OKLA. L. REV. 495, 502 (1997) ("competence is an ongoing requirement that poses a continuing obligation on the trial court to make further inquiry and order an examination if the defendant's conduct during the trial raises a bona fide doubt as to her competence") (discussing *Drope*), it is often ignored by trial courts.

7. *See* Michael L. Perlin, *"The Executioner's Face Is Always Well-Hidden": The Role of Counsel and the Courts in Determining Who Dies*, 41 N.Y.L. SCH. L. REV. 201, 229 (1996) ("Thus, we should not be surprised to learn that a trial judge, responding to a National Center for State Courts survey, indicated that incompetent-to-stand-trial defendants could have understood and communicated with their counsel and the court "if they [had] only wanted.").

8. *See* Chapter 2A, at 55 (on the way that expert witnesses conflate definitions of incompetency and insanity).

9. *See e.g.*, Michael L. Perlin & Deborah A. Dorfman, *Is It More Than "Dodging Lions and Wastin' Time"? Adequacy of Counsel, Questions of Competence, and the Judicial Process in Individual Right to Refuse Treatment Cases*, 2 PSYCHOLOGY, PUB. POL'Y & L.114 , 134 (1996) ("Ward psychiatrists demonstrate a propensity to equate incompetent with makes bad decisions and to assume, in face of statutory and case law, that incompetence in decision making can be presumed from the fact of institutionalization"); Brian Ladds et al., *The Disposition of Criminal Charges after Involuntary Medication to Restore Competency to Stand Trial*, 38 J. FORENS. SCI. 1442 (1993); Brian Ladds et al., *Involuntary Medication of Patients Who Are Incompetent to Stand Trial: A Descriptive Study of the New York Experience with Judicial Review*, 21 BULL. AM. ACAD. PSYCHIATRY & L. 529 (1993).

- In cases involving social control—where a case decision potentially involves the loss of liberty or civil rights as a result of state action; for instance, if the purpose of the assessment is to determine whether to permit the subject to exercise autonomy or to be civilly committed against her or his will[10]—competency decisionmakers are often leery of relying on mental health expert judgment, depending in large part on their fears or apprehensions about possible outcomes that might flow from an expert's recommendations.

- The balance between expertise and judicial decision-making is often a tenuous one. Expert testimony can assist the fact finder by explicating specific facets of an individual's functioning, and then the fact finder can apply that knowledge to the final determination. For example, expert testimony about how an individual's mental retardation affects impulse management may assist the fact finder in determining whether that individual is competent to waive counsel. The ultimate determination should never be (but often is) given away to the mental health expert, who has no special expertise in the value judgment that may underlie how culpable a person with limited competency may be. That does not mean, however, that the mental health expertise should be ignored; rather, the expert should be guided to stay within the confines of mental health expertise and the available data in offering opinion, and not make inferences that, by addressing the question before the court, invade the province of the fact finder.

- Competency decision-making requires that the mental health and legal professions work together in harmony; yet, there is an underlying power struggle both between law and the mental health professions and *within* the mental health professions[11] on a number of issues, including the balance between objectivity and advocacy, the matters about which mental health experts can offer definitive opinion, and whether to introduce expert opinion on the ultimate issue.

---

10. John LaFond & Mary Durham, Back to the Past: Why Mental Disability Law "Reforms" Don't Reform 156 (1992):

> Neoconservative insanity defense and civil commitment reforms value psychiatric expertise when it contributes to the social control functions of law and disparage it when it does not. In the criminal justice system, psychiatrists are now viewed skeptically as accomplices of defense lawyers who get criminals "off the hook" of responsibility. In the commitment system, however, they are more confidently seen as therapeutic helpers who get patients "on the hook" of treatment and control. The result will be increased institutionalization of the mentally ill and greater use of psychiatrists and other mental health professionals as powerful agents of social control.

11. *See, e.g.,* Orit Kamir, *Responsibility Determination as a Smokescreen: Provocation and the Reasonable Person in the Israeli Supreme Court,* 2 Ohio St. J. Crim. L. 547, 548 (2005) (discussing the "legal system in its power struggle against the mental health professions;" Renee Römkens, *Ambiguous Responsibilities: Law and Conflicting Expert Testimony on the Abused Woman Who Shot Her Sleeping Husband,* 25 Law & Soc. Inq. 355, 335 (2000) ("I will argue that the legal decision on conflicting expert testimonies in the field of forensic psychiatry and psychology resulted from a much more complex intersection of power struggles between law and science, but also among scientists").

• Cognitive-simplifying devices such as heuristics are commonly used by courts in deciding questions in which mental status is an issue.[12]

• Sanism and pretextuality predominate decision-making in virtually all of these areas of the law;[13] we will not understand how people view this area of law and policy until we examine decision makers' underlying assumptions and feelings about the extent to which persons with mental disabilities authentically have a right to be autonomous, and whether they view such individuals as infantlike (and in need of hyperprotection), or, conversely, beyond the control of authority and dangerous beyond comprehension, or, startlingly, both.[14]

B. SUGGESTIONS

We believe that consideration of the topics that we have discussed in this volume should logically lead to consideration of other related areas of law and social policy. We hope that this book will spur readers to think about some of these.

First, as a society, we accept the fact that persons without mental disabilities are free to make *terrible* decisions all the time without governmental or judicial intervention.[15] We also accept the fact that a significant number of prisoners who

---

12. *See, e.g.,* Michael L. Perlin, *Psychodynamics and the Insanity Defense: "Ordinary Common Sense" and Heuristic Reasoning,* 69 NEB. L. REV. 3 (1990, Perlin, *Psychodynamics*). On the ways that the vividness heuristic, the availability heuristic, and others contaminate the insanity defense process, *see, e.g., id.;* MICHAEL L. PERLIN, THE JURISPRUDENCE OF THE INSANITY DEFENSE (1994); Michael L. Perlin, *"She Breaks Just Like a Little Girl" : Neonaticide, The Insanity Defense, and the Irrelevance of Ordinary Common Sense ,* 10 WM. & MARY J. WOMEN & L. 1 (2003); Michael L. Perlin, *"The Borderline Which Separated You From Me": The Insanity Defense, the Authoritarian Spirit, the Fear of Faking, and the Culture of Punishment,* 82 IOWA L. REV. 1375 (1997); on the way they contaminate the incompetency-to-stand-trial process (*see generally supra* Chapter 3A), see Michael L. Perlin, *Pretexts and Mental Disability Law: The Case of Competency,* 47 U. MIAMI L. REV. 625 (1993) (Perlin, *Case of Competency*); on the way they contaminate the quality of expert witness testimony; see Michael L. Perlin, *A Law of Healing,* 68 U. CIN. L. REV. 407 (2000); Michael L. Perlin, *"Half-Wracked Prejudice Leaped Forth": Sanism, Pretextuality, and Why and How Mental Disability Law Developed As It Did,* 10 J. CONTEMP. LEG. Iss. 3 (1999) (Perlin, *"Half-Wracked"*); Michael L. Perlin, *"Make Promises by the Hour" : Sex, Drugs, the ADA, and Psychiatric Hospitalization,* 46 DEPAUL L. REV. 947 (1997).

13. *See, e.g.,* Perlin, *"Half-Wracked," supra* note 12; Perlin, *Case of Competency, supra* note 12; Michael L. Perlin, *Morality and Pretextuality, Psychiatry and Law: Of "Ordinary Common Sense," Heuristic Reasoning, and Cognitive Dissonance,* 19 BULL. AM. ACAD. PSYCHIATRY & L. 131 (1991).

14. See Michael L. Perlin, *Hospitalized Patients and the Right to Sexual Interaction: Beyond the Last Frontier?* 20 N.Y.U. REV. L. & SOC. CHANGE 517, 537 (1993–94):

Society tends to infantilize the sexual urges, desires, and needs of the mentally disabled. Alternatively, they are regarded as possessing an animalistic hypersexuality, which warrants the imposition of special protections and limitations on their sexual behavior to stop them from acting on these "primitive" urges. By focusing on alleged "differentness," we deny their basic humanity and their shared physical, emotional, and spiritual needs. By asserting that theirs is a primitive morality, we allow ourselves to censor their feelings and their actions. By denying their ability to show love and affection, we justify this disparate treatment.

15. *See, e.g.,* Perlin, *Psychodynamics, supra* note 12.

are given determinate sentences are likely to make bad decisions that lead them to commit other future crimes.[16] Yet, we have a different view with regard to the decision-making autonomy and capability of persons with mental disabilities. Why is that?

Second, we need to think about what one of us (MC) has referred to as the "evolving standards of forensic decency."[17] Where mental health expertise was once no more than clinical expertise offered in a courtroom, stretched or convoluted to fit the legal question, there is now a highly evolved appreciation for the kind of data that must underlie opinions offered to the court and for the ways that data should be collected, organized, and reported.[18]

Third, we need to consider whether the heightened standards the U.S. Supreme Court has articulated, in cases such as *Daubert v. Merrill Dow Pharmaceuticals Inc.*[19] and *Kumho Tire v. Carmichael*,[20] with regard to the admissibility of expert testimony will, in real life, affect the way fact finders, across the full range of cases we have discussed, construe expert testimony as about competency. An interesting related question is whether these increasingly refined evidentiary standards have paralleled the evolving sophistication of the field of forensic mental health assessment.[21]

Fourth, we need to think about how to mine the richness of the analysis of criminal competency issues[22] for direct application in civil competency and institutional mental disability law.[23] Both courts and scholars have spent decades thinking seriously about these matters in the criminal context, but they are often ignored, or paid simple lip service, in other relevant areas of the law. This must change.

We hope that this book provides the attorney with tools necessary to develop expert assistance and probe its adequacy. We hope that it provides the mental health professional with tools necessary to understand the law and work with lawyers so as to provide the best and most professional assistance that can be rendered. If this happens, we will feel that we suceeded in this venture.

---

16. One of us (MLP) regularly asks his classes, "So, have you ever had a bad date? Chosen a bad restaurant? Gotten a bad haircut?"

17. *E.g.,* on recidivism rates in prisons, *see, e.g.,* http://www.ojp.usdoj.gov/bjs/pub/press/rpr94pr.htm (US Department of Justice's Bureau of Justice Statistics reporting that two thirds of all released felons are rearrested and charged with serious crimes).

18. *See, for example,* KIRK HEILBRUN, PRINCIPLES OF FORENSIC MENTAL HEALTH ASSESSMENT (2001); THOMAS GRISSO, EVALUATING COMPETENCIES (2003).

19. 509 U.S. 579 (1993).

20. 526 U.S. 137 (1999).

21. *See, e.g.,* John Monahan, *Tarasoff at Thirty: How Developments in Science and Policy Shape the Common Law,* 75 U. CIN. L. REV. 497 (2006).

22. *See supra* Chapter 3.

23. *See supra* Chapters 3 & 4.

About the Authors

MICHAEL L. PERLIN is Professor of Law at New York Law School (NYLS), director of NYLS's Online Mental Disability Law Program, and director of NYLS's International Mental Disability Law Reform Project in its Justice Action Center. He is also an adjunct professor at NYU Medical Center and the University of Rochester Medical Center. Formerly the director of the Division of Mental Health Advocacy in the New Jersey Department of the Public Advocate, and deputy public defender in charge of the Mercer County (Trenton) New Jersey Office of the Public Defender, he now serves on the board of advisors of Mental Disability Rights International and on the board of directors of the International Academy of Law and Mental Health.

PAMELA CHAMPINE is a Professor of Law at New York Law School, specializing in wills and trusts and related personal affairs. She is a member of the American College of Trust & Estate Counsel as well as a former chair of the Legislation Committee of the Trusts & Estates Section of the New York State Bar Association. Her writings include books as well as articles, academic and practitioner oriented. Prior to joining the faculty of New York Law School, Prof. Champine served as law secretary to Surrogate Eve Preminger of the New York County Surrogate's Court, and prior to that practiced trusts, estates, and personal affairs in a major New York firm.

HENRY A. DLUGACZ is an adjunct professor at New York Law School, at St. John's University School of Law, and an assistant clinical professor of psychiatry and behavioral science at New York Medical College. He is an attorney, psychiatric social worker, and consultant in private practice in New York City, specializing in mental disability issues. His work includes the monitoring of complex, federal class action litigations related to forensic psychiatric hospitals and correctional mental health. Before entering private practice exclusively, Prof. Dlugacz served as director of mental health for the St. Vincent's Hospital Correctional Health

Program, assistant program director for the St. Vincent's Hospital Correctional Health Program, an expert consultant and mediator for the Special Master appointed by the Chief Judge of the District of New Mexico in a multiparty class action litigation, and, in addition to numerous other appointments, mental health unit chief for the Montefiore-Rikers Island Health Service.

MARY CONNELL is a forensic and clinical psychologist in independent practice in Fort Worth, Texas. She works in a range of forensic practice areas and specializes in child sexual abuse in family, tort, and criminal litigation. She has served as president of the American Academy of Forensic Psychology, chair of the American Psychological Association Committee on Professional Practices and Standards under the direction of the Board of Professional Affairs, and on the board of the American Psychology-Law Society. She writes in the areas of professional development, ethics, and family psycholegal issues. She has been an active participant in the American Academy of Forensic Psychology Continuing Education Workshop series, presenting workshops on forensic ethics and family psycholegal matters, and she served as chair of the workshop series in 2007.

Subject and Case Index